# Slatter Slopey II - A Diamond in the Rough

## *The Angel's Second Visit*

### Toni L. Head

Bloomington, IN  Milton Keynes, UK

*AuthorHouse*™  
*1663 Liberty Drive, Suite 200*  
*Bloomington, IN 47403*  
*www.authorhouse.com*  
*Phone: 1-800-839-8640*

*AuthorHouse*™ *UK Ltd.*  
*500 Avebury Boulevard*  
*Central Milton Keynes, MK9 2BE*  
*www.authorhouse.co.uk*  
*Phone: 08001974150*

*This book is a work of fiction. People, places, events, and situations are the product of the author's imagination. Any resemblance to actual persons, living or dead, or historical events, is purely coincidental.*

*© 2007 Toni L. Head. All rights reserved.*

*No part of this book may be reproduced, stored in a retrieval system, or transmitted by any means without the written permission of the author.*

*First published by AuthorHouse 3/6/2007*

*ISBN: 978-1-4259-6841-0 (sc)*

*Printed in the United States of America*  
*Bloomington, Indiana*

*This book is printed on acid-free paper.*

# SPECIAL NOTES OF THANKS

My heart felt thanks go out to my loving husband Jim, my daughters, Sherry & Dana, my grandchildren, and my sisters Lou Ann & Linda and their families for their constant support and encouragement.

A Special note of sincere appreciation to Pam for all of her time and hard work she so generously donated toward the editing of my book.

A special note of thanks to my Sunday school teacher Bob Fuson, who through his extraordinary presentation of God's word helped me immensely in weaving spiritual threads within my stories.

Thank you Adam Powell for your technical support and expertise.

Dear Reader:

This book is about faith, prayer, love and hope. There is an essence about childhood that fills the world with an exciting, undiminished, enthusiasm for life. Slatter Slopey has a true child-like faith that will captivate you. She receives many precious gifts from God as she makes her journey through life. It is my hope as you read this book, that you too will be given one of life's greatest gifts; the gift of true vision. Vision is so much more than being able to see with your eyes. It is having the patience and understanding to really look at life the way God intended for you to see it. Only God can give you the ability to see life through the window of your heart. One of the greatest realizations known to man is knowing that things which are seen are temporary, but things which are not seen are eternal. God created both the visible and the invisible. You can choose how much you want to see. As you read this book, I envision you feeling the warmth and joy of God's presence as it leaps off of the pages at you. Please keep in mind that in this busy and complicated world we live in, God still sends angels to minister to his people. So, when you've finished reading this book, don't be surprised if you look up into the heavens and catch a glimpse of the breath taking beauty of your very own, God sent guardian angel.

Sincerely,

Toni L Head

# SLATTER SLOPEY

## A DIAMOND IN THE ROUGH

### THE ANGEL'S SECOND VISIT

I dedicate this book to you, the reader. I hope it touches your soul in such a way that causes you to acknowledge God and his everlasting love for you.

Every human being that has ever lived has reached a significant point in their life when they looked up into the heavens and said....
"God, are you truly real?"
Slatter Slopey asked this question and guess what? She found the answer.

# TABLE OF CONTENTS

**1**
THE LOCKET'S SECRET REVEALED.....1

**2**
A FRIEND OF A DIFFERENT COLOR.....17

**3**
A LESSON IN JUDGING.....25

**4**
COOLING OFF SHEKOE .....55

**5**
WHAT IS A DREAM.....91

**6**
A HERO IN THE SUN'S SHADOW.....111

**7**
THE COUNTY FAIR PRINCESS PAGEANT.....157

**8**
WHAT IS MERCY.....217

**9**
A TEARFUL FAREWELL.....233

10
A HOT FALLING STONE.....245

11
A FAIR AND JUST REWARD.....273

12
THE CIRCLE OF LIFE.....295

13
DECORATING FOR CHRISTMAS.....305

14
REKINDLED TROUBLE.....319

15
LOVE YOUR ENEMIES.....329

16
LOST IN A WINTER WONDERLAND.....345

17
ILLUMINATED FOOT STEPS.....351

18
A FRIEND WITH IMMORTAL EYES.....353

19
A HAUNTED LOOKING SANCTUARY.....365

20
THE DOOR TO ANOTHER DIMINSION.....373

21
THE GOLDEN PITCHER.....381

22
FINDING A VALUABLE TREASURE.....399

23
A DIAMOND IN THE ROUGH.....405

24
DASHING THROUGH THE SNOW.....425

25
CRYSTAL MOMENTS.....439

26
WINDS OF WARFARE.....445

27
A LITTLE PIECE OF HEAVEN.....451

28
HOME AT LAST.....461

29
A CHRISTMAS GIFT FOR SLATTER.....477

30
AGAPE'S WATCHFUL EYE.....485

# 1

# THE LOCKET'S SECRET REVEALED

Slatter's sweet young face lay softly on her pillow as the bright sunlight of a late summer's dawn slowly crept through her window. The warmth of the sun's rays beaming on her face awoke her from a peaceful sleep. She awakened slowly and looked around her room. She collected her thoughts trying to piece together what had happened the night before. She felt a sense of excitement as she remembered finding the old yellowed piece of paper inside the gold locket that belonged to Granny B. She smiled to herself as she remembered hiding it under her mattress. "I am sooo very clever," she said out loud as she smiled and stretched out her toes. She delighted herself in thinking that no one else in the Slopey house knew about the secret paper except for her; and she was going to keep it that way. She devised a plan to get out of bed, hurry and get dressed, and go to grandpa's store. Once there, she would sneak behind the store where she would be all alone to examine the paper.

She quickly jumped out of bed and looked at the old, metal alarm clock sitting on her dresser. It was a special clock because Granny B had given it to her as a gift when she first came to live there. She wanted Slatter to have something to call her very own. Scratching her head, she yawned and mumbled to herself, "Why it's only 7:00 a.m. I wonder if grandpa has gone to the store yet." She picked up her big old wooden hairbrush that was lying on her dresser and quickly tried to brush her matted and tangled hair. As she grasped the brush's handle, she remembered how much she hated the old thing. Her dad had beaten her many times with it and she remembered the stinging pain like it was yesterday. She never tried to tell anyone about the way her dad mistreated her because she didn't think anyone would believe her. She hated having to lie when someone asked about the big red whelps that puffed up on her arms and legs. Even now, the painful memories still floated around in her mind every time she looked at the brush. As she fought back tears, she kept forcing the brush through her thick matted hair. No matter how much she brushed, she couldn't get the static electricity out of it. She finally gave up trying to make it smooth down and look pretty. She decided her hair looked good enough for where she was going. After all, she was just going up to Grandpa's store. She figured if she didn't brush her hair at all, she would still look much better than the old loafers that hung out there. Slatter had high hopes of sneaking past Granny B so she wouldn't notice how unkempt her hair looked. She didn't like the way Granny B was always making a fuss about the way she and her grandpa looked. Granny B was always quick to remind Slatter and her grandpa how old Kally Hudd looked and smelled. As Slatter made her bed, she bobbed her head from side to side, mocking aloud her Granny B. She used a shrill voice as she screeched, "It's Sunday mornin' and everyone be sure to look your best. Now remember. The way you look on the outside reflects what ya think of yourself on the inside. We all represent each other when we go out in public. There ain't nothin' wrong in takin' a little pride in yourself by being clean and presentable." Her thoughts were interrupted when she glanced out her bedroom window and noticed her grandpa's old blue goose was not in the driveway. She breathed out a big sigh of disappointment.

"Shoot," she remarked as she slapped the side of the wall.

"The old blue goose is already gone.

I reckon I done missed the boat.

Oh, well," she shrugged her shoulders.

"Nooo problem.

I reckon I'll just walk to the store."

She quickly jerked off her nightgown and looked around the room to see if Granny B had laid out some clothes for her to put on. Sure enough there on the end of her bed lay a pair of clean overalls that had been cut off at the knees. The denim material was thin and threadbare in places. She looked at the patches that Granny B had so neatly sewn onto the knees to cover up the worn out holes. She immediately remembered the pretty dresses some of the girls in her class had worn to school. She wondered if they had to wear shabby clothes to play in or if they looked all pretty and prissy all the time. Frowning, she grabbed a clean pair of underwear out of her old dresser drawer, put them on and slid into the overalls. She couldn't help but notice how nice and clean her clothes smelled as she hurriedly buckled the straps. The clean scent made her remember something she heard Granny B frequently say to her grandpa. As Slatter stood with her hands on her hips in front of the mirror, she once again mocked her Granny B in a southern high pitched voice.

"Now J.E.," she scornfully gestured as she pointed her forefinger toward the mirror.

"Ya ought not let that old Kally sit out in front of the store on Saturdays.

It jest ain't good fer business.

That's our biggest profit day of the week.

I don't care how poor she is, there ain't no excuse fer her a stinkin'.

It ain't a sin to be poor, but it is to be dirty.

That old girl jest needs a good soapy rag took to her skin."

She giggled to herself as she pictured old Kally splashing around in a big tub of soapy water with Granny B wrestling her around trying to give her a bath. As she continued getting dressed, she started thinking about all the times Granny B had gotten angry at grandpa. Sometimes when Granny B and grandpa argued over little silly things, Slatter would put her hand over her mouth to hush her giggles so they wouldn't hear her laughing at them. In the midst of her thoughts, she reached under her mattress and pulled out her secret treasure, the old yellowed piece of paper. She stuck the paper in the back pocket of her overalls and ran toward the kitchen.

Granny B was in the kitchen doing the breakfast dishes and her other usual morning chores. As Slatter entered the doorway to the kitchen, she smelled the aroma of fresh fried bacon and toast. She saw breakfast on the table and decided it looked way too good to pass up. Granny B had fixed her a plate of two fried eggs, bacon and fresh baked biscuits. She quietly sat down at the table and began putting butter and jelly on her biscuits. Granny B heard Slatter fumbling around at the table. Turning around to face her, she spoke to Slatter in a matter of fact way.

"Well, it's about time ya got up this mornin', ya ole sleepy head," teased Granny B.

"I was jest about ready to come and wake ya up.

I wanted to remind ya about somethin' I reckon you've plum already forgot about."

Slatter looked up at Granny B with jelly smeared all over her mouth. With a mouth full of food, Slatter mumbled.

"Oh yeah, what would that be?"

Granny B flipped the front page of the morning paper in front of Slatter's face for her to see. The headlines read,' COUNTY FAIR TO START NEXT WEEKEND.' Granny B had a delighted smile on her face as she used a drawn out tone of voice.

"Why, look-y here.

The county fair will be here next week."

Slatter, with a what in the world are you talking about look on her face, just stared at Granny B.

"Ah ha!" screeched Granny B.

"I was right!

Ya have forgotten all about it."

Then her voice softened as she bent over and put her arm around Slatter.

"Oh, surely you remember that the county fair comes around every summer honey child."

Then she paused a minute to see Slatter's reaction.

Slatter was not sharing Granny B's excitement about the fair.

She just looked back down at her plate and kept on eating. Granny B bit down on her bottom lip and tried once again to get Slatter's attention.

"Uh .........say Slatter," said Granny B in a pleasant voice.

"There's a Little Princess contest being held at the fair this year.

I was a wonderin' if ya might like to enter it."

Granny B raised her eyebrows as she waited for Slatter's reaction. Slatter grabbed a napkin and made an attempt to wipe the sticky jelly off her mouth. She was so startled at Granny B's question she almost choked on her food. Then, forgetting how awful her tangled hair looked, she gave Granny B a glaring look. Using a hateful tone, she yelled at her.

"Did you say a princess contest? C'mon now, ya gotta be kiddin' me. I ain't no princess Granny B.

Look at me!"

Granny B tried not to laugh as she noticed Slatter's hair sticking straight up all over her head. Slatter looked more like a circus clown than a well groomed princess, but, Granny B knew that this was not a good time to scold her granddaughter about her scraggly appearance. Slatter continued trying to convince Granny B she didn't want any part of a beauty contest.

"Besides," added Slatter getting more aggravated by the moment. "I'm brand new around here and ain't nobody goin' vote fer me anyways."

Granny B wanted very much for Slatter to enter the pageant, so she tried her best to encourage her by explaining further. "Ya never know," said Granny B as she threw a napkin at Slatter.

"It might be kinda fun. All ya have to do is stand up on stage with some other little girls and sing or maybe read a poem that ya wrote yourself. You're creative ain't ya?"

Slatter just rolled her eyes at Granny B and stared at her. "Come on and say ya will do this fer me and your Grandpa." Then in a tender, pleading tone of voice Granny B tried to appeal to Slatter's softer side.

"Oh, honey. You're a pretty girl. Won't ya at least try?

This contest is not all about how a person looks on the outside. It's more about what a person's heart looks like on the inside. Ya know, kinda like the makins' of who a person really is. No body ever said ya had to be the prettiest girl in town to win." Slatter could see delight in Granny B's eyes as she spoke with excitement about the contest. Slatter didn't have the heart to disappoint her. So after a few seconds of hesitation, she wilted like a week old plucked flower and then reluctantly whined, "Oh, Alright. I'll do it. I'll start workin' on the poem tonight before I go to bed."

Do I write a short one or long one?" Granny B gave Slatter a big hug and thankfully said, "Oh I reckon just a short one will do. Ya jest might be surprised young lady. I'm a thinkin' that ya have jest a good a chance to win as anyone else. I'll bet you'll win that contest if ya put your mind to it."

Slatter with a bad attitude grumbled under her breath as she got up from the breakfast table.

"Yeah right.

There are so many girls my age around here that are so much prettier than I am it ain't even funny, and they have real pretty clothes to wear too. All I got to wear is that one old raggedy brown dress I wear for dressin' up, and I tore the hem out of it chasin' some boys after church last Sunday."

As she took a drink of her milk, she squinted her eyes in anger as she made a mean face at the thought of the boys making her tear her dress. She said aloud, "Huh. If'n I'd a caught 'em I'd a shore taught 'em a good lesson 'bout makin' fun of me. I bet ya I could've whipped 'em all.................the scrawny little brats."

Granny B put her hands on her hips as she questioned Slatter. "What in the world is all that mumbo jumbo about I jest heard."

With a snarl look still on her face, Slatter replied, "Ah, it ain't nothin' I don't reckon. I was jest a sayin' that I'll jest bet one of them other pretty girls that's lived 'round here longer than me will win that princess contest." Granny B frowned and ignored Slatter's negative remarks. Then she acted as if she had just noticed Slatter's hair sticking out ever which way and nonchalantly started picking at it.

"Uh hmm," Granny B cleared her throat. Patting one foot on the floor she sneeringly ordered, "I think one of the first things we need to do to get ready fer the Little Princess contest is to practice combing our hair. Slatter didn't want to waste any more time on such trivial matters as her hair so she quickly spoke up.

"Nah.

Ya go on ahead and practice on yours first Granny B. I've got to hurry up and get up to the store. I've already missed my ride with grandpa and I'm quite sure he's a needin' me to help him by now." Granny B didn't say a word back to Slatter. She leisurely walked into Slatter's bedroom and came out with Slatter's big old wooden hairbrush. Slatter, trying to hurry and sneak out the front door, turned around just in time to see Granny B come back into the kitchen holding the dreaded, ugly old hairbrush.

"Alright young lady," spoke Granny B in a harsh tone.

"If ya don't want me to use this here hairbrush on your little hiney, I suggest ya come back in this kitchen right now and let me brush your hair." Slatter stopped dead in her tracks when she heard Granny B speak so sternly. She knew she meant serious business when she used that tone of voice. Granny B pointed in a downward motion to the chair directly in front of where she was standing. Slatter knew her silent order meant for her to take a seat so the hair brushing ritual could begin. Slatter let out a big sigh, giving into Granny B's demands. She slowly walked over to the chair and plopped down. She put her hands over her face as to brace herself for a lot of pain. Granny B had to dip the brush several times into water as she tried to brush out the tangles in Slatter's matted hair. Slatter kept squirming in the chair making it difficult for Granny B to do her job.

"Ouch you're a hurtin' me," yelled Slatter.

"I hate this!...............ouch!....ouch!"

In spite of Slatter's carrying on and wiggling all around, Granny B kept right on brushing.

"Jest sit still a minute," demanded Granny B.

"I'll get done quicker if ya cooperate a little. Your hair wouldn't get in such a mess if'n you'd brush it more often." Granny B was on a mission and nothing short of an earthquake was going to stop her from finishing her quest. Finally, after several minutes of excruciating pain, the task was finished. Even though she had a sore head, Slatter didn't dare complain because she knew that a hairbrush used on her head was less painful than a hairbrush used on her hiney. Slatter had a hard time understanding why Granny B always wanted her to be so clean and have her hair brushed all of the time. Granny B with a snarl look on her face said, "There. Now, that wasn't so bad was it?

I think you're just a little tender headed. Ya need to toughin' up a bit."

Slatter, who was still suffering in pain from her throbbing head, mocked Granny B in a loud, hateful tone.

"Yes!

It was too....... soooo bad and I ain't tender headed neither!"

Slatter felt very angry inside.

Trying her best to hold back tears, she spoke loudly, "Granny B! I'm tellin' ya right now. Who ever invented those old ugly wooden hairbrushes must have hated kids. Especially kids with lots of hair. I jest hate that old thing! It's...it's ugly and it's only good fer hurtin' people. Maybe I need to cut all my hair off. There's some boys at my school that don't have any hair at all to comb 'cause their moms shave their heads. Boy are they lucky." Slatter kept fidgeting and sniffling as she hung her head and stared at the floor. After a few minutes of trying to figure out what to say to Slatter, Granny B decided that pity was not the answer. Instead, she gave her a direct order in a jokingly sort of way.

"Oh come on now Slatter........... Quit your whinin'.

Before ya die, you're goin' have to go through a lot worse things than gettin' tangles brushed out of your hair. Jest get over it and go on. Now get to goin' on up to the store and help your grandpa. He'll be a lookin' fer ya. Go on now and do as I tell ya. Get ta goin'."

When Slatter stood up, Granny B gave her a quick smack on the seat of the pants. When Slatter looked up at her, she winked and cheerfully said, "Oh, wipe your tears and put a smile on your face. Life's a way too short to go around mad. Ya can't always have your own way 'bout things. Ya can't have a good day if ya don't have a good attitude. Ya need to remember young lady that ya can't change what life throws your way, but ya can change how ya react to it."

Some things ya just have to make light of and let go of. You're a better person fer it."

Slatter, red faced and glad the whole ordeal was over, wiped her tear stained face on the breakfast tablecloth and furiously stomped through the living room. She almost tore the old squeaky screened door off of its hinges as she stormed out. She could tell by the way it bang up against the house that she probably broke it. "Stupid old squeaky door," she growled under her breath.

"Ain't nobody ever goin' to fix it. It squeaks so loud, I'm ashamed of it when anybody comes to visit. I hope I did break it. Maybe then grandpa would either fix it or get a new one." She ran as fast as she could toward the store. She was more than ready to get out of the house and away from Granny B and that old ugly hairbrush.

As she ran down the road to the store, she felt into her back pocket to make sure that her treasure was still where it was supposed to be. After she had a few minutes to catch her breath she walked inside the store and grabbed a couple of bags of peanuts for Gibber and her other pet squirrels. Then, she headed down the path that led to the back of the store. She ran as fast as she could down the old narrow beaten path that led to the edge of the woods. She ran like she was running away from the world. She couldn't help smiling to herself as she thought about why the path was made in the first place. It was made by people walking to the outhouse behind the store. Everyday people with everyday problems just like her. She knew it was silly to be thinking about an old outhouse, but somehow, it was helping her to forget her own problem. She had a smile on her face as she continued to concentrate on thoughts of the old outhouse. It was a two seater outhouse, she thought to herself. Slatter had never known any two people to use the outhouse at the same time, so she never understood why grandpa had two seats built in it. The holes were so big that a very small person could easily fall through. It was a big job to keep the wasp nests out of the top of it and ya always had to hurry and do your job because of the honey bees that swarmed inside the hole you were sitting on. Slatter had gotten a few stings herself and boy did they hurt. She remembered the time she used the bathroom out in the woods behind the store and unknowingly wiped with Poison Ivy leaves. Boy was that a mistake. She'd rather battle a few bees than to take a chance on that happening again. She learned real quick what a Poison Ivy leaf looked like. She was sure the old outhouse was used a lot over the years by customers and people just passing by. She figured if that outhouse could talk, it sure could tell some good old stories about its' visitors. The old dirt path to it never had a chance to grow any grass. The path could be easily seen in the summertime when the green grass grew tall all around it. Slatter thought that everyone in the county at one time or another had used her grandpa's old outhouse.

She pulled an old broken orange crate off of a big trash pile, brushed the dirt off of the top of it and sat down. Then, she reached into her back pocket and pulled out the yellowed piece of paper. With much anticipation, she carefully unfolded it. She couldn't believe her eyes. The long wait was over. She could clearly see what was on the yellowed paper.

It was definitely a map!

She just sat and stared at it for a very long time trying to figure it out. All of a sudden, Gibber the squirrel jumped into her lap and started squealing at her for peanuts. Slatter had become so engrossed with her new treasure she had forgotten to open the peanuts and feed Gibber and the other squirrels. She quickly opened the bags of peanuts and, without looking up, carelessly threw them onto the ground.

Gibber instantly jumped off of her lap and began eating the nuts like he was starved to death. It didn't take long for the other squirrels to join Gibber in the free meal and then they were off running up into the trees. Slatter didn't even notice when the squirrels left as she was still staring at the map trying to figure out what it was all about.

It looked like a big winding dirt road with several trees on both sides. There was a smaller road that turned off of the big winding road. She noticed the smaller road had crooked trees growing on each side. There were big fields on both sides of the road that had something growing in them. Slatter thought maybe the fields were farmer's fields with corn growing in them. The paper was too old and faded to make out what it was. Right at the end of the smaller road was a big old wooden, house surrounded by so many trees it looked like the house was sitting in the middle of a big forest. There was a big "X" placed right in the middle of the big old house. There were some letters beside the X that read DIT. On the right hand side of the map near the bottom, was the date, May 23, 1854. A name was written at the bottom left hand side of the map. The name was A. Peabody.

"A. Peabody", whispered Slatter.

"Mmm.

I ain't ever heard mention of that name before." She instantly knew that she had her work cut out for her. She was going to have to ask around to see if she could find someone who was familiar with that name. She couldn't tell by looking at the map if the name belonged to a man or a woman. She sighed great big as she knew she didn't have a clue where anything was that was on the map. One thing she knew for sure, she was going to have to find help from someone that knew how to read it. But that someone would have to be someone she could trust. Then she noticed a sign on the map by one of the small roads. The sign read: **HUMPREY'S LANE** and the letters seemed to jump off of the paper at her. She became distracted when all at once a big green grasshopper jumped up onto the map. She picked up a stick and began chasing it. When it leaped into the tall grass beside her, she made an ugly scowl face and screamed, "Ooh! I hate you!

Don't ya be a jumpin' on me.

I hate bugs that jump!"

She started beating the grass with the stick hoping to smash the grasshopper. She kept on talking to the weeds as she searched for the insect.

"I reckon God put these here weeds for stinkin' bugs to hide in cause they ain't good fer nothin' else except to make me itch. I hate not knowin' when a grasshopper is goin' to jump on me. It's a good thing you're a hidin' in these tall weeds you ugly green thing cause if I see ya again, I'm gonna smash ya with this big stick! Then ya won't be a scarin' me no more.

Jeepers Creepers!

I wonder why on earth God saw fit to make icky creatures like spiders and grasshoppers. They're sooo ugly too!" She stopped smacking the grass and said, "Oh, I jest give up. The stupid bugs blend in with the weeds. Anyways, it's way too hot to waste time and energy a chasin' somethin' that moves so fast." She kicked the orange crate over and sat back down on it. She stared up into the clear, blue sky. She used the sleeve of her shirt to wipe the sweat from her brow. She began to talk out loud to God, just as if she could see Him somewhere in the sky.

"Oh God. Are ya truly real?

Are ya so way up high somewheres in that great big old sky that you're always gonna be invisible to me?

If ya are really there, jest maybe ya can help me figure out this here map I found...er..uh...I should say stole from my Granny B. Last time I prayed and asked ya to heal my mommy and ya didn't see fit to do that. Maybe Ya can answer this prayer for me. Maybe there's a lot of money hidden somewhere around here close by. Jest maybe, I could end up really rich! Please, please God. I'd go through most anythin' to find a real treasure. Please answer my prayer and lead me to the most wonderful treasure that I could ever find. A treasure so valuable it would change my whole life."

Then she started explaining to God what all she would do if she had a lot of money.

"Ya see God.

I would do good if ya saw fit to give me a bunch of money. I'd give some of the money to people like Old Kally Hudd, ya out to remember her if'n from nothing else, just the way she stinks so bad all the time. I 'd buy her a brand new washer and dryer so she could clean up her clothes and I'd buy her lots of fruit to eat. Oh, and I fer sure would buy a new pump fer Granny B's kitchen, cause I know she dreams of havin' runnin' water right inside the house. That would really make her happy. It would make me happy too cause I wouldn't have to spend so much time a drawin' water out of the well. I would even buy everyone at school all of the candy and ice cream they could eat.

Yep!

Even that old mean bully, Lodden and his yucky friends." With each request she made to God, she pictured it in her mind how it would be. She looked around to see if anyone heard her talking, but as she peered down the beaten path all she saw was the trees swaying in the summer wind. She was all alone. The strong hot summer breeze reminded her of her friend, Gappy. She remembered him telling her ............ You can't see the air, yet you still breathe it. Just because you can't see somethin', doesn't mean it ain't there.' She sadly muttered out loud, "I can't see the wind either Gappy, but I see proof it's there cause I can sure see it blowin' the leaves on the trees. I reckon ya can't always see God's way of doin' His miracles, but He let's us see the results.

Ah, gee wiz Gappy.

I'm so lonesome.

I wish I could talk to ya again.

I wish I could talk to my mommy again, but she's in heaven. I reckon heaven is someplace very, very far away.

I wonder if mommy's happy there.

I hope she is...reckon I'll never know fer sure if she is or ain't. I jest got a feelin' heaven is closer than anyone knows. Maybe it's right here in front of my eyes, but invisible to me. She let out a big deep sigh as she bit her bottom lip and said, "Oh, well.

I guess nobody knows the answer to that question.

Well, nobody but God that is.

But God won't tell me. At least not yet anyways.

Someday He might though.

The preacher says we'll find out soon enough when we die.

I suppose he's right."

# 2

# A FRIEND OF A DIFFERENT COLOR

    She was so deep in thought about heaven she barely heard the crackling sound of the sun dried grass as it was being crushed by someone walking up behind her. She quickly folded up the old map and stuck it back into her pocket. For a moment she was startled. She sure was hoping it wasn't her grandpa walking up behind her. She didn't want him to catch her looking at the secret paper. She thought this unknown intruder was probably just someone looking for the outhouse. She quickly jumped up and turned around. Slatter was shocked at what she saw. She had a surprised look on her face because she couldn't believe what she was seeing. Standing right in front of her was a little girl she had never seen before. She looked to be about the same age as Slatter. She was wearing an old worn-out, tattered looking red dress with holes in it. She was barefoot too. When Slatter looked down at this little girl's bare feet, she took a liken to her right off. For a few seconds, Slatter and the little girl stood staring at one another. Slatter knew this little girl had to be kin to Mr. Fritz. Her skin was very dark, like his, and her dark hair was very long and curly. Slatter thought this intruder's big brown eyes looked like two big marbles that lay on a bright white sidewalk. The little girl finally got brave enough to walk up closer to Slatter. As she approached, she boldly asked, "What is ya doin' a way back here ahind dis here store all bys ya self?" Slatter, still in a surprised state, hesitated a few seconds before she replied. However, since this little stranger spoke with the same drawl as Mr. Fritz, she immediately felt comfortable in her presence. Slatter flashed a great big smile at her.

"Oh, not much a nothin'," answered Slatter in a friendly voice. "But if you're a lookin' fer Mr. Fritz," she pointed toward the store.

"He lives up there in that great big shed next to my grandpa's store." The little girl nodded her head and politely replied, "Oh, I ain't a lookin' fer him, cause I know where he is. He be my uncle Fritz.

I know where he live cuz I'm his niece and Iz comes here to stay wif him fer a short spell.

He be the one dat sent me a way back down here ahind dis here old store to look fer ya.

He say dat youz would be a friend fer me to play wif.

My momma say Iz had ta come here and stay wif my uncle Fritz till my daddy come back fer me."

Once again the girls stared at each other each one waiting for the other one to speak. Slatter, snapping off a weed that was tickling her arm, broke the silence. Twiddling the weed around in her hands, she curiously asked, "How come ya have to stay with your uncle Fritz fer a while anyways?"

"Cause my daddy say to," spoke the stranger as she shrugged her shoulders and twisted her body back and forth in a nervous manner, "Ya seez", continued the intruder, "my mamma is real sick and she gots to go stay with my aunt Shaneese fer a spell soz she can git well agin. My daddy say she a needin' some time fer privitation and solitude."

Then she stuck out her hand for Slatter to shake as she introduced herself. Acting a little shy she commented, "Ah, Iz sorry.

I reckon Iz plum forgots my manners.

Why, my daddy say da polite thang to do when Iz meets somebody is to shake dare hand."

The stranger continued to extend her hand for Slatter to shake as she said, "Howdy. My name is Pydalean Jackson.

My folks just call me Miss Pydie.

What be yore name?"

Slatter smiled back at her as she grabbed her hand and shook it very hard. With excitement in her voice, Slatter gratefully responded to Pydie's greeting.

"My name is Slatter Slopey, but I reckon ya can just call me er... uh..............Miss Slatter.

I'm so glad to meet ya. I was back here all by myself, just a longin' fer a friend to play with.

Uh ...er..... uh," still startled, she stammered as she found herself grasping for the right words.

"I live with my grandpa and Granny B Slopey.

They own this here General store and it is the only one in this whole town. We just live down the road a piece."

Slatter was trying very hard to make conversation as fast as she could, so she would make a good first impression. She stopped shaking hands and started bragging on herself.

"Sometimes I help my grandpa run the store.

He says I 'm a good worker."

Pydie didn't show much of a response to Slatter's attempt to toot her own horn, so Slatter decided to try another approach. She decided to ask Pydie about herself. She thought asking her about her mother would be a good way to find out more information about her new friend.

"Say Miss Pydie, what is your Mommy's name anyway?"

Pydie eyes dropped toward the ground and after a few seconds of hesitation she said, "Well, her name be Mrs. Rosa June Jackson. My grand pappy, I mean my Momma's daddy, say when my momma was born, she was as pretty and fresh as a new rose in June. Dat is why she got da name of Rosa June."

Slatter smiled at Pydie to let her know she liked her story about her mother. Then she pointed toward some busted orange crates that were on top of of a big pile of wood stacked beside the old withered outhouse. Trying to entice Pydie to stay for a while she politely asked, "If ya wanna sit down and visit with me a while, I'll go over to that old wood pile and git ya one of those old orange crates to sit on. We can pretend we're loafers and tell each other big lies if ya want to. I hear my grandpa's loafers tell big windy stories almost every day."

Pydie had a blank look on her face as she asked, "What in da world is a loafer, and what is big, windy stories?"

Slatter half heartedly replied, "Oh there just some old men that hang around grandpa's store mainly on Saturdays, and they make up stories about all kinds of stuff. My Granny B says they're a might lazy and just lie around the store like an old loaf of bread lies around in the kitchen. She also told me they make up lots of phony stories just to get attention 'cause they don't get much of it at home. She says she thinks they jest want to feel important."

Pydie sat and listened to Slatter ramble on and on about the old loafers because she had never heard of anyone being called a loafer before. It didn't take long for Slatter to realize she very much liked Pydie and Pydie had taken a liking to Slatter. They were both very happy to have found a friend.

The fact that Slatter was white and Pydie was black didn't make one bit of difference to either one of them. They were two little girls looking for a friend. Neither one cared if they had found a friend of a different color. Slatter found a big stick for Pydie to play with and all afternoon they both sat on the orange crates and dug in the dirt with their sticks laughing and giggling together. They both liked discovering their new found friendship. They talked and talked about one thing and then another. Slatter told Pydie her story about her mother dying and how her dad had left her in the care of her grandparents. She also told her all her secrets about the old junk hole pond, the big, yellow, talking snake named Mingler, and how her friend Gappy had saved her life. They found they had a great deal in common. They both were very lonely and needed a friend. When Pydie told Slatter how poor her family was, Slatter could hardly believe it. Pydie remarked, "Iz have a big family and weez all live in da hills of Kentucky. Weez iz so poor that weez have dirt floorz and weez have only one big room in our house. Our dishes are old and broken and we use big tin cans fer drinkin' glasses."

Slatter rubbed her finger along her top lip then interrupted her by saying, "Don't ya cut your lips on the edges of the can when you go to drink out of 'em?"

Pydie rolled her eyes and replied, "Nope.

My daddy beats the edges down with a hammer and dat's makes 'em good. Uncle Fritz say he has real drinkin' glasses to drink out of.

I done seez where he live and it's real nice.

Knows what else?

"What," asked Slatter abruptly?

"Iz is only seven years old," answered Pydie, "and so fer, Iz only gots ta go ta school fer one day and dat was fer a visit."

I shore would likes ta go to school.

I can't wait to learns how to read and write."

Slatter's mouth dropped open in disbelief. She tried to be pleasant as she yelled out."

"What in the heck do ya mean ya only got to go to school fer one visit?

How come ya don't have ta go ever day?

I have to whether I like it or not."

Pydie shrugged her shoulders and shyly replied, "Cause silly.

Iz is the youngest of ten kids.

I has ta wait my turn. My brudders and sisters git ta go first cause day iz lots bigger dan me. When my Momma got sick my daddy decided dat Iz was a way too small to be of much help round home, so to keep me from being a burden on da family, my daddy brought me here ta uncle Fritz's nice place to live fer jest a while til thangs gets better. My daddy, he been out a work fer a while 'cause he been a takin' cares of my momma."

Slatter felt sorry for Pydie thinking that Mr. Fritz's shed was a nice place. Slatter had spent a lot of time in Mr. Fritz's old shed and she didn't think it was very nice at all. She sure hated to see Pydie have to live there. But if Pydie liked it, that's all that mattered. Who was she to tell her otherwise? Slatter put her arm around Pydie and showed her sympathy by saying, "Gee, I'm real sorry your mommy is so sick. My mommy got bad sick like that and she died." Pydie, with big tears in her eyes, stared at Slatter. Slowly she mustered up the nerve to speak.

"Miss Slatter," whimpered Pydie softly, "Duz youz think my momma's gonna die too?"

Slatter just sat there for a few seconds because she didn't want to answer. However, Pydie pressed her for one.

"Well, duz ya?"

Slatter couldn't bear to see her new little friend in such agony and pain. She knew she had to say something to give her hope. So, she perked up and looked up in the sky as she cheerfully stated, "Ah, your momma is gonna be alright.

Have ya prayed to God and asked him to heal her?"

Pydie's frown turned to a smile as she responded, "Iz shore has and, Iz is believen' that God is gonna heal my momma." Slatter spoke softly with doubt in her voice.

"Yeah, I believe God will heal your momma too."

Slatter, still trying her best to cheer up her friend, said, "Say, I got a good idea. Why don't ya come down to my house and spend the night with me? I've never got to have someone sleep over. Pydie with excitement in her voice replied, "Duz ya think my uncle Fritz will let me do dat?"

Slatter optimistically said, "Why I don't see why not. I bet he'll let ya come over. Your uncle Fritz is a good friend of my grandpa's. I'm sure my Granny B won't care a bit.

Let's go ask him."

Pydie said, "If'n yore granddaddy owns dis here store, I bet dat means ya get a pretty good supper ever night huh?"

Slatter gave her a giggling reply, "Yep and my Granny B is an awful good cook too. She makes cakes and pies..... jest about anythin' I want. Sometimes ya have to watch out though, cause tryin' to sneak somethin' pass her is like tryin' to sneak daylight pass a rooster."

The girls started giggling at Slatter's funny comment.

The girls stopped giggling long enough for Slatter to announce, "C'mon Miss Pydie!

Let's go right now and talk to your uncle Mr. Fritz.

While we're there, I'll ask him if ya can go to church with me sometimes."

Pydie smiled. Grabbing Slatter's hand she happily agreed, "OK.

Iz would shore likes dat!

Let's go!

Let's race!"

They both jumped up and ran towards Mr. Fritz's shed.

# 3

# A LESSON IN JUDGING

Out of breath, they stopped just short of the shed's door. They noticed two men standing around the corner of the store building. It was very apparent the men didn't want to be seen. They were trying their best to whisper to one another as if they were telling each other some sort of secret. Slatter kept staring at them. They looked very familiar to her. She knew she had seen them somewhere before. All at once, she drew in a big sigh and her eyes widened. It hit her like a bomb when she suddenly realized who they were. Their names were Joe Beeser and Butane Craney. They were members of her church. As she watched the men laughing and snorting, she noticed each of them had an unopened carton of cigarettes in their hands. The men were laughing so hard, they didn't pay any attention to the girls as they quietly walked up behind them. They continued their conversation, totally unaware the girls were listening to every word they were saying.

Mr. Beeser only had two teeth in his mouth and he talked kind of funny. He had a speech impediment that caused his words to have an "ith" sound when he spoke. His big ears looked dirty and crusty. He was almost totally bald headed and had deep, crater pits all over his face. He had a bushy moustache he wore to hide the fact he did not have a top lip. Slatter was thinking she sure would hate to meet up with him in a dark alley. He was so ugly he could scare someone to death. She remembered hearing little Jimmy Dee tell his loafer friends about the time he had a girlfriend that was so ugly, she'd make a train take a dirt road. Slatter wasn't for sure what that meant, but she had a pretty good idea Mr. Beeser had to be the perfect match for little Jimmy's ugly girlfriend. Slatter and Pydie quietly tiptoed a little closer so they could listen more closely to the men's conversation.

Trying to keep his voice down to a loud whisper, Mr. Beeser was half-way laughing as he bragged, "Yeah, ain't we thumthin'. We thure did fool old J.E. He was tho bithy a waitin' on cuthomers he didn't even thee uth get behind the counter and steal these here thigarettes."

He continued his hillbilly laugh, "Hee hee hee." Mr. Craney had a great big belly and when he laughed, it shook up and down like a great big bowl of Jell-O. He had a deep rolling laugh that vibrated through his big chest causing his big belly to dance up and down. He was shoddy looking too. Because he was so fat, his shirt always hung out. He couldn't keep it tucked inside his pants. He always looked like he needed a haircut because his greasy hair always hung over the collar of his shirt. His long, scraggly beard looked dry and wiry. Just about every time Slatter saw him, he was chompin' on a big wad of tobacco chew. He kept it stuck in one corner of his mouth which caused his jaw to pooch out like he had the mumps. When he would spit out the juice, it would get hung up in his beard. Every once in a while he would wipe his face with his shirt sleeve to try and wipe the gooey brown spit off. His face was so big and round it made his eyes look small and squinted. He reminded her of a big hog. He often stuck his tongue out one side of his mouth when he talked. His eyes habitually darted back and forth when he grinned. The girls watched him prop one elbow against the side of the store building as he sarcastically replied to Mr. Beeser's remarks. "Yup, not a soul saw us take 'em either.

So, my good friend, Joe.

Since we got what we came here to get or steal rather, I reckon we can leave now."

He started laughing harder as he continued to make fun of Slatter's grandpa's kind ways.

"Just stop and think about how easy it was to pull the wool over old J.E.'s eyes," cackled Mr. Craney.

"When we came into the store, we didn't know the old fool would be so busy he would tell us to 'just help ourselves.' This ought to teach him not to be so trustin' and not give his customer's so much freedom in his store. He gestured with his hands as he mocked Slatter's grandpa using a high pitched tone of voice, "C'mon in folks, and help yourself.

If'n I'm busy just go on ahead and pick up what ya need and put it up on the counter."

Mr. Beeser, laughing so hard he could hardly talk, finally managed to regain his composure long enough to add his two cents worth to the conversation. He stuttered his words out.

"Y...yeth. Y..yeth thir.

And by golly that's juth what we did too!

We helped ourthelves alwight.

Wittle did we know when we goth here, how eathy it was gonna be to get these here thamokes fer fwee.

Why, I bet we thaved $10.00 or more.

That's enough savin's to buy gas fer my twuck fer two whole weeks.

Maybe we orta go back in and pick up some of them there new fangledy, filtered kind. I heared thumbody thay jest ta other day that ya ain't as apt to die tho young if'n ya thamoke that new stuff. Did ya ever here tell of sich a thang afore?

Hardy har har," he snorted and laughed. The two men just shook their heads as they inhaled their cigarette smoke and blew it out their nostrils. They acted as if they had heard very little about the new filtered cigarettes that were being advertised on the radio and appearing on billboards along side the roads. They were one of the newest items fresh out on the market and only the big grocery stores in major cities carried all of the new varieties of tobacco.

The longer the two men talked, the angrier Slatter became. She wanted to get them back for making fun of her grandpa and for stealing from him. She didn't know how much more she could take of their disrespectful wise cracks. However, she was afraid to try on her own to accuse them of stealing, because they might make a big scene in front of her grandpa. Slatter figured he would take the side of the two men because they went to church with him. She also knew if the two men had a chance to hide their cigarettes out in their truck, grandpa would for sure believe them over her; because the evidence would be hidden. After all, she was just a little ole kid and who would believe a kid over a grownup. She knew her Granny B wouldn't.

"Psssst," Slatter quietly made a noise to get Pydie's attention. "Let's go to the other side of the shed."

Without question, Pydie followed behind her. When the girls knew they were completely out of sight, they sat down in the scorching hot dirt. Pydie, with her eyes as big as half dollars, spoke in a concerned soft whisper.

"Well, Miss Slatter," she seriously asked.

What is ya gonna do about dem dare two men a stealin' from yer Grand pappy Slopey?"

Slatter was deep in thought for a few seconds.

She whispered back to Pydie in a very grim tone.

"I don't know just yet.

I gotta do some thinkin' on this."

As sweat ran down her forehead, she folded her arms together and began to think about what her friend Gappy would do if he was in this situation. She grinned as she thought about how smart he was. He always had an answer to every question she asked him. All at once her facial expression changed. Her face lit up and she snapped her fingers together. It had taken a moment for her brain to get around to a solution, but she thought she had a good idea going on.

"That's it," She exclaimed.

I just figured it out!

Gappy would simply find a way to outsmart those two mean varmints."

She jumped up and danced around in a circle causing her bare feet to stir up a cloud of dust.

Pydie bopped her head back and forth watching Slatter dance around in circles.

"What iz ya doin' a actin' like that.

Did ya step on a bee and get stung?" asked Pydie curiously.

Slatter giggled as she whispered excitedly.

"No silly.

I didn't get stung.

I just figured out what we can do to those scoundrels!"

We will do to them what they did to my grandpa.

We will steal the cigarettes back from them."

There was a scared tone in Pydie's voice and her body stiffened. Her voice quivered as she asked, "H-how iz .....uh, w-weez gonna d-do dat?" Dayz will seez us fer shore! Slatter leaned over to Pydie and quietly whispered in her ear, "Well first thing we gotta do is go tell your uncle Fritz what we jest heard those two men a talking about. He might be able to help us out. Besides if we get caught by them, Mr. Fritz can come to our aid.

He's so big and strong ain't nobody fool enough to want to make him mad.

I guarantee you that."

Pydie nodded her head in agreement with Slatter.

Then, they joined hands and quietly tiptoed around the corner of Mr. Fritz's shed. Cautiously looking behind them, they crept inside the door.

They could see Mr. Fritz wasn't very busy. He looked like he was just doing some cleaning up around his shop. He was using an old rag to wipe off dust off some old boards. He noticed, however, the girls were sneaking around trying to be very quiet. He started to ask them what they were up to when they both put their finger to their lips to give him the sign to be quiet. He smiled at them showing his big pearly white teeth. He was so pleased to see Pydie had met Slatter and they were already becoming good friends. He sat down on an old whiskey barrel and motioned for the girls to come over to him. They quickly obeyed him and tiptoed up to his side. He perceived Slatter was trying to tell him some sort of a secret so he bent forward as she placed her small hand over his ear so no one could hear what she was saying. She whispered, "Mr. Fritz. There's two mean men a standin' right behind the corner of grandpa's store and they've stolen some cigarettes. Pydie and I heard them talkin' about it and we have a great idea. We want to steal the cigarettes back.

Do ya have any ideas how we could do it?

I mean without them a knowin' what we are a doin'?"

Mr. Fritz said,

"Well, now let me see.

Is day still a standin' over dare by da store buildin'?"

Slatter and Pydie quietly ran back over to the doorway to see if the men were still standing in the same place. Pydie said,

"Day shore is still dare and day is a lookin' dis a way."

Slatter yelled at Pydie in a hushed tone," Quick Pydie! Get away from the door. We don't want them to see us a lookin' at 'em." The girls ran back over to where Mr. Fritz was sitting. The three of them were so close together, Slatter could feel Mr. Fritz's hot breath on her face when he spoke.

He commanded, "Ok now.

Listen up youngins'.

Iz has an idie that jest might work."

Slatter and Pydie huddled closer as they listened.

"Now, here is what weez iz a gonna do with dem dare bad fellows over dare," said Mr. Fritz with a big grin on his face. Weez is gonna fix 'em good." Mr. Fritz put an arm around each of the girls and each of the girls put their arm around him. There the three of them stood in a huddle just like they were organizing a big plan to solve a mystery.

Mr. Fritz's speech kept getting faster as he hurriedly explained his plan. He said, "Now, weez gotta act fast. Pydie youz go all da way round the back of da store and keep a lookin' toward dis here shed. When the time is right, I'll give ya this right hand signal." He put his right hand up in the air like he was waving at someone. Mr. Fritz pointed toward an old dilapidated yellow truck parked in front of the store. He continued, "Now Miss Slatter. Does ya seez that big old rusted out, old yeller truck parked over dare by da gasoline pumps?" Slatter nodded her head up and down.

"Well, continued Mr. Fritz.

"Dat dare truck is what dem two fellars drove up to da store in. Here ya go, Miss Slatter."

Mr. Fritz handed Slatter a two gallon bucket.

Wide eyed Slatter took the bucket from Mr. Fritz and didn't ask any questions.

"Youz take dis here bucket out there, said Mr. Fritz, and stand by the driver's side door of that big old yeller truck. Youz just keep on a keepin' watch over here at dis here shed fer dis same hand signal only it'll be wif my left hand." Mr. Fritz waved his left hand up in the air. He wanted to make sure both girls knew what signal to watch for.

"Weez all got to be on da same page about dis here plan if'n it goin' to work. Do ya girls know what Iz is a sayin'?" Both Slatter and Pydie nervously nodded their heads up and down. Mr. Fritz began to speak real slow as he said, "Now Miss Slatter. In dat dare bucket is some firecrackers left over from da 4$^{th}$ of July. Dare is also a big box of kitchen matches in dat bucket. Now, Iz is not a teachin you two that it's alright to be a playin' with matches. Iz is supervisin' dis here operation and Iz better not ever catch eader one of youns a playin' with matches after today, or I'll fer shore tan your hides good. Dat is one promise youns can count on from old Mr. Fritz. Now when I gives da left hand signal to Miss Slatter, she gonna strike a match and light five or six of dem dare firecrackers and throw dem as fer as she can under dat old truck. Then she gonna strike a nutter match. Only dis time, she gonna throw two or three of dem dare firecrackers in da front seat of dat dare old truck. Then, I will holler out to dem two fellars that their truck is on fire. I'm a bettin' days will forget all about dare stolen cigrettes and drop 'em on da ground. Day will go a runnin' fer dare old truck.

Now Miss Pydie, dis is where yuz will come in on da plan. When I raise my right hand and wave to ya, yuz run up behind the two fellars and grab dare stolen merchandise. Day will be as good as caught and den we will call out to J.E. and see what he wants us to do wif 'em. Pydie and Slatter were excited. They felt like real live cops after bad bank robbers. Mr. Fritz grinned great big and saluted the girls like an army sergeant. The girls saluted Mr. Fritz right back. As the three of them planned their scheme, they didn't pay any attention to how hot it was in that old shed. Beads of sweat oozed from their heads and run down the back of their necks. Mr. Fritz sounded serious when he asked, "Now is everybody set to go? Does anybody have a question 'bout what day is supposed to do? Now is da time to ask questions, not later."

Pydie eagerly said, "Iz is ready."

Slatter, wiping her sweaty hands on her overalls, responded with a worried look on her face.

"I reckon I'm ready too", she bravely said.

"Mr. Fritz chuckled at little as he chimed in with the girls.

"Ok.

If youz both is ready, den I is ready too.

You girls git to goin' now."

Slatter hurriedly ran out of the shed carrying the firecracker bucket. When she approached the old yellow truck, she squatted down beside the driver's side. She wanted to follow Mr. Fritz's orders to the letter. She immediately became aware she could watch for Mr. Fritz's signal through the rear view mirror of the truck. Pydie ran all the way around the store building to the back of the store. She stayed hid behind the building never taking her eyes off of Mr. Fritz as he stood in the doorway of his shed.

 Mr. Fritz raised his left hand high up in the air to signal Slatter. Pydie was so nervous. When she saw Mr. Fritz's hand go up, she became confused. She was much too excited to stand still. She thought the left hand signal was for her and she started running up behind Mr. Beeser and Mr. Craney. The two men were startled to see Pydie running toward them. At the same time Pydie was running toward the two men, Slatter saw Mr. Fritz's hand signal and lit the firecrackers. She threw them under the truck just like she was supposed to do. Then she thought about how angry she was at the two men for stealing from her grandpa. Thoughts were racing through her mind about how awful these two men were and how they deserved to be punished. She just couldn't stop herself from wanting revenge. She lit another match. Then, meanness began breaking out all over her. Grinning to herself, she decided to light three more firecrackers just for good measure and quickly threw them inside the truck. They landed right smack dab in the front seat. Slatter yelled out, "Hey! This is a lot of fun!"

 Then something totally unexpected happened. Just as she lit another match, she burned one of her fingers causing her to accidentally drop the burning match inside the bucket of firecrackers. She was so excited she forgot to watch where she was walking. In all the excitement, she tripped over something and the bucket flew out of her hands and landed inside the front seat of the truck! Just as the fireworks started blowing up inside the truck, she fell face down in the gravel and rolled underneath a parked car in the parking lot. The firecrackers kept igniting one another causing loud exploding, popping noises. The smoke very quickly became so thick it actually hid the truck. Glass from the truck windows was flying through the air making loud crashing sounds as it landed onto the ground. Mr. Fritz started yelling at the two men that their truck was on fire. Mr. Fritz started laughing at the two men as they ran toward their truck. Mr. Beeser and Mr. Craney did exactly what Mr. Fritz said they would do. They were so worried about their truck catching on fire they forgot all about their stolen merchandise and dropped the cigarettes on the ground. In just a few seconds, something happened that was not in Mr. Fritz's plan. Mr. Beeser saw Slatter running away from the truck and ran after her. He caught up with her, grabbed her by the arm and held on to her tightly. In the meantime, Mr. Craney used one hand to catch Pydie by her long curly black hair and with his other hand held her around her waist. Pydie was so scared. She was squealing and carrying on for all she was worth. Mr. Fritz stopped laughing when he saw the two men grab hold of the girls. His temper got the best of him and he picked up a long piece of metal pipe, about the length of a baseball bat, and ran to help the girls. He ran up behind Mr. Beeser and with one hand grabbed him by the shirt collar. Sweat was rolling down his dark face and he was out of breath from running. His eyes were wide and wild with anger. He picked Mr. Beeser's up by the shirt collar and held him up in the air. Mr. Fritz spoke loud and clear in a boisterous demanding voice, "Hold on here now. I jest thinks dat you two men better take a long look at who youz is a messin' wif and decide if ya wanna keep on tanglin' wif me and dis here piece of steel pipe.

Cuz if'n youz don't be a lettin' go of deese two sweet little ole girls right now, dat is jest what youz is gonna be a tanglin' with.

Now, youz two jest better back off or youz is fer shore a gonna gets into some real bad trouble.

Somebody's a goin' to get bad hurt and it ain't goin' to be old Mr. Fritz."

The girls were now very scared. It wasn't a game of cops and robbers anymore. Because the robbers had caught the cops instead of the cops catching the robbers. Their hearts pounded in their chests. Their sweat had matted their hair against their neck and their faces were beet red. Pydie was crying in pain because Mr. Craney was pulling so hard on her hair. Slatter was scared but she wasn't crying. She was still very angry. She was doing everything else but crying. She was kicking and biting Mr. Craney trying to make him let go of Pydie. She screamed at the top of her lungs, "Ya two ain't nothin' but thieves and hypocrites. My grandpa's better than both of youns put together could ever be. You're caught now and you're goin' to get in big time trouble when my grandpa finds out what youns have done!"

She felt very brave with Mr. Fritz standing close to her side. When Mr. Craney saw Mr. Fritz pick up Mr. Beeser with one hand, his mouth dropped open and instantly he let go of Pydie's hair. He was afraid of Mr. Fritz because he was so big and strong. Both men stopped what they were doing and stood very still. They knew both of them together were no match against a big brawny man like Mr. Fritz.

There were many customers inside the store and they came running outside to see what all of the excitement was about. Slatter's grandpa was the first to arrive on the scene. When he saw Mr. Fritz holding Mr. Beeser up in the air, he blurted out in a very loud and demanding tone, "What in tarnation is a goin' on here Fritz? I've never seen such a mess! Put that man down!" Everyone got real quiet. Mr. Fritz let go of Mr. Beeser. As Mr. Beeser fell to the ground, he started coughing like he was choking. He had a very scared look on his face. Slatter's grandpa looked around at all of the customers whispering to one another as they walked around the scorched truck. Everyone stared in disbelief as they fanned the smoke away from their faces.

As the smoke cleared, it was easy to see the seats inside of the old truck were completely destroyed. It was a sight to see. The color of the truck was more black than yellow and there wasn't a piece of glass left in it anywhere. The truck's shattered windshield lay on the ground underneath the truck. Slatter's grandpa took off his cap and scratched his head. He put his hands on his hips as he bent over and sternly addressed Slatter, "Young lady. I think you've got a whole lot of explainin' to do. Did ya or did ya not throw fire crackers into this customer's truck?" Slatter had a hot, troubled frown on her face as her eyes looked upward to Mr. Fritz for help. She didn't want to have to answer his question. Mr. Fritz knew it was up to him to help the girls. He calmed down and started volunteering information.

"J.E."

He said in a passive tone as he motioned for grandpa to walk toward him.

"Iz think Iz have da answer fer ya.

If'n ya could step right over here jest a minute, Iz will try ta explain dis here mess da best Iz can."

Grandpa turned to the crowd of customers that were gawking at the burned truck and as he waved his hand in the air at them he yelled, "All right now folks. Show's over. If ya got your tradin' all done, ya can get in your vehicles and go on home now; that is everyone except Joe Beeser and Butane Craney. I want to have a word with ya two men about what went on here."

The two men weren't going anywhere in that old truck anyway. It was so damaged, it would have to be towed to where ever it needed to go.

Grandpa wiped his hands on his apron and walked over to the front of the store where he sat down on a 100 pound sack of chicken feed. Grandpa demanded, "Ya two girls go on inside the store and wash off your hot faces.

There's a clean rag a layin' over by a bucket of fresh water sittin' behind the counter. Go ahead and help yourself to a cold soda too. A cold rag to your face and a cold soda ought to cool youns off some."

Slatter knew her grandpa was trying to get rid of them so he could talk to Mr. Fritz in private. Slatter was reluctant to leave. She wanted to hear Mr. Fritz explain to her grandpa about what had just happened. She started pleading with her grandpa.

"Ah, gee, grandpa, aren't ya gonna call the police or the sheriff? These two men are robbers. They are bad men and they deserve to go to jail. I tell ya, they deserved to be punished."

Grandpa motioned for Slatter to go on in the store and very sternly said, "Ya do just what I told ya to do and I mean do it right now!

Youngins are to be seen, not heard."

Slatter knew grandpa meant business when he used that kind of a voice so she quickly obeyed.

Mr. Fritz walked over to where grandpa was sitting. As he started to speak, he propped his foot up on an old orange crate and sincerely said, "Well, J.E. Dis here is da honest to God truth 'bout what happened jest now. Ya know Iz ain't ever lied to youz or anyone 'bout anythin' since ya knowed me..........and I don't intend to start now. Da good Lord knows dat Iz has always told da truth no matters what. Ya seez Doze two ya- hoos men, the ones ya called Joe Beeser and Butane Craney." Grandpa just nodded his head in agreement. "Well, day was a stealin' demselves some cigarettes outa yore tore while youz wasn't a lookin'.

Da girls, day overhered dem two a makin fun of da way youz do business. Iz means, dese here two little girls, my Pydie and yore Slatter, day didn't figure youz wouldn't pay no mind to what day had to say 'bout it. So, day ask me to help em out a bit. Ya knows what I mean. Day wanted me ta help em steal back dem dare stolen cigarettes. Day was jest tryin' to help ya."

Mr. Fritz walked over and picked up the cartons of stolen cigarettes and brought them to grandpa. Grandpa just shook his head in disbelief as he handled the cartons of cigarettes. He called the two men over to him. They hesitantly walked over to where he was sitting. Grandpa shook his finger in their faces as he spoke in a disgusted tone of voice.

"Did ya two men pay me fer these cigarettes?"

The men just looked at one another.

Grandpa could tell by the look on their faces they were consumed with anger. They didn't show one ounce of remorse. Finally, Mr. Craney thought he had a good come back answer and hatefully remarked," Well, jest ya never mind those cigarettes J.E. What ya gonna do about a payin' to get my truck fixed? Why, it ain't even drivable now thanks to that little mean brat granddaughter of yourn. It's been burned all to heck; besides, me and my buddy Joe don't have a penny to our name. We're broke flatter than a snake through a ringer. Grandpa shook the stolen cigarettes in Mr. Craney's face and in an unyielding tone bellowed, "Now, ya listen here. Ya two no good varmints don't need to be a givin' me any back talk!

Havin' no money is no excuse fer takin' stuff that don't belong to youns.

I know of lots of people that are poor and they wouldn't even think of stealing a postage stamp ifn' they needed one.

Ya know. Some people don't have to wait to stand in front of the good Lord to pay fer their sins.

It looks to me like you and your old buddy Joe Beeser here, has paid a high price fer these little old smokes.

I reckon youns wanted awful bad to go and steal 'em.

I hope they were worth it.

I seen ya two a sashsayin' around my store.

I never dreamed youns would pull a stunt like this.

My advise to you two fellers is to make a deal with me and the deal is this.

I won't call the sheriff on ya if you take your stolen merchandise and that old burned out yeller truck and git on out of here. Ya can just consider your shopping spree is over here at old J.E. Slopey's general store.

I had better not see either one of your faces round here again." Mr. Fritz agreeably added, "Yeah, dat goes fer me and dese here two little girls too.

Ya ought to be plum ashamed a doin' what ya did and ya

ought to be embarrassed too.

Dese little ole girls should'na have to be a showin' ya that ya done wrong.

Youz been actin' like da kid and dese here sweet little girls was a actin' like da grown ups.

Mmm .......mmm....mmm !

Dat shore is a shame.

Shame...shame.....shame."

Mr. Craney whispered under his breath to Mr. Beeser, "I'd like ta catch that little brat Slatter alone sometime without that big old blacksmith around.

I'd tan her hide good.

I could shore teach her a lesson or two!

Just ya wait and see.

One of dese days, we'll catch up to her and fix her good!

I don't know how or when, but I'm a tellin' ya right now, the day'll come when we'll have our chance to get even with her fer a messin' us up like this. Yes sir. We'll jest watch our tongue and bide our time 'til then.

And another thing, Joe. If'n she has the little nigger kid with her that belongs to big ole Fritz, it'll be a big bonus to get her too." Mr. Beeser nodded his head as he shot a mean grin back to his partner.

Mr. Fritz motioned to the two men to come and help him push the damaged truck out of the way of the gas pumps. As the three men diligently worked to move the truck beside the store building, they didn't speak a word to each other. They only exchanged hateful glances toward Pydie and Slatter.

Mr. Beeser and Mr. Craney started walking down the road like two whipped pups with their tails tucked between their legs. Mr. Beeser angrily yelled back at grandpa.

"J.E.

I weckun we'll be back thumtime tomorrow ta get da twuck."

Grandpa, Mr. Fritz, Pydie, and Slatter started laughing at the two men as they were walking down the road carrying their stolen merchandise. They weren't laughing at them, but rather at the fact they paid a high price for the stolen treasures they were so carefully hanging onto. As everyone was walking back inside the store, grandpa pulled off his cap and scratched his head. He was in deep thought as he commented, "Man oh man. Those two fellers shore showed themselves today. I'll bet ever time they go to light up a smoke they think about what it cost them to steal those cigarettes. Where ever a man's treasure is that's where you'll find his heart. I'm so glad I am not controlled by the desire to smoke. That's gotta be the nastiest habit a person can have. I reckon I'm a thinkin out loud, but I wonder why would a man in his right mind, on a hot day, want to put somethin' that's on fire next to his lips.

Oh well. It's not fer me to judge." He walked over to the window to get another look at the old burned up truck. He shook his head and said, "I'm sure its goin' to cost them several dollars to fix that old yeller truck out there."

Mr. Fritz smiled great big at grandpa and nodded his head in agreement.

Grandpa picked up a fly swatter and started swishing flies off the big bags of potatoes that were leaning up against the counter. He was careful not to kill one on top, because he didn't want the dead flies to fall down inside the burlap bag.

Pydie had a sly grin on her face as she turned toward her uncle Fritz. As she batted her long dark eyelashes and twisted her body back and forth in a bashful fashion, she spoke in a pleading tone.

"Say uncle Fritz.

Howz 'bout me spendin' the night with my new friend?"

Please, pretty please," she begged.

Mr. Fritz leaned over and picked her up in his big stout arms and gave her a big hug. He used a loving tone when he responded to her request.

"Oh, now Iz was jest a thinkin' maybe youz and Miss Slatter has had enough excitement for one day.

Maybe youz can stay some utter night wif' her."

Pydie smiled great big and waved goodbye to Pydie as Mr. Fritz carried her outside. She liked being held tight in Mr. Fritz's big arms. She rubbed his cheeks with her hand and let out a silly squeal.

"Ok. Ok," Giggled Pydie as she spoke.

"What ever ya say is ok wif me I reckon cause my daddy say fer me to do what ya say.

I knows my daddy duz what's bestest fer me."

Pydie and Mr. Fritz waved goodbye to grandpa and Slatter as they walked back to Mr. Fritz's shed for the night.

Slatter and her grandpa started carrying in the outside merchandise. After they had finished grandpa tipped back his cap and sat down on the old wooden counter. He had something to say to Slatter and was having difficulty finding a way to start the conversation. Slatter noticed her grandpa had stopped working and seemed to have something on his mind. She was learning his ways very well and she figured his quiet behavior had something to do with her, but he was waiting for Mr. Fritz and Pydie to leave. That way, he wouldn't embarrass Slatter. She nervously started picking at her fingers trying to build up enough courage to ask him what was wrong.

Finally, she slapped her hands on her lap, rolled her eyes toward the ceiling and boldly exclaimed,

"Ok.

What's on your mind, grandpa? Let me have it. I've seen that look before. You're actin' like ya want to ask me somethin'. What have I done wrong this time?"

Grandpa was glad Slatter was learning to be sensitive to people's facial expressions and body language. He tried to be very tender in is approach. He twisted his ball cap back and forth on his head as he collected his thoughts. He shifted his false teeth around in his mouth as he thought of different ways he could start his conversation. Slatter knew that such a long pause could only mean one thing. She had done something to displease her grandpa. She didn't have a inkling what she had done wrong, but she wanted to hurry up and get it over with whatever it was. With a serious look on his face he began making conversation. He looked her in the eye and tactfully said,

"Well young lady, I'm glad ya asked me that because I do have somethin' on my mind I need to discuss with ya."

Slatter jumped up on the counter and nervously started fumbling with the strings on his apron. She liked the way he crossed them from behind, and then tied them into a bow in the front. In a carefree attitude she urged him to speak up.

"Oh what is it," she demanded.

"I hate waitin."

What on earth do ya want to talk to me about?

If it's about throwin' the firecrackers in that old truck, I only did what Mr. Fritz told me to do."

Grandpa quickly replied.

"Well, Slatter.

The first thing I want to say to ya is, ya should've used your common sense and came and told me that ya saw those two men a stealin' from me.

I could've taken care of this situation in a manner that didn't require so much unnecessary excitement and attention. I reckon we'll be the talk of the whole town for a few days. But more importantly, I was surprised at ya for wantin' to call the sheriff on those two men."

Slatter acted surprised at her grandpa for saying such a thing. Curling up her lips she asked,

"Why not grandpa?

They were thieves!

They stole that stuff from ya and there ain't no tellin' what else they've stolen that ya don't know anything about."

Grandpa replied, "Alright. That's jest what I thought. Now, I see your way of thinkin'. Let's just see if ya can pick up on my way of thinkin'. Now, ya just stop and think about what ya just said young lady. Ya know I reckon you've got a real short memory. Ya know it was just a few weeks ago that ya stole somethin' from this store too.

Have ya forgotten about that?

Do I need to remind ya what it was?"

Slatter hung her head as she looked down at the old wooden floor.

"No." She humbly whispered.

Grandpa continued on with his lecture.

"Ya see Slatter.

It is human nature for people to think that it's just fine for them to do something wrong, but it's not alright for someone else to do somethin' wrong. What I'm trying to say to ya is we try to justify the wrong things that we do, but, when we see other people do wrong things, we think terrible things about em'. God loves everyone the same and he gives us all second chances ........every single day of our lives. I gave you a second chance. Doesn't your Sunday school teacher teach ya that we should always try our best to act like Jesus?

Didn't ya think I needed to give those two men a second chance too?"

God gives you and me lots of second chances, all the time.

Don't ya think we should set an example of ourselves.

Jesus wasn't quick to condemn people.

I've learned over the years that usually, if ya give enough rope to a person that's on the wrong path, sooner or later, he'll hang himself and without any help from us. God has a way of allowing our wrong doings to catch up with us."

Slatter just shrugged her shoulders. She didn't quite know what to say. She knew her grandpa was right and she had been wrong. She sat quietly and kicked her heals against the counter as she listened. Grandpa continued trying to show her the error of her way.

"People like you and me aren't perfect people either.

We need to get the log out of our own eye before we start tryin' to get the spec out of other people's eyes."

Slatter laughed out loud as she pictured someone trying to push a big log into an eye. Still laughing she said, "What do ya mean by that, grandpa?

C'mon now.

Ya know a big tree log won't fit in somebody's eye.

It's way too big."

Grandpa folded his arms and thought for a few seconds before he replied to her remark.

"Well, sis.

I reckon that does sound funny to ya, but it simply means ya shouldn't be so quick to judge others when ya do wrong things too. We've got a great big job a tryin to fix all of our own problems before we start a tryin' to fix other people's problems. Ya see, sis. When we do somethin' that displeases God, He'll use the same rod to measure our wrong doin's that we use to measure other people's wrongs.

We really do need to be careful about findin' fault with others.

That's as simple as I can put it. Ya got a big job ahead of ya just tryin to take care of yourself." Slatter stopped smiling and replied.

"Oh, I see.

Wow.

I sure didn't know all that.

I sure don't want God to judge me the same way I judged those two mean fellers. I want God to forgive and forget all about the wrong stuff I do."

Grandpa stood up and picked up Slatter off of the counter and then stood her down on the floor. He looked at her for a few minutes as he observed her child like appearance.

Her bright eyes were full of love and innocence.

Her willingness to learn and accept his answers to her questions made him realize how vulnerable and totally dependent she was on him. He was hoping she understood what he was trying to teach her. He felt teaching her God's ways was sometimes more challenging that he had originally bargained for. He gazed into her eyes and looked for some assurance that she was comprehending his little talk with her.

"I'm sure hopin' ya got my message about all this mess that went on here today, Slatter," her grandpa sternly stated.

"Ya know, God has compassion on his people and we are to have compassion for others if we want to be Christ like.

Compassion is love in action.

Everyone has the need sooner or later to reconcile with God. Believe me when I say that there will come a time in those two men's lives when they will have to reconcile with God; whether they like it or not. When God created mankind, He left an empty space inside the human heart that only He can fill. God put eternity in everyone's hearts. Usually, after people have tried everythin' in the world to fill that void, they come to realize they must turn to God in order for their lives to be completely fulfilled.

It doesn't matter who ya are or where ya live, there ain't no true happiness without God.

Always remember that.

No matter what.

Don't let anyone ever try and tell ya any different.

During your life time you're goin' to meet all kinds of people from all walks of life. Ya may even run across someone who'll try to tell ya there ain't no God.

If'n that happens, ya jest remember what your old grandpa has taught ya. Every time ya see a new born baby, smell a flower, or look up at the big spacious sky, you're reminded there really is a God. Every time ya see new life begin in the spring and the storm clouds come and go, you'll know He's real 'cause only God has such majestic powers to create life in all creatures and control His very own universe. And mostly," he pointed to his chest, "down deep in your heart," ya know he wonderfully created ya and all that you feel and all that ya are. Jest feel sorry for the people who choose to be blinded to God's ways and when they cross your path in life, pray fer them. Don't argue with them because your quarrel is not with them, it's with principalities and power. That's grown up things you're way too young to understand and maybe I've gotten way off the main road 'bout all this. As ya grow up, ya will find out that things of the world that the devil wants promoted, will prosper and grow. However, the old devil will do his best to put a stop to anything that promotes God and all of his goodness.

Back to what I've been sayin', right now the main thing I want ya to always remember is to try your best not to judge people until you've walked a mile in their shoes.

Ya know, sometimes I feel like I'm a hangin' out on a limb when I'm a tryin the best way I know how to teach ya God's ways while you're a youngin.

Then, when ya are all grown up, what ya do with your learnin' is up to you. If ya don't understand somethin' I'm a tryin' to tell ya, I expect ya to speak up about it."

He paused a few seconds in case Slatter needed to ask a Question, but she remained silent.

"Ya know, Slatter".

Grandpa breathed in a deep sigh and began speaking again.

"I've learned over the years, it's teachin' youngins how to do things the right way, God's way, while they're young that helps them cope with big problems in their life when they are grown.

You'll learn that too when ya get older.

Now enough said, let's go on home.

It's been a very long day and I am very tired.

I will be glad to get home and rest a while."

Slatter took grandpa by the hand and together they turned out the lights and locked the door behind them. Then, like they had done every evening all summer long, they got into the old blue goose and drove home.

Granny B was sitting in the swing on the front porch waiting for them. When she saw the old blue goose pull into the driveway, she groaned to herself as she rose up out of the swing to go into the kitchen. Just as she was getting the warmed up food on the table, Slatter and grandpa came strolling through the doorway. She used a sympathetic tone when she greeted them.

"Well, well. Good evening, my tired weary lookin' travelers. Ya two are a little extra late tonight, aren't yunz?"

Grandpa just smiled at Granny B and patted Slatter on the head.

As he washed his hands, his voice sounded very tired as he spoke. Jokingly he said, "Yeah, I think Slatter has a cops and robbers story to tell ya about."

Granny B was surprised at what grandpa had said.

She had a puzzled look on her face as a wave of interest flooded her mind. She inquisitively replied, "Why what do ya mean by that?

Did someone try to rob the store or somethin'?"

Slatter happily responded to her question, "I'll tell ya all about it while I'm eatin' can't ya tell I'm starvin' to death!" Granny B shook her head and laughed at Slatter's remark. After Slatter and grandpa washed their hands, they sat down to eat their supper. Slatter rattled on and on about her new found friend Pydie and the two men they had caught stealing. Trying not to talk with her mouth full, she didn't leave any details out including how Mr. Fritz had helped the two girls catch the thieves. Granny B listened very closely to the story as she sat next to Slatter sipping her cup of coffee.

When Slatter had finally finished rambling, she took a deep breath and blurted out a surprise ending.

"And Granny B, I want ya to know that grandpa said we needed to give those old boogers a second chance.

So, he didn't even call the sheriff.

I guess they really were punished enough for what they did, cause now they're gonna have to spend a bunch of money to fix up their old truck that got burned up."

Granny B let out a big sigh as she sat her coffee cup down on the table. She calmly responded.

"Yeah, I reckon so.

But, I never did have much use for them two fellers anyway. One time at a Sunday night church service, I saw that old Mr. Beeser take money out of the offrin' plate. He knows I saw him do it too, but that didn't seem to bother him none. Now that's steppin' down pretty low if'n ya ask me."

Granny B shook her head and started cleaning up the supper dishes. She noticed that Slatter had started yawning. She started giving Slatter orders.

"Ya had better go on to bed, now.

I think you're about wore out.

Besides, I got some things to talk over with your grandpa and youngins don't need ta here everythin' that grown ups have to say."

Slatter was glad to get out of doing the dishes so she was quite agreeable.

"Oh, ok. Granny B.

What ever you say.

Well, I guess I'm out a here.

I want to get up early tomorrow anyway so I can play with my new friend Pydie.

Granny B. Did I tell ya her real name is Pydalean Jackson, but folks mostly call her Miss Pydie."

Slatter got up from the table and put her dishes in the sink. Then she took a sponge bath and brushed her teeth before she went to her room for the night. She yelled out to her grandpa, "I'll say my prayers by myself tonight grandpa 'cause I know you're extra tired."

Grandpa shook his head back and forth and chuckled in a proud way. He liked the way he was getting so attached to his granddaughter. He liked the way she needed him, and he knew he needed her.

Slatter, very tired from such an exciting day, stumbled as she took off her overall shorts. Suddenly, she remembered to pull out the old yellowed map from her back pocket and hurriedly slid it back under her mattress. She smiled to herself as she climbed into bed. Her thoughts drifted to the time when she first came to live with her grandparents. She had felt alone and out of place. She gazed around her room. Now, she couldn't imagine living anywhere else. As she thought about what a wonderful day she and Pydie had, she remembered how she had started the day out with anticipation of trying to find out what secret was in the locket. She smiled to herself as she was amazed at how the secret map had somehow became of less importance to her after she had met her new friend Pydie. She remembered what her mother had told her one time, always think of the little insignificant things in life 'cause they're really what make life worth the living. Always look around ya at what God has given ya to be happy with instead of expectin' more. She smiled to herself. Slatter was happy that God had given her a new friend to play with. Even if it was just for a little while. She kneeled beside her bed and closed her eyes. She earnestly prayed,

"Dear God.

Thank ya for a wonderful day.

I really do thank ya so very much for sendin' me my new friend Pydie.

God bless grandpa and Granny B, Mr. and Mrs. Hudd, all the old loafers at the store, Gibber and all of the animals, and oh yeah, my good friend Mr. Fritz. And thanks so much, God for helping me, Pydie, and Mr. Fritz catch those two old stealers. Oh, and I can't forget to pray for my old friend Gappy. Please help me to see him again sometime soon. Please bless him real, real good where ever he may be. Amen."

She started to get into bed when she remembered one more thing she needed to pray about. Dropping to her knees once again she added,

"And God, I almost forgot somethin' very important. Please say hello to my mommy and tell her I still miss her very, very much. And one more thing God, please help my mommy to like her new home as much as I like mine and somehow, please let me know that my mommy is in a beautiful place.
Amen."

She was so excited about having a new friend to play with she could hardly wait for tomorrow to come. While she was contemplating on whether or not to let Pydie in on her secret map, she closed her eyes real tight, snuggled up next to her pillow and quickly fell sound asleep.

# 4

# COOLING OFF SHEKOE

The night passed quickly and Slatter was up and dressed at the crack of dawn. She did not want to get left behind by grandpa today. She couldn't wait to go to the store and see her new friend. Slatter and grandpa hurriedly ate their big hot breakfast Granny B had so graciously prepared for them. Slatter was right on her Grandpa's heels as he headed out the old squeaky front screen door.

They quickly hopped into the blue goose. Grandpa pushed in the clutch and revved up the motor. Slatter watched as the black smoke rolled out of the car's exhaust pipe and surrounded the car. Grandpa, quite aggravated at the situation began speaking in a harsh tone.

"Ah. This thing ain't a idlin' right at all.

I ain't got time fer car trouble again.

I need a real mechanic to work on this car, instead of a young whippersnapper that thinks he knows everthin' there is to know about a car when he really don't know what the heck he's a doin'. I reckon I'm goin' to have to get it back in the shop before long and get it fixed again.

If it ain't one thing it's another.

Money money money.

Everythin' takes money and it seems everybody wants my money.

Seems I ain't never got enough to go around."

Slatter paid no mind to grandpa's complaints about the car. Thoughts were dancing around in her head about how she and Pydie could spend the day playing.

Once on the road, the car began bucking back and forth each time grandpa let the clutch out. Every time he shifted gears, the car made a loud grinding noise. Slatter was embarrassed, so she slid way down in the front seat so no one could see her.

As they rounded the curve toward the store, Slatter was quick to ask grandpa what she thought to be a most important question. The first item on her agenda for the day was to ask grandpa if she could have most of the day off so she and Pydie could play and have some fun.

Slatter crinkled up her nose and closed her eyes.

She crossed her fingers tightly and spoke in a brave, But humble tone.

"Say, grandpa.

How about my takin' the day off today so I can show Pydie around the store a little?"

Grandpa smiled at Slatter.

He could see her fingers crossed so tightly they were turning white on the ends. He could plainly see that having a new friend to play with was very exciting for her. He could tell by the way she asked him about taking the day off she felt her work at the store was very important. He tried to respond to her in a business sort of way because he wanted to confirm to her how important her work was to him. He knew she was feeling like she was an important part of his business and he didn't want to take that feeling away from her. Rubbing his chin between his thumb and his forefinger, he tried to respond to her question in a professional manner. He squinted his eyes and cocked one corner of his mouth to the side and said, "Well, let's see now."

I reckon it would probably be all right this one time, but don't get to thinkin' that ya can take every day off.

Ya know you're a big help to your old grandpa now and school will be a startin' before long."

Slatter felt proud he acknowledged her work as being important to him. She excitedly responded with a big grin.

"Yeah, I know.

Maybe I can help ya by workin' at the store after school and on Saturdays."

The drive to the store was very short and the car bounced into the store's parking lot before it came to a screeching halt. Grandpa, struggling with the gear shift, looked over at Slatter and smiled which was his way of showing his approval of her enthusiasm. He was having difficulty keeping up with Slatter's conversation because he was disgusted with the way the blue goose was acting up.

Grandpa frowned as he said, "This car's enough to make a preacher cuss."

Slatter could see his mind was on the car, so she asked her question again.

"Grandpa, didn't ya hear what I jest asked ya?"

I said maybe I could work for ya some on Saturdays."

"We'll see," he replied still fumbling with the gear shift.

"It all depends on your school work.

Ya know your Granny B is real big on gettin' homework done on time.

School work is very important," he stressed.

"An education is somethin' that nobody can ever take away from ya."

Slatter did not respond to Grandpa's statements regarding her homework. Instead, she rolled her eyes and pushed the heavy car door open.

She leaped out of the car and ran as fast as she could up to Mr. Fritz's shed. She jingled the big lock and pounded on the big wooden door. Mr. Fritz came to the door and unlocked it. When he opened the door, his face beamed when he saw Slatter's smiling face. He promptly greeted her cheerful.

"Well, well," he said,

"If it ain't our little friend Miss Slatter," swishing his hand out in front of him as he bent over and bowed to her as if she were a princess entering a ball.

"C'mon in. Miss Pydie's been a waitin fer ya.

She's jest now a finishin' her breakfast.

Den she be ready to go out and play which ya."

Pydie was sitting on Mr. Fritz's big checked quilt that lay on the end of his bed. She was holding a big plastic bowl with one hand and a spoon in the other. Slatter walked over to Pydie to see what she was eating. As she leaned over and looked inside the bowl, Slatter commented as she scrunched up her nose and made an ugly face.

"Yuckie Poo, Miss Pydie!

I can't believe that you're a sittin' there a eatin' that slimy lookin stuff!

It looks like thick snot!

It looks just awful.

I'm glad I don't have to eat that.

I'd puke!

What is that stuff anyways?"

"Grits," Pydie kindly replied as she kept on eating and ignoring Slatter's insulting comments.

"I like 'em.

I like dem a whole lots."

Slatter had wondered where Pydie was going to sleep in the one room shed. She could see Mr. Fritz had made him another bed out of empty feed sacks and she could see where he had slept on the floor. He used an old sack cloth for a pillow. Slatter thought Mr. Fritz's bed actually looked a little comfortable; maybe a little dirty, but comfortable. The old shed wasn't much to look at by any means of luxury, but Slatter could feel love in it.

Mr. Fritz noticed Slatter looking around the room.

He commented,

"Miss Pydie shore do like stayin' wif me and I shore do like havin' her here too.

I reckon ya two girls got somethin entertainin' up yore sleeve to do today."

He reached into what looked like a very large worn out cloth hand bag that clasped together at the top. He pulled out a big black comb with pretty pink flowers on it. Slatter had never seen such a beautiful comb before. She realized the bag must be Pydie's suitcase because it had her personal belongings in it. Mr. Fritz winked at Slatter as he made his way over to Pydie. Slatter closely watched Pydie's face and waited for a dreaded look to appear. When Pydie saw Mr. Fritz walking toward her with the comb, she took her fingers and flipped all of her hair toward the back of her neck. She sat perfectly still. She didn't mind a bit to have her hair combed. Mr. Fritz began combing Pydie's long curly hair. Slatter watched his huge calloused black hands as they awkwardly caressed the small comb sliding it ever so gently through her hair. Slatter walked over to Pydie and touched her long, tight curls as they fell behind each turn of the comb.

Then Slatter thoughtfully said, "Gee Pydie. Your hair is as soft as rainwater. My hair is as stiff as a board when I get up in the mornings. I hate to have my hair brushed because it always hurts so bad. My hairbrush is so big and ugly it can be used for a spankin' paddle."

Pydie smiled at Slatter as she softly replied to her compliments.

"Thanks.

I like to look pretty.

My momma is pretty and I want to look like her."

Pydie was not used to someone saying something so nice to her about her hair, because she got very little attention in her big household. Mr. Fritz was so very proud to have Pydie visiting with him. He put his arm around his niece and spoke as if he was making an announcement.

"Miss Slatter, Iz get ta treat Miss Pydie here, just like a princess.

Iz let her take over my very own bed while she a visitin' me.

Dat a way she's gots lots of room to move around in while she a sleepin' in dat big ole bed.

She be a guest in my home and Iz want her to have the very best of all Iz got.

Ain't that right Miss Pydie?"

Pydie thought Mr. Fritz had combed her hair long enough, so she grabbed the comb away from Mr. Frits, stood up and said,

"Why Iz not used ta havin' ever thin' so good.

Uncle Fritz is gonna spoil me fer shore.

Me and him was a eatin' Fig Newton cookies jest afore weez went ta bed.

I slept jest like a princess too.

There shore was a nice cool breeze a comin' in through dat dare winda over dare by da bed.

Iz plum got chilled by mornin'."

Pydie looked to Slatter to take the lead and inform her of what they were going to do next.

"Say Miss Slatter, what's weez gonna do today?"

"Slatter had a sly grin on her face as she replied.

"Well, I been a thinkin 'bout that and I think I got it figured out.

I think we're gonna play with my grandpa's tomcat that he keeps in his feed room at the store."

Pydie had a curious look on her face.

"Why does your grand pappy have an old tomcat in his feeds room anyways."

Slatter had a quick answer.

"Well, grandpa says that anytime ya have feed around, ya got mice around. So, he found him a cat to keep in the back room. We call him Shekoe."

"Shekoe!

Giggled Pydie.

"What a funny name."

Slatter felt she needed to explain the cat's unusual name.

"Well, that's the name he had when grandpa got him.

He's kinda Indian lookin' anyway."

Pydie giggled and curiously asked, "Oh yeah. How's dat?"

"Well," said Slatter very boldly, "He is yellow and white with a dark band of hair around the top of his head.

He looks like he's wearin' a headband jest like

Indians used to wear."

Pydie brushed off her little wrinkled burlap dress and said excitedly, "Let's get ta goin' so I can seez an Indian cat!"

Mr. Fritz knew Pydie would be thrilled to get to pet a real live animal. Patting her on top of the head he encouragingly said,

"Now ya be a good girl and don't be a gettin' in Mr. Slopey's way at the store. Ya here me now and do as Iz say."

Pydie looked up at her uncle and nodded her head.

Slatter was more than ready to go play. She proudly grabbed Pydie's hand and yelled,

"Well, If'n ya are ready to go play then let's get ta goin!"

Slatter glanced at Mr. Fritz as they both remembered her promise to him about not ever going into the feed store the back way.

Mr. Fritz winked at Slatter and bent down to whisper in her ear.

"Remember yore promise to me Miss Slatter.

And remember that big ole black snake Iz killed in da corn bin."

Slatter's eyes widened and she slowly nodded her head.

She would never forget the awful, cold, rubbery feeling when the big ole black snake rubbed against her leg while she was trapped in the grain bin next to her grandpa's feed store.

Pydie's eyes widened with excitement.

"Iz can tell that youns two has a big secret?"

Mr. Fritz said, "Yeah.

Ya might says dat we do and dis secret's only fer me and Miss Slatter to know."

As they walked out of the shed holding hands, they both waved goodbye to Mr. Fritz. It was a beautiful summer day with the sun shining brightly.

The wind, exhaling a refreshing cool breeze, gently blew the girls' hair away from their eager young faces.

They ran over to the front of the store so they could enter the feed room through the front door. The morning had came and gone very quickly and the heat from the hot sun was bearing down hard. The old metal handle on the big wooden door to the feed store was so hot it burned Slatter's hand when she grabbed it. Pydie wanted to help so she took a corner of her dress tail and turned the door knob while Slatter pushed on the door. Finally, after several hard pushes the door opened.

The odor in the feed room smelled of dry pet food.

The girls wrinkled up their noses and Slatter was the first to speak up, "Yuck," Slatter exclaimed as she used her right thumb and forefinger to hold her nose.

"It sure stinks in here."

Pydie wanted to be like Slatter, so she held her nose too as she nodded her head up and down. They looked around the room for Shekoe. It didn't take Slatter long to spot the cat. She pointed to the back of the room. There he lay on the very top bag of a stack of horse feed. He looked quite content all curled up into a big ball. Pydie stared in amazement as she gazed at the great big tom cat. Slatter acted as proud as a peacock as she asked,

"Miss Pydie. Did ya ever see such a big old cat in your life? Grandpa says he weighed him on his feed scales the other day and he weighs twenty five pounds!"

Pydie reached over to pet Shekoe and he stood up and stretched. Shekoe had plans for his day and they did not include playing with Pydie and Slatter.

He jumped down onto the old wooden floor and began to cry.

"Meow. Meow."

Pydie had a puzzled look on her face as she asked Slatter. "What is he a sayin?"

Slatter, in a matter of fact tone of voice replied without hesitation.

"Oh, who knows.

He probably just wants us to get him some more food.

All he does is eat and sleep.

I don't even think he catches very many mice.

Granny B thinks he's a real mouser cause he's so big, but my grandpa says, he's just big because he has access to so much cat food."

Slatter pointed over to the big twenty pound bags of cat food stacked in one corner of the room.

It was plain to see there was one bag in particular that had been torn open.

And it was very apparent, that old Shekoe had not been missing any meals.

As the girls stroked the cat, Slatter continued talking.

"Grandpa says he's got some customers that act just like Shekoe."

Pydie acted puzzled at what Slatter had said.

"Oh yeah.

Howz dat?"

Slatter was eager to explain.

"I heard him tell the loafers one time there are some people that think the world owes 'em a livin' and they ain't never gonna work to get ahead."

Pydie liked Slatter so much she seemed to soak up every word that Slatter spoke to her.

Shekoe began to pant because he was so hot.

Pydie had never seen a cat pant before and she thought he was getting sick.

She watched his tongue hang out the side of his mouth. She abruptly stopped stroking his fur.

With wide eyes she proclaimed, "Well I declare. Maybe I iz a makin' him hotter by rubbin' 'eem. I ain't never seez nothin' like dis afore. Is he gonna throw up or somethin'?"

"Na", replied Slatter in a know it all sort of way.

"He's just really hot.

He's jest pantin'.

Dogs do that too.

My grandpa says when animals get too hot, they have trouble breathin'...just like people do."

Pydie had a look on her face like she wanted to do something to help Shekoe, but didn't know of anything to do for him. After they both stood there for a few minutes watching the cat pant, Pydie joyfully spoke up, "Say, I gots an idea. Let's takes him outside and try to cool him off a bit."

Slatter quickly replied.

"We can't cool him off without some water.

There ain't no way to get any water here at the store."

Suddenly, Slatter got a bright idea.

Her eyes lit up as she exclaimed.

"Hey.

I know.

Let's carry him down to my house.

We've got a well and I fer shore know how to draw a bucket of water.

Surely we can figure out a way to cool him off with some nice cool well water.

But we gotta be careful and not let my Granny B know what we're a doin' cause she says old Shekoe ain't nothin' but a flea bag and she'd get real mad if'n she saw us a packin' him around the house."

Slatter and Pydie tried to pick the cat up.

But, he was way too heavy for them to carry all the way to Slatter's house. The cat was so gentle he let the two girls wrestle him all around and he never once offered any resistance. He was either too hot to fight with them or too fat and lazy to care much about anything. Both of them were working up a big sweat trying to find a way to carry the cat. Slatter first tried to wrap him up in Pydie's dress, but that idea didn't work because the front of her panties could be seen. Pydie, with both arms around the cat, struggled to hold him close to her chest. The cat was way too big for her to carry. He was so long his feet drug the ground.

Slatter even tried to push him down in the front of her overalls. But no matter what they did, he just didn't fit.

Then Slatter remembered seeing an old broken down metal wagon leaning up against the side of the store building in the back.

She eagerly gave Pydie an order.

"Wait right here fer just a minute Miss Pydie.

I'll be right back.

I got me an idea."

Pydie thought Slatter was the brains of their mission.

Since Shekoe was too heavy for her to stand and hold by herself, she sat down on the ground with him on her lap. She waited for Slatter to tell her what to do next.

Even though the hot summer sun was bearing down, the agonizing heat did not seem to alter any plans that these two girls had in mind. Pydie kept wiping the sweat off of her brow as she bent over the cat and gently spoke into his ear.

"What does youz think about us a goin' to cool youz off Mr. Indian Shekoe cat?"

Youz is one big ole kitty cat dat can't take da heat.

Me and Miss Slatter here, is a gonna do ya a real good deed and get ya cooled off da bestest way weez can.

Dat is, as soon as Miss Slatter finds us a way to get ya down the road a piece."

As Pydie patiently waited for Slatter's return, she continued to talk to Shekoe, as if the cat could understand every word she was saying. He looked up at her and yawned as if he could care less about anything. Poor old Shekoe just wanted to be left alone. The more Pydie wrestled him to keep him on her lap, the hotter he got and the more he panted.

After what seemed to be a very long period of time, Pydie saw Slatter walking toward her pulling an old rusty, metal wagon behind her. Slatter had wired one of the back wheels onto the wagon by using several short pieces of wire and the wagon was very wobbly. Like a drill sergeant, Slatter started giving more orders to Pydie.

"Miss Pydie, you get into the wagon and hold Shekoe on your lap so he won't jump out.

We need to get on out of here as fast as we can."

Pydie felt the urgency in Slatter's voice, and quickly obeyed her commands. She handed Slatter the cat and then climbed into the unstable wagon. It almost turned over when she sat down. Pydie suddenly spotted a piece of cardboard lying on the ground. It triggered a memory about a special person in her family.

"Miss Slatter, she politely asked.

"Would ya hand me that ole piece of cardboard over dare aside ya on da ground?

I just remembered somethin' about my old Aunt Adaline." Slatter had a puzzled look on her face as she tenderly placed Shekoe on Pydie's lap, picked up the cardboard, and handed it to Pydie.

"What about your Aunt Adaline and what are ya gonna do with this piece of old cardboard anyway?"

asked Slatter in a friendly, yet demanding tone.

"Well", continued Pydie.

"She be my aunt and she real big and heavy. Ever time she come over to visit, my momma would have all us kids collect pieces of cardboard.

Den, we all would sits around and fan her while she visited momma.

She was one hot momma.

She was all da time a fannin' herself. One time, she even stole a cardboard fan from da church.

She say the good Lord didn't care if'n she take dat fan, cause He knows she been a needin' a travelin' fan cause she's always hotter den anyone she ever knowed.

She'd wear us kids out a talkin' so much.

She talked all da time.

Us kids and momma, shore did dread a might when we would seez Aunt Adaline a comin' downs the road.

"Jest when my momma would get a word in edge wise, Aunt Adaline would but in."

Pydie began mocking her aunt in a squeaky tone.

"She say, "Honey child, does ya have da heat on?

I iz a gettin" awful hot."

My poor sick momma was glad to seez her leave.

My daddy say dat ever one has an aunt Adaline in dare family. Ya know someone dat talk all da time but doesn't ever say much dat really matters."

Pydie giggled as she continued telling Slatter about her family.

"She shore did like it when all of us was a makin' a big ole fuss over her.

Dat must've shore looked like somethin' all us a sittin' around a fannin' her.

Weez jest keep on fannin' and she jest keep on a talkin'.

She talked so much, we never could get her all da way cooled off.

Oh wozey me.

Da more she talk, da hotter she got and the harder we all fanned. We was all worn out by the time she went home. So ya seez, I'll use dis here piece of cardboard to fan old Shekoe. I knows how to fans real good.

I shore will try and keep him cool while youz keep on a figger'n a way fer us to git him down to yore house."

Slatter, shaking her head back and forth at Pydie's story, picked up the old heavy wooden tongue of the wagon and began pulling it toward the front door of the store. As Slatter was struggling to pick up speed, she noticed grandpa standing outside the front door of the store.

He was using his apron to wipe off potatoes. She waved her hand up in the air and tried to get his attention by yelling.

"Yoo hoo!

Hey grandpa.

Me and Pydie are needin' to go on home for a while."

Slatter could tell by the way her grandpa acted he did not hear what she said. He kept on working and did not acknowledge her presence.

About the same time Slatter was trying to get her grandpa's attention, a customer drove up in a brand new shiny car and parked it in front of the gas pumps. Slatter thought he looked like a rich family man. He was wearing a shirt and tie and was clean shaven. He impatiently honked the horn several times for grandpa to come outside and put gas into his car. The man didn't act very friendly and he was complaining and griping about the price of gas. As he was getting out of his car, he grumbled hatefully.

"Why J.E. Slopey!
Thirty five cents a gallon is highway robbery!
Can't ya do somethin' to get the price down a bit?
People have to eat too ya know.
Your customers can't spend all of their money on gas.
We have to buy groceries too."
A man's gotta feed his family."

Grandpa tipped his hat and grinned at the customer. He ignored the man's sarcastic remarks. He walked up to the man and in a polite, friendly manner tried to be of assistance to him.

"What can I do for ya today, buddy? "grandpa asked.
"It sure is a nice warm day.
Did I hear ya say ya are a needin' some gas?
I'll sure fill yer tank up fer ya.
I've got cold soda in a cooler inside the store there, if you're thirsty."

Grandpa walked all the way around the new car and whistled at it like he was whistling at a pretty girl.

"Whew-ee! Now that's one good lookin' piece of machinery ya got here."

"Thanks," said the customer very proudly.

Grandpa kept walking around the car as he admired it. He put his hands on his hips and struck up a conversation with his customer.

"By the way, speakin' of high prices, I reckon the price of big new cars ain't too cheap these days either are they?

I see ya jest bought one.

She sure is a beauty.

It's a new Chevy Impala ain't it?"

Again, the customer proudly replied.

"Yep, jest got her today and she's a beauty alright.

Be real careful now and don't spill any gasoline on it."

Grandpa couldn't resist the timing to comment about the car's big gas tank.

"Looks like she's got a big old gas tank on her too," grandpa politely commented.

"Ya know ya would think someone who worries 'bout the price of gasoline so much would buy a smaller car that had a smaller tank!"

The customer knew grandpa was making a point, but he didn't quite know how to respond to his remarks. He finally quit complaining long enough to say,

"Ah, just give me three dollars worth of gas I reckon."

As he stood there watching grandpa pick up the pump handle, he spoke under his breath.

"Surely, three dollars worth of gas ought to last me all week especially, if I can keep my wife and kids from runnin' to town to show it off."

"Ya know J.E.

I think I will go on inside a buy me a cold soda pop.

Maybe that would make me feel better.

I'll just leave my money on the counter."

Grandpa knew this man had a bad attitude and needed a lot more than a cold soda to make him feel better. After Slatter listened to the man smart off to her grandpa, she wondered how on earth her grandpa could be so nice all the time to such rude people. She noticed he was always kind and friendly to his customers. She didn't think he deserved to have to put up with people's hateful comments. She remembered him saying to her one evening as they were closing up the store.

"Slatter."

I jest don't know what kind of a day a person is a havin' by the time they get to me.

When people are dealin' with a lot of bad things in their life, by the time they stop by my store, they could be at the end of their rope.

I don't reckon anybody intentionally means to be hateful, they jest don't always stop and think about what they're a sayin'. Sometimes it's not what ya say but how ya say it.

I jest try to be as kind as I can to 'em and maybe a kind word at the right time will make their life seem better for a little while. We're all God's people and we need to learn to get along."

By the time Slatter could get the old rickety wagon pulled up next to the gas pumps, where her grandpa was standing, she was out of breath. As grandpa began pumping gas, out of the corner of his eye, he caught a glimpse of Slatter and Pydie walking toward him. Pydie tried her best to stand in front of the tied up wheel so her grandpa wouldn't notice the wire ties. "Well hello there pretty little ladies," said grandpa cheerfully. It sure is hot today, isn't it?"

Slatter was frowning as she wiped the sweat from her brow. "Yep.

It sure is," commented Slatter.

Grandpa continued pumping gas as he stared at the girls' hot, blistery faces.

After a few seconds, he broke the silence with a curious question.

"Why do I get a funny feelin' that you two youngins have a hankerin' to talk to me about somethin' ya think is mighty important.......er maybe you're jest up to no good.... which is it?

I've got to get back inside the store and get busy.

So spit it out.

I ain't got all day.

What is it ya want to say?"

The girls were afraid to speak up. Grandpa's tone of voice let them know real quick that at that moment, he didn't have much time to give to them. He was very busy with customers and whatever it was they needed to say, they needed to say it quick. They gave each other a quick glance and looked up toward the sky. Grandpa could see the girls were a little uneasy about talking to him so he thought he would console them by using a more yielding tone of voice.

"I'm sorry kids," he affectionately said as he tugged at the front of his cap.

"I didn't mean to be so short with youns.

Maybe, ya two would like to go over to the soda cooler and get a cold soda pop?"

Slatter pointed to Pydie and Shekoe as she casually remarked.

"Nope.

Thanks anyways.

But we don't want any soda right now, cause Pydie and Shekoe are goin' home with me.

Ya see, grandpa," Slatter explained.

"Me, Pydie and this here old Shekoe cat are all real hot and we would like to go home for a while and see if Granny B will make us some cold lemonade.

Then we could find us an old shade tree to sit under and cool off."

Grandpa immediately realized that for a moment he had forgotten the innocence of childhood and how hard children work at playing....at simply just pretending.

Trying to be organized and making the most of time was not very important to a child. Time seems endless to children. He thought Pydie's idea of drinking lemonade under a cool shade tree sounded like a very appealing idea. Grandpa pushed his cap back on his head as he bent over to Pydie. He brushed the long locks of sweaty, curly hair out of her eyes. In a soft pleasant voice he asked,

"Is that what ya would like to do little Miss Pydie?"

Pydie acted bashful as she batted her eyes at him and nodded her head. She nervously squeezed Shekoe up next to her chest. Cat hairs were flying everywhere and Grandpa fanned them away from his face as he chuckled to himself. Grandpa offered a suggestion to the girls about the cat.

"You girls need to let that poor old cat go.

He's old and he's hot.

He's goin' to get tired of bein' held so much and he might scratch the dickens out of ya when he jumps out of that there old wagon."

Slatter giggled when her grandpa used the word dickens.

She cheerfully argued.

"Ah grandpa.

He ain't a gonna scratch us.

He likes bein' held all of the time.

He's like a big baby.

Granny B says cats like their backs rubbed, so we keep rubbin' on him.

He won't go nowhere."

Grandpa took off his ball cap he was wearing to keep the sun out of his eyes and ran his fingers through his thin grey hair.

"Well, I can see your minds are made up," replied grandpa nonchalantly.

I reckon it's alright if ya girls go on home and call it a day.

There's no doubt today is a scorcher.

Watch out for cars so that ya don't get run over.

Everyone's in a big hurry these days.

Oh and say Slatter.

I want ya ta tell your Granny B I'll be home early for supper tonight."

As the girls started to leave, he yelled out to them.

"Ya girls be sure and help Granny B around the house when ya get home.

Pydie it'd be real neighborly of ya if ya helped your friend Slatter with her chores."

Pydie was so glad to get to go to Slatter's house that she yelled back at Slatter's grandpa.

"Weez shore will do jest as ya say Mr. Slopey."

Slatter rolled her eyes at what her grandpa said, but reluctantly agreed.

"Yeah, yeah," whispered Slatter in a slow lazy tone under her breath.

"We'll get the work done. C'mon Miss Pydie.

I got my work cut out for me just trying to pull this old heavy wagon with you and this big old cat in it.

Ya guys feel like ya weigh a ton."

Grandpa heard Slatter's comment so he thought it necessary to speak up and offer his advice on how to get the pitiful looking wagon home.

"Well, Slatter.

Ya can do what you want to, but the easiest way to get that wagon down the road is for ya to pull and Pydie to push." Slatter shrugged her shoulders as she replied.

"Na.

I'm afraid that won't work."

Grandpa looked puzzled as he asked.

"Oh, and why won't it work?"

Slatter looked very serious as she explained.

"Well ya see.

Somebody's got to hold the cat down or else he'll jump right out of the wagon.

Best I can figure, that's Miss Pydie's job 'cause she's the littlest one in this cat haulin' business."

Grandpa could see that Slatter had given a great deal of thought to her plan. He decided not to interfere any further. Laughing at the whole situation, he agreeably said,

"Alright. Alright.

Ya girls just go on and do it the hard way.

It's your venture.

Old grandpa was jest tryin' to help ya out a little.

Git to goin' now."

Slatter and Pydie waved goodbye to grandpa and started walking down the hot paved road. Slatter was working as hard as she could at pulling the old wobbly wagon. She knew Pydie was much too small and frail to be of much assistance.

The heat from the hot afternoon sun was almost more than she could bear. She could feel her skin burning from the sun's heat. Slatter knew it was up to her to make sure Pydie and Shekoe arrived at her house as quickly as she could get them there.

After what seemed like hours, Slatter finally pulled the wagon up to the old screen door in front of the house. She immediately fell down on the ground and lay lifelessly on the hardened, sun scorched grass. She was absolutely exhausted. Pydie, till sitting in the wagon holding the cat, stared at Slatter. Pydie wasn't tired at all. She noticed Slatter's clothes were wringing wet with sweat. Pydie still gently stroking the cat's back, calmly began talking to Slatter.

"Miss Slatter.

Youz and dis here cat must beez real tired cause youz is a layin' on da ground like ya could goes to sleep and dis here ole Shekoe cat is already a sound a sleep."

Shekoe had curled up into a big round ball with his head tucked between his back legs. He looked totally undisturbed. The rough ride home did not bother him one bit.

Granny B was outside in the garden picking green beans and tomatoes for supper. She happened to look up at just the right time and saw the girls as they came into the front yard. Granny B, putting her hand over her forehead to keep the sun out of eyes, started waving at the girls to come over to the garden.

Slatter saw Granny B waving at them and grabbed Pydie by the back of her dress and murmured very firmly.

"Pydie. Quick. Look the other way.

Granny B is waving at us.

I can tell she wants us to go over there and do some work for her.

I'm way too pooped to do anything for anybody right now. I'm a telling ya.

I'm plum wore out.

Let's just pretend we don't see her."

When the girls didn't respond to Granny B's wave, she hollered out to them.

"Yoo hoo!

Ya two girls!

Come on over here and help me!

I've got way too much for me to carry to the house by myself."

Slatter felt bad for ignoring Granny B's gestures so, she quickly got up off of the ground. She grumbled, "Oh, c'mon Miss Pydie.

Let's go see what we can do to help my Granny B."
Pydie replied.
"What about dis here Shekoe cat?

What is we gonna do wif him?

Duz I jest let him go?"

Slatter looked at the sleeping cat.

"Na, ya better not do that," replied Slatter as she looked around for a place to hide Shekoe.

"I see a place.

Let's take him over to the smoke house and put him in a box until we get done with the chores.

He's so fat and lazy, he'll probably just lie around and sleep, until we get back over here to him.

From the looks of him, he for sure ain't goin' nowhere.

He's too busy a sleepin'."

It took both of them to carry Shekoe over to the smoke house. Slatter quickly spotted a big cardboard box to put him in. She didn't want to use her hands to pick up the box for fear of waking the cat. She didn't dare let go of him, so she used her foot to drag the box closer to her. Because of the way they were jolting him around; the cat woke up and looked around.

His ears were laid flat against his head and his eyes were as black as coal. He was waiting for a chance to bolt away from his new founded friends. They gently stuffed the cat inside and folded the cardboard flaps down tight so he couldn't get out. At least they had themselves convinced he couldn't get out. After they hid the cat, they tried to make up for lost time by running as fast as they could over to the garden where Granny B was working. Slatter got on one side of Granny B's over sized wicker vegetable basket and Pydie got on the other. Using all their strength, they managed to pick it up off the ground. Struggling with each step, they managed to carry it into the house.

When the girls saw Granny B was finished working outside, they hurriedly ran over to the box where they had left the cat. To their surprise, the top of the box was wide open and Shekoe was gone. He was nowhere to be found. The girls started looking for him. As they walked passed the well, Slatter heard a noise. It seemed to be coming from a nearby bucket. The bucket was moving back and forth. Slatter put her finger to her lips and made a shh sound for Pydie to be real quiet. The girls then tiptoed over to the bucket. As they slowly leaned over the top of it, they saw Shekoe all hunched down hiding in the bucket. He was so hot and scared he was panting. The girls could tell the cat didn't want to be found, so they slipped around to the other side of the well and squatted down so he couldn't see them. Slatter whispered to Pydie,

"He looks so hot I hope he don't die on us."

Then she got a brain storm of an idea. She grabbed Pydie's arm and softly exclaimed.

"Hey! I got an idea.

Let's leave him in the bucket and lower him down into the well so he can cool off really fast.

He'll really like that."

Pydie trusted Slatter completely and went along with her idea. Both of the girls, at the same time, stood up and leaned over the well curb to look down. The water looked very deep and dark. Pydie's hands shook with fear.

"How deep is dis old well Miss Slatter," asked Pydie with fear in her voice. Slatter had no idea how deep the well was for sure, but to keep her friend from thinking she was stupid; she said the first thing that came into her mind. Slatter spoke in a slow, confident manner.

"Ooooh, I don't know.

I reckon it's probably 70 or 80 feet deep.

Yeah.

I'd say at least that."

Pydie's eyes got as big as they could get when she heard Slatter's answer. As she backed away from the well she shrieked in a loud scared voice.

"Wow!

Dat's a way too scary fer me!

Iz is gettin far, far, away from dare!

Iz a gettin fear all da way down ta my feet when Iz lookin' down in dat ole well!

Iz sure don't wants to be put down dare!

Iz can't even swims yet."

Slatter took the lead to try to calm Pydie's fears.

"Shh. Hush now.

Ya want us to get in trouble!

Don't be so loud!" remarked Slatter in a hushed tone of voice.

"Jest stop your worryin', Pydie.

We ain't gonna fall in.

"We ain't gonna actually put Shekoe in the well, neither.

We're jest gonna lower him down in there a little ways, so he can cool off fer a few minutes.

It's cool down in the well near the water.

As long as he stays in the bucket, he'll be just fine."

Pydie was very uncomfortable with Slatter's proposal.

"Alright," remarked Pydie.

"He's yore cat and youz the boss."

Slatter quickly grabbed the extra long rope that was hanging on the well curb and pulled it through the bucket handle. Then she tied a great big knot in the rope so the bucket was secure. About the time the girls lifted the bucket up in the air, Shekoe got wind of what was happening and decided he wanted out. He sprang up in the air and out of the bucket. He tried to use his claws to climb up the well curb, but he couldn't dig into the slick wet brick. Instead, he slid all the way down the inside of the well until he landed in the water.

Splat!

He made a big splash when he hit.

The girls, stunned at what they saw, stared down in the well in horror. Both of them stood there, with their mouths open wide and their hearts pounding in their chests. They were afraid that Shekoe the cat was going to drown and it would be all their fault. The cat was swimming around and around in circles and neither one of the girls knew what to do to rescue him. Slatter knew she had to try and do something very quickly as she had always been told that cats' did not have the ability to swim, at least for very long periods of time. Without saying a word, Slatter quickly lowered the bucket down into the well and turned the bucket sideways on top of the water.

She was hoping Shekoe could climb in it, but the cat was too scared to see anything. He kept crying a frantic "meow.... meow" as he swam around in circles. Slatter knew the cat was pretty old and he wouldn't be able to keep paddling around for much longer. She kept swinging the bucket back and forth until it landed upside down on top of Shekoe and then it fell on its' side. Pydie stood very still and was careful not to make a sound as she watched Slatter frantically try to get the cat to crawl into the bucket. The cat was not cooperating. He did not want anything to do with getting back into the bucket. Slatter had desperation in her voice when she whispered loudly.

"Pydie.

We'd better pray this works cause otherwise, old Shekoe is a goner fer sure!"

Pydie, scared stiff, dropped to her knees and clasped her hands together. She prayed aloud.

"Oh dear Lord.

Please help me and Miss Slatter save dis here Shekoe cat from drownin'.

We didn't means to kill him.

We was jest a wantin' to cool him off a bit cause he was sa hot."

Slatter's tongue was sticking out of the corner of her mouth as she skillfully maneuvered the bucket. Her arms were getting very tired from hanging onto the rope for so long. She didn't know if she had enough strength left to pull the heavy bucket with Shekoe in it, out of the well. Pydie saw that Slatter needed some help, so she got up off of her knees and began helping her pull on the rope. The rope was old and as it rubbed against the well curb, it began to fray. It was just a matter of time before the rope would snap in half. As they got the bucket within reaching distance, Slatter reached over the well curb and grabbed Shekoe by the back of his neck. He was alive, but scared half to death and dripping wet. She managed to get him to the ground. He didn't dare make a move. He acted like he was submissively grateful for their heroic rescue. Then, as soon as Slatter took her hands off of him, he took off like a shot and ran up to the front door steps where he began licking his drenched fur. Slatter and Pydie ran as fast as they could trying to catch him. They both felt awful because they almost drowned him. When they reached the front of the house, Slatter grabbed Pydie by the back of the dress and gave her a warning in a harsh tone.

"Now ya got to remember Miss Pydie," ordered Slatter.

Not one word to grandpa or Granny B about what jest

happened cause I'll for sure get a bad spankin' with my old wooden hairbrush."

Pydie, wide eyed, nodded her head up and down as Slatter spoke. Pydie could tell by Slatter's tone this was a very serious moment. The girls did not realize their rescue mission had lasted almost half an hour and Granny B was yelling at them to get washed up for supper. The girls quietly went into the house and washed their hands. As they walked by the two half empty buckets that were sitting on the kitchen floor, they looked at each other. Their thoughts were suddenly interrupted by a familiar bossy voice.

"Bout time you two showed up", remarked Granny B sternly. She spun both girls around looking at their unclean appearance. Then she started making clicking noise with her mouth and shaking her head as she started criticizing.

"Why I declare!

Jest look at youns.

Mmm. Mmm.

Ya two look like Filthy Mae and Gommy Lou.

If your hands is clean, I reckon youns will do 'til bath time. I've been a waitin fer youns fer a while.

I reckon youns didn't hear me a callin' ya.

Now I want each one of ya, to take a bucket on out to the well and draw me some more water fer supper.

I used all I had to wash the vegetables."

Slatter and Pydie's eyes met again as they gave each other a funny 'oh oh '.... 'We're about to get in trouble' look. Slatter, with a scowl look on her face, let out a big sigh as she reluctantly grabbed the buckets.

"Ah, c'mon Miss Pydie," remarked Slatter depicting a tired tone.

Here we go again.

We'd better do as we're told.

Let's go get some water."

Pydie and Slatter quickly walked back out to the well. Slatter started swinging the bucket back and forth and then dropped it into the well. Pydie attentively watched every move she made. Pydie noticed Slatter's arms were shaking as she pulled the first heavy bucket out of the well. She snapped the hook off of the first bucket and then snapped it onto the second one. Once again she sank the bucket. Breathing hard, she hesitated several times trying to regain enough strength to finish the task. It was all she could do to pull the bucket up out of the well. Her arms were weak from working so hard to rescue Shekoe. Pydie felt very sorry for her tired friend. She sympathetically offered to help.

"Iz will helps ya carry da water to da house," offered Pydie as she put her hands on the handle of the bucket, slopping water out on the ground.

"Iz jest don't thinks ya got it in ya to git it dare by youz self."

Slatter, fighting back tears, smiled a grateful smile as she gratefully moaned a response.

"Oh golly gee Miss Pydie. Thanks a lot. You're right.

I don't think I can carry it to the house by myself either.

My arms feel so shaky and weak."

She rubbed her hands up and down her arms.

"I sure hope they stop shakin' before supper."

As the girls were carrying the water buckets into the house, they noticed grandpa's old blue goose was sitting in the driveway. The girls wondered if grandpa had seen poor old, wet Shekoe sitting on the front steps licking himself. Hurrying, and not paying attention to what they were doing they sat the buckets down on the kitchen floor, almost turning them over. Some of the water spilled out. Pydie acted as a look out person while Slatter quickly grabbed a towel to wipe up the water before Granny B saw it.

Grandpa was already sitting in his chair at the kitchen table. He and Granny B were discussing how good Granny B's home canned pickles tasted and that she had a good chance to win first prize at the fair. Grandpa noticed how Pydie and Slatter had worked together to bring in the buckets of fresh water into the house.

"Now, that's what I like to see," bragged grandpa.

Two hard workin' little girls gettin' a job done by workin' together."

Granny B giggled to herself as she watched the weary girls sit down at the table.

She noticed the girls seemed very tired. She commented in a snooty tone of voice.

"Huh.

I'll say they're hard workin.'

They've been hard workin at somethin' alright.

Just look at their red faces.

I might have been born at night but I fer shore wasn't born last night. I'll bet these two youngins' have been up to somethin'." Slatter and Pydie exchanged guilty looks. Granny B walked over and put the dipper into the bucket. She dipped enough water out to fill up a pitcher and then she sat it on the table. As Grandpa poured everyone a glass of water to drink, he shared the dinner rules with Pydie.

"Miss Pydie." He firmly insisted.

"First rule ya need to know when ya eat at our house is we always say grace and thank the good Lord for our food. Second rule is we share our day's events with one another, but we don't laugh and cut up at the table.

Ya might say we let the food stop our mouths.

The third rule is don't let your eyes be bigger than your belly; and that simply means don't take out more food on your plate than ya can eat."

Miss Pydie looked over at Slatter and softly replied.

"Yes sir.

We gots da same rules at my house."

Grandpa asked the blessing and then opened up the conversation with a statement.

"Ya know the strangest thing happened at the store today.

A lady came into the store to buy a loaf of bread, but when she laid it on top of the counter; we noticed the end of it was tied with twine instead of the usual wire tie. I thought that was very strange so I walked over to the bread shelf to get her another loaf. I checked the other loaves of bread, and lo and behold, all of them had twine tied on the ends of them too. I've never seen sich a thing. Somethin' else that made the situation look worse was the twine on the end of the bread wrappers was the same twine I use to tie up butcher paper 'round my meat packages. Needless to say, I lost a sale. That lady turned her nose up and high tailed it out of my store. Can't say I blame her.

Somebody could've reached their dirty hands in there and took a piece out of it..... er somethin'.

That'd be plum unsanitary.

Who'd want to buy a loaf of bread with a piece of twine tied on the end of it?"

Grandpa shook his head in disgust.

"Well anyway, I pulled all the bread off the shelf and stacked it under the counter' cause it ain't fittin' to sell now.

The bread man doesn't come for two more days, so I reckon I jest won't have any bread to sell 'til then.

I can't imagine who'd do sich a thing nor why."

He stopped eating and with raised eyebrows he looked across the table at Pydie and Slatter as he asked a simple question.

"Say, ya two girls wouldn't happen to know anythin' about this little mishap would youns?"

Pydie and Slatter didn't respond to his question. Instead, they kept on eating and never looked up. Granny B came to their rescue by changing the subject.

Slatter had worked up quite a thirst. She had a taste for lemonade, but was afraid to ask for it. She decided to be satisfied with the water and grabbed her glass to take a drink. She couldn't help but notice something floating in the water. She immediately recognized what it was and kicked under the table at Pydie's legs. Pydie jerked when she felt the kick and gave Slatter a puzzled look. Slatter's eyes turned toward Pydie's glass of water and she gestured with her head toward her drink. She wanted Pydie to pick up her glass and look in it. Pydie took the hint and slowly picked up her glass of water. When she brought it up to her lips, she was shocked at what she saw in her glass. Her big eyes widened. She too instantly recognized what was in the water. It was full of Shekoe's cat fur! Needless to say, neither one of the girls finished drinking their water. They quickly and quietly sat their glasses back down on the table. Grandpa and Granny B paid no attention to the girls as they kept on talking about the day's events while they ate their supper. Slatter and Pydie quietly finished eating and asked to be excused from the table. Hurriedly, they scatted outside. On their way out, grandpa yelled out to them, "Don't ya girls run off now.

I told Mr. Fritz I would bring Pydie home right after supper." Slatter putting her hand to her mouth, giggled as she yelled back at him.

"Ok grandpa. We won't.

We'll just be sittin' outside a waitin' for ya to finish eatin'." Once outside, the two girls sat quietly side by side, in the old broken down metal wagon and patiently waited.

Both of the girls knew that it was just a matter of time before grandpa and Granny B noticed the cat fur floating in their drinking glasses. However, neither one of them dared bring up the subject for fear of being overheard. They both knew they had done something wrong and were hoping no one would ever find out! It would be their own little secret they would keep just between the two of them.

# 5

# WHAT IS A DREAM

As the girls sat side by side in the old metal wagon, they gazed up into the beautiful moonlit sky. Millions of stars illuminated the very humid, warm summer night. Nature's shades of darkness had completely covered the sky, with a subtle midnight black. The girls pointed and giggled at the thousands of lightning bugs that sparkled like diamonds against the dark summer night sky.

Pydie, staring into the sky in amazement, stuttered a little as she asked Slatter a serious question.

"Uh say, Miss Slatter. Have ya....uh... have ya ever wonder 'bout how many stars day iz in da whole heaven a way up dare?"

Slatter gazed up into the sky and thoughtfully replied.

"Yeah, I wonder stuff like that all the time.

Why I even wonder how in the world all of those gazillions and gazillions of stars stay up there a hangin in space all by themselves. I can't even imagine how far away they really are. They all look so small. Yet, my teacher says each one of the stars is bigger than the whole earth. Ya know there has to be a great big God up there somewhere in the heavens a taken care of all of this sky stuff; cause there ain't nobody I ever heard tell of here on earth that can make the moon glow at night and the sun come up ever mornin'. Only a great big powerful God could make all of these stars to stay in their very own space and sparkle like they're a doin' tonight.

Come ta think about it, I reckon most people don't really take the time ta think much about stuff like that.

Heck, Pydie.

I don't stop playin long enough to look up toward the sky much in the day time.

Oh, I guess once in a while I do, but I look more at the sky at night.

It's easier to look at then. The sun's so bright in the day; it hurts my eyes to look up at it. Besides, all I can see is the clouds. Somedays there ain't even any clouds, jest a big blue sky and what I don't understand is, how come it never falls down. It somehow just hangs up there.

Ya know what I mean?"

Pydie responded softly to Slatter's question.

"Yeah.

One of da thangs I wonder 'bout is duz da stars that's weez is a lookin' at right now, duz day shine in da day time too and maybe weez jest can't seez 'em.

Weez shore can seez 'em at night time. Jest look at all of 'em a shinin' down. I wonder how many dare is up dare."

Slatter nodded her head.

"Yeah."

There's a bunch of 'em up there alright.

I bet there ain't nobody here on earth that can count 'em all.

My Sunday school teacher told me that God has a name for every star in the sky 'cause before He made man, he was real busy makin' other stuff in the heavens and namein' everythin'."

Fer the life of me, I don't know why a star needs a name.

They don't never do anythin' to get into trouble so why would they even have to have one.

God could jest start with the number one and call all of 'em numbers instead of names, but I reckon God don't think like me."

The girls kept gazing into the starlit sky as they continued to share their thoughts.

"Ya know," said Slatter as she scratched the top of her head. "Come to think of it, I can't remember ever seein' the stars out in the day time either.

I remember seein' the moon one time during the day.

Oh well, only God knows all of the answers to our kinds of questions.

I reckon we jest need to ask him for the answers.

I bet He'd tell us anythin' we want to know if we jest ask him. He'd give us the answer through a person though 'cause I don't think God does much talkin' on his own. I reckon He likes for us to do all the talkin' and He does most of the listen'.

My grandpa knows a lot about God 'cause he talks to him a lot when he prays.

After me and Granny B go to bed, sometimes I hear him a prayin' way into the night. Sometimes I think he knows more about the bible than our preacher does. But even grandpa doesn't know the answers to some of the questions I ask him. Sometimes he acts like he don't want me to ask so many questions 'cause he has to take time to explain the answers to me and he uses words he says I'm too little to understand."

Slatter had excitement in her voice as she asked,

"Say, have ya ever heard the old sayin' if ya see a fallin' star ya are supposed to close your eyes and make a wish and that wish will come true? But only if you keep it to yourself and don't tell anyone."

Pydie quit looking up into the starlit sky and looked Slatter right in the eyes. Her big dark eyes danced with delight.

"Well, then Iz is gonna watch for one of dem dare fallin' stars so Iz can wish makes me a wish."

She giggled a little.

"If'n Iz be lucky, Iz might even catch some star dust and put it in my pocket."

All at once, Pydie's excitement instantly faded.

She closed her eyes trying to hide her sadness. Tears began to slide from beneath her long dark eyelashes. She put her hands over her face and began to cry. She cried silent tears. Slatter recognized that kind of cry. It was a heart wrenching hollow sound she herself had experienced many times while grieving for her mother. It was a cry that caused a huge painful lump to swell up in her throat. An ache so painful she felt as if her heart was going to break into tiny little pieces. Every once in a while when Pydie would catch her breath, Slatter would hear a soft whimper. Slatter didn't know what to do. She wanted to comfort her friend. She did the only thing she knew to do. She scooted over closer to Pydie and put her arm around her. She hated to see Pydie cry. She started saying encouraging words. "Ah, c'mon Miss Pydie," said Slatter tenderly.

"Don't cry so much.

You're probably just a little bit home sick.

You'll be alright in the mornin' when the sun comes up.

My momma used ta tell me, ya better not let that big old yeller sun catch ya cryin'. I heard Granny B say one time, things always seem worse at night time cause darkness makes ya feel heavy, ya know.... sorta serious about things; but come mornin', daylight will make ya feel lots better cause it makes your troubles feel lighter and ya can think on 'em differently.

Ya know I used ta get homesick all the time when I first come to live with my grandparents.

I was real scared.

I felt like I didn't belong anywhere to anyone.

Now, I feel right at home.

Now.

Ya have to believe your momma is a gettin' well, right now this very minute.

Why, I'll just bet ya your momma is a makin' big plans for ya to come home real soon.

Ya just wait and see.

I bet I'm right.

Just think.

At least ya still got a momma ta go home to."

Pydie nodded her head at Slatter's kind words.

"Iz pleads with God ever night and asks Him to please not take my momma to heaven 'cause Iz needs her here.

Can ya understand dat," replied a tearful Pydie.

Slatter swallowed back her own tears. She hung her head and whispered,

"Yeah.

Sure I understand.

Boy, do I ever understand 'cause I miss my momma a lot too." Slatter dropped her eyes to her lap so Pydie couldn't see her sad face.

Then, Slatter reached over and tenderly gave Pydie a big hug and kissed her on the forehead. As Slatter's face brushed Pydie's cheek, she tasted Pydie's salty tears as they trickled down her face like drops of rain. Slatter patted Pydie on the back and cheerfully changed the subject.

"Ya know what Miss Pydie.

Sometimes I imagine my mommy to be a sittin' way up high on a big poofy, white cloud a watchin' out fer me.

Why, sometimes if I listen real close, I can almost hear her voice. My momma's voice was so soft. She never hollered or screamed at me. Her voice was comfortin'. It always sounded soothin' to me. Kinda like a cool drink on a real hot summer day. When I'm lonely I think about the sound of her voice and it quenches my loneliness like water quenches my thirst.

Pydie, with a look on her face like she was about to cry, rolled her big eyes up at Slatter. She seemed to hang onto every word Slatter spoke. Pydie continued to talk about her mother.

"Miss Slatter," said Pydie in an inquiring tone, "afore yore momma died, did ya ever wish on one of dem dare fallin' stars that she'd get all better?"

Slatter, flicking specs of rust off the old wagon immediately replied.

"Oh ya bet I did.

I shorely did.

More than once too, but I think I must've told my wish to someone, cause it never ever came true.

Miss Pydie, I just want ya to remember somethin' I heard once.

There's always sunshine after the rain.

That means even when bad things happen to us, somethin' good will come along to make us be happy again. Just like the sun comin' out after a dark dreary, rainy day. I think that's such a nice thought. I think thoughts like that a lot since I moved in with my grandpa and Granny B."

My Sunday school teacher said it's best to keep our mind a thinkin' on good things instead of bad things.

She says that's how kids gets into bad trouble.

They get to thinkin' about the wrong things, then before they know it, they're a doin' wrong things.

Slatter wanted to talk about something happy because she could see that all of their conversation about Pydie's mother being sick was making both of them very sad.

She decided once again to try to change the subject.

She inquisitively asked Pydie a question about an unusual subject.

"Miss Pydie.

I'm wonderin' somethin'.

What would ya say a wish is anyway?"

Pydie immediately cheered up. Wiping her tear stained face with her dress tail, she managed to reply.

"Well.

Only thing I know 'bout wishes is what my momma told me once. She say a wish is like a dream.

Ya know.

Somethin' ya dream about dat's sooo good youz is fer sure, it ain't a goin' happen to ya.

Iz think wishin' for somethin' is kinda like dreamin' bout' somethin'.

I reckon it's kinda like wishin youz had enough money to go anywheres youz wanna go and buy anythin' youz wanna buy for yourself or for uther people in yore family.

Ya know, like when ya wish for somethin real hard and den believe it can come true.

I believes dat some people's wishes duz come true.

But when yore wish finally duz comes true, ya still jest can't believe it."

Pydie gave Slatter a sly grin and asked, "Would ya likes to know one of my best secrets Miss Slatter?"

Slatter grinned back at her and replied.

"Yeah!

I love secrets."

Pydie brushed her hair out of her eyes and scooted over as close as she could get to her new found friend. She looked all around her to make sure no one was listening then she leaned over just inches from Slatter's face and whispered quietly.

"Well, one time, when Iz went with my momma to see da doctor, Iz saw a pretty little black baby doll in a store winda. She was the prettiest lookin little ole baby doll Iz ever did see.

My momma say her hair look jest like mine.

Dat little doll was just a sittin' in dat big ole winda, jest like she was a waitin' for me to comes along and buys her.

She looked all alone cause she was da only doll in da whole winda.

Dare was big ole mean lookin' stuffed animals a sittin' all around her.

I was a figurin' she might be a scared of dem animals.

So, I asked my momma if'n we had some money ta buy dat baby doll and she just shook her head no.

Den later dat night, when she thoughts Iz was a sleepin', Iz heard her a cryin'.

I knows she was a cryin' cause she didn't haz no money ta buy dat doll fer me.

I wanted dat doll real bad, but, I shore didn't want it bad enough to makes my momma cry.

So, Iz just keep on a dreamin' about gettin' me a little black baby doll someday. Iz ain't never hads a real baby doll before. Ever night, Iz pray to da good lord and ask Hims to sends me one." Slatter saw hope in Pydie's big bright eyes as she pointed her finger toward the ground and boldly said,

Iz really believes dat one of deeze days, the good Lord's gonna look down here on earth at me and say,

"Dat little ole Pydie girl has been a real good little girl and she needs herself a little black baby doll to plays wif and Iz gonna seez she gets one.

Den, He gonna give it ta me.

Until den, Iz will jest keep on a wishin' and a dreamin' bout' it. I jest wished He'd hurry up and dude it cause I doesn't like dis waitin'."

As Pydie talked, Slatter was in deep thought. Frowning, Slatter shrugged her shoulders and asked,

"Well, then what's a dream?"

Ain't there no difference in a wish and a dream?"

Pydie breathed a deep sigh and smacked her hand against her knee. She rolled her eyes and put her hands on her hips. "Miss Slatter." Pydie's voice began to get louder.

"Ain't ya heerd a word Iz been a tellin' ya?

I was a sayin'........a dream is a wish from yore heart!

A wish is a yearnin' in yore heart fer somethin' special or fer somethin' to happen that ya know ain't never gonna happen, but it'd be sooo wonderful if'n it did.

Uncle Fritz told me one time dat I should follow my heart' cause the good Lord leads people by speakin' to dare heart.

He also told me dat most people think with dare head, but people who loves the Lord...well, Christian folk dat is, day is supposed to thinks wif dare heart."

My daddy say one time a dream is somethin' ya has to build. Jest like buildin' a great big house, only youz is a buildin' it in your head.

Ya has to be able to seez it in yore mind.

Ya dream about howz ya goin' to build one room at a time in yore life.

He say dreams should last yore whole life.

Ya should always be a lookin' fer ways to builds one more room onto yore great big house.

A dream is when ya keep makin' one room at a time in yore head."

She mocked her father by using a deep low voice.

"My daddy say, Miss Pydie.

Youz dream is yore very own place.

It's somethin' dat belongs to jest youz and youz can make it anyway youz wants to."

Slatter nodded her head. She was listening very seriously to what Pydie was saying to her and she believed every word her best friend had said.

All of a sudden, the girls spotted a blazing streak of white-capped haze shooting downward out of the sky. Slatter was first to express excitement. She quickly leaped to her feet, and pointed up into the sky.

"Look! Look!"

She exuberantly shouted as she jumped up and down.

It's a real fallin' star!

Hurry Pydie make your wish!

But don't ya dare tell anyone what it is, and I mean not even me, or it won't come true."

Pydie's big dark eyes danced with enthusiasm as she stood up next to Slatter. Pydie confidently spoke up and said,

"ok.

Here Iz goes."

Grabbing hold of Slatter's hand, she closed her eyes real tight and made her wish. After that, both girls slowly sat back down. The excitement was quickly over and it didn't take long for them to notice they were scratching their arms and legs because they were being bitten by annoying mosquitoes.

Just as Pydie began to yawn, grandpa came walking out of the house and sat down on the steps next to Slatter. He jokingly asked.

"Well, now children.

Is the stars a puttin' on a free show fer youns tonight?"

The girls didn't respond. They were too busy scratching their arms and legs. Grandpa smiled as he watched the girls swat at the mosquitoes. "Ya two girls had better watch out.

You'll get eat up by mosquitoes if ya stay outside much longer. Your both so sweet, I bet you'll draw 'em from a mile away."

As he looked up into the starlit sky, he teased them again.

"Do youns think youns have had enough adventure for one day or are ya stirrin' up your imaginations for tomorrow," inquired grandpa. The girls just giggled at him. He stood up and made a grunting sound as he knelt down on one knee in front of them. He rubbed his leg for a few seconds as if he was in pain. He was just a few inches from their faces when he began to speak.

"Say," spoke grandpa in a soft, tender voice.

"If ya girls think youns can keep a special secret, I know a good one.

Would youns like to know what it is?"

With big eyes, they looked at one another and at the same time yelled, "yes."

They put their hands over their mouths to muffle their giggles. Grandpa tenderly put one arm around each of them and pulled them close to his chest. The girls could feel his end of the day whiskers tickle their cheeks. He eloquently whispered to them.

"The wind of heaven is that which blows between the breaths of children's secrets."

Again, the girls looked at one another and giggled; only louder this time.

"Oh grandpa," replied Slatter as she threw her arms around him and gave him a big kiss on the cheek.

"You're jest being silly."

Slatter's grandpa laughed as he stood up. Then, he took Pydie by the arm and spoke in an insisting tone of voice.

"Come along now.

Get into the car Miss Pydie, so I can take ya home to your uncle Fritz.

He'll be a lookin fer ya bout' now."

Pydie hugged Slatter goodnight and hurriedly jumped into the front seat of grandpa's old car. Slatter couldn't see short little Pydie sitting in the wallowed out seats of the old blue goose. As the car backed out of the driveway, Pydie stuck her arm out of the window and waved goodbye. She watched the old blue goose go down the road until its' tail lights faded out of sight. Slatter had a sad expression on her face. She had enjoyed her new friend's company so much she hated to see her have to go home at the end of the day.

Granny B walked out onto the porch and saw Slatter standing on the porch steps, looking down the road.

She thought Slatter looked lonely and pitiful. She slowly walked outside and stood next to her. She tenderly put her arm around her. The summer night air was sticky and muggy. She touched the back of Slatter's head, and then smoothly ran her hand down her neck. She smiled as she lovingly pulled Slatter close to her side.

"Don't fret none child," said Granny B.

"Tomorrow is a new day.

A day full of life and fun.

It'll be here before ya know it.

We've done all we can do in this day.

We've milked as much life out of it as we can.

C'mon let's go on in the house and get ready for bed."

Slatter couldn't help but notice the tired look on Granny B's face as they both turned to go inside. The wrinkles under her eyes seem to silently suggest life had not been too kind to her. She knew Granny B was getting old and she hated the thought of her dying. The thought of death was never very far from her mind. She pushed the dreaded thoughts out of her head and took one last glance at the beautiful night sky; mainly to make sure she didn't see any storm clouds before she closed the door behind her. She always dreaded thunderstorms, especially at night. The bright flashes of lightning and the loud rolling thunder seemed more powerful in the dark. She hated everything about darkness because it made her feel exposed to danger she couldn't see.

The evening seemed empty now and the illuminating liquid light of the full moon offered her little comfort. She whispered out loud to herself as though she was making conversation with an invisible person.

"There is somethin' so lonely about darkness.

Even though the sky is so aglow and beautiful tonight, I know in my heart, there is nothin' outside to be afraid of. Yet, I am still afraid. I guess maybe it's because things can easily be hidden in the darkness. Sometimes hidden things are ugly and creepy lookin' and they can jump out at ya unexpectedly. Night time has a way of making me feel alone and scared. It makes me feel heavy. I like sunshine a whole lot better. I like being where there is light. I like to be able to see what's around me." Slatter had a habit of talking out loud to herself. It was an odd sort of way of coping with her loneliness.

Slatter's serious thoughts were suddenly interrupted when Granny B yelled at her from inside the house.

"Quit a talkin' to yourself.

Hurry up now.

Ya need to shut the door and come on inside.

You're lettin' bugs in the house.

Was ya raised in a barn or somethin'?"

Slatter quickly slammed the door shut.

On the way to her room, she shifted her thoughts to what she had heard the preacher say one time.

God says there is joy in the morning.

Slatter hung onto that thought. She knew she would get to see her friend again in the morning and that for sure would bring her joy. She quickly went inside to get ready for bed. When she reached the kitchen door, Granny B handed her a dish pan filled with warm water and instructed her to take a sponge bath before putting on her pajamas. Granny B patiently waited while Slatter walked to her room and jerked her pajamas out from under her pillow. Then she walked back over to Granny B and took the pan of warm water. She headed for the back porch where she would have the privacy she needed to bathe.

When she had finished bathing, she quickly put on her pajamas, said goodnight to Granny B, and climbed into bed. As she lay in her bed she remembered how she used to look forward to waking up in the mornings. She would jump out of bed, and quietly slip into her mother's room. While her mother slept, she would slip into her bed and snuggle up as close as she could get. She could still remember the lingering scent of sweet lotion on her mother's skin. She thought about how happy Pydie must be to be able to look forward to seeing her mother again. Slatter could not understand how one day her mother was so alive, laughing and talking, then the next day be gone forever; without any kind of a warning. She thought about seeing her friend Pydie. Fear began to tug at the strings of her heart. She hoped that nothing would happen to Pydie during the night. At least, nothing like what had happened to her mother.

"ooooh" cringed Slatter, talking out loud as she glanced up at the ceiling.

"There I go again.

I can't let myself think about such bad stuff.

I must remember to think on good things, pure things..... things that make us think happy thoughts.

I won't let myself dwell on bad ugly stuff that can happen to me without any warnin'."

As she said her prayers, she prayed that God would protect her friend Pydie during the night and she would still be at Mr. Fritz's house in the morning. Slatter realized at a very young age that death is only a heartbeat away, and each day is all anyone ever really has. She shivered as she thought about how absolutely no one has any kind of a guarantee they will be alive from one moment to the next. She always remembered in the back of her mind what her friend Gappy had told her. Because of Gappy's unusual voice, his words echoed in her mind several times a day; 'Life is but a vapor compared to eternity.' She somehow felt protected and secure in thinking the people she loved would always be there for her to touch and show them affection. But, deep down inside, she knew better.

She shifted her thoughts to the poem she had to write to enter into the beauty contest at the fair.

"That's it!"

She snapped her fingers, after receiving what she considered to be an inspirational thought.

"That's it.

That's what I'll write about!

I'll write somethin' up about how people need to act more like Jesus.

I'll try to tell people how they should look for Jesus in the small things in life and that Jesus wants us to be good to one another-watch out and protect one another. I want to share with people in this town how God is really here with us on the earth and He's carefully watching over everybody.

If people really believed Jesus was watchin' 'em every day in all they say and do, they'd live their lives a whole lot different. They wouldn't be so hateful to grandpa and they wouldn't give mean stares to Pydie and Mr. Fritz."

She smiled as she remembered her Sunday school teacher telling her class about Jesus' birth. Her teacher said in Jesus' day people were looking for Him to come as a king with all the attention centered on money and power. But Jesus came into the world as a little baby, born in a plain, old stable where animals lived. He was raised as a regular poor kid; not a rich one. He never owned a diamond ring or a fancy house either. I'll jest bet Jesus shows himself to people in little ways a lot more often than he does in big ways.

She was very deep in thought when she rolled over onto her side and stroked her hand along the edge of her mattress. All of a sudden, she sat straight up in her bed and exclaimed,

"Oh my gosh, my secret map!

I left it in the back pocket of my dirty overalls!"

Her eyes suddenly opened really wide as she envisioned Granny B picking up her dirty clothes and going through her pockets. She quickly sprang out of bed and tiptoed very quietly to her doorway to see if anyone was nearby. She snuck back into the kitchen where she had taken her bath and there were her dirty clothes still lying in a pile beside the wash pan full of dirty water.

"Whew.

Man was that ever a close call."

She sighed out loud. She pried the old yellowed map out of the back pocket and ran to her room. She quickly stuffed it under her mattress and jumped back into bed.

She fell asleep thinking about what she and Pydie had said about dreams. She even wondered if her life was really a dream and when she died, maybe that was when her real life would begin. She thought about a song she had heard the church choir sing before entitled Death Is Only a Dream. She thought to herself that maybe she needed a dream to hang on to in this life-right now. As she thought about what kind of dream she would desire. She decided her dream would be a hopeful one.

Hopeful that someday she would find a buried treasure by using the old map she had found.

Hopeful that her treasure would belong to just her and no one else.

Hopeful that she would have enough money to be able to buy anything she wanted for anyone she wanted and not have to worry about the cost. She wondered if God would hold it against her because she wanted to be rich. She remembered hearing her Sunday school teacher say one time that money wasn't the root of all evil; it was love of money that makes people turn away from God. The last thing she was hopeful for was to have enough money one day to be able to repay her grandpa and Granny B for taking her in and letting her live with them. She was old enough to know that raising children require a great deal of money. After all, her own father couldn't afford to raise her by himself. She felt obligated to give something back to them in return for helping her. In her young mind, she thought by giving them money, she would be repaying them for the kindness they had shown her. She wondered how she could ever come up with a price that would represent how grateful she was for their love. In her mind, she could never come up with a fair price. She could pay them gazillions of dollars until she died and it still wouldn't be enough. She finally came to the conclusion on her own that love was priceless.

She wished in her heart that her mother had not died.

She wanted her real family together again. She realized she couldn't change her past but she couldn't stop such longings in her heart either. She had lived through enough changes in her life already to know that just because things change, doesn't mean life still can't be good.

Grandpa always made Slatter sit next to him during the church service so she had no choice but to listen very close to the preacher's sermon. Somehow, the preacher's words always seemed to stick in her mind and at least once every day something would happen to make her recall his sermons. He most recently stated that people cannot change their past. The past is dead. She pulled the covers up over her head. Because she feared death, every time she thought of the word dead, she shivered. A person's future is the only thing that can be changed. She wanted to be careful to only wish and dream about the future, but she wondered how in the world she could ever be able to forget the past.

The sounds of the window fan as it pulled in the cool night air caused Slatter to become sleepy. As she closed her eyes and pulled the clean, cool sheet up to her chin, her mind pondered over the day's events. She had to smile to herself as she remembered neither grandpa nor Granny B had said a word to her about the cat fur in the drinking water. Maybe they hadn't noticed or maybe they didn't know what it was for sure. Whatever the reason, Slatter thought she was in the clear and she wasn't going to worry about that situation any longer.

# 6

# A HERO IN THE SUN'S SHADOW

Slatter was rudely awakened by the grinding sounds of a great big truck backing up into the back yard. She quickly scrambled out of bed to look out her window to see what was going on. The truck looked very old and it had a big white tank on the back. Slatter glanced over at her alarm clock sitting on the dresser. She rubbed the sleep out of her eyes to make sure she was seeing the time on the clock correctly.

"Why it's jest seven o'clock in the morning," she spoke aloud.

She could not imagine what in the world this truck was doing at her house at such an early hour. She saw a big heavy set man get out of the truck and walk over to the well where her grandpa and Granny B were standing. She could see the man's name was spelled out in bold black letters on the pocket of his shirt. She read the words aloud, "Bub's Water Service..... You Call We Haul."

All at once Slatter realized what was happening. Bub's Water Service was there to pump out the well. She remembered Shekoe falling into the well. She quickly realized she was in big trouble. Curiosity got the best of her, so she quickly got dressed. She gave her hair a couple of quick strokes with her old hairbrush and ran outside. She didn't even take time to put on any shoes. As soon as she stepped outside, she noticed how hot and steamy the day had already become. The sun was barely up and she was already dripping wet with sweat from running outside. She came to a screeching halt right beside Granny B. They both watched as the big truck slowly backed into the yard.

"What's goin' on around here Granny B," asked Slatter innocently. Slatter knew perfectly well what was going on, but she thought playing dumb was the best course of action to take at this point. When Granny B didn't respond to her question, Slatter pointed to the truck and asked Granny B again, "What's this big old truck doing in our back yard? Is there somethin' wrong?" Granny B put her arm around Slatter and with a tone of aggravation, she finally replied.

"Just never you mind child.

Ya jest go on back inside and eat ya some breakfast.

Your grandpa is a takin' care of things out here.

Kids don't need to know about everythin' all the time."

Slatter started digging her bare toes into the grass. She liked to wrap the cool clover grass underneath her toes and pluck it out of the ground. Her curiosity was not satisfied, but she didn't know quite how to ask Granny B another question without making her mad. So, she decided to obey her and go back into the house. As she reached the back door, she turned around and saw Granny B walking right behind her. Granny B, volunteered the information Slatter wanted to know.

"Hey.

Wait up fer me Slatter," ordered Granny B.

I reckon ya have a right to know what's a goin' on."

Granny B, periodically gasped for air as she hurriedly caught up with Slatter. As she walked, she used a complaining tone of voice. "I'm so aggravated," she said as she wiped her hands on a dish towel she had carried with her outside.

"Your grandpa and I think a wild critter must've accidentally fell in the well the other night."

"Why do you think that Granny B," asked Slatter with her teeth clenched together. She fearfully waited for Granny B's reply.

Granny B looked right into Slatter's eyes as she answered.

"Well, when we was a finishin' up with supper last night, we saw some kind of fur floatin' around in our drinkin water. We were afraid that whatever it was that fell in the well was drowned and probably was still a layin' down in the bottom. We could get real bad sick a drinkin' contaminated water, so jest to be on the safe side, we called the water man to come and drain the well."

Slatter made an awful scrunched up face as Granny B spoke. She felt so bad about hiding the truth from Granny B. She stared at the ground because she didn't have the nerve to tell her the truth. Slatter had one question on her mind and she had to ask it or bust. She spoke in a concerned stutter.

"Er, uh, Granny B. I was jest wonderin'.

D...does ....does that cost very much money to have all of that cleanin' stuff d...done?"

Granny B shot her a mean look.

"Your darn tootin it does," she replied as she backed up to Slatter for her to tie on her apron.

That's an expense your grandpa and I wasn't a plannin' on havin to pay out.

Why, havin to call Bub over here will pert near take all of this month's savin's.

He ain't cheap ya know.

Money don't grow on trees neither.

It has to be earned."

Granny B felt a need to explain how Bub would clean out the well so Slatter would have a better understanding of the procedure. As Slatter tied Granny B's apron strings into a bow, she listened to her explain how Bub cleans out a well.

"Ya see Slatter," began Granny B in an aggravated tone.

The first thing the man's gotta do is drain all the water out of the well.

Then, the second thing he's gotta do is clean it and put fresh water back in."

Granny B let out a disappointed sigh.

"Oh I reckon it don't matter none, but my problem is I may not get to enter my pickles in the fair this weekend cause of this little deal. I don't know if I'll have enough cash left over to pay my entry fee." Slatter, leaning up against the kitchen counter, slowly responded to Granny B's remarks.

"W-e-l-l golly gee, Granny B.

I'm sure sorry ya had to call the water man."

Granny B patted Slatter on the back and assuringly said, "Oh, don't ya go a worryin' your pretty little head about it. It's not your fault."

But Slatter knew it was her fault.

She hung her head to hide the guilty look on her face.

Slatter's bottom lip began to quiver.

Granny B thought it strange for Slatter to be so upset. She reached over and gave her a great big hug.

"Ah, now don't ya go a frettin' and feelin' sad fer me.

Your grandpa will find a way to pay my entry fee.

I've no doubt.

He'll take care of me. He's takin' care of me for a lot of years now.

This ain't none of your doins' anyway.

It ain't the end of the world.

If this is all the trouble I ever have to worry about before I die, then I got it made. Ya go get dressed now and I'll fix us a bite to eat." After Slatter had gotten dressed, she came out of her room with a gloomy look on her face. Granny B made them some toast and eggs and set their plates on the table. Together, they sat down to eat. Slatter did not have much of an appetite. She knew something Granny B didn't. She actually did have something to do with the water man having to come to the house and she felt really bad about the whole thing. Slatter sat very quietly at the table as she tried her best to tell Granny B what she had done with Shekoe the cat, but every time she opened her mouth to confess, the words just wouldn't come out. She had already resigned herself to the fact that she would rather have bad feelings in her head than to have them on her hiney. Finally Granny B decided to break the long silence. She reached over and pushed Slatter's long stringy bangs behind her ear.

"Slatter." Granny B cheerfully said.

"I saw Mr. Fritz early this mornin'.

He was out in the fence row behind the house a pickin' berries. He walked on up to the house and asked me if it would be alright if Pydie could come here for a while this mornin'. He's got a man a comin over to his place that's a bringin' some big draft horses that need to be shod and he doesn't want Pydie in the way. He said the horses are worth a lot of money and he's afraid Pydie might do somethin' to scare 'em. Ya know that man has been so good ta help me and your grandpa over the years. He's an amazin' man and it's a privilege jest to know him. He never complains about nothin' and seems to me he always thinks before he speaks. I told him we'd love to have Pydie come down and play. I already spoke to your grandpa and he said ya don't have to help him at the store today. So, you and Pydie can play right here at the house."

Slatter remained silent. Granny B hesitated a few seconds and then changed the subject.

"By the way, did ya know that old flea bag Shekoe cat slept in the old blue goose last night?"

She carefully observed Slatter's reaction to her question. Slatter didn't even look up. She kept staring into her plate. Granny B continued on.

"Your grandpa is goin' to take that cat with him back to the store this mornin' when he goes to work.

I told him that cat is a real good mouser and he belongs in the feed store room where there's lots of mice; not here under foot.

I'm afraid he'll trip me and make me fall."

Suddenly Granny B heard the old blue goose start up and she quickly looked out the kitchen window just in time to see grandpa leaving for the store.

"I reckon Bub must be finished.

Your grandpa's a leavin' now."

Slatter kept on stirring her scrambled eggs around in her plate. She was sitting there wishing she had never brought that Shekoe cat home with her. He was a big bunch of trouble. Granny B could tell something was bothering Slatter, but she didn't ask her any questions. She was not in any mood to put up with Slatter acting pouty. Frustrated, she began fussing at her.

"Young lady," she scorned.

I'll have ya know I done scrambled them eggs once.

Now, you're tryin' to scramble 'em again.

What's the matter with ya anyway?

I ain't never seen ya so quiet.
Has the cat got your tongue?
Ya ain't a sayin' much.
Ya usually gab my ear off."

Slatter shrugged her shoulders. She did not want to talk about Shekoe any more than she had to. All of a sudden, they both heard a light, tapping sound on the front screen door. Slatter jumped out of her chair and ran through the living room to see who it was. As she approached the door, she could see through the screen that it was Pydie.

She was glad to see her. She yelled back to Granny B. "Pydie's here!
I'm gonna go on outside and play with her."

Pydie took one look at Slatter's very sad-looking face and with raised eyebrows said, "Man o man, Miss Slatter. Youz look as if 'n youz has lost yore bestest friend."

Slatter opened the screen door and stepped outside.

She sat down on the front steps and Pydie sat down beside her.

Slatter's voice sounded shaky as she spoke quietly.
"Oh Miss Pydie, I feel just awful.
See that big old truck in our back yard over there?"

Slatter pointed toward the well in the back yard.

Pydie nodded her head yes.

Slatter almost in tears kept talking.

"Well, 'cause we dropped poor old Shekoe cat down in the well, Granny B called the water man to come and fix our well.

They think a wild critter, like a skunk or a possum', fell in the well and drowned and is a laying down in the bottom of it. Granny B called the water.......... contaminated."

Pydie's eyes widened and her mouth dropped open when Slatter said such a big word and she didn't have a clue what it meant. She didn't even ask Slatter to explain what it was. Judging from the despair in Slatter's voice, she knew it meant something bad. Slatter could not take her eyes off of Bub the water man. For a few minutes the girls sat and watched him work. Slatter wanted him to hurry and do his job and leave. She became so nervous she took a hold of Pydie's hand and demanded, "C'mon. Let's go play or somethin'. Maybe we could go out to the edge of the driveway and look for some pretty rocks, until that Bub guy leaves." Pydie didn't say a word. She followed Slatter out to middle of the front yard. They sat down on the stiffened, late summer grass that had turned an ugly brown from the summer sun's intense heat.

The girls sat there on the ground for a long time watching an army of ants build big mounds in the dirt. For a long time, neither one said a word.

Finally, Pydie got tired of sitting around doing nothing. Her patience grew thin and she decided to let Slatter know she was bored. She sounded a little aggravated when she spoke.

"Say, Miss Slatter.

Iz a gettin' tired of sittin' here a doin' nothin'.

Why doesn't we goes out dare, back behind your house and play in dat old barn?"

Slatter, was starting to get very bored too. She sprawled out on her back and put her hand over her eyes to block out the blinding rays of the sun. She had a weed hanging out of one corner of her mouth as she tried to use an understanding tone of voice when she responded to Pydie's question.

"Ah Pydie.

There ain't nuttin' out there worth seein' or playin' with.
Believe me I know.
Remember I live here."

Slatter watched Pydie get up off of the ground and brush the dirt off of her burlap dress. Slatter couldn't help but notice Pydie always wore the same clothes every day, but they always looked clean. Slatter knew the feeling of not having pretty clothes to wear and she didn't dare say anything to Pydie for fear of hurting her feelings. Slatter began thinking about what a good uncle Mr. Fritz was to Pydie. She knew she had a few aunts and uncles, but so far no one had come forward and offered to show her any care. He was sure taking good care of Pydie. It seemed to Slatter, he was acting more like a dad to Pydie instead of an uncle. He took the time to laugh with her and teach her things she needed to know about everyday things in life. He was teaching her things like being polite and considerate of other people's feelings. He was showing her Godly things by the way he lived his life. Slatter had heard her grandpa say more than once, that Mr. Fritz is the most honest man he has ever met and he would rather see a testimony any day than hear one. Then, Slatter realized something very special. She realized her grandpa and Granny B were using their lives to teach Slatter the same lessons.

Pydie noticed that Slatter was in deep thought.

As she folded her arms across her chest, she spoke up in a half angry tone,

"Well, Miss Slatter.
Where Iz come from, we has ta make our own fun."

Slatter just kept staring out into space as Pydie talked.

"Miss Slatter.
Iz is a talkin' to ya.

Is youz just gonna lays there, or is ya gonna get up and do somethin' with me?"

Slatter blinked her eyes and apologetically replied, "I'm sorry.

What were ya sayin'?"

Pydie, pointed her finger toward the back field. She acted a little more disgusted with Slatter than she did the first time.

In a loud voice she said, "I says dat Iz think weez ought ta be out yonder a playin' in dat old barn!"

Pydie rolled her eyes and replied, "Well ya don't have to holler. What can we do out there?"

Pydie put her hands on her waist and stomped her foot.

"Like I say before.

Iz just bet we can pretend that old barn out a yonder is a big ship and weez can have a lots of fun a playin it.

Let's goes and gives it a try!

It shore does beat a sittin out here in dis here hot sun a doin nothin' except gettin' hotter and hotter!"

Slatter could tell by the way Pydie acted she was getting angrier by the minute.

Slatter didn't want her to get mad and go home so she was happy to oblige.

"Oh, alright, replied Slatter.

Let's go."

Pydie gave Slatter a great big smile and the two girls started running toward the old barn.

When they reached the edge of the back yard, Slatter suddenly stopped dead in her tracks. She noticed something in the back field behind the barn she had not seen before. Some one had left a big old piece of farm equipment in the field. It was partially hidden because the weeds had grown so tall. All the times she had played in the back field, she had somehow managed to overlook it. It was so dirty and rusty you could hardly tell it was ever a green color. It was about 16 feet long and looked to be very heavy. It had several big disc blades underneath it that looked rusty and sharp. On top, it had steel bars the shape of a square box that looked like a bar used in a flying trapeze act at the circus. Slatter really liked the way the thing looked.

Grinning from ear to ear, she pointed toward the barn and said, "Hey.

Check out that great big farm thing.

I bet we could pretend the old barn is a circus tent and we could sit on that thing and pretend we are performin' a circus act. I'll bet we could swing real high on this thing!

You know way high above the chimney tops.

We could even pretend we have on shiny sparklin' clothes and we are stars of the show!

Why I'll bet we could swing so high we could fly over the rainbow! Ya know.

Like in the Wizard of Oz movie."

Both of the girls laughed at such a thought.

Pydie excitedly clapped her hands together and continued to giggle as she said, "Miss Slatter. Youz is sooo funny."

Pydie could see Slatter had a smile on her face and a gleam in her eye once again. She was not thinking about Shekoe falling in the well. Instead, her mind was on having fun. Pydie thought Slatter's idea sounded like fun but she still wasn't sure she wanted to participate. She cocked her mouth to one side of her face in an encouraging way and said, "Ok.

But youz goes first.

Iz doesn't know how weez is gonna gets a way up dare on dat big old thing.

Iz reckon youz will has to figure dat out.

Iz will goes over and try to finds a way to clean up dis here old barn soz it can look like a real circus tent!"

Slatter half heartedly agreed as her mind was in a whirl about how much fun it would be to sit on that old piece of farm equipment and pretend she was swinging on a trapeze.

She had seen a picture of a circus once in a book at school.

She very much liked to swing and she wanted to be the first one to sit on the swing. She had already decided that she would be the boss of the circus and Pydie would have to be the assistant boss. She kept walking around and around the farm implement trying to figure out a way to climb on it. It was sitting so close to the fence there was no way she could get on it from the back. Then, she hit on a great idea. She would get Pydie to hoist her up so she could get on top of it. She yelled for Pydie at the top of her lungs.

"Pydie! Pydie!

Come here quick!

Hurry!

I need ya to come over here!"

Pydie had found an old broom and was sweeping the dirt and trash out of the barn. She wanted her circus tent to look clean. She created a fog of dust, and it was flying everywhere. She heard Slatter yelling but couldn't see her for the grimy fog. Thinking something was wrong, she instantly threw her broom down and ran over to see what she wanted. Pydie's face and hair were covered in dust and she was out of breath. Aggravated because she had to leave her job and gasping for air she demanded, "What in da world duz ya want Miss Slatter?

Whew! Iz was a workin' hard.

I am plum out of breath."

Slatter's eyes glistened with excitement. In the blazing hot, noon day sun, she put her arm around Pydie and explained her scheme.

"Ya see," said Slatter with her face all aglow with a bright idea.

"I got me a plan on how to get up on this trapeze lookin' thing.

"Slatter could tell by the concerned, puzzled look on Pydie's face she was afraid to ask about the plan.

"Oh yeah.

"Well how's dat," asked Pydie in a puzzling tone of voice?"

"Ya make your hands into a circle like this," Slatter confidently replied as she made a circle with her hands.

"Ya know, kind of like a stirrup on a saddle."

Ain't ya ever seen anybody mount up on a horse?"

Pydie shook her head no and shrugged her shoulders.

Slatter looked disgusted because Pydie didn't understand what to do.

"Well anyways, Ya jest do what I tell ya.

Ya make the circle and I'll put my foot in it.

Then you give me a big boost up in the air as hard as ya can." Just as she was getting into position to help Slatter, she saw the blue goose drive up the driveway.

Slatter grabbed the back of Pydie's dress and pulled her down into a squatting position.

She whispered,

"Stay down! Don't move!

We have to hide."

The girls both squatted down and hid themselves in the weeds so grandpa could not see them.

Pydie whispered back to Slatter, "Why is we a hidin' anyways?" Slatter quickly replied, "'Cause silly.

I'm sure grandpa doesn't want us a playin' around on this here equipment.

If he sees us out here, we could get into some real bad trouble.

Ya don't want to get into trouble do ya?"

Pydie, with her big dark eyes dancing back and forth responded fearfully,

"No.

Iz shore doesn't needs no trouble."

She didn't want any trouble from anybody because Uncle Fritz would tell her dad and then she would get a big spanking.

Pydie kept staring at Slatter as she shook her head back and forth.

"We'll jest sit here and wait," continued Slatter in a bossy tone.

"He'll be gone in a few minutes.

He's just a comin' to pick up Granny B.

He's gonna take her up to the store to stay so he can come home and eat a bite of lunch."

The girls' legs got tired of squatting down, so they sat on the ground and remained very quiet. As the girls patiently waited for grandpa to leave, they became hotter and hotter. They were sitting in very tall weeds so thick they couldn't even feel the stir of a breeze. Their faces became as red as beets, but neither one breathed a word of complaint. Pydie was so scared and nervous about getting into trouble that

Slatter could hear her heart pounding in her chest. Slatter didn't want Pydie to be so scared, so she leaned over to her and casually tried to deal with her problem.

" Ah, don't worry so much Pydie," remarked Slatter breaking weeds off as she talked.

"We ain't gonna get caught and get in trouble.

Grandpa will be comin' back home in a few minutes.

He'll just let Granny B out of the car and come right back.

He always does.

Heck, we can't get into much trouble in just a few minutes anyways.

So, ya see, there ain't nothin' to be afraid of."

By the time Slatter finished her sentence, the blue goose was gone and out of sight.

Slatter and Pydie stood up.

They both let out a big sigh of relief as they felt the fresh air hit their blistering faces.

Slatter had an urgent tone in her voice as she spoke.

"Quick Pydie.

Make a stirrup for me and help me get up onto this thing.

I want to have a little bit of fun before grandpa gets back."

Pydie hesitated. She wasn't sure if she should do what Slatter asked of her. She stuck her finger in her mouth and tried to talk Slatter out of getting on the farm implement.

" I dunno 'bout dis Miss Slatter", replied a reluctant Pydie.

"Maybe weez better not play on dis old thing if'n yore grandpa doesn't want us to."

Slatter frowned and without hesitation pleaded with Pydie.

"Oh don't be silly Miss Pydie.

Don't ya know that grown ups forget how to have fun when they grow old.

Sometimes I think they jest don't want us doin' stuff jest ta keep us from havin' fun.

We ain't gonna hurt nothin'.

Nobody will ever know we were playin' on this thing.

We're just gonna play on it for a few minutes and then we'll go play somethin' else out in the barn."

Pydie could feel trouble a brewing.

"Youz a askin' for trouble Miss Slatter.

Iz can feel it in my bones."

Pydie could see the determination on Slatter's face, so, she didn't say anything else.

She quickly did as Slatter told her to do.

She made a circle with her arms and clasped her hands together to form a stirrup.

Then, Slatter grabbed hold of the implement and Pydie gave her a great big push up in the air.

With one big jump, Slatter had made a successful landing right smack dab in the middle of the bar; right where she wanted to be. She grasped a hold of both sides of the railings with her hands. From where Pydie was standing, she could see something Slatter couldn't. Both sides of the implement were supported by a stack of concrete blocks. The blocks kept it balanced so it wouldn't fall. When Slatter jumped onto it, her weight caused the blocks on one side to shift sideways. She was way too engrossed in trying to make the trapeze looking object swing forward to notice the top blocks were starting to slide. Slatter hollered out.

"Yee haw!

Hey Miss Pydie, watch this.

I am really goin' to have some fun now.

Then it'll be your turn and I'll give ya a boost so ya can get up here."

Pydie waved her hands in the air as she tried to warn Slatter the implement was falling off the blocks, but she couldn't get her attention. Slatter thought Pydie was waving at her in fun and she totally ignored Pydie's gestures.

Then, something totally unexpected happened.

The stack of blocks on the other side of the implement began to slide causing all of the blocks to collapse. The heavy piece of equipment slowly slid into the fence. Slatter could see she was falling backwards and tried to jump off, but every time she moved, she caused the implement to slide faster. Pydie began screaming at Slatter.

"Jump off, Miss Slatter!

Youz gotta jump off of that thing!

Right now!"

But it was too late. Pydie could tell by Slatter's face that she was scared to death! She tried to grab hold of Slatter's feet to keep her from falling backwards with the implement, but she was just not strong enough. Slatter's weight had caused the implement to become off balance enough to cause it to slide backwards.

Then, in just a few split seconds, it was all over. The implement slid backwards pinning Slatter between it and the fence. The top bar of the trapeze looking object had her neck tightly pinned against the old rusty, wire woven fence. Slatter's face immediately began turning a bluish color as her oxygen supply was being shut off. The pressure of the implement pushing against her wind pipe kept her from yelling for help. She began fighting to breathe. Gasping for air, She began kicking her legs and clawing at the ground. Every time she tried to make the slightest move, the bar pushed tighter against her neck. She was forced to lay perfectly still. To complicate matters, she had fallen into a thick patch of sticker bushes. Pydie, frightened out of her wits, started jumping up and down as she screamed,

"We needs help Miss Slatter!

Tells me whats to do!

Ain't nobody home!"

But Slatter couldn't tell Pydie what to do, because she could not speak with that metal bar pressing against her throat.

Slatter began to think that she was going to die because she knew there was no one around that could lift the heavy implement off her. Since she couldn't breathe in very much air, she knew she wasn't going to be alive for very long.

Suddenly, Pydie heard a car drive into the driveway and she could see it was Slatter's grandpa. Screaming at the top of her lungs, Pydie ran as fast as she could toward the car.

Mr. Slopey! Mr. Slopey!

Help! Help!"

Grandpa saw Pydie running toward him.

He barely got the car stopped before he jumped out.

He did not see Slatter anywhere around, so he knew something was bad wrong.

He grabbed Pydie by the shoulders.

He had a panicky look on his face as he questioned her.

"Where is Slatter?"

Pydie was crying so hard that he could hardly understand what she was trying to tell him.

"Oh Mr. Slopey.

Miss Slatter is in a whole heaps of trouble.

I think she's dyin'.

She mights even be dead by now!

She can't get no air.....she can't breathe!"

Grandpa had a very worried look on his face as pulled her close to his chest and sternly demanded,

"What on earth are you talkin' about child?

Show me where Slatter is!

Take me to her now!

Hurry!"

As Pydie started running, she pointed toward the old farm implement. Grandpa began praying out loud.

"Oh no.

Dear God. Please tell me she didn't try to climb on that old implement that's out in the field!"

Tears began to fill grandpa's eyes as he kept pleading with God.

"Oh dear Father in heaven.

Please make her be alright!"

She's just a little child. Just a baby!"

When grandpa arrived on the scene, he saw Slatter sprawled out on the ground. As he approached her, he could plainly see her neck was tightly pinned between the old woven wire fence and the farm implement. He could not tell if she was still alive. So, he knelt down beside her to see if she was still breathing. She was. He heard her moan and he saw her fingers clamped together making a fist. He could tell she was in pain. Fear gripped his heart. He tried not to show on his face what he was feeling. He could see her face was turning a bluish color from lack of oxygen. She was struggling to breathe. He also knew she was getting weaker by the moment. He had to act fast or he was going to lose her. He patted her face firmly and with a shaky scared voice started speaking to her.

"Slatter", he tenderly said. Slatter honey. Can ya hear me?"

He waited for her lashes to flutter, for her eyes to open and smile back at him. But nothing happened. His precious little granddaughter that was so full of life now lay totally lifeless in front of him. He was desperate for help. He knew he had to somehow get the implement off of her or she was going to die and very soon. He quickly stood up and made his way through the high weeds to the middle of the implement. He grabbed hold of it with both of his hands. Then, with all of the strength he had in him, he pulled on it.

Nothing happened.

It did not even move an inch.

He tried several times to lift the implement. But no matter how hard he tried, in his own strength, he just could not lift it. The sound of Pydie's crying and whimpering was overwhelming. He wanted stop and comfort her but, that would take precious moments away from time he was already short of. As he stepped on the dry weeds, Slatter heard a loud crackling sound that was magnified in her ears. Because the implement was putting pressure on her wind pipe, she was on the verge of losing consciousness. Slatter could not speak, but she could still see. Her eye lids were becoming heavier and it was all she could do to focus her eyes. She watched her grandpa take off his apron, throw it on the ground and kneel down next to her. Grandpa noticed Slatter had opened her eyes a little bit. They both exchanged fearful glances as she looked for hope in her grandpa's face. He took his apron and gently wiped the sweat from her brow. Then, he calmly whispered in her ear, "Now sis listen very carefully to me. I'm goin' to try one more time to lift this big old thing off of ya. As soon as you feel it bein' lifted off of your neck a little bit, I need for ya to slide off to the side a little and then you'll be out from under it and you'll be free.

Did ya hear me?

I say Slatter.

Did ya hear what I said to ya?"

Because she was in so much pain, all Slatter could do was move her eyebrows up and down. Even though she had watched her grandpa make several futile attempts to pull the implement off of her, she had hope in her heart as she watched him make another attempt to try again. She knew if her grandpa didn't get the implement off of her pretty soon, she was going to die. As she lay there so helplessly on the ground she wondered how could something so simple and innocent turn into something so tragic. All she wanted to do was have a little fun. She knew she was paying a high price for her disobedience. She also thought to herself that the fun she thought she was going to have was not worth all of the trouble she was now in.

The intense heat from the sun coupled with not being able to breathe complicated Slatter's condition. With great difficulty she strained to keep her eyes open so she could be alert enough to do what her grandpa had told her. She was going down hill fast and she knew it. She was absolutely helpless. She realized real quick she was at the mercy of her grandpa. Pydie stood next to him, sobbing so hard she was speechless. He picked up one of Slatter's small sweaty hands and cupped it into his. He knew she realized the seriousness of the moment because he could see tears pouring out of her squinted eyes.

He felt as if a dark cloud was hovering over the three of them. He began thinking about spiritual warfare. If the devil had anything at all to do with this situation, grandpa was not going to let him win. He knew God would fight this battle and win.

He had to hide his fear from the girls. He wanted to keep their spirits up. Even though he felt like his heart was breaking, he was not going to give up trying to help her. He knew just where to go to get the help he needed. Without a doubt, he knew God was the only one that could save his granddaughter. He lifted her head and dried her tears with his forefinger. Looking up toward heaven, he swallowed back his own tears. His voice had a pleading submissive tone as he boldly approached the throne of God.

He earnestly prayed.

"Dear heavenly Father,
 Ya are my Father which art in heaven.
 Ya are the great I AM.
 My almighty and powerful king of kings and Lord of lords.
 Right now, I need a miracle from ya.
 I have read in your word where Ya said, ya have not because ya ask not.

Your word also tells me I can do all things through God who strengthens me.

I do not ask this prayer for myself.

Rather I ask it for my granddaughter because she is not able to ask.

Please help me Lord.

I am jest way too old and too weak to lift this heavy thing off her by myself.

I need your strength.

It's jest you and me against this big old implement.

Please, I beg of you.

Give me the strength that I need to do this task set before me.

Please send me help from above because I can do nothing without You.

I believe your word to be true and ya know my heart.

Ya know I believe in ya.

I ask ya for this great miracle in the name of Jesus, your precious son.

Thank ya Lord.
Amen."

It was all he could do to finish his prayer as he choked on his tears.

He let go of Slatter's hand and stood up. Slatter had a difficult time watching him, because it was hard to see with the sun shining directly in her eyes. With great faith, he grabbed hold of the implement. What happened next was unbelievable to the human eye. Slatter, watching her grandpa's every move, could not make a sound, but in her heart, she could hardly contain herself. Right behind where her grandpa was standing, she saw a huge overshadowing image of what looked like an angel. She thought to herself, could I be seeing a real angel. Did God actually hear my grandpa's prayer and send help? She was having difficulty believing what she was seeing.

She had seen a picture of an angel one time in her grandpa's old family bible Granny B kept on the table beside his chair.

This huge shadow looked to be three times taller than her Grandpa with wings stretched out higher than the big sassafras trees that were growing in the fence row next to the implement.

Slatter silently watched as the angel reached around and placed his hands over her grandpa's hands and lo and behold, the implement began to lift off the ground.

As it was being lifted, Slatter began to feel some relief from the pressure of being pinned against the fence.

Suddenly, in the blink of an eye, Slatter noticed an intense silence in the air; it was like all of time stood still.

Not even a leaf dared to move.
Then, she heard a familiar sound.

A sound she had heard one day as she waited to get on the school bus. The sound was like a breathless rustle of leaves followed by a swishing, whispering sound as it echoed in a cool summer breeze.

Slatter didn't know if she was so near death she was seeing and hearing things, or if God was allowing her to witness sounds from a heavenly portal.

She wanted to wipe the dripping sweat and tears from her eyes, but she didn't dare make a move for fear of making her situation worse.

As she stared at what she thought was the huge shadow of an angel, thoughts began racing through her mind.
"What else could something that big be....but an angel!" contemplated Slatter.
With the glistening sun in her face, all she could make out of the image was it looked like a huge shadow of a person .............only with huge wings.

She mulled over in her mind.
"My oh my.
This is a real angel.....an angel sent from God!
Wow!"
She formed her lips to whisper the word, but no sound came out. She started feeling a grateful love toward God. Her mind continued to ponder,
"God must really love me if He sent one of his heavenly angels just to help me.
Heck.
I'm just a kid.
I'm nobody special.
Everyone I know thinks that angels are invisible.
Yet, I'm seein' one right now!
I bet no one will believe me.

Maybe I'll not tell anyone what I'm seein'.
That way I won't get accused of being crazy."

Slatter managed to raise her finger up in the air to point to the angel so grandpa could see it too. But because he was too busy watching to see if the implement was moving, he never bothered to look up. Gritting his teeth together, Grandpa was very short winded in his voice as he managed to grunt out the words with great anticipation.
"Hurry Sis.
Slide on out from under the thing.
Hurry.
Do it now!"
Slatter managed to grab hold of some of the tall sticker bushes growing next to where she was laying. She used them for leverage as she somehow found the strength to pull herself out from underneath the implement. In just a few short seconds, she was free. Grandpa was amazed at the way the implement lifted up in the air so easily. He knew God had answered his prayer and sent him help. He knew without a doubt God had sent him heaven aid. Slatter did not have the strength to get up off of the ground, so she just lay there, moaning. Grandpa wasted no time. He swooped her up in his arms and carried her toward the house. He wanted to get her out of the hot sun as quickly as possible. As he walked, she lay limp. The whole ordeal left her totally exhausted.

On the way to the house, for just a brief moment she was able to half open her eyes. It was during this time she saw something that left no doubt in her mind that she had actually seen a real angel.

In the sun's shadow, she saw the huge angel hovering above them. He swooped down so close to her the tip of his wings almost touched the top of her grandpa's head.

The loud deafening sound of his massive wings fluttered loudly in her ears.

The deep soul stirring view that she experienced next would be imbedded in her mind for all of eternity.

She actually caught a glimpse of one of the angel's wings as he flew directly overhead. She saw numerous layers of bright white, transparent feathers that unfurled like petals of a rose. She tried her best to raise a hand to reach out and touch it, but she was too weak. As they rushed toward the back door of the house, Slatter looked up and saw the shadow of the angel still lingering over them, with wings outstretched in a protecting way.

As soon as her grandpa stepped inside the back door, Slatter looked behind him and saw the angel take flight. He was gone in a flash. He disappeared so quickly it somehow reminded her of a pigeon she once saw taking flight from atop of a tree.

In her mind, she was also remembering a time when she had stood all alone in the middle of a dirt road and watched from a distance, as her friend Gappy suddenly disappeared into thin air.

She noticed something else that seemed strange. She was feeling the same peaceful easiness in the air she had felt when she was around her lost, but not forgotten friend Gappy.

She knew the difference between real and make believe. Yet, she couldn't help but wonder why strange things keep happening to her. Her throat hurt so bad she couldn't even speak. But in her heart, she felt all aglow, because she knew God had came to her rescue by sending one of his angels to help her in her hour of need.

As grandpa carried Slatter's limp body, she looked as though she was sound asleep. However, she wasn't. Her heart was smiling even though no one could tell by the solemn look on her face. She had the satisfaction that no one could ever take away the heavenly sights she had seen and she would always ponder them in her heart. She felt like she was sharing a secret with God and there was a holiness about her new spiritual awareness that made her not want to share it with anyone.

Struggling, grandpa managed to carry Slatter into the house. He headed straight for her room and laid her down on the bed. The skin was broken on her throat and blood was trickling down her neck. He quickly went into the kitchen and grabbed a wet towel to put on her throat. Using one end of the wet towel, he wiped the sweat from her face. He could clearly see she had an ugly, red mark across her neck along with a big bruise that was beginning to take on a bluish, yellow color. Slatter began to cough as she started to breathe in more air. Her natural skin color had returned and she was feeling much better. Grandpa comforted her with a kind, soft spoken voice. "There, there now.

It's all over sis.

You're gonna be alright now.

Just try to lie real still and slowly breathe in some big deep breaths. Can ya speak a word or two for your old grandpa?"

Slatter whimpered a little and shook her head back and forth. She started coughing so hard she tried to prop herself up with her elbows to be able to breathe. She coughed up some blood and spit it in her hand. Without thinking, her grandpa quickly unbuttoned the cuff on his long sleeve shirt and used it to wipe the blood out of her hand. She lay back down and closed her eyes. She was very thankful to be alive. She stopped sniffling and started breathing deep and slow just like her grandpa instructed her to do. Wide eyed Pydie, standing beside Slatter's bed, watched her friend suffer. She wanted to do something to help, but was afraid to even speak. She wanted to make sure Slatter knew she was by her side. So Slatter would hear her, she bravely spoke in a happy tone of voice, "Mr. Slopey.

Does ya think Miss Slatter is goin' to beez alright now?"

Grandpa put his arm around Pydie and pulled her close to his side. He could feel the heat coming through her dress from her sweaty body. He knew Pydie was very upset too, and she needed a little comforting assurance that her friend was going to be alright.

He patted her on the back and gave her a great big hug.

Smiling, he winked at her and then optimistically responded to her question.

"Oh yeah.

I think Miss Slatter is going to be just fine now.

You two will be back playin' together in no time.

Now, I'm gonna have to go on back up to the store and pick up Granny B so she can come home and tend to Slatter.

She's a better nurse than I am.

Can ya sit right here beside Miss Slatter and play like you are a nurse until Granny B gets here," he asked.

I will bring her back home as fast as I can.

Pydie's face lit up and she cheerfully replied, "I shore can.

I will beez Miss Slatter's nurse til youz come back."

Grandpa used a scolding tone as he whispered to Pydie.

"Just remember Pydie.

Ya need to be real quiet.

Slatter just needs to lay here on her bed and rest for a while."

Pydie felt important and honored he would ask her to watch over her injured friend until he could bring Granny B Pydie back home.

She reassuringly agreed.

"Iz will take good care of my bestest friend," said Pydie.

I iz sooo glad that she gonna be alright.

I shore was scared."

As grandpa waved goodbye to Pydie, he couldn't help but notice what a beautiful child she was. When Pydie smiled the contrast of her dark skin and her beautiful coal black hair next to her pearly white teeth was striking. Her skin tone was so smooth and shiny and her facial features had a perfect contour. She looked like a great big pretty doll as she stood next to Slatter's bed. He knew Slatter would be in very good hands while he was gone. Because he was confident Pydie would not think of leaving her friend's side, not even for one second.

Grandpa hurriedly got into the old blue goose and headed toward the store. He realized he didn't even take time to eat his lunch, but he didn't care. His first priority was to take care of Slatter and for the moment, that was the only thing on his mind.

After he left, the room became very quiet. Slatter, weak and tired, had drifted off to sleep. Pydie softly tiptoed over to the window and looked out toward the back yard. She noticed something looked very different. Something was missing. The implement that had caused so much worry and trouble was gone. The weeds were still smashed down where it was sitting, but the implement was simply no where to be found. It just seemed to have disappeared out of sight. Pydie could not believe her eyes. She couldn't wait until she saw Slatter's grandpa again so she could tell him the implement was gone. Pydie knew Mr. Slopey hadn't moved it because he had not left Slatter's side since the accident. Pydie had a very puzzled look on her face as she stood gazing out the open bedroom window. The room was so quiet all Pydie could hear was the sound of the katydids singing. They sang as if they were a loud full-throated choir celebrating the end of summer. She began to feel a little sad because she knew what that sound meant. It meant summer would be coming to an end very soon and she and Slatter would have to say goodbye. She would miss her good friend, but she also knew she was ready to go back home and see her beloved mother. Pydie's eyes scanned all around Slatter's room. She thought Slatter to be very lucky to have such a nice room all to herself. She knew she would probably never have a room of her own, because everyone in her family had to share just about everything in her house.

Pydie noticed Slatter had rolled over on her side, so she walked over to the bed to check on her. She bent over Slatter to get a close look at her injuries. Pydie moved her head back and forth as she spoke in a sympathetic whisper.

"Poor Miss Slatter.

Howz in da world is ya ever gonna wins a beauty contest with them dare old ugly marks 'round your neck?

Ya can't beez no beauty queen a lookin' like dat.

Dat's for shore.

Mmm, mmm, mmm."

Pydie was so deep in thought about how awful Slatter's scratched up neck looked; she didn't even hear the old blue goose drive up the driveway. Pydie was glad to hear Granny B's footsteps as she came running into Slatter's room. The room was steaming hot and smelled of sweat. Pydie very intently watched Granny B gently touch Slatter's neck as she examined her very thoroughly. Granny B's tender loving care and kind gestures made Pydie think about how much she missed her own mother. Pydie didn't want to wake up Slatter so she leaned over to Granny B and whispered, "Miss Slatter done gone and got herself hurt real bad, but her grandpa say she gonna be just fine."

Granny B could tell Pydie was looking for some assurance, but she never spoke a word until she had thoroughly inspected Slatter's injured neck. She left the room for a minute and came back with a small window fan and a pan of warm water that had a wash cloth in it. She set the fan in the window and turned it on. The wind gently blew across the room toward Slatter. As Granny B put her arm around Pydie, she tried to comfort her by using a long suffering tone of voice. Without taking her eyes off Slatter she calmly replied.

"Yes, little Miss Pydie.

Slatter seems to be a doin' jest fine now.

She's breathin' real good.

But I do think she needs to rest for a while."

With a big sigh of relief Granny B continued, "Yeah. We've done all we can do for her right now, I reckon the rest will be up to the good Lord. She should be just fine in a couple of days. Keep her in your prayers tonight. She looks as though she is going to have an ugly bruise on her neck for a few days, though. She is a very fortunate little girl.

She just as easily could've been killed.

God spared her life for a reason."

As Granny B took off Slatter's bloody shirt, and wiped her off with a warm wet cloth, she tearfully said, "Yep.

She's me and her grandpa's very own special little girl.

Our very, very special little girl."

When she had finished bathing Slatter, Granny B reached out her hand for Pydie to take hold of. Smiling, she tenderly said, "How about you little Miss Pydie. Are ya doin alright yourself? I'm sure this whole ordeal was pretty scary for you too."

Pydie started picking at her fingers. She had a repentive attitude as she nodded her head and said, "Yes'm. Iz was real scared. Iz didn't want ta play on that big old thing.

But Miss Slatter, she say it'd be alright cause weez gonna have lots of fun on it.

I shore is sorry."

Pydie started crying.

"Iz was so scared dat Miss Slatter was gonna die and Iz jest didn't know whats ta do?

Dare was nobody home.

Youz and Mr. Slopey was up at da store.

Weez was only by ourselves fer jest a few minutes.

Everthin' happened so fast.

I shore was glad to see Mr. Slopey comes home when he did."

Granny B patted Pydie's hand as she comforted her, "Well, stop a cryin'. It's all over now. Be glad things ain't any worse than they are. I hope ya girls have learned a lesson from this little incident. In the first place, you girls are big enough to know better than to play around dangerous farm equipment.

Most old farm equipment a sittin' around like that one, is usually broken. Old broken down equipment like that ain't good for nothin', except fer somebody to get bad hurt on. It's not meant to be played with. It's used for workin' not playin'.

There's plenty of things for ya girls to play with 'round here without a messin' round on somethin' that don't belong to ya. I know of one little girl that's a gonna get a talkin' to when she gets to feelin' better.

And I think grandpa Slopey is a talkin' to your uncle Fritz right now.

I suspect your uncle Fritz will be a comin' down the road to get ya any minute now to take ya on home.

But for right now, enough said."

Her voice became more stern.

"Don't ya go a heapin' coals of fire on your own head, 'cause I know it wasn't your fault Slatter got hurt.

One thing I've learned about her is she has a way a gettin' into trouble all by herself.

She don't usually need too much encouragement from anybody." Pydie knew that Granny B was giving her a scolding in a nice way.

Granny B walked into the living room to get a needle to get the stickers out of Slatter's hands, when she returned she handed Pydie a tissue and kindly ordered, "Miss Pydie. Ya go on outside now and wait for your uncle Fritz. Ya might wanna brush some of that dust off of ya before he gets here too. I'm sure he'll be directly." Pydie wiped her nose with the tissue and respectfully replied.

"Yes mam."

She hung her head and walked to the front door. She tried to wipe some of the dust off of her dress, but her sweat caused it to stick to her skin. She finally gave up trying to get it off and sat down on the steps and waited. The more she thought about what Granny B had said to her the more she began to pout. She felt unwanted in a strange place. She started to cry again. Because she felt so alone and out of place, she yearned in her heart more than ever to be with her mother. She wished she could curl up in her mother's lap and feel happy and wanted again.

She had only been waiting for a few minutes, when she looked up and saw her uncle Fritz come walking through the yard. He greeted her with a big smile. Slatter was relieved to see he was not mad at her. He grabbed her and threw her up into the air so high she lost her breath. They giggled and laughed together. Pydie used both hands to rub Mr. Fritz's cheek and then she asked him a question.

"Ya means ya ain't mad at me for a bein' with Miss Slatter whenz she gots hurt?"

Mr. Fritz shook his head back and forth as he answered her.

"Ah, now youz knows yore Uncle Fritz better n dat.

I ain't mad at ya.

Iz ain't mad at nobody.

Iz could never beez mad at my favorite little niece no matter what she done.

Now let's get ta goin on home and Iz'll fix us a mess of fresh greens and fried chicken for supper tonight."

That sounded good to Pydie. Now that she knew Slatter was going to be alright, she suddenly realized she was very hungry.

The afternoon sun had slanted as if sinking into a hidden ravine and just for a few scant moments, the sun's rays cascaded down from the sky like streaks of shimmering golden strands. The heat from the scorching hot sun was still lingering in the air as Pydie and Mr. Fritz walked arm in arm down the road. Pydie began to talk about how hot the sun was.

She sounded angry as she complained about the weather.

"Uncle Fritz. Dat ole hot sun is sa hot it's a makin me mad.

I think the good Lord should've gives dat dare hot sun a people name.

Iz means a nutter name, somethin' besides the sun."

Mr. Fritz smiled and looked down at Pydie as he humored her.

"Well, jest what name duz ya think the good Lord should've give dat big ole sun," he jokingly asked.

Pydie, carefully walking on the stiff, dry grass so she didn't have to walk on the hot asphalt road, quickly replied.

"Ah, uncle Fritz, dat's easy.

Dat ole hot sun's name should a been Ray.

Yep.

It oughts ta been called a man's name.

Iz thinks a name like Ray Beamim' Sun would be fine.

Dat name suits da sun.

Dat Mr. Ray Sun must get real mad at everthin' here on earth in da summer time cause he makes everthin' to shribble up under its' sizzlin' heat.

Kinda like he likes ta burn things til dare ain't no life left in 'em.

Even da trees squiggle up and turns brown."

Pydie bent over and pulled some of the dead blades of grass that were growing along side the road. She used a pitiful whiney tone as she held the grass up in the air for him to see, "Looky here at dis here poor ole grass, Uncle Fritz.

Dat sun just killt it all.

It used ta be pretty and green.

Now it's brown and dead lookin' and it's a stickin' to my bare feet likes sticker bushes."

Then Pydie grinned great big at Mr. Fritz as she pleaded.

"Would ya mind a carryin' me for a piece uncle Fritz?

Please............. pretty please.

My feets iz hot and the dirt's sa hot, I can't hardly walks no further."

Iz do believe dat Iz is plum wore out."

Pydie began to limp a little so Mr. Fritz would feel sorry for her. Mr. Fritz realized that Pydie really was having a hard time walking, so he stopped for a minute and took a long look at her. Her hair was stuck to her face from sweat and her body was covered in dust. He shook his head and grinned as he compassionately picked her up in his arms and sat her on his shoulders. Pydie squealed with excitement when he slung her up into the air. She liked being way up high. The two of them began to sing:

"Swing Low, Sweet Chariot, a comin for ta carries me home,
Swing Low, Sweet Chariot. Comin for ta carry me home."

Pydie suddenly stopped singing. She couldn't get out of her mind the way the old farm implement had suddenly disappeared. She decided to ask Mr. Fritz a very strange question.

"Does ya believe in magic uncle Fritz?"

Mr. Fritz was surprised Pydie would ask him such a strange question. He immediately stopped walking. Then, he reached up and pulled Pydie over his head and stood her on the ground right smack dab in front of him. He knelt down on one knee and put both of his hands on her shoulders. His voice sounded very stern as he spoke. His smiling face changed to a serious look.

"What ever in dis world made ya ask such a question as dat Miss Pydie?"

Pydie shrugged her shoulders a little, "Oh, Iz dunno.

Iz was a wonderin' why one minute dat big old farmin' thing dat Miss Slatter got hurt on was out in da field in front of da barn and den when Iz was a standin' in Miss Slatter's room a lookin out towards da barn, dat thing wasn't dare.

It was gone... I mean...it just up and disappeared.

Jest as if it was magic!"

Mr. Fritz's dark eyes widened as he sternly spoke.

"Miss Pydie. What in dis world is ya talkin' 'bout?

Iz wants ta get one thing straight which ya right now. Da good Lord can make things happen supernaturally any time he sees fit to do so, but anythin' to do with magic, does not come from the good Lord. If'n ya ever see somethin' that some body tells ya is magic, ya gets as far away from dem as ya can get."

With a frightened look on her face, Pydie didn't say a word. With big eyes, she nodded her head yes. Mr. Fritz could see by the expression on her face she was frightened, so he put a big grin on his face and in a matter of fact way he said, "If'n dat old farm implement is gone, den there is a good reason it's gone and dat is dat. I'll speak to J.E. about it when I seez him again.

Now Iz think enough has been said 'bout dat."

Pydie seemed agreeable with what Mr. Fritz had said to her. So, they quietly walked the rest of the way home holding hands. Neither one of them had much to say to each other from that point on. They both seemed to have a lot on their minds. Mr. Fritz was thinking about how he hoped he was teaching Pydie right. He never dreamed he would be having a conversation about magic, of all things, with such a young child. He also hoped he had said all of the right things to her in the right way. He knew he would have to talk with Pydie about Slatter's accident, but he was waiting for the right time. He wanted to let Pydie get over the horror of it all before he brought it up again. Mr. Fritz just wanted to get Pydie home among familiar surroundings.

After Pydie left, Granny B devoted the rest of the evening to caring for Slatter. She finished digging out all of the stickers in Slatter's hands and then she carefully rubbed some ointment on Slatter's neck. Next, she covered her up with a fresh, clean sheet. Granny B brought a chair from the kitchen into Slatter's room and sat next to her bed. She did not leave Slatter's side for one minute. Even when she heard grandpa's old blue goose drive into the driveway, she remained by Slatter's side. When grandpa came into the house, he walked straight to Slatter's room to check on her. As grandpa took off his hat he leaned over and whispered in Granny B's ear.

"How's our little girl a doin'?"

Granny B had tears in her eyes as she replied.

"Well, J.E.

I think she's gonna be alright, but her neck is gonna need some time to heal.

She sure had a close call.

Ya know.

I've been a thinkin' about that old farm implement she got hurt on." She looked up into his face with a bewildered frown on her face.

"Fer the life of me, I jest can't figure out why in the world ya would park that thing so close to the house anyway?"

Grandpa wiped his face with his hand and shrugged his shoulders. He felt like he should have an answer for her, but he was struggling for one. He paused before he spoke. Then with an attitude of a child that just got caught with his hand in the cookie jar, he defended himself.

"Now don't ya go a blamin' me fer this," argued grandpa.

"All I can say is it's just an old piece of junk I never seem to find the time to get rid of.

Ya know I've always got way too much work to do and I never seem to have enough time or money ta get 'em all done.

I never gave much thought to a kid gettin' hurt on that thing.

They didn't have no business a playin' on it.

Besides what's done is done and there ain't no changing it.

Ya can't unring the bell, Granny B."

Granny B sarcastically replied.

"Well J.E.

I know ya can't unring the bell, but ya could've hung the bell up a little higher so kids wouldn't be able to ring it.

Don't ya think it's just a matter of priorities to get rid of a dangerous old piece of junk when ya got youngins' around?"

Her voice began to get louder.

"I've told ya and took ya out and told ya that you're a big pack rat.

Ya keep stuff til it rots whether it's any good or not.

If ya ain't gonna use somethin' it's time ta get rid of it!

Especially if ya ain't used it in over a year.

That thing has laid out there til the weeds have taken it over and it's so rusty we'll be lucky if Slatter don't get that lock jaw disease. I'm sick and tired of havin' old junk just sittin' around 'cause ya think some day you're gonna make a buck or two off it.

I think that first thing tomorrow mornin' would be a good time to move that thing and get it off of our property."

She clenched her teeth together and pointed her finger at him.

"I really don't care what ya do with it J.E......... just get rid of it!" She wiped her nose with her handkerchief as she finished her speech. Grandpa stared at her. It had been a very long time since he had seen his wife so upset. After a couple of minutes, she quieted down. Her voice became softer.

"I've had my say now.

I ain't gonna say no more about this.

One thing's fer sure.

Our a fussin' ain't gonna change a thing."

Grandpa was tired of talking about the whole mess, so he patted her on the back and nodded his head in agreement.

With puckered lips he replied, "Well, come to think about it, I do remember jest the other day a talkin' to old man Kaneke. He stopped by the store for gas. Ya remember him don't ya? He married that red headed Curry lady that used ta bring those delicious home made apple pies to the homecoming dinner at church. Well anyways, he's the one that fixes up and resells old farm equipment. Him and his sons own Kaneke's Farm Implement Repair just south of the store a little ways."

Granny B kept staring at Slatter and did not respond to his comments. She whispered under her breath.

"Yeah, I've heard tell of him.

He owes a big grocery bill at the store and he ain't paid a dime on it in months."

Grandpa heard her mumbling and asked, "What's that you're a sayin'? I didn't hear it."

Granny B sighed and said, "Never mind, it wasn't important." "Well, anyway", he continued, "I'll go over to his place in the mornin' first chance I get and tell him he can have that old thing for parts if he wants it. He'll probably come and pick it up sometime tomorrow."

Granny B seemed satisfied with his answer and decided to change the subject. She had her say and was not going to discuss anything any further about the implement.

"Well, J.E.," said Granny B as she smoothed out the covers on Slatter's bed.

"I reckon you're hungry, but I just didn't feel like a fixin' any supper tonight.

I can scramble ya some eggs and make ya some toast if your hungry."

Grandpa walked over to Slatter and stroked her face with the side of his hand.

He looked down at her sweet, innocent little face and said, "I don't believe I'm very hungry tonight.

If I get hungry, I'll fix me a few crackers in some milk before I go to bed."

Granny B tearfully replied, "Ok. Suit yourself."

Then grandpa said something to Granny B that made her stiffen up. He confidently stated, "Ya know the Lord saved her life today, Granny B. I just know He did. There is no way in the world I could've lifted that big old heavy thing off her by myself. Why, that piece of equipment has to weigh well over a ton. Besides, I know I felt a heavenly presence surrounding me after I prayed to God and asked Him for his help."

Granny B had no response to his statements as she continued to pick up the wet cloths and clean up Slatter's room. She knew all too well if Grandpa had felt a heavenly presence, then it was surely so. After a long pause, Granny B turned to walk out of Slatter's room. As she looked back behind her, she could see the tiredness in her husband's face as he stood beside Slatter's bed. She felt compassion for him. She thought about how small his shoulders looked compared to the big strong ones he had when she married him. The years of hard labor had caused his posture to become slumped making him look much shorter than he really was. Even though his face showed lines and wrinkles, she thought he was just as handsome to her now as he was the day they married. She walked back over to him, took him by the hand and in a sweet voice said,

"J.E.

I jest want ya to know I'm real sorry for a growlin' at ya.

I jest get so aggravated at ya sometimes.

Seems we never have enough time or money to do the things we feel need done.

But I want ya ta know I love ya with all my heart.

I know ya do the best ya can with what we got.

I know ya never promised me a rose garden when we married.

I guess I jest get a little tired sometimes a pluckin' the weeds out of life, but I shore wouldn't have things be any other way if'n it meant havin' a life without ya."

She gave him a quick kiss on the cheek and tugged at his arm.

"C'mon", she whispered.

"Let's go on out and let her rest.

We'll see how she's a doin' in the mornin'.

If she ain't able to get up and play, then we'll have to call the doctor. They both bent down and kissed her on her forehead.

As they were walking out of the room Grandpa reached over and pinched Granny B on her behind. Granny B, shocked at her husband's teasing behavior, turned around and scolded him.

"Oh, J.E. stop it," said Granny B as she blushed and smacked at him.

"You're way too old to be a actin' like a kid."

Grandpa grinned as he pulled her into his arms.

"Have ya forgotten somethin' my sweet bride?"

Granny B, pretending she didn't like what her husband was doing, tried to push him away. She managed to let out a flirtatious giggle as she spoke.

"No.

I don't reckon I've forgotten anythin'.

What on earth are ya talkin' about? "

Grandpa kept holding her tight as he whispered in her ear, "I think you've forgotten the old sayin'....the older the fiddle, the sweeter the tune."

" Oh yeah."

Said Granny B with a big smile on her face.

"Well I declare.

I'm a thinkin' you've forgotten somethin' too."

Grandpa's eyes lit up as he chuckled.

"Oh, and jest what did I forget, "he asked.

She jokingly responded to his question as she smacked him on the arm once again and pointed her forefinger in his face.

"Sometimes ya have to jump start the motor to get the car a runnin' and our jumper cables are old and worn out."

They both had a good laugh and then they retired to their room for the night.

Slatter was sound asleep and totally unaware of all of the love surrounding her. If love has a color, it must be a very bright white, because that night, Granny B and grandpa's faces put off a brilliant white glow from all of the love they were feeling for each other and for their granddaughter. Slatter had no way of knowing she was receiving the same quality of love and care her mother would've given her if she had been there herself.

# 7

# THE COUNTY FAIR PRINCESS PAGEANT

When Slatter awoke, she opened her eyes to a brand new morning. She breathed in the fresh country air as she looked around her room. She began gathering her thoughts of what happened the day before. She was having difficulty remembering her accident. Suddenly, she felt a stinging sensation on her throat. As she caressed the cut with her hand, she felt like she had one big, long scab across her neck. Suddenly, memories of the awful accident flooded her mind. She sat straight up in bed and tried to yell. She instantly realized she didn't have a voice. Overnight, she had developed laryngitis. Frightened half out of her wits, she managed to push out a loud, scratchy whisper.

"Granny B.

Come here," she kept trying to yell louder.

"Hurry!"

Granny was in the kitchen cleaning up the breakfast dishes when she heard Slatter trying to call out to her. She wiped her hands on her apron and ran into Slatter's room to see what was wrong.

"I'm right here Slatter," she remarked as she entered the room.

"How do ya feel this mornin'?"

Slatter pointed to her throat as she spoke with a scratchy sounding voice.

"I feel ok.

But why can't I talk?

Am I gonna talk like this forever?

I sound awful."

Slatter, almost in tears, sounded whiney as she continued to try to speak.

"I'm scared!

I want to talk normal."

As Granny helped Slatter out of bed and into her clothes, she tried to calm her fears by declaring she would get her normal voice back in just a few days.

"You're gonna be just fine", said Granny B in a reassuring tone of voice.

You'll be talkin' normal again in a few days.

So, don't worry any more about it.

Ya just bruised the inside of your throat.

It'll heal up before ya know it.

Your grandpa and I are just thankful to the good Lord that ya are alive.

That accident could've killed ya, ya know."

Slatter shook her head yes, as she stood and gazed in the mirror at the ugly scabbed over wound on her neck.

Her thoughts quickly shifted to the upcoming beauty pageant.

She was hoping maybe she wouldn't have to be in it since she now had an ugly wound on her neck.

She complained, "What about the princess pageant at the county fair this Friday, Granny B.

Do I still have to enter the contest?"

Granny B walked up behind Slatter and started brushing her matted hair with the old wooden hairbrush. She sternly replied to Slatter's question.

"Why sure ya do.

You're not gonna let a little ole thing like this keep ya from having a lot of fun are ya?"

Granny B was trying to make light of Slatter's accident.

Slatter rolled her eyes toward the ceiling at what Granny B had said to her. She replied to her question in an aggravated half hearted way.

"Well no.

I don't reckon.

But don't ya think that everybody there will be a starin' at this cut on my neck?

It looks awful!

I'll be so embarrassed.

What if I see some kids from my school there.

They already don't like me and think I'm ugly."

As she continued to look at her reflection in the mirror, she frowned and stomped her foot as she pointed at her neck.

"Just look at this Granny B.

My neck looks like one great big bruise with some icky blood on it!

Are you sure that dried blood will come off ?"

Granny B, still trying to encourage Slatter replied, "Yes.

I've already washed most of it off.

Ah, quit a starin' at it and don't be a pickin at it either.

That scab will heal in no time.

You'll see.

You've got to remember young lady that pretty is......is pretty does.

You'll learn as you get older that pretty looks always fade with time.

But your prettiness on the inside will stay in ya through all eternity.

Ya just wait and see."

Now, ya don't need to be a talkin' much for next day or so.

I know that'll be hard for ya to do, but the less ya talk, the faster your voice will heal.

Oh, and one more thing.

"You'll not be a goin up to the store today or tomorrow either for that matter.

At least not until that neck heals up a little.

I don't want ta take any chances on ya gettin' infection in that cut.

No need in ya a goin' up to that nasty old place so much any way.

Ya might pick up a lot of old nasty germs from those old lazy loafers.

No tellin' where all their hands have been.

Ain't none of 'em ever looked too clean to me."

Slatter just stood with her hands on her hips and with an ugly frown on her face, staring at Granny B. Granny B, pointing her finger in Slatter's face declared,

"Now, don't be a given me a mean face about this whole mess.

If ya would've obeyed your grandpa and stayed off of that old farm implement, ya wouldn't be hurt right now and ya would be up at the store a playin' with your little friend, Miss Pydie.

But, what's done is done and ya just gotta make the best of it.

No need in cryin' over spilt milk.

Ya need to let this be a lesson to ya.

Ya can't change yesterday.

Ya can only change things that's a goin' on today, right now. Yesterday is for learnin'- learnin' from your mistakes and today is for doin – doin' everythin' ya can to make the most of what ya learned. Well, enough about that. Young lady. I think ya need to be a workin' on the poem you're gonna' be enterin' for the talent part of the beauty contest."

Slatter threw herself onto the end of her bed. She really didn't feel like going anywhere or doing much of anything right now.

She especially didn't feel like trying to write a poem.

It hurt her throat to cry and she knew she was straining her voice when she tried to talk. She didn't have it in her to talk back to Granny B. So, she sat there and waited until Granny B left her room.

As soon as she was alone, she reached under her mattress and opened up the old yellowed secret map. She thought to herself it seemed like forever since she found the map. She earnestly wished she could find someone who lived in the area for a long time. Perhaps there was someone... somewhere ..that could help her figure out the directions on the map. The map was old and could be easily torn. So, she very carefully put it back under her mattress. She was always very cautious when she took it out from its' secret hiding place. She always made sure no one was around, because she didn't want anyone to know she had it.

She slowly walked over to her dresser and opened the top drawer. She reached in side and pulled out a pencil and a tablet of paper. Before she started working on the poem, she thought it would be a good idea to write Pydie a note. She thought she could send it to her by way of her grandpa. Slatter asked Granny B to help her with the spelling of some of the words. Granny B told Slatter to first write the note and then she would correct her spelling. Slatter sat down at the kitchen table and began to write. On top of the page, she drew a picture of a stick man making a big circle in the air with a rope. Then, she drew an arrow from the word hoopin' up to the circle. The note read:

"A big hoopin hello to my friend Pydie.
   I am doing just fine.
   I hope you are having fun and not getting bored since we cannot get together to play.
   Granny B says I will be able to come up to the store to see you in a day or so.
   She is afraid I will get infection in my throat if I get around the nasty loafers or play with Shekoe or touch all of the dusty, dirty stuff in the store. I miss you a bunch and I want to see you soon.
   P.S. I want you and Mr. Fritz to come with me to the beauty contest at the County Fair. I wish that you were going to be in the contest too. I think you are much prettier than I am and I think you would win. Granny B says I have to write a poem for this stupid contest so that is what I am doing today.

Your friend, Slatter.

   When Slatter had finished her note to Pydie, she folded it up into a small square and gave it to her grandmother. Granny B promptly asked.
   "Is this all you're gonna write to Pydie?
   This little note?"
   Slatter shrugged her shoulders and replied.

"That's all I feel like writin'.
Anyways, Pydie will understand.
Will you make sure grandpa gives it to her?"
Mr. Fritz will have to read it to her, cause she don't go to school yet and she don't know how to read. Granny B stuffed the note to down in her apron pocket and remarked, "Yes. I'll make sure Pydie gets your note." Slatter politely moved to her lips to form the word
"Thank you."

She went back into her room and sat down on the floor.
She started thinking about what she could write her poem about.
She started to write......

Roses are red and violets are blue...Shoppin' at Slopey's store is a smart thing to do.

"That sounds dumb," she remarked in a repulsive tone of voice. Then she scratched it out. She thought that sounded way too silly to read out loud. She surely could come up with something better than that. She didn't want to embarrass her grandparents. She wanted to make them proud of her. Her grandpa would probably want her to write something about Jesus. Then she had a great idea.

She would write a poem about lookin' for Jesus.

She rolled over on her back and began to think.
She started whispering to herself out loud.
"Let's see now.

Where can I look for more stuff about Jesus.
I know.
I will go to my grandpa's big old family bible and
see if I can find somethin' in there to write about."

She hurried into the living room and sat down on the floor beside grandpa's chair. She picked up the big bible that was on the table next to his chair and very carefully laid it down on the floor. She could tell someone had been reading it because it was on a different page than it was the day before. Slatter made it a point to walk by the bible several times each day and she always noticed when the pages had been turned. The pages were now opened to the book of Psalms and someone had used a red ink pen to underline some verses. Slatter assumed her grandpa had been the one to mark the scripture. She immediately began to read the underlined verses out loud.

"Psalm 34:7 The angel of the Lord encamps around those who fear Him and rescues them."

Tears began to swell up in Slatter's eyes. Suddenly she vividly remembered seeing the angel while she was pinned under the farm implement.
"Oh, my gosh!" She exclaimed.
"I can hardly believe what I just read!"
She managed to get a ..........WOW!
out of her weak, scratchy voice.
"I really wasn't seein' and hearin' things.
I remember everythin' real good now.
How excitin' this is!
Golly Gee.
I really did see a real angel.

I don't give a care if anyone believes me or not.
I know what I saw."
She became overwhelmed with excitement.
Then she had another thought that made her hesitate for just a minute.
I wonder why I didn't see the angel's face though.
She continued with her delightful thoughts.
Aha!
It's all comin' back to me now.
I do remember seein' a beautiful angel's wing.
Now I know grandpa must've seen the same angel that I did yesterday.
I wonder if he saw the angel's wing as close as I did.
It was the most beautiful thing I have ever seen in my life.

I wonder why he's not said anythin' to me about it.
I know he'd think I was a fibbin' big time and he probably thinks no one around where we live would believe him if he made it known, he saw a real angel.
I sure can't blame him for keepin' quiet.
I sure am glad I came in here and noticed where he has been readin' about angels in the bible.
I've got to be real careful and not let on to anyone what I saw.
I think this can be me and grandpa's little secret.
Oh well, some day I will have to ask him about it.

She felt real good about herself. She was so pepped up and full of enthusiasm that she started talking to God, out loud, in her rough, whispery tone of voice. She rattled on and on talking to Him as if he were an invisible best friend.

As she talked, she looked across the room at a chair as if she could actually see God sitting in it.

"Let's see now, God.

I want to find here in your book where the preacher said Ya wrote a bunch of stuff about everybody a lovin' everybody, no matter who they are or what they look like.

Ya know.

I've been a noticin' when Pydie goes to church with me how some of the people stare at us.

Some of the people around here sure treat her different than they treat me. They think she's different 'cause her skin is darker than mine. I don't think people treat her rude 'cause she doesn't have any pretty dresses to wear to church 'cause I don't have pretty clothes to wear either. Heck. Come to think of it. None of the kids at my church dress fancy. It has to be cause of her dark skin."

Then Slatter leaned over closer to the bible and in a quiet whisper tried to coax God into helping her write her poem.

She spoke in a pleading whiney voice.

"I sure would like fer ya to help me out with writin' this here poem.

It sure would pleasure me a heap.

I promised my Granny B that I'd write one for this stupid beauty pageant.

It's a comin' up quick....in about one more day and I ain't come up with the first line yet.

I really don't want to write this poem, but I can't let her down.

I gave her my word.

I know ya understand about givin' people your word.

I learned at church when Ya give your word about somethin', Ya always keep it.

No matter what.

I reckon that's easy fer Ya to do cause you're God.

Sometimes it ain't very easy for some folks.

I reckon what I really mean to say is, it ain't easy fer me.

I really do want to be like You and Jesus.

I want to be a good girl, but sometimes things jest happen and seems I'm always gettin' into trouble.

I jest got a lot to learn about lots of things.

My grandpa and Granny B tell me all the time I should try to be like Jesus.

I really do want to be like Him; except He's a boy and I'm a girl.

So if you could please see your way clear to even help me out a little on this here poem; I'd be mighty grateful.

I'd like to put somethin' in my poem that will sort of sound like a preacher's sermon.

Ya know.

Kinda like when he reads somethin' out of the bible that makes people think about what they're a doin' wrong.

Like when people go around hurtin' other people's feelings.

I don't really think that people want to be mean to my friend Pydie, but when I see people stare and look down their noses at her all the time....ooh eee," she nodded her head back and forth.

"I get real mad .....'cause I can tell her feelins' are hurt.

She gets a real sad look on her face.

Maybe if people knew how much they hurt Pydie's feelins, they'd treat her better. I jest think if people knew ya were a watchin em every day all the time, they'd treat one another a whole lot better.

I think people forget about ya sometimes and forget you're real."

Pydie noticed the bible had a big index in the back.

She decided to make use of it. She very carefully turned the bible on its' back side and started looking up words such as kindness and love. Everything she was looking for seem to jump off of the pages at her.

Granny B walked into the living room and curiously asked.

"Who in the world are ya talkin' to Slatter?"

Slatter hesitated to answer her. She remembered she was not supposed to be using her voice. She didn't want to get into trouble for talking, so she didn't respond. Instead, she shrugged her shoulders and cocked her head sideways. Granny B could see Slatter had no intention of talking to her, so she started walking back into the kitchen. Slatter reached out and jerked on the string of her apron. When Granny B turned around to see what she wanted, Slatter motioned for her to come over to where she was sitting.

Granny B walked back over to her and asked, "Well, what is it Slatter. What do ya want?"

Slatter took her ink pen and wrote her a note that read, Do you think Jesus is right here in the room with me?

Granny B leaned over Slatter's shoulder to read the note. She replied in a matter of fact tone.

"Why yes.

He's probably a sittin' right there beside ya.

Why do ya ask?"
Slatter wrote her another note that read:

I just wanted to make sure cause I've been talking to him quite a bit."

Granny B sympathetically smiled as she bent over and patted Slatter on the shoulder.
"Well, that's alright.
Just remember you can always talk to Jesus.
He hears everythin' ya say and one of these days when ya are older and understand more, ya can invite him in your heart. Then, He'll never forsake ya or leave ya.
Let me show ya where that's at in this big bible and ya can read it fer yourself.
Then Granny B turned in the bible to the book of Hebrews chapter 13, verse 5 for Slatter to read.
In a soft whisper, Slatter read the scripture out loud.

"I will never forsake you or leave you."

Then, Granny B went back into the kitchen.

As soon as Slatter knew that she was alone, smiling, she scooted over on the floor as far as she could next to her grandpa's chair. She once again started whispering out loud to Jesus.
"There now Jesus.
I made ya some more room to sit by me so ya won't get squished while ya help me search for somethin' for me to write about for the contest.
Ya know.

I think I'm gonna like havin' ya for my friend.

I like the thought of ya never, ever leavin' me.

It sure seems to me every time I learn to love someone, they always have to leave me for some reason or another.

I know Pydie's my bestest friend now, but she's gonna be leavin' me soon to go back and live with her mother.

Ya know, God.

I loved my mother and she left me.

I kind of had a dad for a while and I loved him some.

He left me.

I made a new friend named Gappy.

He left me too.

Yep.

Seems to me everybody is always a leavin' me to go somewheres else.

But Granny B just now showed me in your bible here that Ya are the one and only true God, and ya will never leave me.

One time I remember hearin' my grandpa tell one of the loafers at the store that Ya are always faithful to Your word.

He also told them the Bible says the grass will wilt and flowers won't fade, but Your word will stand forever.

I sure do like that about Ya.

Seems to me, when Ya decide to do somethin', Ya make it a point to make it last forever.

Ya know God.

I think ya got a whole lots of friends here on earth, cause I hear plenty of people talkin about how good ya are.

I hope one day ya can say somethin' good about me.

Yep.

I think we're gonna be great friends."

She hesitated and took a deep breath, then continued right on talking.

"Even if I can't see you right now, I know for sure
.........someday I will.
.........I don't know how I know it.
...........I just know it.

Slatter was absolutely sure Jesus was in the room with her and He was going to somehow, help her write her poem. Without thinking, she picked up her pencil and began to push it against the paper. As she wrote, her face took on a peaceful countenance. Deep in thought, she kept talking to herself.

"Maybe," she spoke aloud.

"If people spent more time lookin' for Jesus, they could somehow get to know him better. Sorta like get a little glimpse of him to see how He'd like fer things to be done."

All of a sudden, the words started to flow out of her mind and onto the paper. She smiled to herself as she felt like someone else, instead of her, was actually writing the poem. Her pencil smoothly began to move all by itself against the paper. All she did was hang onto the pencil. When the pencil stopped moving, the writing didn't look at all like Slatter's child like print. The poem was written in less than ten minutes. Granny B walked back into the living room as Slatter was folding up the piece of paper she had written her poem on. Granny B walked up to her and kindly asked,

"Are ya finished writin' your poem already?"

Slatter didn't try to speak. She knew Granny B wanted her to save her voice for the pageant, so she nodded her head yes.

Granny B then held out her hand for Slatter to give it to her. Slatter did not hand her the paper. Instead, she tried to hide the paper by sticking her hands behind her back. She lowered her eyes to the floor. Again, Granny B inquired, "C'mon now," she pleaded.

"Let your Granny B read your poem?
Ya don't have to hide it.
I won't tell a soul what ya wrote about. "

Slatter shook her head no and clutched the paper tightly to her chest.

Granny B was insulted. She had a shocked look on her face.

"Well my goodness." She said in a hurtful tone.
"What's gotten in to ya child.
I only wanted to read it!"

Slatter could tell by the expression on Granny B's face she had hurt her feelings. Slatter quickly grabbed another piece of paper and wrote Granny B a note that read:

God helped me write my poem.
I don't want anyone to know about my poem until I read it at the contest. I saw hurt in your eyes and I didn't mean to hurt your feelings. I'm sorry.

Granny B glared at her.
She didn't know quite what to say.
She never expected Slatter to treat her like a stranger.

Even though she was disappointed, she politely responded, "Well, alright then. I'll respect that. The poem is yours to do with as ya see fit. I'll get busy and get your best dress pressed and ready for ya to wear tomorrow night."

Granny B, still upset, wiped the palms of her hands on her dress and walked away. Slatter quickly folded the piece of paper and stuffed it in her pocket. Then she walked out onto the front porch, curled up in the big swing, and fell asleep.

The next thing she knew Granny B was waking her up to eat supper. Slatter still wasn't feeling very good and she was still having trouble swallowing, so Granny B made her drink some home made warm chicken broth. The broth really did make her feel a little better. Since she couldn't use her voice, she preceded with her bedtime ritual which consisted of a sponge bath, and brushing her teeth. As she put on her pajamas, she remembered to put her poem under her mattress. She jumped into bed, dreading for morning to come because she knew tomorrow night was the county fair beauty pageant. She was afraid everyone would make fun of her ugly, red, scabbed over neck. She felt very ugly and ashamed and the dread of people laughing at her was overwhelming.

It was mid morning when Slatter finally awoke from her restful sleep. The penetrating heat of the sun had already caused her room to become hot enough to cause sweat to drip off of her forehead onto her arm. She kicked the wrinkled covers off of her bed as she rolled over and over, trying to find a cool spot to lie on.

Finally, she decided to get up and look in the mirror to see if the wound on her neck had healed any more. She managed to force a smile on her face as she stood staring at herself in the mirror. She snickered as she took a long, hard look at herself. She tried practicing how she would stand at the contest. She turned to one side and then the other sticking out her chest and holding in her stomach.

She shook her head and let out a big sigh as she whispered to herself.

"Huh.

Look at me.

I guess mirrors don't lie.

I sure wish mine did.

When I stand up in front of all of those people, they'll probably think that I look ugly and pitiful.

The kids at school say I walk like a boy.

I don't know any other way to walk.

My hair always looks a mess.

Oh golly gee.

This has got to be one of the worse days of my life.

Ain't nobody gonna vote for me with this ugly ole red ring

around my neck.

I'd rather take a beatin' than be in this beauty contest.

But, grandpa always says that a person is only as good as

his word.

If'n I want to be like the good Lord, I have to do what I'd

say I'd do.

And I did give Granny B my word that I would enter the contest.

Soooo"......................... She let out a big sigh.

"I guess that means I have to go through with it, no matter what."

It was time to give her voice a try.

If her voice was still scratchy, there was a slim chance Granny B would let her back out of her word. She cleared her throat and out came her words as clear as a bell, "How do ya do.

My name is Miss Slatter Slopey."

She plopped down on the edge of her bed and in a half-hearted disappointed tone, she said "Shucks.

I might a known my voice would sound just fine.

Now, I have ta go to that stupid beauty pageant."

Granny B heard Slatter talking to herself and yelled for her to come to breakfast. Slatter sat at the breakfast table with a frown on her face. Granny B cheerfully exclaimed, "Eat your breakfast little lady and don't ya be a pretendin' ya still can't talk, cause I've already heard ya talkin' to yourself in the mirror this morning.'

She giggled as she handed Slatter her breakfast.

"I have a very nice surprise for ya.

I told your grandpa that Pydie could come down and play for a while this mornin'.

But, you two girls will have to start gettin' ready to go to the fair about four o'clock.

We have to be there by six o'clock, so ya better get your playin' time in this mornin'."

Slatter grabbed a piece of toast and ran to the front door.

She could see Mr. Fritz and Pydie were already walking across the yard toward the front door. Slatter yelled out to Pydie, then flew out the squeaky screen door. Slatter grabbed Pydie and gave her a great big hug. The girls started playing ring around the rosy together.

Slatter cried out, "Pydie. Oh Miss Pydie, I've missed ya so much!

I feel like I haven't seen ya in months."

The girls hugged one another and jumped up and down. Granny B was drying her hands on her apron as she walked up behind Slatter. She and Mr. Fritz at the same time exchanged a good morning, how do ya do. Then Mr. Fritz told Pydie he would be back to get her around four o'clock and left.

Granny B had a stern but pleasant look on her face when she blurted out, "Now, I want ya girls to play quietly today.

Slatter will need her voice for tonight to read her poem."

The girls joined hands and headed toward the back yard. Granny B feared the girls would get into mischief again, so she made sure the girls did not leave her sight. She grabbed both of them by the seat of their pants.

"uh, uh, uh.

I meant for you girls to play quietly....inside the house," ordered Granny B.

Slatter folded her arms and whined, "Oh, Granny B.

There ain't nothin' to do in their.

We'll be bored to death.

It's way too hot to play in there anyways.

Can't we go outside jest for a little while?"

Pydie just stood beside Slatter and didn't say a word.

Mr. Fritz had already given her a talking to that morning about obeying her elders.

Granny B remained insistent, "Now Slatter. Don't talk back to your elders. Ya remember what happened the other day when ya disobeyed. Ya jest need to keep a civil tongue in your mouth and do as I say.

Besides, I think I know of somethin' you girls can play with.

It's somethin' ya ain't never played with before."

C'mon inside the house."

The girls looked at one another and followed her back into the house. They both were wondering what in the world she had in mind for them. They thought she was so old she couldn't possibly know anything about playing and having fun. Once they were inside, Granny B went over to the table beside her chair and picked up an old Sears and Roebuck catalogue. Then, she walked through the kitchen out to the back porch and picked up a big cardboard box. The two girls followed close behind her and watched her every move. They wondered what she fixing them to play with. There eyes widened as Granny B opened her big butcher knife drawer, beside the kitchen sink, and began to cut square holes in the box.

As Granny B furiously worked, Slatter couldn't help but notice how calloused her hands were from years of hard work. She proceeded to cut off the flaps that were on top of the box. When she had finished cutting on it, the girls could see it resembled a big doll house. Then Granny B made slits in the flaps she had cut off the top of the box. The flaps were now tightly fitted crossways inside the box and they looked like walls with doorways. Slatter and Pydie were simply delighted. They couldn't believe such an old person would know how to make something so neat to play with. With the skill of an artist, Granny B had fashioned a very unique looking doll house. They had not seen a home made doll house before. Straitening her shoulders and throwing her head back, she proudly handed Slatter the box and declared,

"Now.

There ya go.

Instant fun and it didn't cost one red cent either!

How about that.

Fun doesn't always have to cost ya money.

Remember that girls.

Now ya girls have yourselves a big doll house."

Pydie was quite impressed with Granny B's masterpiece. She looked down inside the box and curiously asked,

How's we gonna play wif it Mrs. Slopey?

"We ain't got nothin' to put in it.

It's a real fine lookin' doll house, but it's kinda bare."

Granny B winked at the girls then walked over to her sewing kit. She quickly turned around to face them after she pulled out a small pair of scissors from the drawer like a cowboy pulls out a gun from his holster.

"Ya can pick out and cut out," remarked Granny B in a teasing gesture. Then, she handed the scissors and the Sears & Roebuck catalogue to Pydie and Slatter. The girls took them from Granny B and gave her a puzzled look. Slatter softly asked, "What are we supposed to do with this stuff?"

Granny B giggled a little and said, "Ya weren't listen' to me was ya. You youngins these days need to use your imaginations for somethin' besides gettin' into trouble. Now, you two sit down right here in the livin' room floor and think jest a minute or two about this stuff I just gave ya.

I declare.

I've fixed up all the hard part fer youns and that's as fer as I'm a goin' with it.

I'm a drawin' the line now.

I ain't about ta tell ya how to play with it.

You two can surely figure it out."

Slatter started turning the pages of the catalogue. She saw pictures of men and women and children. She ooed and awed at the pictures of beautiful living room furniture and clothes for the whole family. Granny B walked back into the living room with some old newspapers, two wet clothes and a bowl full of home made paste.

Pydie, crinkling up her nose, was the first to speak, "Ooh yuk!

What is dat yucky lookin' stuff?

It looks like a bowl of gravy!"

Granny B chuckled a little as she said, "Yeah it does sorta look like it.

But it ain't.

This, my dear child, is paste.

Ya know, glue.

It's home made glue.

I just now made it out of flour and water and don't you two try to eat it!

It's not edible.

Oh, and here is a rag to wipe your hands on."

Granny B pleaded with the girls.

"Please, please try your best not to make a mess with this paste."

When Granny B had finished speaking, Slatter excitedly yelled, "I got it Granny B!

Ya want us to pick out pictures and cut them out of this catalogue then paste 'em in our doll house.

Wow!

Ain't this somethin' Miss Pydie.

We can dress it up and make it as fancy and beautiful as we want to."

Granny B used her apron to wipe the paste off her hands as she watch the girls being delighted with their new toy.

"Ya guessed it right", replied Granny B as she patted Slatter on the back.

"You girls can spend all mornin' a playin' like your rich.

Ya can paste curtains on your windows and cut out furniture for your rooms.

Ya both can use your imagination and have lots and lots of fun. Remember, I'm just a holler a way in the kitchen if ya need me for somethin'."

Granny B set up a floor fan beside the girls so they would keep cool while they were playing, then went back into the kitchen to finish her work.

Both Pydie and Slatter were very content to sit on the floor and create their very own doll house. The girls spent all morning pretending they were rich and buying everything they wanted to furnish their house. They made play money by cutting short strips of newspaper and pretended Granny B's old buttons were coins. Handling the play money and pretending to be rich caused Slatter to have pleasant thoughts about her secret map that was hidden under her mattress. What if she really does find out the map is real and ends up finding a buried treasure somewhere. Then, some day she could, for real, buy anything she wanted. The girls had made a big mess with cut up pieces of paper all around them, but, Granny B never said one harsh word to them. She was really enjoying listening to them as they talked and laughed together; like they didn't have a care in the world. As she listened to Slatter's happy giggles, she remembered what a sad child Slatter had been when she came to live there. Granny B knew Pydie would soon be going back home to live with her mother and Slatter would miss her little friend something terrible. But until that time came, Granny B wanted the girls to spend as much time as they could together. Granny B thought Pydie was one of the sweetest little girls she had ever met and when the time came for her to leave, she would be sorely missed by everyone in the Slopey household.

As the old saying goes, time flies when you are having fun and today was no exception. When four o'clock rolled around, Granny B came strolling into the living room to announce the time.

"Alright you two girls.

It's four o'clock and that means it's gettin' ready time."

The girls knew exactly what she meant.

It was time to get ready to go to the fair and attend the dreaded beauty pageant. They weren't ready to quit playing, but knew they didn't have a choice. They immediately started cleaning up their doll house mess. Just as they finished putting the last piece of paper in the trash, Mr. Fritz arrived and was knocking on the front screen door. Pydie excitedly ran outside to greet him and jumped into his big arms. He was just as happy to see her as she was to see him. He laughed out loud and said, "Whoa is me youngin'.

Iz think maybe youz got a lots bigger since dis mornin'.

"How about a big squeeze for your old uncle Fritz."

Then, as Pydie was giving him a great big hug, he made a loud 'mmm, mmm, mmm' sound. It was quite apparent Mr. Fritz had so much love for Pydie. You could hear it in his voice when he talked to her. Mr. Fritz and Pydie waved goodbye to Slatter and Granny B as they headed down the road toward home. Pydie, walking backward, happily yelled out to Slatter, "Youz be shore to get all fancied up for dat beauty pageant tonight and me and uncle Fritz will be dare to vote for ya.

Seez ya later alligator."

Slatter, with a blank look on her face, looked at Granny B and asked,

"What was all that about an alligator?"

Granny B laughed a little at Slatter's question.

Then as they walked back into the house, Granny B commented, "Oh, that's just an old sayin' Mr. Fritz has told to Pydie.

When one of your friends say, see ya later alligator.

Ya are supposed to reply back to them with, after while crocodile." Slatter smiled and said, "Oh yeah? Well that's nice. It rhymes. "Hey, I like that.

I will start sayin' that back to Pydie every time I see her."

Granny B hugged her and gave her a loving pat on the back. She took her by the hand and led her into the kitchen to start getting her set up for her bath.

Granny B had heated some water on top of the stove in a big, heavy, metal tub. She had brought another long, deep tub into the house for Slatter to use as a bath tub. There were two big fluffy towels hanging on the back of a kitchen chair and a new bar of soap lying on the counter. Slatter stood and watched every moved Granny B made. She poured warm water into the long tub and then told Slatter to take her clothes off and get in it. Slatter reluctantly obeyed without saying a word. She knew it was way too late to try and get out of the contest now. Granny B handed Slatter a wash cloth to place over her eyes so when she tilted her head back to rinse her hair, she wouldn't get any soap in her eyes. When Granny B had finished washing Slatter's hair, she handed her another wash cloth and giggled a little as she said, "There, young lady. My part is done. You're gettin' to be a big girl now. So, ya can take things from here. You wash as far down as possible and then as far up as possible and then wash possible."

Slatter blushed. She didn't have to ask what possible meant. She knew. When Granny B turned to go out of the room, she turned toward Slatter and jokingly added, "Oh yeah. I almost forgot. Don't ya be getting' any bright ideas about makin' bubbles with your hiney while you're a sittin' in that water cause I may want to take a bath in that same water when your done."

Slatter giggled and threw her wet wash cloth over her face. After she had finished bathing she was more than ready to get out of the tub. She yelled out to Granny B.

"I'm all done.

"I need fer ya to come and help me dry off!

Granny B stopped what she was doing, grabbed a towel and tossed it at Slatter.

"There ya go," remarked Granny B in a matter of fact way.

"I think your surely big enough to dry yourself off."

Slatter gave her a pouty look and Granny B grinned back at her.

"Oh, alright, compromised Granny B.

"I'll help ya dry off."

She patted Slatter dry and dusted her with bath powder. Then she took the towel and fluffed her hair until it was almost dry. Slatter thought this was quite a ritual to go through just for the county fair. She thought nothing could be worth this much trouble. She preferred to take her regular sponge bath with a pan of water. Granny B kept turning her in a circle until the towel was completely wrapped around her. Next, she made Slatter sit in a chair at the kitchen table while she put big brush rollers in her hair. The rollers hurt Slatter's head because Granny B used bobby pins to pin them to her head. After her hair was all rolled, Slatter had to sit in a chair in front of the floor fan for about an hour so that her hair would dry faster. Granny B could tell by the look on Slatter's face she thought she was being tortured. Slatter kept picking at the rollers trying to make them loose because they were making her head sore. She was trying her best to be a good sport about the whole situation. She never complained one time. She helped pass the time by reading her grandpa's Saturday Evening Post magazines. Granny B kept coming over to her and unrolling one of the rollers, as she checked to see if Slatter's hair was dry yet. Each time she checked, Slatter asked, Am I done yet?"

Granny B would giggle and shake her head no. Finally, after what seemed like hours to Slatter, the time for the unveiling of her new hairdo had arrived. Granny B turned off the big fan and took the rollers out. She began brushing Slatter's clean, fluffy hair with long hard strokes. She began to smile to herself because she was so pleased with the way Slatter was shaping up. She held her finger up to Slatter and said,

"Wait here.

"I'll be right back in jest one minute."

She walked into her bedroom and reached into her old jewelry box and pulled out a beautiful hair comb. It was covered in big, royal blue rhinestones and trimmed in sterling silver.

She walked up to Slatter and as she spoke, she delicately laid it in the palm of her hand. She said, "Would you like to wear this tonight?"

Slatter's mouth opened wide with excitement, "Wow!" she exclaimed.

"I would love to wear this.

Are ya sure ya want me to wear this beautiful comb?"

Granny B was pleased that Slatter liked her comb. She swallowed back her pride as she continued.

"My mother gave this to me to wear in my hair on my weddin' day when I married your grandpa."

Slatter was honored that Granny B would let her wear such a memorable piece.

"Oh...........I would be proud to wear this comb tonight!

It's soooo very beautiful.

I promise to be very careful with it.

Are ya sure I won't lose it.

Gee, I'd feel jest awful if I lost your comb."

Granny B took a small section of Slatter's hair and French braided it.

Then they curled it up into a bun on top of her head.

She slid the comb into the French braided bun.

"I'm putting the comb in real tight for ya," remarked Granny B.

That way ya won't be as apt to lose it."

When she was finished she backed up a few steps and proudly announced, "Well, Well, Well. Don't ya look all spiffy now." Slatter couldn't wait to see her new hairdo. She jumped up and ran into her room so she could looked at herself in the mirror. She liked what she saw. She could hardly believe that the person in the mirror was her. She took her hands and started playing around with her new hairdo. Granny B followed close behind her.

"Now quit a fiddlin' with your hair," said Granny B smacking at Slatter's hands.

"You'll jest mess it up.

Keep your hands off of it.

Here.

I ain't done.

I'm goin' to put hair spray on it so it won't get messed up."

To prevent the spray from getting in her eyes, Slatter put her hands over her face.

"Oh alright," said Slatter, "but not very much."

When Granny B finished spraying Slatter's hair, Slatter put her hand on top of her head and said, "I can't stand for my hair to feel sticky."

Granny B replied, " Well ya can stand it for a little while for jest one night I reckon."

Slatter kept staring at herself in the mirror.

All she could see was the sparkling blue rhinestones on top of her light, blonde hair.

She didn't even give another thought to the red marks around her neck.

Granny B caringly put her hands on Slatter's shoulders and announced, "Honey. I got somethin' very special fer ya jest fer this special occasion. It's in my closet. I'm goin' to go and get it and I'll be right back."

Slatter was full of anticipation. She kept primping in the mirror until Granny B waltzed back into the room holding a beautiful, new royal blue dress in one hand and a small brown sack in the other. Slatter's mouth dropped open as she grabbed the dress away from Granny B. She was ecstatic. She screamed, "Oh, my...goodness!

Jiminy Jahosaphat! I've never seen such a beautiful dress!

Is this for me?

I mean, can I put it on?"

Granny B smiled at Slatter and said, "Why, yes. It's yours.

It ain't gonna fit nobody else.

I made it just for my little girl.

I've been workin' on it at night after ya go to bed.

Your grandpa helped me some.

There is not another dress in the whole world made like this one.

The pattern didn't call for a ruffle at the bottom or on the sleeves, but I added 'em anyway.

Aren't they pretty?"

Slatter grabbed Granny B and gave her a great big hug.

She couldn't stop the tears as they spilled from her eyes.

She had a lump in her throat from the gratitude she was feeling.

She was speechless. After a few seconds of hesitation she spoke in a stuttering way, "Oh, my oh my. Oh, Granny B!

I ...I don't know what ta say.

I ...I was dreadin' this beauty contest 'cause I knew I didn't have anythin' pretty enough to wear, but this dress is the most beautiful dress I've ever laid my eyes on.

Can I try it on?"

Granny B, overwhelmed with the way Slatter carried on about the dress, replied,

I reckon my feelins' would be hurt if ya didn't."

"I'm real glad ya like it sa much.

Oh and here in this sack is a new pair of shoes to wear with it." Granny B reached down inside the brown sack and pulled out a shoe box.

"I got 'em on sale here while back.

They should fit.

Me and your grandpa measured your feet one night while you was a sleepin."

Slatter grabbed the shoe box and jerked the lid off. When she saw the shiny new white Patent leather shoes, she grabbed her throat and exclaimed, "Oh my golly gee.

Granny B they're jest beautiful.

I ain't never had anythin' like this before."

She quickly slid them onto her feet. They were a perfect fit. She leaned over and stroked them with her hand.

"C'mon now, enough gawkin' at them shoes.

I'm anxious to see if'n this dress fits ya.

I used one of your old ones as a pattern.

It should fit ya jest right."

Granny B helped her slip into the dress and then Slatter slowly turned around and stood in front of the mirror. She gasped when she saw herself. She thought she looked absolutely beautiful. For the first time in her life, she thought she looked like a beautiful princess ready for the ball. She twirled around and around the room in her new dress. She cried out, "I think I look like a movie star right out of a magazine. Jest look at me! My hair is all curly and fixed with shiny blue rhinestones on top.

I look like I'm already a wearin' some kind a crown."

She smoothed her dress with her hands as she bragged on her dress, "I can't believe I get to wear this nice-lookin' fancy new dress.

It's the color of a perfect blue sky on a perfect cloudless day."

Her light blonde hair and her striking bold blue dress complimented each other like a freshly opened golden daffodil reflecting against a solid blue sky. Granny B had a proud look on her face as she put her arm around her and boasted, "Ya look as pretty as a princess right out of a story book."

"I couldn't have my little princess wearin' a plain, tired lookin' old dress to a beauty pageant.

What would everyone say?

People will be so busy a lookin' at how pretty ya are they won't even notice that red mark around your neck.

Your grandpa and I are so proud of ya."

Granny B walked over to Slatter. As she caressed Slatter's cheek with her hand she said, "Ya know. Ya look a lot like your momma a standin' there, all gussied up. Ever time I saw her she always had a smile on her face. She was never one to complain about nothin'.

She was always a willin' to help anyone do anythin' and when she started to work, Whew-ee! She'd work like a house a fire, fast and furious. As long as I live, I'll never understand why the good Lord saw fit ta take her while she was so young, but we ain't supposed to question God.

Heaven has a way of shapin' our destiny that sometimes looks very peculiar to us."

Only He can see the big picture of our lives when we can't."

Slatter stopped smiling and turned toward Granny B.

She thought that was a strange comment for Granny B to make. Especially since she had heard it before. She remembered her friend Gappy explaining to her about the big picture of life. She had an inquiring look on her face when she said, Granny B. What did ya mean when ya said God can see the big picture of our lives?"

Granny B blew off her question by saying, "Oh nothing I don't reckon. I really don't have the time right now to explain it.

We've got ta hurry and get ready or we'll be late. Ya know how I hate to be late for anythin'."

Granny B glanced over at the old alarm clock and started talking faster, "Oh dear. I had better get to goin' and get ready myself. Time's a gettin' away.

I'll have to hurry.

Your grandpa will be here in just a few minutes to get cleaned up.

He'll probably just come in and put on a clean shirt and freshen up a little bit.

It don't take a man very long to get ready to go somewhere. Slatter, you go on out to the front porch and sit in the swing and wait for me there. I won't be very long. Don't ya dare go outside and get dirty."

Slatter quickly responded to Granny B's orders.

She headed toward the porch swing just like she was told.

She did not want to be in Granny B's way while she was getting ready. Slatter couldn't wait to get to the fair now. She wanted to show off her pretty new hair style and new dress. She felt like she looked just as pretty as any of the other girls that had entered the beauty pageant.

As Slatter sat in the porch swing and waited, she eagerly anticipated the appearance of the old blue goose. Finally, after only a few short minutes, she saw it coming up the long driveway. Slatter was quick on her feet to open the old squeaky screen door for her grandpa. She couldn't wait for him to see her new look. Grandpa immediately noticed how pretty she looked and he could tell by the way she acted toward him she wanted him to compliment her. He wasted no time. He winked at her and his kind words were like music to her ears. He bowed in front of her and said,

"Well now. Excuse me beautiful lady, but have you seen my, Slatter?"

Slatter smacked her grandpa on the arm and in a bashful sort of way said, "Oh, grandpa. Ya know it's me.

Do I really look beautiful?"

Grandpa leaned over and whispered in her ear.

"My dear, ya are the prettiest little girl in the county and I'll bet ya win that Little Princess pageant hands down."

Slatter looked down at her feet as she nervously picked at her fingers. She swayed back and forth. She was overcome with pride. She wanted him to compliment her again, so she put her arm around his waist and walked him to the front door. She spun around in a circle and said, "Granny B made me this new dress. I ain't never had anythin' so beautiful.

I don't ever want to take it off."

This dress makes me feel so pretty.

I wish this night could last forever."

Grandpa winked at Slatter and as he turned to walk away, he stopped and rubbed the back of his hand against the front of the sleeve of her dress. He tilted his head and mentioned, "No doubt, it sure is a pretty one, but just remember... pretty is...is pretty does.

Lots of girls look real pretty, but when ya get ta know them, they can become pretty ugly."

Slatter nodded her head. She had heard that saying before. She watched her grandpa walk on into the house, and then she walked back over to the swing and sat down. She smoothed out her dress and flipped her head back and forth so she could feel her curls swaying. She patiently waited for her grandpa and Granny B to get ready. Granny B was already dressed and ready to go and she had a clean shirt already laid out on the bed for grandpa. As he changed his shirt they began talking about Slatter. Since their bedroom was next to the front porch, they didn't realize Slatter could clearly hear their conversation. Granny B was so pleased with the way Slatter looked. She began bragging on her.

"J.E.

Did ya ever think that little thing out there could ever clean up so good to look as pretty as she does?"

Grandpa smugly replied, "Yes I did.

I have seen her beauty all the way along.

She's smart too.

And I'll tell ya something else.

If her poem she wrote for this pageant reflects even half of the beauty she has in her heart, she'll be sure and win.

I've been watchin' that little lady a lot lately and she's very sensitive to Godly things.

She's different than most kids her age.

Her heart seems to be straight in line with God's word.

When she hears about a bible story or when her Sunday school teacher reads scriptures aloud to the class, she remembers 'em.

Not only does she remember 'em, but she believes with all of her heart that God's word is true.

No ifs, ands, or buts about it.

I can see faith in her eyes when she talks about the bible.

She's totally convinced that God is absolutely real and whatever God says in his word is a done deal.

I've never seen so much faith in anyone in my whole life.

I think that it's **the way** she believes that makes her so special."

Then grandpa chuckled to himself because he liked that quality in his granddaughter. He was tired but his mood was chipper. As he changed his shirt and combed his hair he said, "All I know is God must have a special purpose for that child.

I can see it comin'.

Can't you?"

Granny B smiled and then thoughtfully said, "Yes, but seems to me everything's either a wedding or a funeral to her and there's no in between. Sometimes I have to actually walk into the room where's she's at to see if she's laughin' or cryin'. It's hard to tell.

Oh, but there's no doubt she is a very curious child.

Why jest the other day, she didn't know I was watchin' her and she scooted over on the floor so Jesus would have room to sit beside her. When I walked into the room, she was a talkin' up a storm to what looked like thin air. She even asked me if Jesus was in the same room with her. I told her yes 'cause He said in his word that He'd never leave us.

I could tell she really believed that Jesus was right there in the room with her."

Grandpa finished tucking his shirt inside his pants and took Granny B by the hand and looked into her eyes.

He lovingly said, "I'm sure Jesus was in the room with her; Not seein' is believin' ya know.

Maybe a little child sees a lot of spiritual things that are invisible to us old folks.

A young person's mind isn't clogged up all of the time with the cares of the world."

Granny B smiled at grandpa as she flattened his shirt collar down, "Ya jest might have somethin' there, J.E.

Say, we better get to goin' now or we are going to be late for the pageant. After all this time sayin' she didn't want no part in the beauty contest, she's bustin' at the seams to hurry up and get there." They laughed together as grandpa reminded Granny B to be sure and take her jar of home canned pickles with her, for the pickle contest. Granny B was way ahead of grandpa on this one. She shook her finger in his face and jokingly said, "I'll have ya know Mr. J.E. Slopey; I've already sent a jar to the fair, by way of Mrs. Raker."

Grandpa rolled his eyes and asked on a disbelieving note,

"Ya mean the one in your Sunday school class who was kiddin' ya last week about not havin run-in' water in your house yet?

Huh.

I figured ya was still mad at her. Reckon that's one fer the books! Ha!"

Granny B replied,

"Well, I always say overcome evil with good.

Anyway, her time is a comin'.

The good Lord will make a footstool out of my enemies.

I'll jest bide my tongue and watch it all unfold."

Grandpa snorted a little and patted her on the back as they walked out the door.

"That's my Granny B," he said.

Slatter had heard every word that Granny B and grandpa had said about her and she was so pleased to think they thought of her as being a special little girl. She felt guilty because she had not been honest with them about Shekoe falling in the well. So, in her mind, she vowed to do better. She managed to hide her look of shame as the three of them got into the old blue goose and headed for the county fair.

The fair was just a few miles from the house. Slatter got excited when she saw all of the lights and carnival rides. The glittery spectacle and bright lights of the midway intrigued her. She hadn't been to a county fair before. She didn't know what she had been missing. She couldn't get over how many people were there just walking around having fun doing nothing. After grandpa had parked the car, the three of them got out and walked toward a big red barn where the beauty contest was going to be. It was easy to find because it had a great big picture of a huge sparkling crown hanging on the front door. Slatter kept stumbling as she kept staring at the people instead of watching where she was walking. She gave lingering looks to the people walking beside her as she watched them eat cotton candy and fiddlesticks. She saw people playing games and carrying big stuffed animals. Everyone seemed to be having a very good time. She wanted to ride some of the carnival rides but she knew she'd have to ask permission.

"Say Granny B," asked Slatter very politely.

Can I go have some fun after the contest is over?

Ya know ride some of the rides and stuff and maybe buy some ice-cream?"

Her grandpa shook his head and shot Granny B a quick look of disagreement. Granny B regretfully denied Slatter's simple request.

"No.

I'm sorry.

Not tonight honey," replied Granny B in an apologetic manner.

"The fair carneys are just out ta get your money and you'll end up goin' home broke with nothin' ta show for it."

Slatter was disappointed but she understood they didn't have much money to spare. She felt like she had caused enough extra expense by having to have the well cleaned out. Her eyes quickly shifted toward the ground so she could continue to hide the guilty look on her face. She could feel Granny B's eyes closely watching her every move.

All of a sudden Slatter saw the two mean bullies from her school, Newton and Lodden. They didn't recognize her at first because she was so dressed up. Slatter, however, recognized them at a first glance. She would know their taunting, freckled faces anywhere. Just as she was going into the barn, the boys ran up to greet her. Slatter wanted the boys to see her pretty new dress and hairdo, so she stopped to talk to them. Granny B kept on walking. At first, they just stared at her for a few seconds like they wanted to be sure she was who they thought she was. Then Newton spoke up with a snide remark.

"Well, well.

Look who's here!

If it ain't Miss Slatter Sloppy Mess...........ooh...Teacher's pet!"

She tried to smack the boys, but they quickly darted to and fro.

Slatter's proud smile was short lived. Her face instantly took on a wrinkled up mean look as she squinted her eyes and scrunched up her lips. She stood with her arms folded as she yelled back at Newton's smart-alecky remark.

"Ya listen here ya no count bullies.

For your information, my name is Slatter Slopey!

Sticks and stones may break my bones but your words will never hurt me."

She remembered her grandpa's comment to her about pretty is-pretty does. She wondered if that phrase was intended for boys too.

Newton, enjoying every minute of his playful teasing, had to make another sarcastic comment.

"Well well," said Newton as he made a circle around Slatter looking her up and down.

"What are ya all slickered up for.

I think this county fair has got enough clowns."

Then both the boys started laughing as hard as they could.

Lodden, who always followed Newton's lead, had to put his two cents worth in too.

"Yeah.

Ha-Ha," laughed Lodden.

"Ya aren't plannin' on enterin' that Little Miss Princess pageant here at the fair tonight are you?

Cause if you are.

You ain't gonna win with that big red ring around your neck!"

As they yelled out, they raised their arms high in the air, made a big circle with their hands and wiggled all around.

"Hoopty do! Hoopty do!

Look at her new hairdo!

Hoopty do!

She's wearin all blue!

Ha-Ha.

Bootsy boo....Bootsy boo."

They continued to laugh at Slatter as they taunted her. They kept grabbing at her hair from behind, trying to mess up her hair. She kept slapping at them.

"What happened to ya!" shouted Newton.

Lodden began to tease Slatter with a made up song.
"Slatter, sloppy Slopey.....somebody tried to hang her!
Somebody tried to hang her and used a wire hanger!
Nan a nan a nan a!
Ha Ha Ha."
They kept on laughing louder and louder.

The boys started pointing at Slatter's neck. She was caught off guard and was so upset she didn't know how to respond to such spitefulness. Finally, she looked down at the ground and started to cry. The boys had no sympathy for her. They were so loud they were bringing attention to themselves. People were stopping and staring at them. It didn't take long to draw a crowd. The boys unknowingly had twirled themselves into a position where they had their backs turned toward the front of the barn's outside door. They were totally unaware of what was going on around them. Out of nowhere, a show horse had quietly walked up behind them. Without warning, the horse decided to relieve himself. He raised his big black, fluffy tail and dropped a big pile of fresh manure right on the back of the boys' head. Slatter with tears in her eyes, started laughing.

Now, it was her turn to point and laugh at Newton and Lodden.

The boys weren't laughing anymore. They were too busy trying to wipe the manure off of their heads and the backs of the their shirts. They were covered in fresh, green, manure and the smell was appalling. The boys didn't like the way people were pointing and laughing at them.

It didn't take long for Granny B to notice Slatter wasn't by her side anymore and she promptly went back to find her. As she walked up to where Slatter was standing, she held her nose because of the terrible odor. Wrinkling up her nose she complained, "P-hew. What in the world is a goin' on around here?

Young lady.

I hope ya didn't get any of that horse manure on your new dress." Granny B grabbed Slatter's hand and gave her a jerk.

"C'mon now with me.

We've got to hurry.

Ya are the third contestant."

Slatter stopped laughing and Granny B handed her a tissue to wipe the tears from her face. She hurriedly walked into the pageant building and walked up the stage steps where she took her place in line. A lady walked over and pinned a big square piece of white paper on the front of her dress that had a big black number three on it. Slatter started fidgeting and picking at her fingers when she saw the huge crowd that had gathered inside the barn for the event. Her new found confidence had suddenly grown shaky and she wanted to put her hand on her throat to hide her ugly red mark. She knew it was better not to touch her throat because she knew she would only draw more attention to it.

As she gazed around the room, she noticed something that really bothered her. All the girls on the stage were white. She didn't see one single little black girl in line competing for the Little Miss Princess title. She wondered if Miss Pydie was the only black girl in the whole county. She gazed out into the audience and saw Granny B and her grandpa sitting in the front row. Then, she looked around for Pydie and

Mr. Fritz. It wasn't hard to find them, because they were the only black people there. She figured they must've came into the barn late because they were sitting in the very back row. It meant so much to her that both of them came to give her their support. She gave them both a great big howdy wave. Slatter could see almost everyone in the audience had proud smiles on their faces. She figured everyone there was somehow related to each of the contestants.

Slatter hadn't been standing on the stage very long when the announcer walked out and welcomed everyone to the fair pageant. He was a short, bald, fat man and liked to talk a lot. He must've been awful hot, because he kept wiping his forehead with his handkerchief. Every now and then, Slatter would see him wink at some of the other girls, but for some reason, he never did wink at her. She started to get a bad feeling about him. She thought he was up to no good. He had a fake way about him that made her distrust him. She thought he put on a front and he really wasn't as nice as he wanted the audience to think he was. He managed to speak very loud with a deep whispery voice that had a thunderous impact.

As the announcer strutted across the stage, he went on and on about having the ten prettiest little girls in the county on the stage with him. After several minutes into his opening speech, he finally got around to telling the audience that all of the contestants picked their own talent and when the audience went to cast their votes, they needed to consider everything about the candidate not just their cute little faces. He also finally got around to showing everyone what the prizes were.

First prize was a $20.00 bill and a beautiful, silver crown with the words LITTLE MISS PRINCESS engraved on the front of it. The crown sparkled with hundreds of tiny rhinestone jewels with sterling silver filigree.

Second prize was a new little doll. When the announcer held up the little doll for all to see, Slatter noticed it was a little black baby doll. As he walked back and forth across the stage, waving the little black doll into the air, his speech changed and he started talking with a sarcastic southern dialogue. He mockingly announced, "Now, ladies and gentlemen. Don't ya knows dat every little white girl should wants ta **owns** one of dese here little ole black baby mammy dolls.

Iz understands dat it's the latest kind of doll outs on da market today.

Da winner will gets ta beez a mammy to dis here little black baby doll."

What the announcer said, and the way he said it, made Slatter very angry. He was making fun of the way Pydie and Mr. Fritz talked. She stomped her foot and with laser eyes, glared at him. She wanted to walk over and smack him in the face, but she knew she would embarrass her grandparents if she misbehaved like that, so she made herself just stand there. She didn't attempt to hide the hostile expression on her face. Everyone in the audience, except for Granny B, grandpa, Mr. Fritz, and Pydie, laughed and snickered at what the fat announcer had inappropriately said. Slatter leaned over to the little girl to her right and sternly said, "How would he like it if someone stood up and made a remark about his being fat and bald."

The girl frowned back at her.

Slatter was slowly beginning to get the big picture, as her friend Gappy would've said.

Apparently, not only did the town's people not like Pydie. But they really didn't like Mr. Fritz either. Slatter whispered out loud to herself.

"How awful!

Mr. Fritz has worked like a dog for some of these people and this is the thanks he gets fer it.

I see the truth, now.

People really don't like Miss Pydie and Mr. Fritz 'cause their skin color is black instead of white.

I just can't believe it!

Why, these people don't know anything about 'em.

I'll just bet some of the men over by the front door made 'em sit in that back row."

Some of the girls standing on stage next to Slatter gave her a funny look because she was talking to herself. Slatter didn't care. She stuck her tongue out at the contestants each time one of them glared at her. Slatter was trying not to get mad, but her attitude was not getting any better. In a mean tone she whispered, "What are ya girls a starin at?

Ain't ya ever heard a person whisper to themselves before?"

No one dared to respond to Slatter's questions.

They acted like they were afraid of her. One thing was for sure though. Slatter's anger overcame her nervousness. She patiently waited for her turn to step out in front. In her mind, she was concentrating on creating a plan to somehow get to the announcer and tell him off.

The first contestant stepped forward and said her name and who her parents were. She spoke in a tiny little voice and she picked at her dress as she swayed back and forth. She softly announced, "My name is Darlene Cassidy and my mommy and daddy are Frank and Lula May Cassidy and they own Cassidy Furniture Store." She had a pretty red ruffled dress on that looked way too short for her. When she bent over Slatter could see her underwear. It was red ruffled too. Slatter felt sorry for her. She thought that whoever made that little girl's dress, must've run out of material so they made panties to match. Her hair had so many tight banana curls they bounced with every step she took. She must've ran out of things to say because after she stated she owned a dog named pootie, she just stood there and twisted the bottom ruffle on her dress. Her mother came running out on stage and helped her start singing a song without any music. The name of the song was You Are My Sunshine. She sounded pretty good, but she kept forgetting the words and had to start over two or three times. Slatter thought Darlene's mom did a pretty good job of singing her daughter's song for her. She giggled to herself thinking that instead of voting for Darlene, maybe the people would vote for the little girl's mother for Little Miss Princess.

 Then, the second contestant stepped out from the group and announced her name. Her name was Bertha Brander. She was a great big girl for her age. She was much taller than the announcer. Slatter thought a good nickname for her would be Big Bertha. Bertha had pigtails and her four front teeth were missing. She told everyone that she had a pet cat that was solid yellow in color, and it's name was Misty. Slatter could tell she had a cat at home because the back of her black dress was thickly covered in yellow cat hair. Slatter thought her Granny B would never stand for that. Big Bertha had a big belly and her dress must've been way too tight for her cause she kept pulling down on it as she talked. Her talent was twirling a baton. The girl's mother played a record so her daughter could have music to twirl to. The title of the song was 'When The Saints Go Marching In.' The record must've been old because it kept getting stuck. To make matters worse, Bertha kept tripping over her dress. She only fell down two or three times. Things got a little tense when all of the contestants had to duck every time she threw the baton way up in the air because big Bertha wasn't able to catch it when she was supposed to. But, fortunately, the baton never did hit anyone standing on the stage. Slatter didn't know what the other seven girls were like, but so far, her chance of winning this contest was looking pretty good.

Finally, it was Slatter's turn to step out and tell about herself. She took a deep breathe and stepped forward. She just stood there for a few seconds, and looked around at the audience. Everyone remained quiet as they waited for Slatter to speak. Finally, her anticipation had come to an end. She remembered Granny B saying that it's better to overcome evil with good. She decided to give it a try. Controlling her temper, she started to speak in a kind, sweet voice.

"Hello everyone.

My name is Slatter Slopey.

I live with my grandparents, Granny B and J. E. Slopey.

They are my parents now and they own Slopey's General Store.

My mommy has went to heaven to be with Jesus and my daddy is off a workin' somewhere. So far I don't have any pets except for an old cat named Shekoe, but Granny B says he has to stay up at grandpa's store cause she don't want him under foot. When I came to live with my grandparents, I shore was lonely cause I had to change schools and I didn't have any friends. I didn't have anyone to play with me, so

I asked Jesus to come and play with me." The audience responded with slight laughter.

"I reckon He couldn't come, but He sent me a very special friend instead.

He sent me the best friend I could ever hope to have.

I would like for my best friend, Pydalean Jackson, to come up here right now and stand beside me on this stage. I want you all to see her." Mr. Fritz leaned over to Pydie and said, "Go on now, Miss Pydie. Go on and do whats Miss Slatter has asked ya to do. She's proud of ya and she wants ta shows ya off."

Pydie, wearing her little sleeveless burlap dress, stood up and started walking down the aisle toward the stage. The room became so quiet you could've heard a pin drop. Most of the women started jerking their heads around and straightening their shoulders and the men started nervously fumbling with their hats. Slatter stopped talking as Pydie walked down the middle of the aisle. The startled crowd murmured as all eyes were on this little dark skinned girl as she proudly stepped up onto the stage and took her place next to Slatter. Smoothing her hair away from her face, Pydie clasped her hand into Slatters and smiled. The two girls hugged one another and then Slatter continued her speech.

"Folks," began Slatter as she continued to proudly show off her new friend.

"I want ya all to meet my very special friend Miss Pydie.

"Her skin may be a different color than mine, but Jesus made her heart the same color as mine.

And by the way, He also made her heart the same color as yours." She raised her eyebrows as she made a face to the audience that made a silent statement.

She was trying to say to them.....take that and put it in your pipe and smoke it.

"My Granny B," continued Slatter, "says pretty is ..is pretty does.

I think Miss Pydie is the prettiest girl on this stage tonight, cause she acts as pretty as she looks."

Slatter remembered how Pydie had talked about how much she wanted a little black baby doll. Slatter wanted to take advantage of this opportunity to get her one. She wanted Pydie to have that doll. The room was still very quiet. The audience watched as Slatter pranced across the stage toward the announcer. The only sound that was heard was the clacking of Slatter's patent leather shoes, as she marched across the old wooden stage. When Slatter reached the announcer, she hatefully jerked the black doll out of his hands. She stuck her tongue out at him and in a harsh tone of voice proclaimed,

"I'll take that doll.

You and the devil have had it long enough."

Then she walked back over to Pydie. Not one person made a move to try and take the doll away from her. As she handed Pydie the doll, Slatter hugged her friend and said, "Here Miss Pydie.

I believe this belongs to you.

I think Jesus wants ya to have this fer your very own."

Slatter then walked back up to the center of the stage, and turned toward the audience.

"I feel in my heart, that Jesus wants Miss Pydie to have this little doll for her very own since she didn't get a chance to be in this Little Miss Princess Pageant tonight."

Fighting back tears she lovingly said, "You see folks. Pydie has a great talent too.

If ya would take time to get to know her, ya would see it.

Her talent is teaching."

She looked at her friend and gave her a heart felt smile.

"She taught me a lot about love.

She taught me what love feels like.

Have ya ever wondered what love really feels like?

Have ya ever felt alone in the darkness and then suddenly felt the touch of a person's hand as they reached out to help ya?

Well, that's what love feels like.

The touch of a hand when you're stumblin' around in the darkness.

Ya really don't care what color that hand is.

You're only glad that it's there.

She also taught me what love sounds like.

Have ya ever heard a faint, heart breaking whimper in the night from someone who is pleading with God for the life of someone they love?

That's the sound of love.

What about taste.

Did you ever think that love has a taste.

Well, I can tell ya I know what love tastes like.

It tastes like salty tears.

Have ya have ever hugged someone so tight while they were cryin' ya could feel their tears a slidin' down their cheeks like rain drops as they dripped onto your lips?

If ya have......Then, you've tasted love.

And lastly, Miss Pydalean Jackson here has showed me what love looks like.

If ya think ya can see love on people by lookin' at their outward appearance........ ya can't.
It just ain't there.

My grandpa told me one time the bible says God is love.
He also said a person's love is reflected from a person's heart like a mirror onto their face.
Ya have to have love in your heart to be able see love in someone else's face.
Ya have to feel love before you can give it to someone else.
Love ain't somethin' ya can keep fer yourself.
Love ain't love until ya give it away.

But, thanks to Pydie, I've learned that ya **can't** see love on a person by lookin' at the color of their skin or by the color of their eyes. That's just science; like what we study in school.

Ya can only see love in a person though the eyes of the heart.

My grandpa told me that only God can see a person's heart, but ya can hear what's in a person's heart if ya take the time to listen....... Cause whatever is in there, comes flyin' right on out of their mouth when they go to talkin.'

Love is how ya talk to others. Granny B calls it keepin' a civil tongue in your mouth. Least said, least mended. Everyone needs to remember that.

Love is givin' back to others when they have given to ya.
Love is allowin' your hands, to become Jesus' hands.

.........Givin' of your time to reach out to people in need like Mr. Fritz a takin care of his niece while her momma's sick.

And makin' your feet, become Jesus' feet...........Ya know.
Doin' things for others when they can't do for themselves.
Sorta like when my grandpa delivers groceries to old people that ain't able to get out and go to the store and get groceries anymore.

And the way Mr. Fritz goes ahead and fixes things fer people even when they ain't got any money to pay him.

In the short time, that I lived with my Granny B, she has taught me that actions speak louder than looks.

They've been teachin' me to learn about people by listenin' and watchin'.

My friend Miss Pydie here is jest like me.

She ain't got fancy clothes to wear but she wears the most beautiful thing she could ever wear; and that's the cloak of love.

Ya can't wear nothin' any prettier than that.

Love is a priceless garment and it can't be bought anywhere.

It's worth as much to the giver as it is to the one receivin' it.

Pydie became my friend first even though my skin was a different color than hers."

Slatter swallowed back her tears as she paused for a few seconds to regain her composure before continuing on.

The audience could not believe such a young, simple, little country girl could speak such a powerful and sophisticated message to them. She had their immediate attention because everyone there knew she was giving them a message that seemed to be flowing through her from a much higher source. She continued speaking to a silent, captivated audience. She cleared her throat and said, "I asked Jesus to help me write my poem and He did." The audience snickered a little.

"Honest He did," said Slatter in a hurtful defensive tone when she heard the audience's reaction to her statement.

"My Granny B wanted to read it before tonight," she growled.

"I reckon she thought she might need to fix it up a little bit fer me so it'd sound alright, but I wouldn't let her.

I wanted to be able to say that no one but me and Jesus knew what was in this poem.

I didn't want anyone sayin' that my Granny B helped me write it." Slatter stood very still as she unfolded her paper. Granny B took her handkerchief out of her purse and held it against her nose. She was nervous for Slatter. She drew in a deep breath as she absorbed every word that Slatter's was saying. Slatter boldly continued speaking,

"I've never written a poem before, but I think that Jesus might be tryin' to send ya all a very important message through this one. So, please listen."

A hush had fallen over the crowd. Even the young children sat perfectly still and waited for Slatter's next move. She licked her lips and brushed her hair away from her sweaty face. She stared at the huge fans in the back as they tirelessly worked to create a breeze inside the hot, humid room. She noticed every eye in the barn was fixed upon her. She looked over the audience. She saw women fanning themselves with paper fans and men using their handkerchiefs to wipe sweat from their faces. She cleared her throat and in a caring, clear voice began reading her poem aloud.

**"HAVE YOU SEEN JESUS TODAY?"**

"Have you seen Jesus today, was He within your sight?

Was He in the shadows that faded with the night?
Did you see Him pass by your window in a sudden burst of light?
Was He in the silence of your sleep?
Did His presence wake you with a fright?
Did you feel a flutter down deep in your heart?
As He searched for a place to land, did you feel a tug in your mind as He gave you a silent reprimand?
Did you feel Him in a gentle wind, as it blew back your hair?
Did you try and convince yourself, that He really wasn't there?
Just ask God to open your eyes and I'm sure you will see
His very special angels watching over you and me.
You can see Jesus every single day, if you read His word and pray.
But, if you close your eyes to the smallest of things,
He'll never let you hear the rustling of His heavenly angels' wings."

When Slatter finished reading, there wasn't a dry eye in the place. She put her arm around Pydie and pulled her close to her side. All of a sudden, everyone in the audience stood up and began applauding. She noticed the women in the front row were using their handkerchiefs to wipe the tears from their eyes. Pydie stopped clapping long enough to give Slatter a big hug. Then, tightly clutching the little black doll to her chest, Pydie nodded at Slatter and jumped off the stage. She made her way back to her seat and stood beside Mr. Fritz.

When the overwhelming applause had ceased, Slatter stepped back in line with the other contestants. She felt in her heart she had made her point to the audience. She didn't really care if she won that contest or not. She had given her friend something she wanted very badly and hopefully shamed the whole town. She felt really good about herself.

By the time the contest was over, everyone on stage had grown very tired and was sitting on the floor. The announcer told everyone to go over to a big box in the back of the room and vote for their favorite contestant. It only took about twenty minutes for everyone to cast their vote and return to their seats. When everyone was finished voting, two men took the box behind the stage and began counting.

After a few minutes had passed, the two men came out and handed a note to the announcer. Everyone had been eating cookies and drinking Kool-Aid while they waited for the results of the vote. Their socializing came to an abrupt stop when the announcer stepped back onto the stage and enthusiastically started telling everyone to please take their seat because the votes had all been counted. As soon as everyone was properly seated, the announcer walked onto the stage and yelled into the microphone, "Ladies and gentlemen.

The votes have all been counted and I have the name of the first prize winner."

Slatter's fingers were crossed and so were Pydie's.

"Will Miss Slatter Slopey please step forward.

You are our new Little Miss Princess winner for this year."

Suddenly, everyone in the audience stood up and started applauding. Slatter was surprised. She couldn't believe she had won the contest. A few of the contestants started crying because they didn't win and some of them gave Slatter dirty looks. The contestant Slatter thought of as Big Bertha, strutted over to her and hatefully stated,

"You shouldn't have won because you ain't even got a real mom and dad." Slatter put her hands on her hips and sarcastically replied, "Oh yes I do.

My Granny B and grandpa are my mom and dad."

Big Bertha hastily walked away from Slatter, then turned around stuck her tongue out and remarked, "Everybody knows you're jest an orphan and besides your grandma and grandpa are way too old to be real parents." She let out a mean laugh and said, "They're so old, they'll probably die real soon and leave ya jest like your mommy did."

Slatter had had enough of her smart remarks. She wanted to smack her in the face for being so nasty to her. Just as she started to run after her the announcer motioned for Slatter to come over to the center of the stage so he could award her first prize. Slatter still had it in for the announcer. She slowly walked up to him. Even though she stood perfectly still and didn't say a word, he acted as nervous as a cat on a hot tin roof as he carefully placed the sparkling crown on her head. Then, she took a step forward and intentionally stomped on one of his toes with the heel of her shoe. He grunted like he felt a sharp pain. He gave her a mean, dirty look and leaned over toward her. A slow, mean looking smile spread across his face and he loudly whispered in her ear.

"Young lady.

I wouldn't push my luck if I were you.

If looks could kill, you'd be dead."

Slatter bit her bottom lip to keep from laughing out loud at what he'd said. He handed her a crisp, new twenty dollar bill and she grabbed it out of his fat little hands. She walked away from him with a satisfied smile on her face because she knew that he knew there was nothing he could do about her stepping on his toes.

The moment became overwhelming to Slatter. She was so proud of herself for having won, she began to cry. She knew she had made Granny B and her grandpa very proud. She had won the contest and Pydie had finally got her very own little black doll. Granny B and grandpa hurried up on stage to get their picture taken with the new little princess. The audience formed a line and shook hands with Slatter as they congratulated her for winning. She could not believe how many compliments she received on her poem. Some people wanted a copy of it and one lady even suggested she try to have it published. When all of the kool-aid was gone and the last home made cookie had been eaten, the time came for everyone to go home.

As Slatter, Granny B, and grandpa walked to the parking lot where the old blue goose was parked, Slatter heard some people talking about how two freckled face little boys were trapped at the top of the rocko plane carnival ride earlier that evening. The boys had been throwing soda pop and ice onto some people walking on the ground below. The ride attendant kept telling them to stop causing trouble, but the boys wouldn't listen. Somehow, the cage they were riding in got stuck high in the air and would not quit spinning backwards. A fire truck had to be called in order to get the boys down from the carnival ride. They didn't get hurt, but they were so sick and dizzy their parents had to take them to the hospital. Slatter started giggling to herself, when she heard the story; because she had an idea the two boys were probably those two mean, naughty boys, Newton and Lodden.

# 8

# WHAT IS MERCY

The evening had been an exceptionally happy time for the Slopey family. All the way home, Slatter had a big smile on her face. She kept trying to look in the car's rear view mirror at the sparkling crown the announcer had placed on her head.

Granny B was the first one to go in the house and Slatter pleaded with her grandpa to take a few minutes to sit with her on the porch swing. He was very tired, but he could see by the look on her face that she did not want the night to end. As Slatter waited for grandpa's response, she noticed he had a special kind of smile on his face. She had no way of knowing that when her grandpa looked into her sweet innocent face, he could see the hope of a new tomorrow in her eyes. He wanted to hang onto the evening just as much as she did. He just expressed it in a different way.

Without saying a word, he sat down in the swing and Slatter plopped down right next to him. He put his arm around her and patted her on the shoulder. Embracing her, he hugged her tightly, tenderly rocking her gently. She buried her head into his chest. She loved to smell the Old Spice aftershave cologne on his neck. She knew in her heart her grandpa was getting older and she would not always have him with her to share such a tender moment, but she had him with her tonight; and for the moment, that was all that really mattered to her.

He asked, "Well young lady. Are ya happy tonight?"

Slatter nodded her head yes.

She was so full of love and excitement that she couldn't even speak. She wanted to tell him she was very happy for winning the pageant, but in her heart, she was just as happy and grateful to be living in a home where she felt she belonged. But somehow, she just couldn't think of the right words to say. She could not begin to express how important it was to her to feel she belonged to a family. Big Bertha's words were still ringing in her ears about her grandparents being old. What her grandpa said next summed up everything she was feeling. Somehow he had a way of knowing how and when to say the right thing to her and at the right time. He softly said,

"I jest bet ya I know what your feelin right now.

You're beginnin' to realize how important belongin' to a family is. Ya know somethin honey.

Ya don't have to live with both of your parents to have a happy family.

Oh, it's true that's always an ideal situation, but sometimes ya have to learn to adjust to a different kind of family.

Whoever is the one takin care of ya and lovin ya is your family and that's who ya have to obey.

Me and Granny B are takin care of ya now.

We're your mommy and daddy now.

Being part of a family is all about belongin' to someone and feelin' loved.

I know lots of families that don't share love in their home the way we do.

There's lots of lonely people out in this old world that have big families, but they don't know how to share their love.

Sharin' love is what happiness is all about.

Sharin' is somethin' everybody has to pitch in and work at.

Now little sis, your old grandpa wouldn't lie to ya.

That's what I think is the key to a happy family.

Ya know Abraham Lincoln once said people are usually as happy as they have a mind to be.

I reckon that's true."

For a moment, there was complete silence between them.

As the cool late night air swooshed across Slatter's face, she took pleasure in feeling the warmth radiating from her grandpa's chest. She pulled her legs to her chest and snuggled close to him.

They began discussing small talk and Slatter listened closely to her grandpa as if he was telling her a goodnight story.

"Are ya still worried about makin friends at school?"

Slatter only nodded her head yes. He kissed her on the forehead and chuckled a little.

"Well, no need in worryin' about that.

It takes time to make real friends.

You'll learn as you grow older, it takes a long time to really get to know someone.

I'll tell ya a little secret, Slatter.

A person's heart is the key that unlocks their mind and reveals who that person really is.

When you love someone enough to open up and share your heart with them without fear of condemnation, ya have entrusted them with your most fragile inner being.

Can ya even begin to understand that?

Or does it just sound like a confusion of words?"

Slatter listening very intently replied softly, "Oh, I think I understand what you're trying to tell me. I understand a lot more than you may think. You're tellin' me to be patient with the kids at school until I get to know 'em better."

Grandpa patted her arm and said, "Well, no matter.

Even if ya don't understand it now, someday ya will.

Maybe your old grandpa has given you some food for thought anyway."

Slatter was thinking of her friend Pydie and Mr. Fritz when she sat straight up in the swing and stared into her grandpa's face. She angrily said, "Grandpa. Why did that old fat, bald headed, announcer mock the way Pydie and Mr. Fritz talked?"

Grandpa scratched his head, hesitated for a few seconds and after he drew in a deep breath said.

"Well, Slatter.

Ignorance I reckon is as good a answer as any.

Some people are jest educated fools.

Ya will find as ya get older that some people are like owls.

The more light ya shine on 'em, the less they see.

The best way I can explain it to ya is a long time ago, black people were kept in bondage and bought and sold like pieces of furniture.

But after many years of scrappin' and fightin', they now have equal rights. That's the way it should've been all through history.

People are people, regardless of their color or nationality, but some people still to this day look down on them just because their skin's black.

It's sad."

There was silence between them as they rocked in the swing.

Then Grandpa continued,

"Oh, I reckon there's always gonna be a few people around that think black people should still be kept in bondage.

I think it's probably human nature to fear someone that looks a little different.

That's man's way though, not God's."

Patting Slatter on the hand he boasted, "I know I was very proud of what ya said tonight and I could sure tell that ya have been readin' the bible a lot lately because of what ya said to all of those people." He chuckled a little, "Yeah, Miss Slatter.

Ya sure put on a grand performance tonight.

I reckon ya gave the gossipers in this little old town plenty to talk about fer a good long while."

Slatter knew this was a good time to talk to him about her punishment for playing around on the old farm implement.

She abruptly jumped out of the swing as she said, "Wait here. I'll be right back. I have to go get somethin'."

She quickly ran to her room and grabbed her old ugly wooden hairbrush her dad used to beat her with and ran back out onto the porch. She handed the brush to her grandpa and tearfully said, "Here grandpa.

I know if I hadn't climbed up on that old farm thing out in the field, I wouldn't have gotten hurt.

I know you have to punish me, so I'm ready to get it over with." She slowly turned around so her back would be toward him and made a dreaded expression on her face. She clinched her fist together and bit down on her lower lip as she prepared for the pain she was about to feel. She then bent over and touched her knees. The old familiar mixture of love and guilt was written all over her face. Her grandpa could not believe what he was seeing. He could clearly see she had been spanked with her hairbrush before. He slowly laid the hairbrush down in the swing and took hold of her little hand. He had a puzzled look on his face as he turned her around to face him.

"Whoa.

Slow down here jest a minute young lady," said Grandpa tenderly. "I'll be the one to decide what kind of punishment ya need to have, not you."

Slatter seemed relieved at his response, but she was still very apprehensive. She plopped down in the swing next to him and nervously crossed her arms over her chest. She acted half-way embarrassed, burying her face into his chest. She sat quietly as she anxiously awaited his next move. She waited for her grandpa to say something, but he didn't. In the silence of the night, the two of them just sat quietly as the old porch swing squeaked with each swaying movement.

Her grandpa picked up the hairbrush and ran his hands across the stiff bristles. After a long silence, he swallowed hard before he delicately asked, "You've been spanked with this old thing before haven't ya Slatter?"

Slatter shamefully nodded her head yes. Grandpa raised his eyebrows and asked, "Was it your daddy that spanked ya?"

Again, she nodded her head yes and then looked down at the floor. Slatter didn't have the heart to tell her grandpa that his son had not only beaten her with that hair brush, but he had also beaten her with a leather belt and a wash pan too. He would grab whatever was handy at the moment. It didn't seem to matter what the object was, as long as he could hold it in his hand. Her grandpa kept shaking his head back and forth as he breathed a deep sigh. He was having trouble finding the right words to express the compassion he was feeling for his granddaughter. Wiping the tears from his eyes, He tried to swallow the lump in his throat. He had pity in his voice as he spoke, "You're such a little thing.

I know that had to have hurt ya really bad.

I'm feelin a lot of shame for what my son did to ya.

Do ya hate him fer what he done to ya?"

Slatter did not respond.

"Well," said grandpa not wanting to push her for an answer.

"I think tonight would be a good time for ya to learn a lesson about mercy."

Slatter perked up and sat up straight in the swing. She wrinkled up her nose as she repeated his last word and curiously asked, "Mercy?

What in the world does mercy mean?"

Her grandpa was quick to give his reply, "Well, sis. I'll do the best I can to explain it to ya. In simple terms it means compassion.

Compassion simply means to withhold punishment from someone that has done a terrible deed that deserves to be punished.

It's sorta of like a strong power under control.

I reckon that's hard fer ya to understand.

Let me say it another way.

The Hebrew word translated into English means to love from the womb.

It means to show others the same tender love a mother shows her own helpless child.

God loves His people with a deep compassion and love that is almost beyond description.

In the bible, God tells us in Luke 6:36 that we are to be merciful.

Just as our heavenly Father is merciful."

Slatter happily butted in, "Does that mean ya got some of that compassion stuff fer me and ya ain't gonna spank me with that old hairbrush?" Grandpa looked into her eyes and smiled.

"Yes, Slatter," answered grandpa softly.

"That's exactly what it means.

I really do think ya suffered enough punishment the other day when ya hurt your neck."

Her grandpa's voice suddenly grew stern.

"Honey," he said in a correcting way.

"Ya jest need to realize that when parents tell their kids not to do somethin, it's for their own good.

Parents aren't tryin to be mean, and they're not tryin' to stop their youngins from havin' fun.

They've jest lived a lot longer and know more about danger. Parents don't want to see their kids get hurt or into trouble. They want what's best for their family.

When ya get a little older and understand more about God, you'll understand that He loves his family the same way.

Some people get mad at God 'cause things don't always go their own way.

But God knows the future and sometimes he stops us from doin' things we think is right, cause He can clearly see all the way to the end of our lives. He can see things, good and bad, a comin' to us a way on down the line;

things we couldn't even think of ......jest 'cause He knows the future.

He doesn't want us to get hurt.

I've seen people hold grudges against God their whole life.

Sure is a shame they have to be so ignorant about spiritual things. People miss out on many blessings of life jest by being an ignorant Amos.

Your daddy's one of them very people.

Ya need to pray fer your daddy.

Pray that he'll quit runnin' away from the Lord.

Seems to me he's been a runnin' away from God like an unending river fer most of his life.

He's always runnin' against the wind."

"What do ya mean by that grandpa?" Slatter innocently asked. Grandpa carefully thought before he answered. He didn't want to say something that would belittle his son, but rather tried to present a good answer that would sound caring and concerned. His remark was caring.

"Oh I reckon it means he thought he was taking control of his life by never surrendering to any kind of authority.... being his own boss. He was always tryin' to go a different direction than I wanted him to go; ya know, sorta like swimmin' upstream. He jest wanted to do things the hard way instead of listening to Godly advice.

He was always lookin' fer somethin' to go up against so he could start a fight.

Some kids are jest like that.

Those kinds of people are what I call late bloomers.

They usually learn late in life how much they've missed out on jest because they were so stubborn and hard headed in their younger years.

Your daddy never did want to listen to me when I'd try to talk to him about God.

He's like a lot of people I've seen over the years.

He lives with a starved soul always thinkin' he needs one more thing to bring him happiness.

People like that feed their bodies, but never feed their soul."

Slatter interrupted him and curiously asked,

"what do ya mean by starvin' your soul?"

Grandpa knew he was way over Slatter's head on this one, so he tenderly replied,

"Well, honey.

He never takes the time to read about God and explore life from God's point of view.

When a person starves his soul, he looks happy on the outside, but he lives in fear on the inside.

Slatter, nervously picking at her fingers, looked up into her grandpa's face and asked,

"Well, what do people look like when they're full of fear?"

Grandpa chuckled,

"Oh, a rebellious look I reckon-sort of uncaring and always tryin' to bring attention to themselves. Anything to be different from everyone else. That way their fear stays hidden from others 'cause everyone's focusing on how different they look instead of who they really are inside. The thing they fear the most is responsibility; especially the responsibility of love.

Love requires a lot of hard work and givin' of yourself.

It's folks' nature to be selfish and not want a lot of responsibility because there's always afraid of failing....ya know, fallin' short of what's expected of them.

I don't expect ya to understand all this, but ya are never too young to start learnin' about things in life."

It seemed to me your daddy was always unhappy.

He thought having a lot of money was the answer to being happy. He didn't like it much when I made him work fer me.

He always wanted money, but didn't have the desire to make his own.

He liked my money better I reckon.

It's always easier to like someone else's money.

He carried a chip on his shoulder and acted like he needed to prove somethin' to somebody.

Oh, I jest don't know where I went wrong with him, but I've never stop believin' he'll grow up one of these days and realize what's really important in life.

There came a day I had to quit a blamin' myself for your daddy's wrongs and trust the Lord to be the one to adjust his life to where he'll gain enough heart knowledge about God to turn his own life around.

Only God can change lives sis.

We don't hear from your daddy much, so I reckon he's a doin' alright.

At least he's tryin' to earn his own way now.

That's why me and your Granny B couldn't trust him to take care of ya when your mother passed away.

It's all he can do to take care of himself right now, let alone take care of a little child.

Dad blame it sis.

If kids are goin' to grow up stable adults, they need to be raised in a stable home.

That don't mean they always have to live with both parents, it means whoever is bringin' them up, needs to be stable.

Always remember this.

Birthright doesn't make somebody be a parent.

Oh well. I didn't mean to get into all of this talk about your daddy. I reckon it jest slipped out."

He sighed and kept on talking.

"I jest reckon it takes a lot longer for some folks to figure life out than it does others."

He bent over and untied his steel toed black work shoes and slid them off his feet. With his socks still on, he wiggled his toes.

"I must be a gettin' another corn on my little toe.

It's givin' me a heck of a lot of pain tonight."

Slatter, eager to please, dropped to the floor and took off his socks. She began to softly rub the top of his feet.

"Does that feel real good grandpa?" she asked.

"Ah, it sure does honey, but be mighty careful and don't hit that corn stickin' up there.

I'll have to soak it in a pan of warm water and Epsom salts before I go to bed."

He stroked the back of Slatter's head as he tenderly finished his conversation.

"Ya see sis," He began again.

"The older ya get, the harder it is to become submissive to God; or to anyone else fer that matter.

That's why it's so important to give your heart to the Lord while you're young.

Most youngins' know they have to answer to a higher authority and sometimes be disciplined.

Did ya know that the very first glimpse children has of God is through their parents?

If there's no respect for the parents, there'll be no respect for God. Children become what they live in, no matter what they're taught in the home.

That old saying, 'do as I say not as I do' doesn't hold water.

I've found out through experience that a kid will do as ya tell him to do when he's around ya, but most kids, the minute ya turn your back, they do as you do.

Kids need role models.

I've found it to be true in most cases that whoever a kid spends the most time around when they're a growin' up, that's who they become like........ when they grow up.

There's always exceptions, but kids are always a watchin' folks; especially their own.

I've seen preacher's kids grow up to be no counts and I've seen kids of no accounts grow up to become preachers.

Parents have to lead their youngins by example and that's all there is to it.....that's all any parent can do.

It takes a great deal of patience and energy to raise kids up right.

Parents have a great accountability both to their children and to God. It's terrible that some of us learn a little too late about our mistakes, but I reckon late is better than never."

He used his middle finger to flick away the tears running down his face. Slatter was afraid she had hurt him by accidentally hitting his sore toe and that was why he was crying.

"Are ya crying cause I hit your corn grandpa?" she caringly asked. "No sis," he tenderly replied.

"Ya didn't hit my corn.

Your old grandpa's jest a thinkin' about things that's all.

Slatter could tell her dad had done something very bad to hurt her grandpa and it must've been a long time ago; maybe when he was a young boy. She wanted to ask what it was, but she didn't. Her heart was tender toward her grandpa. She gave him her undivided attention. After a couple of minutes, he cleared his throat and regained his composure. He continued speaking,

"But back to what I was a sayin to ya before I started chasin' rabbits, your grandpa has lived a long time and I've seen God be merciful with his people everyday, all of the time.

I reckon I'd have to define mercy as God's love in action.

Ya see, Slatter.

God knows that we deserve to be punished for our sins, er ..uh ..I mean the wrong things that we do in this life; that's what the bible calls our sins.

Because Jesus died on the cross for our sins and took all of our punishment, He forgives us of those sins and we don't have to worry about being punished for 'em.

When ya ask him to forgive ya for doing wrong, He not only forgives but He does somethin' you and I can't do.

He forgets all about your wrong doings.

If ya pray to him and bring up to him about your forgiven sins, he doesn't remember them.

Mmm. Mmm.

Now that's somethin' I tell ya.

God is good.

He's so good to us; we don't even have one inkling of all of the good He does fer us.

Most people just take His goodness for granted.

We should always be thankful for God's compassionate kindness.

Since God is just and quick to forgive me when I do wrong, He holds me accountable to be quick to forgive others when they do wrong. God's word tells us that if ya don't forgive others, then He won't hear your prayers. Now, keep in mind, Slatter, your part in this situation, is to be thankful that I'm not going to spank ya for doin' wrong. Ya have seen the wrong ya done and ya have repented. From now on, ya should want to do right and please me and your Granny B. That way I'm good to you and by your being obedient, you're good back to me and your Granny B. Ya should listen and do as you're told and since I'm being so kind to ya, ya shouldn't want to disobey me and cause me disappointment and heartache. Always keep in you mind it is a commandment from God for children to obey their parents. Now, I'm gonna forgive ya for doin wrong and show ya mercy. I'm not gonna give ya a spankin this time for disobeyin' me. But keep in mind young lady; ya might not be so lucky if there's a second time. I do believe in spankin's, but with my hand on your behind-not with a big wooden brush. Now, are we settled about your punishment?"

A relieved Slatter took a deep breath and shook her head yes.

As she scooted over closer to her grandpa, she lay her head back down on his chest and began to cry. She felt so bad for disobeying him. She was glad she had repented to him and he had decided not to punish her, even though she knew she deserved to be punished. He showed her a good example of mercy. An example she would always remember. Grandpa slid both arms around her and as he softly caressed her hair with his hand, she quietly sobbed.

After a short while, the squeaking sound of the old swing swaying back and forth caused Slatter to become very sleepy. She fell asleep thinking how unbelievable it was for black people to have been bought and sold like a piece of furniture, just because their skin was black.

Slatter loved spending time with her grandpa. He always talked to her in a way that made her feel special, like she was grown up. Slatter was learning one of the simplest pleasures in all of God's galaxy was sitting on a porch swing under a beautiful summer night sky, with her head on her grandpa's chest listening to his heart beat in rhythm with the whippoorwills. She knew in her heart these precious moments spent with her grandpa would one day be just a memory; just like the few vague memories she had left of her mother. Her mind always seems to flash back to what her friend Gappy had once told her……. life is but a vapor…… compared to eternity. With each passing day, Slatter understood what he meant. Her summer had gone by so fast; she could hardly believe it was already time to start back to school.

They had only been sitting in the swing a few minutes, when grandpa noticed Slatter had drifted off to sleep. He picked her up in his arms, picked up his shoes, and carried her in the house. As he walked through the front door, he motioned with his head for Granny B to follow him to Slatter's room. They carefully took off her pretty blue dress and slid her pajamas on her. Then, they both kissed her, scooted her over to the middle of the bed, and turned out her light. Without saying a word, they quietly tiptoed out of the room.

# 9

# A TEARFUL FAREWELL

The next morning, Slatter was awakened by a slapping sound made by her curtains, as the wind blew them against the sides of her window. The strong breeze felt wonderfully refreshing as it swished across her feet. She lay sprawled out on her bed in perfect comfort. For a moment, she thought maybe she dreamed she'd won the Little Miss Princess title. Then, she glanced over at the beautiful sparkling crown sitting on her old dresser. She had a gleam in her eye as she stared at her pretty blue pageant dress hanging on her bedroom door.

Granny B suddenly came walking into her room carrying some clean play clothes for her to put on. Slatter could tell by the dreaded look on Granny B's face that something was wrong. Granny B laid the clothes on Slatter's bed and placed both hands on Slatter's shoulders. She looked her in the eye and in a matter of fact tone said, "Slatter. Ya need ta hurry up and get dressed. We've got company this mornin'."

Pydie and Mr. Fritz are in the living room.
They want to talk to ya."

Slatter's heart skipped a beat. She knew without a doubt why they had come. It was time for Miss Pydie to go home.

Slatter grabbed her play clothes and quickly got dressed. With a lump in her throat, Slatter half heartedly walked toward the living room. Granny B reached out and grabbed her by the arm as she boldly stated, "Young lady." Slatter stopped dead in her tracks and turned around to face her. Granny B spoke in a very kind but stern tone of voice. She said, "I know you don't want to hear this, but I have to tell ya before ya go in there."

She took a deep breath before she forced out the dreaded words, "Pydie's father has come to pick her up.

Now, I want ya to be a big girl about this and please try not to cry in front of little Pydie.

It won't accomplish a thing.

In fact, it'll jest makes things worse.

I know I'm askin' a lot of ya, being such a little girl and all, but please try to remember all of the fun you two have had this past month and how happy Pydie will be to see her mother again.

Think of makin' things easy on Pydie instead of yourself."

Slatter knew Granny B was right. She had big tears in her eyes as she listened. She turned back around and slowly walked into the living room. She was dreading what Pydie would say. She noticed Pydie was holding her little black baby doll tightly to her chest. When she walked up to Pydie, neither one said a word. They both started crying and hugging one another. Mr. Fritz and Granny B were fighting back tears too. Slatter, with tears raining down her face, and her bottom lip quivering, glanced over at Granny B and blurted out, "I tried Granny B. I tried really hard to be a big girl for ya. I just couldn't do it." Granny B knelt down beside the girls and wrapped her arms around both of them. Her words were kind hearted.

"Oh that's alright," she said reaching into her apron pocket for a handkerchief.

"You girls can cry all ya want to.

Pay me and Mr. Fritz no mind."

Slatter wiped her nose on her sleeve and slid her hand into Pydie's as she tearfully ordered, "C'mon, Miss Pydie.

Let's go outside by ourselves so we can talk a few minutes."

Like so many times before, the two girls held hands as they walked outside. They sat down beside one another on the front steps. Pydie, still sobbing, timidly finger twirled her little doll's curly hair as she tried her best to say goodbye, "Iz shore gonna miss ya Miss Slatter," sobbed Pydie.

I ain't never had no friend like youz before.

If'n I get ta goes ta school dis year, Iz will learn howz to write and den Iz can sends youz a letter.

Iz promise I will.

Iz will even make youz a pretty Christmas card and have my daddy put it in da mail fer me."

Slatter quit crying and tried to regain her composure.

She blew her nose on her shirt, making a loud honking sound.

Both of the girls thought that was funny, so they began to giggle loudly. When Granny B and Mr. Fritz heard the girls laughing, they figured the girls were finished crying. So they quietly walked out onto the porch and sat down on the swing. They could hear every word Pydie and Slatter were saying to each other. Slatter, still wiping her eyes, whispered,

"I reckon your gettin' to go home means your momma is all well now, huh?"

Pydie happily replied.

"Yeah, my daddy say dat my momma is all better now and she's a achin' to seez me. My daddy is up at yore grandpa's store right now a gettin' him some gas in da truck and den he's gonna come down here and picks me up. He's gonna be here real soon cauz he say I only gots a few minutes to say goodbye."

Pydie, nervously kept talking. She happily said, "I shore did have a sight fer sore eyes dis mornin' when Iz waked up and seez my daddy a havin' coffee with Uncle Fritz.

Mr. Fritz say my daddy come in late last night while Iz was a sleepin. My daddy told me dis mornin' dat Mr. Fritz bragged ta him all about how youz and me got to be such good friends and how good yore Granny B and grandpa Slopey has been ta me.

He say it'd be a rightful thing ta do fer Mr. Fritz ta bring me down here ta tells ya all goodbye and thank ya for bein' sa good to me. I already say goodbye to yore grandpa."

Pydie stood up and stared at Slatter with an empty heart, as fond memories of days gone by flooded her mind.

She looked into her best friend's sad eyes. Trying to cheer her up, she gave her a great big smile.

"Ya know," said Pydie as she held her doll up in the air.

"Iz jest can't thank ya enough Miss Slatter for dis here baby doll.

Iz will keeps her forever.

Iz promise I will.

I can't wait ta show her off to my momma.

Iz want ya to know before Iz go dat dis here baby doll is what Iz wished for da other night when ya helped me wish on dat fallin' star.

Iz reckon it's alright to tell ya bout it now, since my wish came true."

Slatter smiled at Pydie and said.

"Yeah, sure.

It's alright.

I'm glad ya got your wish.

I kinda got one of my wishes too."

Pydie, still picking at her doll's curly hair, sincerely asked, "Which wish was dat?"

Slatter replied,

"Well, I wished from the bottom of my heart for a friend and God sent me you, even if it was just for a little while.

I meant everythin' I said at that beauty contest last night.

I wasn't just a sayin' that stuff so I could win."

Pydie, twisting back and forth in a bashful way, responded to Slatter's kind words, "Ah, I knows dat. Youz iz the bestest friend I ever had in da whole world. Uncle Fritz say dat maybe Iz can come up and seez ya again sometimes. Maybe even next summer if'n my daddy say it's ok."

Suddenly, a big old, wobbly, grey truck with wooden sides on the back, drove up the drive way. Pydie started waving and ran up the driveway to meet it. When the truck stopped, a great big stout black man got out of it. Slatter could tell he was Mr. Fritz's brother because they looked very much alike. They both had the same big smile and both were gigantic looking men. Granny B and Mr. Fritz came outside to greet Pydie's father. Granny B prompted Slatter to get up off the steps and walk in front of her. Mr. Fritz was proud of his brother and he eagerly introduced him to Granny B and Slatter. "Granny B Slopey," said Mr. Fritz, "I wants ya ta meet Mr. Arlington Joe Jackson.

Most folks just call him Arlie.

He be Miss Pydie's daddy and my brother."

Granny B was cordial as she reached out to shake his hand, "I'm pleased to meet ya Mr. Jackson.

We sure have enjoyed havin' Pydie visit us this summer.

I hope ya let her come back and see us again sometime soon."

Mr. Jackson, smiling from ear to ear, replied, "Yes, mam.

I shore will.

I jest wanted ta come by here myself on behalf of me and Mrs. Jackson ta thank ya fer bein' sa good and kind ta our Pydie while she stay with Fritz."

Mr. Jackson turned to Slatter, and stuck out his hand for her to shake, "Well, well, well, remarked Mr. Jackson smiling from ear to ear.

"Dis must be da one and only Miss Slatter Slopey.

Boy, I shore has heard lots of good things 'bout ya.

I shore do wanna thank ya fer makin my little girl's stay here a happy one."

With a tear stained face, Slatter politely reached up to shake Mr. Jackson's hand. She thought Granny B would be proud she hadn't forgotten her manners. She spoke in a broken sad voice,

"Y...your most welcome Mr. Jackson.

I'm sure gonna miss my best friend an awful lot."

Mr. Jackson continued to smile at Slatter with his big white shiny teeth.

"Well, Iz shore figure Pydie will be a missin' youz a lot too.

Don't ya fret none child.

Iz jest knows ya two girls will be a seein' each utter again one of deez here days.

Iz will beez a comin' back 'fore too long to visit with Fritz again and Iz will bring my Pydie wif me.

Well, Weez got a long journey aheads of us and Iz wanna get home afore dark if'n Iz can.

So, weez better get on down da road now.
C'mon Pydie.
Let's go."

Pydie's father quickly swooped Pydie up in his big arms and sat her in the front seat of his truck. After he shook hands with Mr. Fritz, he leaned forward and tipped his hat at Slatter and Granny B.; as a gentleman's way of saying goodbye. As Pydie and her father backed out of the driveway, Slatter followed behind the truck and kept waving at Pydie. Pydie stuck her head out of the passenger side window and yelled to Slatter,

"Sees ya later alligator!"

Slatter yelled back at her.

"After while crocodile!"

Slatter stood out in the middle of the driveway and watched the truck wobble down the road until it was completely out of sight.

Pydie was gone.

Slatter's heart sank and immediately felt empty.
She agonized in silence over the loss of her best friend.
She didn't think anyone could understand what she was going through, so she didn't speak a word. Mr. Fritz quietly waved goodbye to Pydie and Granny B and started walking down the road toward home. As Mr. Fritz walked out of the yard, Slatter noticed he had pulled out his handkerchief and wiped his eyes. She felt sorry for poor old Mr. Fritz. She knew he too would be very lonely with Pydie gone.

For a few minutes, she compassionately watched him walk down the road, then she ran into the house to her room. She sat down on her bed and stared out of the window. All at once, she burst into tears. The empty, lonely feeling in her heart had overwhelmed her. She was hoping maybe she could numb the pain she was feeling by allowing her tears to flood down her face. She was once again all alone now and her feeling of unhappiness had returned. After a while, Granny B noticed Slatter was still in her room so she went to check on her. Granny B was not very tactful in the way she tried to cheer her up. When she saw how hard Slatter was crying, she teasingly remarked,

"Oh, stop your belly achin' child.

You'll get to see her again someday.

It's not the end of the world ya know.

Save your tears for when ya really need 'em."

She could tell she was not doing a very good job at cheering Slatter up but, she kept on trying anyway.

"Ya know what," said Granny B as she tried to get Slatter's mind on something else.

"School will be a startin' real soon.

You'll make ya some new friends then.

Besides, now ya can start helpin' your grandpa up at the store again.

I know he could really could use your help."

Slatter was heartsick and she didn't feel much like talking.

"Yeah.

I suppose so," replied heartbroken Slatter.

"I just miss my friend.

Ya know, Granny B.

I was just thinkin'.

Would it be alright if I wait a few days before I start workin' again for grandpa?

I think I 'd like to spend some time alone."

Granny B walked over to Slatter and hugged her.

"Oh, I don't see why not.

Everybody needs a little time to themselves once in a while.

Spendin some time alone helps a person to sorta, ya know, sort things out in their mind and get their priorities in order; put the things that are most important to 'em, first on their list.

I'll talk to your grandpa about it tonight.

I'm sure he'll understand."

Granny B leaned over and teasingly said,

"keep in mind now........ Idle hands are a devil's workshop."

Slatter smiled at her as she gave a down hearted reply, "Yeah. I heard that in Sunday school class last week. Don't worry. I'll keep busy."

As soon as Granny B left her room, she pulled out her secret map from under her mattress and started studying it. She tried to focus her thoughts on figuring it out. She was determined to accomplish the mission of finding out if the map was some sort of treasure hunt; no matter how long it would take.

For the next few days all she did was mope around the house. She read her bible and kept pretty much to herself. She thought about how her friend Gappy who just seemed to have disappeared off the face of the earth, but mostly she thought about her little friend, Pydie. She also spent some time cleaning her room and doing chores for Granny B. She also studied her secret map each night before she went to sleep and dreamed of being able to use it to find a valuable treasure; hopefully either gold or a pot full of money.

One cool misty August morning, Slatter decided she had hung around the house long enough and needed get to the store to talk to some of the old loafers to see if she could find out any information from them about her map. After she finished her breakfast and did her morning chores, she yelled to Granny B as she headed for the front door.

"Hey, Granny B.

I'm goin' to walk up to the store and see if I can help grandpa do any work.

Remember, I start school in a few days and then I can only help him on Saturdays."

Granny B was changing sheets on the beds as she yelled back at Slatter.

"Ok."

"Ya be sure and watch for cars a crossin' that road when ya get there.

I don't want ya gettin' run over by a big truck or somethin'.

That traffic round that store is a gettin' to be somethin' terrible anymore. And stay out of those big ditches along side of the road.

I know how ya like to go a pokin' around lookin' for crawdads, but one of these days, you're liable to run onto a snake and get bit." Granny B was putting a pillow case on a pillow when she peeked around the living room doorway. Slatter tried to be quiet on her way out the door because she figured Granny B would go out of her way to step out of the bedroom to see whether or not she had combed her hair.

"Did ya hear what I just said Slatter?"

Slatter, using a nagging tone, casually responded.

"Yeah. Yeah.

I heard ya."

Granny B could see Slatter was still down in the dumps.

"I'm sure glad to see ya gettin' out and a goin' again.
You've felt sorry for yourself long enough now.
It's time to move on.
"I think you're a doin' the right thing.
Jest keep yourself busy and time will go by fast.
You'll see."
"Oh, wait a minute.
I almost forgot to tell ya somethin' excitin'." Granny B was all smiles as she shared her good news, "The judge from the fair stopped by to see me today, to let me know I won first prize with my pickles.

He said I tied for first prize with someone named, Erwina Stokes. He said both of our pickles were so good he just couldn't decide between us, so, he gave us both a first prize blue ribbon.

I'm so proud I could bust.

Now, don't forget to tell your grandpa my good news."

Slatter smiled at Granny B and softly said, "I'll be sure and tell him." Then she realized she wasn't acting like she was very proud of Granny B's good news. As she put her arms around her waist and hugged her, she happily said, "I knew you'd win Granny B.

You make the best home canned pickles in the whole world." Granny B blushed a little at what Slatter had said. Then, shaking her head, she turned around and went back into the bedroom. Slatter put her old shoes on, and headed down the road to the store.

# 10

# A HOT FALLING STONE

As Slatter walked down the road, she couldn't help but notice how all of the trees were stripped bare of their leaves. She thought it was odd how trees lost their leaves in the winter and put new ones on in the spring. It seemed to her like the leaves would serve as clothing for the trees on frigid cold days, and would shield them from the winter snow. It made more sense to her for the trees to be bare in the summer, so they could be cooler without all of those heavy leaves hanging on them. She also kept looking around at the different kind of trees in the neighbors' yards to see if anything looked similar to the trees on the secret map. She would slowly walk by each neighbor's mail box and check out the spelling of their names. She was thinking about the letters D.I.T. on the map. Maybe the letters were some kind of special codes.

Her mind drifted off to thoughts about her last Sunday school lesson. The lesson was on Daniel. God had given Daniel the gift of interpreting the king's dreams. She had also learned God had given visions to Daniel. She wished she had a special gift from God like Daniel so she could interpret the secret map she had found in Granny B's old secret locket.

All of sudden, as Slatter was getting ready to cross the road to the store, something very frightful happened. There was an unusual earsplitting noise that sounded like a huge explosion. The whole earth seemed to shake under her feet. Grandpa and several customers came running out of the store to see where the sound was coming from. Out of the corner of Slatter's eye, she saw something fall from the sky. It appeared to be a big black object falling at a very rapid rate of speed. In fact, it was falling so fast that it looked like a black blur. She watched it come crashing down in the soybean field across from the store. No one else acted like they saw anything at all.

Slatter was a little bit afraid, so she went ahead and crossed the road. She ran to the front door of the store just in time to see her grandpa and some other people heading back inside. As she got closer, she recognized the last person walking behind her grandpa. It was her favorite loafer, little Jimmy Dee. He was always very kind and friendly. He was easy to recognize from a distance because of his stooped over posture. He was a very thin, old man that wasn't much taller than Slatter. His skin was blotchy and across the lower part of his chin was a long scar. He looked like he weighed about 90 lbs soaking wet and Granny B had commented once that a big puff of wind could easily blow him away. He wore big thick, black rimmed glasses that looked way too big for his small, slender face and he always smoked a pipe. Slatter could always tell when he was inside the store because when he lit his pipe, she could smell the scent of cherry tobacco all the way outside. She watched him as he kept mumbling to himself as he walked back inside the store. Thinking he might be talking about what just happened, she sat down on an old wooden orange crate and listened to what he was saying. She watched him take out a red polka-dotted handkerchief from his back pant pocket and discreetly mop his face. Sticking the handkerchief back into his pocket, he kept talking in a high pitched, irritating, squeaky voice. He screeched, "I don't care if'n ya all don't believe me. I knowed what I'm a tellin' youns is the truth. I'm a tellin ya the utter day I was a readin' in one of a dem dare fancy city newspapers I found along side the road and... uh... it said that when one of dem big ole jet engine airplanes gets ta goin too fast, it breaks what they call the sound barrier. Ya see them dare fancy airplanes now a days are made ta where they can fly faster than the speed of sound." It seemed no one was paying much attention to Jimmy Dee, but, with his hands stuck down in the front pockets of his pants, he kept on talking anyway. The other loafers gave each other looks like they thought he was talking out of his head. For some reason, little Jimmy felt he had to continue explaining what he thought to be facts. He seemed sincere as he kept trying to convince his pesky audience he was being truthful. As he lit his pipe by striking a match on his shoe his voice was mangled from trying to suck on his pipe and talk too. He mumbled, "Uh, I tell youns, it did say in dat dare paper dat when that happens, it'll make sich a loud boom noise ya can hear it fer miles and miles." Everyone began laughing and shaking their heads at him. He didn't seem to mind their snarling looks. He was convinced he was telling the truth and that was all that mattered to him. He crossed his legs and kept smiling. Since Slatter had never heard of such a thing as breaking a sound barrier, she wondered if little Jimmy Dee was telling a big windy story, or if he really did read something like that in the newspaper. She thought his story sounded very interesting.

As she listened to him rattle on and on, she noticed how dirty and dingy his old coat was. It had holes in the collar and stains on the front of it. He had on a pair of old, worn out dusty boots that had holes in them. Slatter felt very sorry for him. He didn't look like he was of very much importance to anyone. He always seemed to be alone and have on the same old clothes. She thought he was very strange because he wore a heavy overcoat in the hot summer time. Slatter thought people of his generation did some strange things; like her grandpa putting on heavy long underwear in the cold winter and switching to lighter long underwear in the heat of summer. She thought it was a waste of time putting on all of those clothes. She noticed little Jimmy Dee's hands shook whenever he lit his pipe and he always sat with his legs crossed. He had just a few strands of hair on top of his head and he wore a dusty old top hat wherever he went. Slatter had watched little Jimmy Dee on several different occasions and she thought the strangest thing about him was he would walk to the store every day it was open except for Thursdays. She wanted very badly to ask him where he went on Thursdays, but was afraid to ask. She figured he would probably tell her it was none of her business and then tell her grandpa she was being nosey. She thought it best to keep her curiosity to herself. After all, Granny B always says, least said, least mended. All summer long, Slatter noticed little Jimmy came to the store each morning about the same time and sat down on an old cream can right in front of the counter. He didn't bother anyone. He just waited for someone to begin a conversation with him. He acted like all he ever really wanted was to have someone to talk to.

Sometimes Slatter acted disgusted with the loafers because she thought they should, once in a while, offer a helping hand to her grandpa. Slatter thought the least any of them could do would be to offer to work some at the store, at least once in a while; especially since they were there taking up space and getting in the way most of the time.

After she sat there for a while, she convinced herself that regardless of her fears, she had to make herself go look for the falling object. After she had calmed her fears, curiosity got the best of her. While no one was looking, she mustered up the courage to walk softly over to the front door of the store to see if anyone was watching. She didn't see anyone looking. So, she quickly ran back across the road to the soybean field where she saw the object land.

In the distance, she noticed some white powdery smoke coming out of the ground just a few feet from the edge of the field. She could not contain her excitement as she cautiously started running toward the smoke. The closer she got to it, the more she noticed the scent of a very unpleasant odor. The stench reminded her a fresh chicken boiling. Sometimes Granny B would catch and kill a chicken for Sunday dinner. She would make Slatter help her pull off it's feathers and stick it into a big pot on the stove and boil it for a while. The boiling chicken put off a horrible, sickening odor. Slatter pinched her nose together with her fingers so she didn't have to breathe in the awful smell. Cautiously she tiptoed closer. She could hear a sizzling, crackling sound. When she approached the spot where she had seen the smoke, she suddenly stopped dead in her tracks. She could not believe what she was seeing. There, right in front of her eyes, was a huge black hole in the ground.

Whatever had fallen from the sky, must've been on fire. All of the grass and dirt around the big hole was burned black. The black hole was about six feet around and about four feet deep. She looked over into the big hole and saw a huge piece of stone laying at the bottom. The stone looked about a foot wide and about three feet long. It was so hot it was smoking. Slatter stood and stared at the big stone. She could see some markings on it. They looked like symbols. All of a sudden, from out of nowhere, a big black beetle bug appeared. She watched the bug scurry onto the top of the hot stone. Her mouth dropped open from shock as she watched the beetle bug catch on fire and instantly burn up. Slatter was afraid to try and touch the stone because the same thing might happen to her. Her imagination began to run wild. She wondered if she was the only one that was supposed to find this falling stone. Maybe it had fallen from heaven. She wondered if God was trying to send her a message. She thought perhaps God could have written her a letter on the stone and dropped it from heaven. She wanted to run back over to the store and tell her grandpa what she had found, but she did not want to leave the stone. She wanted to sit there and wait for it to cool off. Then she would be able to jump down into the black hole and get a better look at the markings on top of it. She sat there for a long time, daydreaming as she stared at the stone.

Slatter didn't know her grandpa had seen her sitting in front of the store earlier, and now he couldn't find her. He started to worry a little bit and walked outside to check on her. Closing the door behind him, he began yelling her name.
"Slatter............Slatter........Slatter Slopey!
Where in the world are ya.
Come here young lady.
And I mean right now!"
Slatter heard him calling her. She jumped to her feet and took off like a shot toward the store. She could see her

grandpa, standing with his hands on his hips, out in front of the gas pumps. He had an angry look on his face. When she got there she was totally out of breath. Struggling to breathe she asked, "Hey. I'm right here grandpa. What ya need?" I was just over there lookin' around in that soybean field." Grandpa frowned as he twisted the ball cap on his head a little bit and wiped his red face with his apron. Slatter knew the question that was coming next.

"What in tar nation was ya doin' over in an old hot soybean field," he asked in a perturbed voice. Ya can get lost in those beans 'cause they're more than waist high on ya. Slatter looked at her grandpa out of the corner of her eye and declared,

"Well, ta tell ya the truth grandpa; I was over there a lookin' at somethin'. I made footprints in one row as I was goin' into the field, then I followed my own footsteps back.

Pretty clever of me huh."

Grandpa just shook his head back and forth at Slatter.

As he pointed his forefinger right in her face, he angrily said.

"Young lady.

This is partly the reason you're always a gettin' into trouble.

Ya jest can't be a runnin' off by yourself ever time ya take a hankerin' to.

I've told ya and told ya and took ya out and told ya.

Ya ain't supposed to go any where unless ya ask me or your Granny B about it first.

Don't ya know by now there's some mean people out there in this old world and somebody could've kidnapped ya.

I didn't have a clue where ya had got off to.

One minute I looked out and saw ya sittin' out in front of the store, and the next minute, I looked out, and didn't see ya anywhere around.

When I get busy round here, I can't be a watchin' ya ever minute. Sometimes I have so many customers comin' in and out of the store I'm as busy as a fox in a room full of rockin' chairs. You're goin' to have to stay close at hand if'n ya want to hang around and help me here in the store. Do you understand what I'm tellin ya?"

Slatter's bottom lip began to quiver. She didn't mean to make her grandpa so angry.

Fighting back tears she softly replied, "Yes.

I understand.

I'm sorry grandpa.

I didn't mean to make ya so mad at me."

Grandpa realized he was probably being a little too harsh with her so he squatted down on one knee in front of her and lovingly said. "Sis. Me and your Granny B have put a lot of time and care into ya and we plan on keeping ya around here with us for quite a spell. This is your home and ya belong to us.

Everythin' ya do affects us in one way or another.

Ya got to understand that we're a gettin' some age on us now, and we need ya sometimes as much or more than ya need us.

Your young and can do a lot of things that we can't do no more.

If somethin' were to happen to me or your Granny B, we would need to be able to get a hold of ya in a wink of an eye.

It's not that we don't want ya to have any fun , we just need to know where you are......and I mean at all times.

Ya put a little scare into your old grandpa, just now.

I couldn't find ya anywhere.

Do you understand what I've said to ya?"

Slatter just nodded her head yes and used her grandpa's apron to wipe the tears out of her eyes.

Grandpa walked inside the door and came back outside with a broom in his hand. Patting Slatter on the head he insisted, "Now, sis. Here's a broom.

I've showed ya before how to sweep.

If ya do some work around here ya will be close at hand and ya will be a might easier to keep track of."

Grandpa didn't like the way Slatter rolled her eyes with a disgusted look. He raised his head in the air to indicate there would be no compromising and firmly said, "Don't ya start a poutin' either.

Work never killed anybody I ever heard of.

Make yourself busy and sweep off the concrete around here. I don't want the customers a trackin' in anymore dirt than necessary.

People like to do their tradin' at a clean place.

Besides, idle hands are a devil's workshop.

Ya need to remember there's always somethin' around here to do. Sometimes ya have to look fer it, but it's there."

Slatter jerked the broom out of Grandpa's hands and started to work. She didn't want to sweep, but she knew she really didn't have a choice.

While she worked, her mind kept drifting off to thoughts about the hot falling stone. She knew she was going to have to tell her grandpa about the stone, sooner or later. Otherwise, no one would ever believe it was really out in the bean field. After what seemed a very long time, she was finished with her work. She looked around at the front area where she had swept. She was very proud of what she had accomplished. She noticed grandpa wasn't very busy, except for talking to little Jimmy Dee so, she yelled out to him, "Hey grandpa.

Why don't ya come out here and see all of the work I got done for you."

Grandpa came strolling out of the store with a big smile on his face. He immediately started bragging on Slatter's work.

He said, "Whew- ee ! Man o man.

Ya sure have done a good job.

I'm real proud of your work, sis."

Slatter, busting with pride, wanted more compliments, "Do ya really think that I did a good job, grandpa?" she asked.

His approval meant a lot to her. He grinned at her as he replied. "Well sis.

Let me tell ya what my dad used to tell me when I was your age. He said, 'Son. While you're working, always remember this. When ya think you've done the very best job that ya can do then ask yourself this question.' If I was doing this job for Jesus, and He was right here watchin' me. Would He be pleased with my work?"

When he finished talking, he could tell that Slatter was soaking up his words like a sponge. She took his words to heart. In her mind, she began questioning herself whether her work would be acceptable to Jesus or not. He patted her on the back and continued, "Ya see sis. Jesus sees e-v-e-r-y- single thing you do.

Ya can't hide anythin' from Him.

In all that ya do, always do it as if you are a doin' it for Jesus, and ya can't go wrong."

Then grandpa hesitated to see Slatter's reaction.

She just stood and stared at her grandpa for a couple of minutes.

Then as he turned to go back inside, he grinned and said, "In other words Sis. Give it all ya got. Give it your best whether you're pushin' a broom or being president of the United States."

Slatter giggled then she started looking around at her work. She noticed she had not moved things around so that she could sweep behind them. All of a sudden, it was as if she was seeing her work with new eyes. When she realized she could have done a much better job, she became embarrassed about acting so proud of her work. She became motivated and started working harder. She taught herself how to use a dolly to move the heavy items. She couldn't believe how fast her morning had gone by. When she had finished her work, she walked into the store. Her grandpa noticed her beet red face and offered her one of her favorite drinks; a cold Choc-ola soda. He also had a bologna sandwich fixed for her. He put it on a paper plate and handed her a small bag of potato chips. Slatter ate like she was starved to death. Grandpa jokingly said, "Slow down sis.

You're eatin' like a starved harvest hand."

Slatter smiled at her grandpa and kept right on eating as fast as she could.

When she had finished eating she casually walked over to the candy counter. She noticed her grandpa was outside pumping gas for a customer and little Jimmy had gone to the back room. That meant she was alone in the store. This was her chance to steal some candy. She glanced over the store making sure no one was looking. She helped herself to four great big Hershey Bars. She ran behind the tobacco counter, quickly unwrapped them and ate them as fast as she could. Just as she finished eating the last one, she heard her Grandpa call to her.

"Hey Slatter.

Come here.

I've got another job fer ya to do."

Slatter, wiping her mouth off with the sleeve of her shirt, hurried to his side. She said,

"I'm right here.

What do ya want me to do now?"

Grandpa noticed she had chocolate smeared over her top lip, but he never said a word. He had brought out two big boxes of spices for her to mark the price on and then put them on the shelves behind the meat case. Handing her a big black marker, he said, "Now sis. This here is a good job fer ya.

I despise puttin' up these spices 'cause my hands are way too big fer these little cans. Your hands are small, jest the right size for the job. If ya stay with it, it shouldn't take ya very long. This job will teach ya about patience because ya have to work slow and steady. If ya try to work too fast, you'll knock over all your cans. All I want ya to do is use this marker to mark all of the little cans of cinnamon twenty five cents and all of the little cans of cloves thirty-nine cents."

Slatter, still feeling proud of her last accomplishment, happily said,

"Alrightee.

This job looks easy enough."

She found that the job was harder than it looked. The little cans had to be stacked several rows high and they kept falling over. A couple of the cans of spice, had gotten crushed during shipment and the spices had dumped out into the bottom of the box. The spicy aroma immediately began to fill the store. Slatter diligently worked behind the shelves. Because she was so short, she was completely hidden from the customers. She could see out between the shelves, but no one could see her. She overhead a conversation between two lady customers as they waited for her grandpa to fill their meat order. They had no idea their conversation was being overheard by little ears on the other side of the shelves. The first lady, wearing a red flowered dress and white gloves, remarked in an ill-tempered tone as she whispered to the second lady who was wearing a blue checked dress and a big white hat.

"Excuse me.

Is there something wrong with my smeller or do you smell the scent of cinnamon and cloves very strongly?

The second lady fiddled with her hat and kindly replied, "Why, yes.

I most certainly do.

It smells like a wonderful air freshener."

The first lady took off her gloves and stepped closer to the second lady as if she wanted to share some gossip with her. Leaning forward so grandpa couldn't hear her arrogant remark she spoke with a conceited, know it all tone of voice, "Hmm. There just isn't any tellin' what kind of concoction that J.E. Slopey is a mixing up back there.

And he's probably a fixin' to try and sell it too.

I heard he'd sell just about anything to make a buck.

I heard some people say he squeezes every dollar 'til it hollers."

The second lady did not appreciate such a demeaning comment so she turned her head so her big hat would smack the first lady in the face. Then she quickly responded in a sweet, pleasant tone, "Well, it's obvious you have not traded here at Mr. Slopey's store very much or else you would know what a kind, wonderful man he is. I, for one, certainly hope he is cookin' up somethin' special. Can you imagine how great that concoction would be?

Why, I just heard the other day how cinnamon was good for the blood and everyone knows that cloves can cure a bad tooth ache among other things. I'll be the first in line to buy that concoction. Yes mam.

That J.E. Slopey is known to be a healin' man, a godly man.

I've heard a lot of folks tell he's been so close to God that God has used him to heal people. I'd buy any concoction that man would put together."

Then, there was a dead silence between the two women.

Slatter could tell the first lady was offended at what the second lady had said. She had to put her hand over her mouth to keep from giggling out loud. She didn't know the names of the two ladies, but she knew she liked anyone that said such nice things about her grandpa.

Slatter finally completed her tedious task about the time her grandpa was ready to lock up the store for the night. With darkness falling sooner due to the changing of the seasons, her grandpa was closing up the store at a much earlier time now. She didn't like her grandpa offering to give little Jimmy Dee a ride home, because she would have to ride in the back seat. Little Jimmy only lived five or six miles from the store, but it was five or six miles of rough country roads. Slatter jerked open the back door of the old blue goose and with a spiteful attitude, crawled into the back seat. The hateful expression on her face said it all. She thought to herself if little Jimmy wanted to walk everywhere he needed to go, then why couldn't he walk home. Her grandpa chose to ignore her pouting gestures. Slatter realized her terrible attitude had nothing to do with giving little Jimmy a ride home. It was all about her being short. When she rode in the back seat, no matter how straight she sat, she couldn't see out of the back windows. She was very tired and wanted to hurry and get home. School was starting tomorrow and she knew she would have to get up and be dressed by 7:00 a.m. in order to catch the bus. She didn't know why grandpa picked this night to give little Jimmy a ride home. There wasn't much conversation between her grandpa and little Jimmy until they turned down the old country road to where little Jimmy lived. Then in his raspy, squeaky little voice, little Jimmy spoke up and said, "Uh, J.E.

I've been meanin' ta ask ya somethin' fer a spell, but I keep forgettin'.

Did ya ever hear anythin' of what ever happened to old Mr. Humphrey that used to be one of our neighbors across the way?" Slatter's ears perked up when she heard the word Humphrey. She quickly forgot all about her bad attitude as she strained to hear the conversation going on in the front seat. She turned around backwards and leaned up against the back of the driver's seat so she could hear more clearly. Grandpa, wiping his face with his hand, thought for a few seconds before he replied to little Jimmy's question, "No. I can't say that I ever did hear. I reckon we'll never know what ever happened to old Mr. Humphrey. Sad about that old man. He never married, nor had any children. Seems he was always lookin' fer a way to get rich quick. He never had much money and didn't like to work either. I reckon he lived off of the government most of his life. Only time I ever saw him was when he came by the store to get a few groceries now and then. I reckon the only thing he ever owned was that 100 acres or so his daddy left to him. Shoot, I bet he don't even own that anymore. I heard it looks like a wilderness back in the woods around where he used to live. I'm sure by now that old place ain't fittin' for much of nothin'. A hunter stopped by one day a couple of years ago and asked who used to live in that big old run down house way out in the woods. He said that the old house was fallin' in and was hard to find 'cause the trees had grown up all around it. The hunter said he'd never seen such a thick wilderness. He also said that he thought he'd never find his way out of there. It's a shame, but I reckon that old place will just sit there and rot. I heard tell it was a fancy duded up place in its' day. The last I heard, some body else had moved into his place. I can't recall the name, but I probably wouldn't've known 'em anyway.

But, gosh, little Jimmy Dee.

That's been many a year ago.

Ain't nobody used Mr. Humphrey's lane in years.

I don't reckon ya could get a car down it if ya tried."

Little Jimmy nodded in agreement.

Grandpa stopped the car right in front of little Jimmy's house. Moving slow, the old loafer got out of the car and reached back into the front seat to pick up his sack of groceries. He remarked, "Yeah.

I reckon it has been many a year ago.

Boy, J.E.

Time shore has a way of gettin' away from us."

He paused a few seconds like he was trying to remember something important. Then he continued speaking.

.........."Ya know J.E.," said little Jimmy in a serious tone, "It's a darn shame. I kinda liked that old man Humphrey.

He never had much to say.

I remember I was at his place once.

He used ta buy his tobaccy from a guy somewheres a way over in Africa. He was always after me to come by his house so he could give me some. I tried some once but, whew- ee!

I don't know what kind it was, but it shore would knock your socks off. It was very very strong. Way too strong fer my likin'.

Ya could for shore tell he didn't buy anywheres around these here parts. All I know is it shore didn't come from any wheres around our neck of the woods. Yeah, I reckon his'n is the only place left down that old lane?

I too have heerd people tell that old Humphrey's Lane is so grown up with trees and vines now, that ya can't even get a car down it.

When I walk by there, I have to look real hard myself to see where ya used ta make the turn to go down to his house.

It looks a little spooky to me.

A person could sure get lost real easy a goin' down that old lane. I don't much reckon I'll have any cause ta be a goin' down there anymore.

Grandpa sadly replied, "No. I don't have no reason to go down there either.

It's probably full of snakes as big around as your arm and all kinds of wild critters by now."

Little Jimmy raised his hand to wave goodbye as he said, "Well.

I had a good day a visitin' with ya J.E.

Much obliged fer the ride .
I'll be a seein ya."
Grandpa gave him a friendly smile and replied,
"Anytime little Jimmy.
Anytime."
Just as grandpa started backing out of little Jimmy's drive, he abruptly stopped the car, rolled down his window, and yelled back at him, "Say little Jimmy. When's that sister of yourn a gonna come to visit ya anyway.
I ain't seen her in a coon's age."
Little Jimmy, exposing his rotten teeth when he grinned, turned around and walked back up to the car. He stuck his head through the rolled down car window as he answered,
"Ya mean my little Effie Lou?"
Slatter's grandpa replied.
"Yeah.
Does she ever get back over to these here parts anymore? I ain't seen her in years."
Still grinning, little Jimmy said,
"Well, I think she's gonna get ta come fer a visit the week of Christmas this year.
She's been a teachin school over in the St. Louey area and she sent me a letter the utter day a sayin' that she'd be a seein' me at Santa Clause time.
She said she's caught a pretty bad summer cold and she's havin' a tough time a gettin' over it.
She says her doctor's been a treatin' her fer pneumonee fever."
It was easy to see that little Jimmy loved his sister very much because he always smiled from ear to ear whenever he talked about her. When grandpa and little Jimmy finished up their conversation, once again, they waved goodbye to

one another. While her grandpa was putting the car into gear, Slatter quickly opened up the back car door, jumped out, and slipped into the front seat. Grandpa shaking his head, patted her hand and said,

"I reckon you're a might happier now, a gettin' to ride in the front seat.

I seen ya had a pouty look on your face.

Are ya ready to go home, sis?"

"Ok by me." replied Slatter, nodding as she smiled.

She was more than ready to go home. She was beginning to think that little Jimmy and grandpa were never gonna get through visiting.

Slatter could hardly wait to ask her grandpa about Humphrey's lane because she remembered seeing that name on her secret map. Finally, she had some information to go on. She tried not to show her excitement as she curiously asked, "Say, grandpa. Would ya show me where Humphrey's Lane is?

I heard ya and little Jimmy a talkin' about it."

Grandpa politely consented,

"Why sure.

But, ya can't see much from the main road.

It's really all growed up 'round there."

When her grandpa drove near to Humphrey's lane, he pulled off on the side of the road and brought the blue goose to a sudden halt. Turning the car off, he pointed to a densely wooded area and explained, "Well, there it is Sis. That's what we call Humphrey's Lane."

Slatter got up on her knees in the seat so she could see better.

There was a heavy dew that had fallen early that evening causing a lingering, misty fog to float around in the air. Only the very front of the road could be seen as it lay nestled in between two very tall trees with crooked trunks. The rest of road seemed to disappear into the thick dark woods. As she gazed at the spooky looking scene, she felt an eerie feeling come over her. Something about the way it looked gave her a horrible feeling. Shivering, she rubbed the goose bumps on her arms. She became even more frightened when she heard a big old hoot owl make his presence known by his jeering cry, "Hoo......... Hoo.

The sound made her jump and she grabbed her grandpa by the arm. Grandpa made a joshing remark, "Ah. Ya ain't scared of a little old hoot owl are ya?"

Slatter rolled her eyes up at him and snuggled close to his side. As she studied the unusual looking landscape, she noticed huge trees that were shaped very odd and some of their short limbs stuck out like arms on a person. As a balmy night breeze stirred the air, she tugged on grandpa's shirt sleeve and quietly asked, "Grandpa. Why do the first two trees there next to the road have such big crooks in them?

They look very different to all of the others."

Her Grandpa had a troubled look on his face as he awkwardly stammered for an answer.

"Oh....uh...well, gosh honey.

I don't know if I can give ya an answer to that question.

All I remember is Mr. Humphrey's father used to own all of this land around here and he planted those trees a very long time ago.

If my memory serves me right, someone once told me old man Humphrey planted those two trees there especially 'cause they were crooked in the middle.

I reckon he planted 'em there so they'd look different and stand out from all of the others.

That was his way of makin' the turn to his road easy to see."

Grandpa didn't tell Slatter the whole story.

Old man Humphrey had a reputation for drinking way too much whiskey and sometimes he had trouble finding his way home. He needed all of the help he could get finding the turn to his road. But grandpa felt Slatter was better off not knowing all of the details about a person she had never known.

Slatter seemed satisfied with grandpa's answers to her questions, so she sat back down in the seat and said, "This place looks way too spooky fer me. I'm ready to go home now."

Grandpa snickered at Slatter's remarks as he started up the car and drove back onto the road. Slatter remained quiet the rest of the way home.

Just as they were getting ready to get out of the car, Slatter scrunched up her lips and softly said, "Hey Grandpa. I need to tell you somethin'." Grandpa took his hand off of the door handle and with a big sigh replied, "Well, go ahead. What is it? I'm a listen." Slatter knew at this point she had no choice but to continue on with her confession.

She spoke in a regretful tone of voice, "Well, I jest had to tell ya I had a special reason for goin' to the soybean field this mornin'." Grandpa replied, "Oh ya did. Well go on. " Slatter continued, "Well. Did ya hear that real loud boom noise this mornin'?"

Grandpa nodded his head. Slatter, watching her grandpa's reactions, continued with her explanation.

"Well, when I heard that noise, it sounded to me like it was comin' from the sky, so I looked up to see if I could see anything.

That's when I saw it."

Grandpa, intrigued by her story, frowned at her and said, "Well, and jest what did ya see?"

Big eyed Slatter, looked him right in the eyes and replied, "I saw somethin' black a fallin' down out of the sky.

I saw it land in the soybean field across the road from the store and I had to go see what it was."

Grandpa still waiting for an answer started to get impatient.

He said, "Well, I'll ask ya again. What in the world was it?"

Slatter quickly replied, "I'm tryin' to tell ya.

It looked like a great big hot stone and it made a big deep hole in the ground this deep when it landed."

She turned her hand sideways and held it next to her chin to give him an idea of how deep the hole was.

"The hole," she swallowed, "was black all around it.

It looked like it had been on fire before it fell to the ground." Grandpa, trying to picture what the stone looked like, wiped his face with his hand and said, "Oh Slatter. Slatter, Slatter, Slatter.

What in the world am I gonna do with ya?

I'm having such trouble just tryin' to keep up with ya."

He sighed as he spoke,

"Ya had no business goin' out to that soybean field alone.

What if ya would've gotten burned or hurt real bad.

Your jest a little girl.

Granny B and I wouldn't have begun to know where to start lookin' fer ya.

Ya need to learn to think about consequences before ya start a jumpin' into somethin'."

Slatter just sat there in the front seat of the car, nervously, picking at her fingers. She continued trying to explain her actions, "Jest let me finish.

I want to tell ya what I think the stone was."

Grandpa, staring at Slatter in disbelief, hesitated before he spoke.

"Well," he said as he bit his upper lip.

"Go on.

Keep talkin'.

I can't wait to hear this one."

Slatter, reluctant to respond, clenched her teeth together and said, "Well.

I have a good idea what it was.

I think the stone might be a message from God to me.

Ya know tellin' me somethin' about my mommy or maybe a secret he wants only me to know."

After a few minutes of hesitation, grandpa, trying not to be harsh, shook his head and thoughtfully said, "Slatter.

Ya got to stop thinkin' of God as if was jest a human being.

If ya really did see a hot stone land out in the soybean field, then ya have been blessed to witness a very rare event."

Slatter's mouth flew open as she excitedly said, "I have!

What do ya mean by that grandpa?"

He took a deep breath and tried to give Slatter a reasonable explanation for what she had seen out in the field. His voice sounded weak and tired. He asked, "Have ya ever heard or studied in school about meteorites?" Slatter kept frowning at him as she answered, "No.

What's a meteorite?"

Well", began Grandpa, trying to choose words Slatter could understand.

"The best I can tell ya to where ya can understand is it's another name for a piece of a star or a planet that's broken off and fell to the earth. Sometimes stars burn out and they fall out of the heavens. Scientists call these fragments debris. This debris is usually so hot that it burns completely up before it ever gets to the earth.

Very seldom does someone find any fragments of a meteorite.

But, it very well could be that ya found one. I guess that ya could say that God was sending you a message." Grandpa had Slatter's full attention as she got up on her knees in the front seat and leaned over toward him. Frowning, yet hopeful, she seriously asked, "What do ya think my message is, grandpa?" Grandpa scratched his head as he replied, "Well, I think the message God is tryin' to tell ya is; He is real. He is still alive. He is still at work and He is still on his throne.

You see Slatter.

God is constantly at work keepin' His universe perfectly balanced. He is the creator and sustainer of life.

When His stars and planets burn up, it's no big deal for him to create more.

Ya see honey.

God can do anythin' He wants, anytime He wants.

God created a circle of life for all of his creation.

He created the same type of circle of life for his people.

Every time a child is born or someone passes away, God is creating a balance of his people here on the earth.

Only God can create life and He alone has the right to take life away. Remember how we planted our garden this summer?"

Slatter, so involved in what her grandpa was saying, kept nodding her head yes.

As her grandpa tried to explain what he was saying, he used his hands to demonstrate how to plant a seed.

"We put a seedlin' in the ground and covered it up with dirt.

That seed under all of that dirt had to die, in order for it to produce new life.

Jesus died on the cross for our sins; he was buried in a tomb, just like the seeds we planted were buried.

Then, Jesus arose from the dead and is now seated in heaven, at the right hand side of his father, God.

Jest like new life springs forth from the ground, Jesus sprang up from the ground after he was buried.

Because He died and rose again, when people accept Jesus as their personal savior, they can now have eternal life.

Oh Sis.

It's such a privilege to be alive when ya live for Jesus.

Life is indeed one miracle after another.

For instance, jest think on this fer a minute.

God made Adam and Eve from the very dirt he created.

Then he breathed life into them and made them living souls.

Only God can make dirt come alive."

He noticed a far away look in her eyes. She was deeply concentrating on what he had said to her. He wondered if he was talking way over her head. He tenderly asked, "Slatter, honey. Do you understand what I'm trying to tell ya?

Or is your old grandpa a talkin' about stuff your way too young to understand yet?"

Slatter kept nodding her head like she was mesmerized by what she was hearing. She very much wanted to understand every word her grandpa was saying. But, she was not sure she was grasping all of it. Grandpa picked up her small hand and kissed it. Then he chuckled a little as he continued, "Oh don't look so serious about everythin'. Say that reminds me of a joke Jimmy Dee told the other day. Would ya like to hear it?"

Slatter nodded her head yes.

"Well," said grandpa as he wiped his chin, "there was this scientist who was so smart, he thought he knew everything.

One day he made an appointment with God to meet him along side a sandy beach. Once there, he told God that man didn't need him anymore because he and a bunch of other scientists had finally discovered a way to make a human being out of dirt, breathe into him, and make him a living soul.

God replied to the scientist and said alright then let's see ya do it. The scientist walked over to the sand and began scooping up dirt in his hands.

God looked over at him and said, "Oh no ya don't.

Get your own dirt!"

They both laughed at the joke. Then on a more serious note, grandpa looked Slatter in the eyes and licking his lips he said, "Seriously sis.

I reckon what I'm really tryin' to tell ya is, maybe your message from God is this:

Hey little Miss Slatter down there on earth.
I am the one and only true God.
No matter what happens, I am the creator and sustainer of all life. So, stop your frettin' about everythin' cause I'm

a gonna be around forever and I'll be a takin' care of ya all the time even when ya don't think I am.

Now, ain't that a wonderful message?"

Slatter, unappreciative of her grandpa's mild humor, replied in a disappointing tone, "Yeah."

Then, with a delighted expression on her face her eyes danced with innocence as she added, "Grandpa. I jest bet ya that message wasn't jest meant fer me. I think it was meant fer everyone in the whole world who believes in God."

"Ya betcha," said grandpa as he winked at his granddaughter.

"Now ya got your thinkin' cap on.

That simply means people have the assurance that when they pray to God, He 's still on the throne and hears their prayers."

He tilted her chin upward with his hand and kissed her on the nose. He softly said, "No matter what.

I want ya to always remember that God is still in control of the world, not people.

Now, c'mon.

Let's go inside.

I don't know about you, but I'm very, very tired.

And you, my little one, have to start school tomorrow."

He patted her on the leg and firmly said, "Enough said about this hot falling stone stuff."

Slatter, still a little disappointed in her grandpa's answers, slowly followed him into the house. Even if she didn't like her grandpa's response to her theory of the hot falling stone, at least he took the time to talk to her about it. She knew she could depend on him for some kind of answer. She figured he was probably right. He usually was.

After they went into the house and ate supper, they went straight to bed for the night. Granny B noticed that Slatter was extra quiet, but she didn't question her because she assumed Slatter was very tired from working so hard at the store.

# 11

# A FAIR AND JUST REWARD

Slatter awoke the next morning just in time to see the early autumn sun casting fading shadows onto her walls. She rolled over in bed and looked at her old metal alarm clock. It was already 6:00 a.m. and time for her to get up and get ready for her first day at school. She had dreaded this day for a very long time. However, she had decided she would make the best of a bad situation and maybe she would make some new friends this year at school. She mostly dreaded going to school because she would have to sit in class with those two mean bullies, Newton and Lodden.

Slatter washed her face and tried to comb her hair. She wished her hair could always look as pretty as it did for the beauty pageant. But, today, her hair was as straight as a stick. With each stroke the static electricity caused her hair to cling to the brush. She tried to wet it down the best she could, but it still stuck straight out in the back. She put on the newest blue jean overalls Granny B had made for her. She had either outgrown or wore out most of her other clothes over the summer months.

She quickly grabbed her secret map from under her mattress and stuck it in her back pocket. If she didn't have anyone to play with at recess, she could always study her secret map. Now that she knew where Humphrey's Lane was, she thought she might be able to figure out another clue. As she quietly ate her breakfast, she looked at Granny

B's kitchen clock on the stove, 6:45 a.m. She was way ahead of schedule. She had fifteen minutes to spare. After breakfast, she grabbed a glass of water and her toothbrush as she rushed out the back door to brush her teeth. Once outside, she breathed in the crisp early morning air. She was fully aware the season was quickly changing and winter was just around the corner. Once she was finished brushing her teeth, she took a few minutes to admire the beauty of Granny B's pretty yellow and orange chrysanthemums. She giggled aloud as she teased a big grasshopper, poking it with a long stick and making it jump from leaf to leaf. Then, she heard her Granny B yell to her.

"Slatter!

I hear the bus a comin' down the road.

Ya better get out to the end of the driveway so he can see ya standin' out there.

Do ya have your lunch money and book rental money in that envelope I handed ya awhile ago?"

Slatter yelled back at Granny B as she ran to meet the bus.

"Yes, Granny B I have it.

I will see ya this afternoon.

Goodbye."

When the bus stopped in front of Slatter's driveway, she jumped onto the steps and sat down in the first seat behind the driver. She noticed the bus didn't have very many passengers, so she leaned forward to question the driver.

Her voice sounded chipper. She inquired, "Say, Mr. driver man.

How come there ain't very many kids on the bus this mornin'?

Is everybody sick er somethin'?"

The driver, tickled at the way she asked her question smiled as he looked up at her in his big rear view mirror. He replied, "Well, young lady.

You're one of the first ones I pick up every morning.

I'm going to be picking up a lot more children in a little bit.

Just hang on to your tators.

Believe me. I will have a bus load by the time I get this big yellow heap to the school."

Slatter sat back in her seat and stared out of the front window.

She made herself endure each bus stop as she watched every child cheerfully board the bus.

When the bus finally arrived at the school, Slatter was the first one to stand up by the folding door, so she could be the first one to jump off. She slowly made her way into the school building . As she strolled down the hall, she noticed how all of the rooms looked pretty much the same as they did last year. She did notice one big change. The hallway had been painted a bright yellow color and the scent of new paint was still in the air. Slatter walked into the classroom that had the words

# SECOND GRADE TEACHER
# MRS. LOU ANN KOHLER

written on the front of the door. She knew she had the right room. As she pushed the door open and walked in, she saw an older lady standing behind the teacher's desk. She slowly walked up to her. She noticed this lady was wearing a name tag on the front of her dress entitled Mrs. Kohler, second grade teacher. Slatter couldn't understand why she was boxing up all of the books and file folders off of the big desk. Slatter liked Mrs. Kohler right off. She thought this teacher was the prettiest one she had ever seen. She had beautiful long, curly, black hair that shined when the sunlight hit it just right. She was short and petite and had a welcoming smile for Slatter. Slatter decided to be brave and start a conversation with her. She cleared her throat.

"Hmmmm.

Uh, hello there," said Slatter in a very friendly voice.

"My name is Slatter Slopey.

I am in your class this year."

Mrs. Kohler looked up at Slatter and smiled as she kept sorting books. Nervously, Slatter kept on talking, "I see ya are boxin' up stuff off your desk, Mrs. Kohler. It's jest the first day of school.

Are ya leavin' already?

Did somebody make ya mad already on jest the first day of school?"

Mrs. Kohler acted a little nervous when Slatter approached her. In a soft, broken voice she replied to Slatter's question as she stuck out her hand for Slatter to shake as she introduced herself.

"Well, hello there back to you Slatter.

My name is Mrs. Kohler.

Lou Ann Kohler, to be exact.

I don't mean to appear rude, but I am very busy right now.

And to answer your question, well...........I guess I am sort of leaving.

That is, I just found out that I am in the wrong room.

This was the second grade room last year.

But this year since I have a smaller enrollment and I have been told to move across the hall to a smaller room."

Slatter, eager to help Mrs. Kohler, enthusiastically asked, "Hey, can I help? Since my bus got here extra early today, I got time to help ya move some of your stuff across the hall?"

Mrs. Kohler graciously accepted Slatter's offer.

"Well, since you asked, that would be very nice.

I would very much appreciate your help.

To tell you the truth, when all of the rest of the students get here, I am going to ask everyone help me move the desks, books, and well just about everything you see here in this room.

The way I figure it, if we all work together, we can get everything moved in one day. I always say T-E-A-M and that means Together Everyone Achieves More. Then, tomorrow, I can start class.

See that big cardboard box over there by the door?"

As she pointed toward the door, they walked over to the box.

Slatter bent over and looked inside.

"Oh, wow," she loudly whispered as her eyes bugged out of her head.

"It's full of packages of tootsie roll candy!"

Mrs. Kohler in a matter of fact way, quickly replied, "That's right.

That is going to be my students' reward for helping me.

I am going to inform my class that everyone who helps me move, is going to get one whole package of that candy."

That certainly brought a big smile to Slatter's face.

Her eyes lit up as she exclaimed, "Wow!

That's a great reward."

She expressed so much excitement. She acted as if she had never seen a box of candy before.

"Boy, the kids are gonna love comin' to school today," continued a cheerful Slatter.

Mrs. Kohler put her arm around Slatter and winked.

She was glad to find out her candy was an excellent choice for a prize. She breathed a big sigh of relief as she said, "Well good.

If you like my reward then I feel sure everyone else will too.

"Well, that's one load off my mind. Now then, young lady.

Let's get busy and get some work done around here."

Mrs. Kohler pointed across the room as she began firing orders at Slatter.

"Roll some of those nicer chairs over to those wooden book shelves. Then take some cardboard boxes that are stacked by the doorway, and start filling them with all of those encyclopedias on those shelves."

Slatter listened attentively to what her teacher was telling her to do. She wanted very much to please her so she was very careful to follow her instructions to the letter.

Slatter had worked at least thirty minutes before all of the other students got there. Once registration was completed, Mrs. Kohler stood up in front of the class and proclaimed, "Class, I want to welcome all of you to the second grade.

I am your new teacher and my name is Miss Lou Ann Kohler.

Before we get started with passing out this year's books. I have a very special request to make to all of you.

I would very much like for all of you to help me move everything in my class room across the hall.

She pointed over at the cardboard box of candy as she continued her announcement.

"Over in that big box, I have a bag of candy for each of you as a token of my appreciation for helping"

All of the kids smiled and gave her a round of applause.

Then, everyone got up out of their seat and began helping Mrs. Kohler. Everyone in the class was cooperative and Mrs. Kohler kept everyone busy and organized.

At recess everyone but Slatter rushed outside to play. Slatter liked all of the attention she was getting from her new teacher.

She wanted to stay inside so she could say she did more work than anyone else. Slatter saw Newton and Lodden watching her to see if she was going outside for recess. When they saw Slatter was staying in to help the teacher, they went on outside.

Slatter was beginning to feel nervous because she could tell the two boys were plotting something bad against her. She was going to stay as far away from them as she could get.

Lunch time rolled around and Mrs. Kohler invited Slatter to sit with her in the lunchroom. While they ate, Mrs. Kohler noticed several different times Newton and Lodden laughing and giving Slatter mean looks. Finally, just before school let out Mrs. Kohler told the students that they could take a break and go out and play. Again, Slatter chose to stay in the classroom and help the teacher. By now, Slatter had great expectations of getting a lot more candy than anyone else because she had volunteered to stay in and work all during her lunch and at both recesses. She thought she had worked twice as hard as everyone else and deserved a double portion of candy. She couldn't wait to show Newton and Lodden that she had tons more candy than they got. Slatter was just biding her time until the end of the day. Daydreaming, she had herself convinced the teacher would have her come to the front of the class and boldly brag on all of the hard work she had done. Then, she would hand her a bigger reward than she gave anyone else and the entire class would applaud her.

Slatter's daydream was abruptly cut short when she overheard Newton whispering loudly to Lodden as they walked out of the classroom for the last recess.
"Psst. Hey Lodden.
What's that ole Slatter Slopey think she's a doin?
Do ya think she's tryin' to be a teacher's pet or what.
She ain't left Mrs. Kohler's side for one minute today.
What a nerd!
I wanted a chance ta tell her that I've come up with a new name for her.
Splattered Slop!"
Lodden and Newton started laughing as they continued walking. Mrs. Kohler also over heard the boys' hateful remarks. She could tell Slatter was upset by the hurt look on her face. She waited until everyone had left the room, then she walked over to her and put her arm around Slatter. She spun Slatter around so they were looking at each other face to face. Slatter resisted. She quietly stood there with big tears running down her cheeks. Mrs. Kohler wrapped her arms around her and pulled her close to her bosom. Slatter

continued to cry silently. Mrs. Kohler, showing compassion said, "Oh, c'mon now Slatter.

Things aren't so bad.

Don't you pay any attention to those mean boys."

Slatter's voice was muffled because Mrs. Kohler was holding her so close. She managed to cry out, "Ya don't understand.

Nobody understands.

Those two boys are always teasin' and makin' fun of me.

They don't seem to bother any of the other girls in our class. They hate me I tell ya.

They jest hate me cause I ain't pretty like all the other girls."

Mrs. Kohler, was very touched by Slatter's low self esteem.

She very sympathetically replied, "Oh, honey.

Don't be so quick to judge yourself based on what others might think.

Those two boys wouldn't know pretty if it jumped up and bit them in the face.

You are a beautiful little girl.

I can guarantee you those boys think you are very pretty and that's exactly why they've been teasing you.

They're trying to get your undivided attention.

Don't you know when boys your age say they don't like a certain girl that means they really do like her?

And, don't you find it kind of strange that they don't give any of their attention to any of the other girls in class.

They don't even realize they're telling on themselves by the way they spend most of their time focusing on just you.

You must really catch their eye.

Slatter couldn't believe what she was hearing. Could it be that Newton and Lodden really did like her after all? Mrs. Kohler reached over to her purse and took out a tissue for Slatter to blow her nose. She brushed Slatter's hair away from her face and firmly stated, "Now, young lady.

Stop taking to heart something that won't make a bit a difference twenty years from now.

You've been so good to help me work today.

You've been as happy as a lark.

Why don't you pull your chair up to my desk and you can help me give the candy away to all of the kids as they leave to go home." Slatter was pleased her teacher had asked for her help. As she took her seat beside the teacher's desk, she heard the bell ring for the kids to come back inside. After everyone was seated, Mrs. Kohler stood up in front of the class and said, "Class. I want to tell you how much I appreciate all of your hard work. I would have never been able to complete all this work in just one day without your help. You all have done a great job and before you leave, please form a single line right here in front of my desk and Slatter and I will hand you a bag of candy for your reward for your day's work." Everyone excitedly got into a single line and as each child walked past the teacher's desk, they each received one bag of candy.

When everyone had gone out of the room, there was just one bag of candy left.

Mrs. Kohler, reached into the box and handed the last bag to Slatter.

"And it looks like we've saved the last bag for the best student." Slatter had a very disappointed look on her face as she took the bag of candy from Mrs. Kohler.

Mrs. Kohler saw Slatter's disappointed look and curiously asked, "Why Slatter, whatever is wrong now?

Why the sad face?

You look like you've just lost your best friend."

Slatter did not respond. She just looked down at the floor, picked up her books and walked outside to get on the bus. Mrs. Kohler, with a puzzled look on her face, stood in the doorway of the classroom. She did not have a clue what was wrong with Slatter. She wondered if she said something to hurt her feelings.

She shrugged her shoulders and walked over to the second grade sign that was hanging on the old door. She removed it and rehung it on the door to her new room.

Slatter, fighting back tears, plopped down in the first empty seat she could find. She was speechless. She could not believe her teacher acted so ungrateful. She looked down at the bag of candy on her lap. It was all she had to show for her dedication and hard work. She had done twice the work of all of the other kids. She felt she deserved at least two bags of candy. She wouldn't get a chance to flaunt all of her extra candy in front of her classmates. She couldn't let Newton and Lodden know she had received the same amount of candy they'd received. The only thing worth while she had seen those two boys do all day, was dump the trash cans one time. They goofed off most of the time and didn't try to do any work. All of the other kids spent the recess playing on the playground instead of staying inside and working. Slatter thought that Mrs. Kohler was not being fair with her at all. How could this nice teacher, she thought was a new found friend, give her the same amount of reward that she gave all of the other kids, when the other kids hadn't done much work at all! All the way home on the bus, it was all Slatter could do to keep from crying her eyes out. Finally, when she got off of the bus, she ran to the house as fast as she could. Granny B's welcoming smile turned to a concerned look when she saw the look on Slatter's face.

"Well, what in the world happened to ya to make ya come home a lookin' so sad?

Did you have a bad first day at school?"

Slatter, ignoring Granny B's remarks, swiftly brushed past her. She slung her books on the bedroom floor and slammed the door shut.

She threw herself on the bed and started to cry. Granny B followed her to her room and tried to talk to her. Slatter buried her face in her pillow and refused to talk. Granny B gave up hope of finding out what was wrong with her and left her alone to cry it out. Slatter cried herself to sleep. Granny B told grandpa what had happened after school and he went in to talk to Slatter to see if he could find out what was wrong. Slatter awoke from a sound nap as she felt her grandpa sit down on the edge of her bed.

He softy asked, "Slatter. Is there somethin' you want to tell your old grandpa?

Did somethin' bad happen at school today or did someone hurt your feelins'?"

Slatter didn't respond to his questions.

After he felt he had given her ample time to respond, he firmly added, "I'm gettin' mighty tired of playin this guessin' game with ya."

Then he remembered how sensitive she was to harsh words.

As he brushed her hair away from her face he calmly asked, "Is it all that bad?"

She kept her face buried in her pillow and nodded up and down. After a few minutes of silence, he tried sweet talking her again.

"C'mon, I thought we were buddies.

Ya know you can tell your old grandpa anythin'.

Has the cat got you're your tongue?

Your Granny B is worried sick about ya."

Slatter started rubbing the scar on her neck as she spoke.

She didn't want to tell grandpa the real reason she was crying because he might think she was being greedy. So, she decided the best thing to do would be to tell him a lie by pretending something else was wrong. She rolled over onto her back and with a painful look on her face she managed to say, "Oh Grandpa. I don't think this ugly red scar is ever gonna go away.

I know it's the first thing people see when they look at me." Grandpa teasingly said, "Well, there's a bunch of people in this town that thinks you're pretty even with that scar on your neck. Remember ya won the Little Princess title and ya had that red scar then."

Slatter quickly responded, "Yeah. But I think the people mostly liked my poem more than they thought I was pretty.

Nobody else I know has an ugly scar like this."

Slatter pointed to her neck.

Grandpa had a good answer for her, so he cheerfully replied, "Oh but you're wrong about that sis.

Everyone has some kind of scars.

Most people's scars ya can't see.

They have scars on their hearts and scars engraved in their minds.

I can't think of anyone that doesn't have some kind of scar they would like to get rid of.

Take little Jimmy Dee for instance.

He's got a big scar on his face that stretches all the way across his chin.

He got that scar from combat fightin' in World War II.

He says he's proud of his scar.

He got knifed by an enemy soldier while he was defending our country.

Then there's old Fritz up the road a piece.

He's told me many a story about when his grandpa was a slave. He saw his grandpa strapped to a tree one time and nearly whipped to death because he stole a piece of chicken from his master's kitchen. That kind of scar is one no one can see, but Mr. Fritz lives with it every day.

I guarantee ya he'd like to be shed of it.

Now come on Slatter.

This is your old grandpa you're a talkin' to.

You've not said much about that scar in quite a while.

Somethin else is a eatin' at ya.

I can tell."

Slatter hesitated for a minute.

Then she said,

"Well, ok.

I'll tell ya what's really a botherin' me.

Ya see," she started picking at her fingers as she confessed her story.

"I worked extra, extra hard today at school.

I mean I worked a lot harder than any of the other kids in my class. I was helpin' my new teacher, Mrs. Kohler, move our second grade classroom stuff across the hall.

Everyone else went out and played and I stayed in all day and helped her.

Then, when it came time for everyone to go home, Mrs. Kohler gave everyone in our class the same reward."

Slatter stopped talking for a minute as she gathered her thoughts. Her grandpa folded his arms together and chuckled a little as he spoke, "Well, go on.

I can't wait to hear what the reward was."

He started rubbing his chin as he intently listened to her story.

Slatter sarcastically replied, "It was a good reward.

It was a big bag of candy."

She jumped off of the bed and picked the bag of candy off of the floor and handed it to her grandpa.

He looked surprised as he turned the bag over in his hands.

"Well," he commented, "This is a pretty nice reward if ya ask me." Slatter, still pouting, stuck her lips out in a jeering way.

"Yeah," she whined, "Well I thought the reward was alright too, but that's not the problem.

I just thought I should've got a double portion of the reward.

Ya know, somethin' extra special, 'cause I did so much more work than anyone else in our class; including all the stinkin' boys."

After she had poured her heart out to him, she waited for his response. Grandpa still in deep thought used his wisdom to give her his answer.

"Oh now I see what the problem is. You're mad at your teacher, the giver of the reward."

Their eyes met as grandpa continued to explore her reasons for being angry at her teacher.

"Mmm.

Let me ask ya this Slatter.

Did the teacher tell everyone before hand what their reward would be?"

Slatter fell back on the bed and pulled the covers up over her head. She replied in an 'I don't care' tone of voice, "Yes, she did. I don't see why that makes any difference. I jet told ya I did more work than anybody. So what if she told everyone in the classroom they'd get a bag of candy."

Grandpa sighed, "I think your teacher was fair and it sounds like she offered a fair and just reward to all of her students.

She did just what she said she was goin' to do.

Mrs. Kohler bought and owned all of the candy so she could do with it as she pleased.

Slatter, still laying under the covers, started to get angry at her grandpa. She whined harder,

"Oh brother I knew it.

I knew ya would take her part instead of mine.

Well, I don't think she was being fair to me at all.

I did more work than anyone else so I deserved more candy than anyone else; end of story.

She watched her grandpa walked over to her dresser and pick up her new testament bible.

Slatter still aggravated at him, sat straight up in the bed and asked, "What are ya doin' with my bible?"

Grandpa smiled as he replied, I'm gonna show ya somethin' in here.

I'm gonna read ya a story in here and then try to explain it to ya best I can.

Emotions like the anger you're feelin' is a force of nature that God gives us control over and through knowledge ya can learn to control it."

Fumbling through the thin pages, he talked out loud, "Let's see here. It's in the book of Matthew.

Yes.

I've found it.

Here it is.

It's in the Chapter 20.

It is about laborers in the vineyard.

Now listen to this.

As grandpa began reading the story, Slatter abruptly interrupted him and asked,

"Grandpa can't ya just tell me the story in your own words?

I don't like all of those thees and thous in the bible.

Those kinds of words make it hard for little kids to understand.

I will remember it better if you tell me in your own words." Grandpa laughed, "Well, ok.

I'll jest tell it to ya best I can.

"Ya see, Jesus is tellin' the people around Him a story about heaven. The kingdom of heaven is like a landowner who went out early in the mornin' to hire laborers for his vineyard.

This landowner agreed with all of the laborers he would give them a certain amount of money if they would come to work for him for the day. To make things simple, let's jest say he offered them $10.00, for the day. When they agreed to work for that price, he sent them into his vineyard to work. Then as the day went on, he went out about the streets in town and saw others standing idle in the market place. Ya know. Men that were lookin' for work. Kind of like men a standin' in an unemployment line. So, to those men, he said, you too can go work in my vineyard for ten dollars.

All day long, he kept sendin' more workers to his vineyard to work. He told each and every one of the newly hired workers, he would pay them ten dollars as a wage for their work.

So, when evening came, the landowner said to his foreman.

Call all of the laborers and pay them their wages, beginning with the last group to the first.

When those hired at the end of the day, the ones that only worked for a very short while, came for their pay: each one received ten dollars. When the ones that were hired very early in the day, the ones that had put in many long hours came for their pay: they too were paid ten dollars. All at once, the men who had worked longer hours started grumblin' and pitchin' at fit at the landowner sayin', "Hey! this ain't fair. These last men have worked only one hour and you have made them equal to us who have borne the burden and scorchin' heat all day long.

The landowner answered and said to them, "Friend, I am doin' you no wrong; did you not agree with me for ten dollars a day as your wages for workin' for me? Take what is yours and go your way, but I wish to give to these last men, the same as I give to you.

Is it not lawful for me to do what I wish with what is my own? Or is your eye envious because I am generous?"

The story was getting more interesting to Slatter, so she threw back the covers and scooted closer to him. She dangled her legs off of the bed and wiggled her toes as she listened. She wanted to ask him a question so she raised her hand up in the air like she was at school and interrupted him.

"Wait jest a minute here grandpa.

It sounds to me like ya want me to think of my teacher, as the landowner because she owned the candy and she could do with it as she pleased. And, it didn't matter how long or how hard I worked for her because I agreed I would accept one bag of candy for my work, just like everyone else did."

She looked up at him and blinked several times. She grunted, "Huh.

I never thought of it like that."

Grandpa put his arm around her as he lovingly spoke, "That's right sis, but, there's more to learn from this story than that.

You see.

There are some people who are Christians all of their lives, and have spent their entire lives livin' and doin' things for God.

When they die, they have the blessed assurance they will be in heaven with the Lord.

Then, there are people who have lived like the devil all of their lives and then just a short time before they die, they give their lives to God and accept Christ as their personal savior, and they too get to go to heaven to be with the Lord.

Can ya understand sis that salvation is the gift of eternal life from God? It is God's gift to give, and He chooses to give it to anyone and everyone who sincerely asks him for forgiveness of sins and asks Jesus to come and live in their hearts.

It's up to us to not be jealous of others. Jest knowin' that God gives all people the same opportunity to be saved should make us happy. Each person chooses where they want to spend eternity.

God gave man the will to choose either life with him or death in hell. We are suppose to be glad we have our salvation and hope everyone else accepts Christ too. I know it's hard, but you should be glad everyone received a bag of candy, just like you did."

Slatter was listening very closely to what he was saying.

She climbed up on his lap and put her small arms around his neck giving him a big hug. She felt ashamed of making such a big deal over a package of candy. She brushed her hair out of her eyes and said, "I think I understand now, grandpa.

It's very hard for me to believe that God loves those two mean bullies, Lodden and Newton the same as he loves me and you.

But I reckon he does."

He was amused at Slatter's remark. Looking into her eyes he commented, "Well, let me ask ya somethin' else young lady.

What if ya had been one of the students who felt ya did your share of the work, yet ya only did the work that ya were told to do.

I mean, ya didn't do anythin' extra.

Ya would've been jest like all the other kids who obeyed the teacher's rules, and ya would've expected to receive what the teacher had promised; one bag of candy, which was decided by your teacher to be a fair and just reward.

Are ya startin' to get my point?"

Slatter nodded her head yes. He continued with his explanation, "See Slatter.

Your teacher said that everyone that helped her work would get a bag of candy.

She wasn't taking anythin' away from ya when she handed out the rewards.

She was jest tryin' to be fair.

Ya have to always look on both sides of the coin when you're caught smack dab in the middle of a situation like ya are tonight. Lookin' at things from your teacher's point of view is somethin' ya didn't do.

Ya were only thinkin' about yourself and your feelin's.

I hope ya understand what I'm tryin' to say to ya.

Sometimes I feel like we go around in circles when we talk.

Seems like lately we've been a gettin' into some pretty deep conversations.

Sometimes I get frustrated with myself 'cause I'm so old and you're so young.

I find it rather difficult to explain certain things to ya."

Then, after a moment of hesitation, he sternly said, "Sometimes, ya just have to learn to let stuff like this roll off of your back like water runnin off of a duck's back.

Life's way too short to fret over little stuff like gettin' bags of candy, Slatter."

Grandpa wiped his face with his hand and smiled as he spoke.

"Especially when your old grandpa has a store full of it."

Slatter giggled. She assured her grandpa, she would do better about not worrying over little stuff like somebody getting more candy than her.

After they had finished their little talk, she cheerfully stated, "Gee Wiz, all of a sudden I'm hungry.

Let's go eat."

Jumping off of his lap, she slid her small hand into his and looked up at him. She smiled and fondly said, "Golly Gee, grandpa.

I think you're the smartest man in the whole wide world."

Grandpa patted Slatter on the leg and humbly replied, "Oh, I don't know about that, but, I think I might be one of the hungriest men in the whole wide world right now."

Then the two of them started laughing and walked into the kitchen together. Granny B didn't ask any questions, because she could tell by their smiling faces Slatter's problem, whatever it was, had been resolved. The three of them chatted about their day's events and then Slatter helped Granny B with the supper dishes. By the time Slatter's bed time rolled around, she was more than ready to hit the sack.

She took the time to pull out her secret map from underneath her mattress. After she studied it for a while, she stuck it back under the mattress and turned out the light. Then, she got down on her knees beside her bed and said her prayers. She was careful to thank God for her caring grandparents, her friend Pydie, and good old Mr. Fritz. She also remembered to pray for her old friend Gappy. She never lost hope that one day she would see him again. She turned on her night light and as she crawled into her bed she remembered to yell goodnight to her grandpa and Granny B.

"Goodnight to the best grandpa and Granny B any kid could ever have."

Because of her little talk with grandpa, she felt like a tremendous weight had been lifted off of her shoulders. She very quickly fell asleep dreaming of a happier tomorrow.

# 12

# THE CIRCLE OF LIFE

As Slatter road the bus to school each day, she watched the beautiful fall-colored leaves slowly topple to the ground.

Their bright colors always set each day ablaze. Time seemed to be flying by. The days turned into weeks and the weeks turned into months very quickly. Autumn didn't get to linger around very long, because the trees had no choice but to surrender to nature's changing of the seasons.

Slatter was glad the Thanksgiving holiday had come and gone, because that holiday in particular made Granny B feel very sad. In the evenings, Slatter often saw Granny B sitting alone on the porch swing. She would be all slouched over with her head in her hands. Every now and then, Slatter watched her reach into her dress pocket and pull out a handkerchief. She used it to wipe the tears from her eyes as she silently wept. When Slatter asked her why she was crying, she put a smile on her face and replied with some sort of remark about how sad it was to see the beauty of autumn turning into the dreary winter season. Granny B would be embarrassed if anyone saw her cry. Slatter could not tell when Granny B had troubles of her own. She was so good at keeping her personal feelings hidden and bottled up inside. But, Slatter knew Granny B missed seeing her kids and her other grandkids, especially during the holiday season. She kept all of her family pictures in a big box in her bedroom closet. Every once in a while, Slatter would catch her looking through them. When Slatter asked her what she was doing, Granny B would quickly put the box away and pretend to be cleaning out her closet. On occasion, she would ask Granny B why her kids didn't come to visit her during the holidays. She sadly replied,

"Oh honey.

My kids are all grown up now.

They don't have much time to mess with old folks, like me and your grandpa.

Besides, they all live so fer away.

It takes a lot of money to travel home for the holidays.

They all send me nice cards when they can.

It don't matter none, I reckon.

Jest so I know they're all healthy and happy.

Ah, I jest figure they got family of their own to see after.

You'll find out when you grow old Slatter, that after ya raise a family, you're jest not needed very much any more.

Ya jest ain't as important to your kids as ya used to be."

She pointed to her heart as she continued, "Yep. I've got lots of precious memories locked up right here in my heart.

Memories can be like quick silver in a nest of cracks; They can fall down into places ya can't see. Then, all it takes to trigger them into view is some flicker of light like a word or some thing just at the right time." Sometimes ya get a glimpse of 'em when ya least expect it."

Slatter knew all too well what she was talking about. She had a few precious memories of her own. She often wondered if a memory was something she had gained or was it something she had lost. She sat quietly and listened while Granny B continued to share her thoughts. Staring into space, Granny B softly sighed as she spoke, "One of the reasons I'm sad this time of year is because I don't like seeing fall turn the corner to winter.

When I see the leaves fallin', I'm reminded of the fact old man winter is a comin' and so is old man growin' old.

It's sorta sad watchin' yourself go from young to old.

Ya have trouble doin' the simple little things in life that ya jest take fer granted when you're young.

Like drawin' a bucket of water or peelin' vegetables."

Granny B looked down at her hands and rubbed them together. Slatter noticed big knots that had formed on her fingers from arthritis.

"The way I see it," Granny B continued, "when people get old, they sort of become like the fall leaves on the trees.

They've served their purpose for a season and then start becomin' stiff and dried up – lose their zest for life.

Yeah, seems like we flit and blow around in this world a whole life time and all any of us ever do is keep a tryin' to reach out to a higher limb as we struggle to be free, mostly from our own selves and all of our mistakes.

Then, we get tired of all of life's high winds and struggles, so we just hang around until the good Lord sees fit to call us home.

It shore is a comfort to know the good Lord's made a much better place for us to go to than this dirty old earth.

Always remember Slatter.

When God gave you life, it is for all eternity.

This life is just the beginnin'; ya know, the first part of life. Everyone who has ever lived will live long after this physical life is done and over with.

It'll be in heaven or it'll be in hell, but it will be a continued life for all of eternity cause God put eternity in man's heart.

When God creates somethin' it's forever and he created human life forever.

We'll have a new body someday, but we'll have the same soul.

The bible says it'll be a body not made with hands....that means not of this old clay earth.

It'll be a body that can't be destroyed ever again.

Yep." She nodded her head and curled her lips.

"We'll never have to die ever again after we leave this old world."

As Slatter graciously listened, she felt sad for Granny B. She didn't dare interrupt. She knew Granny B needed someone to listen to her and that is just what she did. Granny B rambled on, "Ya see Slatter. One day, when our work is finished here on earth, we'll just drop off.

Just like a leaf a fallin' off of a tree.......about as quick too."

When she was finished talking, she stood up and brushed off her dress. Then, leaving Slatter speechless, she went back into the house without saying another word. Slatter could see 'the big picture' of what Granny B was trying to say to her. Granny B felt neglected by her kids and the disappointment in her voice was leaping out of her heart by way of her mouth .....like a frog jumping off a hot rock. Slatter vowed that day, right then and there, she would never forget to visit Granny B and her grandpa when she grew up and left home.

On school days, she really enjoyed going out at recess and playing in the newly fallen leaves. She realized creating her own fun and sharing it with someone, was really what having fun was all about. She had learned real fun could not be bought with money. Slatter knew if a person didn't have anyone to share the good things in life with, then life isn't as fulfilling as it could be. She missed sharing her life with her mother and she missed spending time with her friend, Pydie.

She passed recess time by gathering as many leaves as she could into her arms and then piled them up in front of the swings. Then she would sit down in a swing and use her feet to kick the big pile of leaves as she swung past them. The wind scattered the leaves way up into the air. As the leaves took flight, some of the kids chased them. Sometimes she raked up big piles of them, and then running as fast as she could, jump right smack dab into the middle of the pile. The indescribable sound that comes from the movement of the rustling leaves would linger in Slatter's mind forever.

One day during lunch period in the glint of a mellow November sun, Slatter sneaked away from her class mates and went behind the school building. She noticed a huge maple tree there and wanted to see if it had shed all of its' beautiful orange leaves yet. The tree was aglow with a bright burnt orange color. Slatter was amazed at the huge pile of leaves that lay on the ground beneath the tree. She plopped down in the middle of the them and curled up like she was in a soft feather bed. She thought she was completely hidden. She started studying each leaf she picked up and was amazed at all their different sizes and shades. She began thinking about what Granny B had said about old people being like leaves. All of a sudden, Slatter saw some unexpected company come walking around the corner of the building. She stood up to get a better look at who was running toward her. It was Lodden and Newton.

She put her hands on her hips and yelled out to the boys.

"Ya better get out of here.

I don't want ya back here with me.

Get out!

I want to be by myself."

The boys just kept laughing as they ran toward her.

Newton yelled to Lodden.

"C'mon, Lodden.

Let's get her.

She likes leaves so well, let's shove her down and make her eat em."

Just about the time the boys got within a few feet of Slatter, the wind started to blow the leaves on the playground causing them to fly up in the air. As they spun around in the wind, they actually formed a big whirlwind. It moved forward like a tornado and smacked Newton and Lodden right in the face with such a hard force, it knocked them off their feet and in an instant, splat! They were on the ground. Slatter started laughing at the boys. The boys didn't like being laughed at. They didn't waste any time before springing to their feet. Once again, they ran toward her. They started to reach out and grab a hold of Slatter, but again the wind picked up and a second whirlwind of leaves, a much bigger one this time, hit the boys again. It was so powerful it kept rolling them over and over again. The boys became frightened. They had a scared, startled look on their faces. They must have decided a whirlwind of leaves once, was not too unusual, but a second, bigger stronger whirlwind of leaves was just way too weird for them. Newton looked at

Lodden and screamed, "Let's get out of here! Every time we get around her, we get into some kind of trouble! Somethin' weird's goin' on around here!"

Slatter laughed at the frightened boys as they ran as fast as they could toward the school building.

Once Slatter was alone, she gathered up the leaves into a big pile again and thought about how much she liked all of the different kinds of trees. She thought trees were one of God's most beautiful creations. Everything about them was fascinating right down to how each had it's own unusual bark. She convinced herself the leaves did look kind of sad. In just one season, they had grown from little buds, sort of like babies, into full grown leaves, like adults. The leaves had lived their whole lives in the same place, dangling on the end of a tree branch. It seemed so easy for the fresh, green, youthful leaves to hang onto the trees as they endured all kinds of storms and intense heat. As they began to age, their young flexible vibrant green foliage slowly became brittle. Their glory seemed to shine as their amazingly beautiful colors brightened every road and hill side in the country. Then one day, without anyone noticing, it happens. The leaves willingly begin to buckle under the slightest little breeze and one by one plummet to the ground; leaving behind empty, barren trees. Once they land on the ground, everyone walks on them and crumples them underneath their feet. Each one of the leaves seemed to have served some kind of purpose, but no one but God really knows when it's time for each one of them to plummet to the ground. Slatter knew in her heart what her Granny B had said was true. People are a lot like leaves. She thought about her grandparents and how they too, like the fallen leaves, were aging quickly. Once again she remembered what her friend Gappy had told her, life is but a vapor compared to eternity.

She began to think on a brighter, happier side of things. She realized Granny B had left out a part about the circle of life. A part that shows there is another side to people that makes them very different to leaves. People live much longer and when they die, they leave behind wonderful changes in the world and changes within people's hearts; because of who they were, what they stood for and the many contributions they left behind that made the world a better place; just because they lived in it for a little while.

The beauty of each person's life, is somewhat like the beauty of the full grown, brightly colored leaves.

Their glory shines all around those who choose to see their beauty.

There are none so blind as those who have chosen not to see.

The changing of the seasons is part of God's plan.
It is a good example of the circle of life and Slatter knew that only God could create such beauty in people as well as in trees.

Slatter thought about her Granny B and how much she loved her. She smiled to herself as she tried to picture what Granny B would look like if she were a tree in a forest. She giggled aloud as she imagined a Granny B tree very short and wide and with long branches sticking out very low to the ground so she could grab little kids, as they ran past her, and make them comb their hair and do their chores. Then she thought about her grandpa and what kind of a tree he would be. He would be a big tall solid oak tree planted beside the water where it's roots would be imbedded so deep no wind could shake or move it. She felt so secure living with her grandparents. She couldn't love them anymore if they were her real parents.

As the afternoon temperatures started to drop, she felt a chill in the wind. She was reminded of the Christmas holiday season that was quickly approaching. She wanted to get a very special gift for her Granny B and her Grandpa. Her grandpa had told her once about a scraggly old peddler everyone called, Peddler Pete. When he came to the store he always managed to make his appearance on a busy Saturday morning; which was a time when grandpa didn't have much time to look at the merchandise he had for sale. Grandpa said the peddler was easy to recognize because he drove an old dirty green and brown station wagon loaded with so much merchandise he wondered how old Pete could see out the car's windows. Grandpa said he had all kinds of neat stuff for sale like jewelry boxes and watches. He told Slatter the next time the peddler came by the store, he would let her know. Slatter had in mind spending her twenty dollar prize money to buy a very special Christmas gift for her grandparents.

She was in such deep thought she barely heard the school bell ring. She quickly brushed herself off and ran as fast as she could so she wouldn't be late for class.

# 13

# DECORATING FOR CHRISTMAS

One very cold snowy Saturday morning two days before Christmas, Granny B decided it was time to decorate the house for the holiday. The heavy snow that had fallen the night before had everything outside almost completely covered. Snow showers were still lightly coming down and Slatter could hardly keep from staring out of the windows. Granny B noticed Slatter's fascination with the beautiful newly fallen snow.

"Come over here Slatter and see what I'm lookin' at," insisted Granny B as she motioned for Slatter to come over to the living room window and stand next to her. Slatter was quick to skip across the room and join her. Granny B put her arm around Slatter and exclaimed, "My oh my. It looks like a perfect picture out there." Granny B's comments let Slatter know they were sharing the same excitement about the snowy scenery.

"A deep snow like this is always somethin' to see," continued Granny B.

"God has a whole different kind of beauty with each and every season?

Ya know, only God could create such beauty.

How in the world can anyone look at this winter wonderland and not believe in the good Lord.

The snow always makes me think that maybe it's the good Lord's way of covering up all of the old sinful stuff in the world with a beautiful coat of pure white newness.

Just look at the ice cycles hangin' on the eaves of the house.

Oh, and look over across the road at the big pine trees," pointed Granny B.

"Jest Look how thick the snow is piled up on the tree branches.

I don't see what keeps them from breakin' off from the weight of the snow."

Granny B's face glistened like a child seeing snow for the first time.

"Hey look out in the front where there's no tracks," she excitedly said as she pecked on the window pane and pointed to the front yard.

Would ya jest look at the way the snow sparkles when the sun hits it jest right.

It looks like thousands of tiny little diamonds a layin' on top of it. It so bright, hurts my eyes to look at it fer very long.

Ya know.

I was jest a thinkin'.

I've seen many snowstorms over the years, but I must say, every time I see one, I think the one I'm a seein' is the prettiest one yet.

"I reckon it's just the good Lord unfurling the beauty of another winter's day.

Slatter, still staring out of the living room window, excitedly replied,

"I sure wish I could go outside and play in the snow."

Granny B said,

"Uh, uh.

No way.

Not today youngin'.

I heard a weather report on the radio this mornin' and we're supposed to get a lot more of this white stuff today.

Don't let that old sun fool ya.

As we speak, we've got snow clouds on the horizon.

I've been a watchin' snow clouds movin' in from the west since early this mornin'.

We only need to go outside today, if we have to.

Your grandpa has taken real good care of us.

He got up extra early, shoveled a path to the old blue goose, and brought several buckets of coal into the house so we could keep the fire in the stove burnin'.

This way our house will stay nice and warm."

Pushing her lips tightly together she sighed as she bragged on her husband.

"Yep.

Your grandpa's a good man," said Granny B as she walked into the kitchen and stared out the window in there.

"Ain't many like him these days.

He's got us all fixed up so that we don't have to go out in the cold for nothin'."

Slatter, still gazing out the window in the living room, nodded her head in agreement.

Slatter was on Christmas vacation from school and like all young children, she was very excited about Christmas. Granny B thought that the best way to keep her entertained was to show her how to decorate the house for Christmas. She had Slatter pull a chair next to her bedroom closet, climb up on it, and hand Granny B the boxes labeled Christmas ornaments. Then, they carried the boxes into the living room and set them on the floor beside the tree.

The night before, grandpa had brought home a big, live, pine Christmas tree from the store. He had placed it in a large bucket of water and wrapped burlap around it to hide the ugly bucket. Granny B then put a beautiful red velvet handmade tree skirt over the burlap. Grandpa set it in front of the picture window in the living room. The tree put off a woodsy pine scent as big as all outdoors. To Slatter, the shape of the tree looked perfect. It was as tall as the ceiling and grandpa had to move furniture around to make room for it. Slatter was so excited she could hardly wait to help Granny B decorate it. Granny B had spent all morning getting her daily house chores done so she and Slatter could spend the entire day decorating the house and baking many different kinds of Christmas cookies.

Early that morning, while Slatter was still sleeping, Granny B had rolled out dough for cinnamon rolls. She sliced them and they had risen to be as big as saucers. She had placed them into the oven just before she and Slatter started gazing at the wonders of mother nature. The delicious scent of cinnamon engulfed the entire house.

Slatter walked over to the tree and carefully started unwrapping Granny B's Christmas decorations. She ran across several home made ornaments Granny B's children had made when they were very young. She carefully evaluated each ornament and could tell at a glance most of them were very old. The dates on the back of them indicated they had been prized possessions thirty years ago. Slatter harmlessly asked Granny B if she wanted her to hang them on the Christmas tree. Granny B was quick to give her a stern answer.

"No."

Realizing she sounded harsh, she changed her tone of voice.

"Honey, don't unwrap the ornaments in that box.

I've not put those things out in years.

Some of them are coming apart.

I keep meanin' to mail them to my kids, but there are so many memories wrapped up in each one of them, I really don't care to go through the trouble of sortin' all that stuff out."

Slatter just shrugged her shoulders and moved on to the next box.

She found a beautiful, white, hand crocheted scarf that had red poinsettias sewn on it. Slatter neatly laid it on top of the fireplace mantel. Then, she dug out three big red candles with fitted holders and put them on top of the scarf. Granny B came into the living room just as Slatter had finished decorating the mantel. They looked at one another and smiled. Granny B's face lit up with pleasure. She used a loving tone as she expressed her feelings, "Why, Slatter.

You've done such a beautiful job.

That mantle looks absolutely gorgeous."

Then, Granny B winked and motioned for Slatter to follow her. They walked out to the back porch.

There on the floor, lay several pieces of fresh cut pine.

Slatter clapped her hands together as she cried out, "Wow!

This stuff smells so good.

It smells jest like our Christmas tree."

She picked it up and put it up to her nose. She softly brushed the pine needles with her hands and said, "As long as I live, I won't ever forget how wonderful this stuff smells.

It's like a woman's perfume."

Granny B agreed,

"Yes.

It makes me think of Christmas when I was a little girl.

Ya know what Slatter.

Your Granny B is a smart old bird.

Yesterday I heard on the radio that we might get a heavy snow.

So after ya had gone to bed last night, I went out back and cut some of this fresh pine off of the trees.

It should be all dried out by now and ready to use.

Let's gather it up and take it to the livin' room."

Slatter was eager to assist in any way she could.

Granny B laid down an old newspaper to keep the pine needles from getting all over the floor and Slatter placed the fresh cut pine on top of it. Then, as Granny B cut the branches in perfect lengths, Slatter laid them on top of the fireplace mantel. Granny B then went into her bedroom and brought out an old wire coat hanger. She took some wire cutters from a kitchen drawer and shaped it into a circle. Then Granny B asked Slatter to hold the round piece of wire so she could affix the pine branches to it. When Granny B had used the last piece of pine, Slatter could not believe what a big beautiful wreath Granny B had made. She told Slatter to dig out a strand of white lights and wrap them around the wreath. Slatter did what Granny B said. Then, to make the wreath complete, Granny B took six old ornaments out of one of the decoration boxes and wired them on the wreath. She walked over to her sewing box and pulled out a piece of wide red ribbon. She took the ribbon and tied it into a bow. She put the bow on the wreath and hung it on the front door. Slatter walked over to wreath and plugged the cord into an outlet. When the lights lit up, Slatter and Granny B clapped their hands together as they stood amazed at their beautiful creation. They hugged one another and Granny B said, "Ok.

Enough excitement over that.

We need to move along.

We've still got a lot to do before we've finished.

I ain't had this much fun in years.

Now, for the tree.

I have made fifty ginger bread men to hang on the tree.

And when grandpa gets home tonight, he is going to pop us a big batch of popcorn and we will string it up onto the tree."

Slatter was amazed at Granny B's creativity.

She watched every move she made. She was bound and determined to learn Granny B's decorating secrets. As she picked up one of the ginger bread men from the kitchen table, she inquisitively asked,

"How are we going to hang these ginger bread men on the tree?

They feel heavy."

Granny B laughed a little as she responded to her question, "Somehow, I knew you'd ask me that and here's my answer.

I have cut fifty strands of pretty white ribbon and we will use the ribbon to tie them onto the tree branches."

She pointed to the ginger bread man Slatter was holding and proudly said, "See here. I'm a clever baker. Before I baked 'em, I made a hole in the top of each one of 'em and then stuck a little wooden peg in 'em so the hole wouldn't seal up."

Slatter smiled with delight as she examined the ornaments.

Then, pointing to a big red plastic container sitting by the Christmas tree, she added, "Next, we are gonna put those big, pretty, white bulbs on the tree.

When your grandpa gets home, we'll ask him to help ya put the angel on top of the tree.

It's over there in a special box, but don't break the string on top of it, 'cause it's made of porcelain and I don't want it to fall out on the floor and break."

Granny B gently patted Slatter on top of the head saying,

"I think it's only fair that our little angel gets to put the Christmas angel on top of the tree, don't you?"

Slatter nodded her head yes. Granny B felt so content, she kept

on talking to Slatter about the angel ornament.

"Some people like to put a star on top, but not me," concluded Granny B as she bobbed her head from side to side.

"My angel has been in our family for many many years. It's been handed down generation after generation. In fact, my great grandmother couldn't remember where it originally came from. I'm sure some old carpenter that was a friend of the family probably made it and gave it to someone in my family as a gift.

It's a very special angel and I shore wouldn't want it to get broken. Someday I'll give that special angel to you for your safe keeping. In the meantime, I'm assignin' ya the privilege to be the one to place it on the top of the Christmas tree.

Ya know your grandpa's a lot taller than we ware and he will be tickled to lift ya way up there and put her in her place.

Besides, we want him to feel like he has a part in decoratin' the tree too.

That sorta thing is important in a family.

That's another thing about life, that ya need ta always keep in mind. It makes a body feel real good inside when they feel like they are a part of the family.

Everybody wants to feel like they belong....ya know share things together.

I think it must be a feelin' that everybody's born with.

Everyone has a need to love and be loved.

I don't care who they are."

Slatter just looked at Granny B and happily said, "Oh, Ok.

I will try and always remember that."

Slatter, scratching her head with a withered look on her face asked, "How are we gonna get popcorn on the string?"

Granny B smiled and shook her head back and forth as she took Slatter over to her sewing box. She picked up a couple of darning needles and patiently explained, "Ya see. We'll each take one of these big needles and run some fishin' line through the eye and tie a big knot at the end. Then the next thing we'll do is take one piece of popcorn at a time and run the needle through each piece.

Then, presto. When ya finish, ya have a string of popcorn.

It will lay neatly right on the tree.

It will be so much fun to make.

You'll see."

Slatter was having so much fun she couldn't remember a time when she felt so happy and content. Granny B and Slatter worked together and put several strands of white lights onto the tree and then plugged them in. The living room, instantly, became aglow. Every time she and Granny

B walked past the decorated tree, they would stop and admire how pretty it was.

Slatter could hardly wait until her grandpa came home so he could pop the popcorn and help her put the angel on top of the tree.

When they were finished decorating the tree, Granny B slapped her hands together and said, "Ok. Now I reckon we're ready to make sugar cookies as soon as I take the rolls out of the oven."

Granny B opened the oven door and Slatter thought the strong scent of cinnamon smelled heavenly. She could hardly wait for them to cool so she could eat one. She thought that no one in the world could bake cinnamon rolls as big and tasty as her Granny B's.

Walking over to her old metal cupboard, Granny B whipped out a big surprise. She had made Slatter an apron to match hers. The hand made masterpiece was red with a big white snowman on it. Slatter, smiling sweetly, let out a short cry mingled with laughter. "Oh Granny B.

I do believe there ain't nothin' ya can't do.

Ya can sew anythin' ya take a mind to."

Granny B blushed as she spun Slatter around to tie it around her. Then she lifted her up onto a little step stool so she could be at the right height to roll out the cookie dough. Just as Granny B turned around to pick up the rolling pin to show Slatter how to roll out the dough, she noticed Slatter dipping her hands into the flour. The powdery dust was all over her face and hair. Granny B was amused at the way Slatter looked. She grabbed up a wet towel off of the counter and lovingly wiped the flour off of her. Granny B turned on the kitchen radio and she and Slatter sang Christmas carols. Slatter never dreamed she could be so happy. With each turn of the rolling pin, Slatter's mind drifted back to the summer day when she heard the words, there's always sunshine after the rain.

Her pleasant thoughts were interrupted by Granny B's sudden flustered remarks.

"Oh, shoot.

I don't believe it.

I'm two cups short of havin' enough flour for this second batch of sugar cookie dough."

Slatter was eager to volunteer her help. She jumped at the chance to get to go outside and play in the newly fallen snow.

"Oh, that's no big deal, Granny B.

I'll just get my coat and hat and run up to the store and get some more."

Granny B was quick to respond. Pointing her finger at Slatter she slowly but firmly snapped, "Ya...will.... do.... no... sich... a.... thing.

Why, there's snow drifts out there so deep that if ya stepped off into one, it would be way over your head.

Besides, I might have an extra bag of flour in the metal pantry out on the back porch.

Ya stay right here and keep rollin' out what we've already got fixed. I'll go look."

Slatter watched Granny B walk out onto the back porch.

She knew this was her chance to go to the store and get Granny B the flour she needed. She knew it would be very cold outside so she devised a plan to run as fast as she could. If it was too cold outside to walk back home, maybe grandpa could give her a ride. Slatter thought perhaps Peddler Pete would be at the store and she could buy a Christmas present for Granny B and her grandpa. Slatter thought she had everything all figured out. She was thinking how clever she was to have created a way for her to get to play in the snow and get Granny B a bag of flour. It was a win win situation in her eyes. Both of them would be getting something out of the deal. Such a simple plan seemed perfectly harmless to Slatter. Once again, in her young mind, she had justified her disobedience.

At that moment, Slatter had no idea that she was following a perfect plan which required her to keep a divine appointment that had been providentially created by God.

She promptly took off her snowman apron and neatly laid it on the counter. She hurriedly grabbed her coat. Then, as she headed out the door, she put on her sock cap, snow boots and gloves. She was in such a hurry and in fear of being caught, she completely forgot to get her prize money out of her room.

She pulled on the string to the hood of her coat as she struggled against the biting, cold wind. She was careful to stay on the road so she wouldn't fall off into any deep snow drifts. She walked as fast as the steps allowed her to.

She was halfway to the store before Granny B came back into the kitchen and discovered she was gone. She began calling out Slatter's name, as she looked in every room in the house. Slatter was no where to be found. Then, as she walked past the big window in the living room, she noticed the snow was starting to come down heavier. She also noticed something else.

There were several small footprints in the snow and they led down the driveway right out onto the road. Granny B, in an aggravated tone said audibly.

"Oh, that youngin.
I told her not to go out in this snow storm.
She'll catch a death of cold.
I hope she remembered to button up her coat.
Oh well.
I reckon J.E. will bring her back home when she gets up to the store.
What in the world was that child a thinkin' when she pulled this stunt?"

Granny B tried not to worry too much about Slatter as she finished baking her Christmas cookies and cleaned up the kitchen. Every now and then she would glance out the kitchen window as she anticipated Slatter's return.

Slatter had not walked very far when she began to realize she didn't have on enough warm clothes to be out in such cold temperatures. She was beginning to realize this winter wonderland was becoming a winter misery land. She had her heavy wool coat buttoned up to her chin and her hat was pulled down tightly over her ears. She tried not to breathe very deep because the cold air made her teeth hurt. The north wind was blowing so hard she had to walk backwards to withstand it. She thought about how warm and cozy her house had been and she wished she had never left.

Suddenly, she thought she heard the sound of a vehicle coming down the road toward her. It was snowing so hard she could only see a few feet in front of her. She could barely see her hand in front of her face. She couldn't see what the approaching vehicle looked like because she constantly had to wipe the snow out of her eyes. The wind was quickly getting stronger by the minute and it was blowing snow around in the air so much it was virtually impossible to see anything. When she saw the vehicle getting closer, she stopped walking. She was hoping it was her grandpa coming to pick her up and take her back to her nice warm house.

# 14

# REKINDLED TROUBLE

All at once, the vehicle stopped right beside her. She put her hand over her brow to block the snow from blowing against her face. As she stepped closer to the vehicle, she could see it was two men in an old truck. All of a sudden, she felt a surge of fear that started at the top of her head and went all the way down to her feet. She recognized the two men to be none other than Mr. Joe Beeser and Butane Craney. The two men grinned at Slatter as they instantly recognized her too. Joe Beeser was driving and Mr. Craney was sitting in the passenger seat of the truck. Slatter stood with trembling arms wrapped around her body in a useless effort to get warm. She felt like she was frozen in her tracks. The snow was over the top of her boots. She could feel the cold liquid from the melting snow as it ran down the inside of them. She was too scared to move. Taking advantage of her weakened state, Mr. Craney rolled down the window of the truck and grabbed hold of her arm. He let her squirm for a moment before he said anything.

"Well, well, well," he growled as his rotten yellowed teeth appeared when he opened his mouth to speak. He was holding Slatter so close to his face, she could smell his bad breath. It smelled like an old dirty ashtray. His eyes were red and bulging as he continued to teasingly scare her. With a snarl look on his face and his eyebrows pointed downward he mockingly said, "If'n it ain't old J.E. Slopey's little trouble makin', mean brat of a granddaughter.

Where are ya goin' ya little trouble maker?

Are ya walkin' out here in the snow jest fer the fun of it? Ha Ha.

Ain't it funny how we get ta meet up with ya again and you're all by yourself this time.

There ain't no big ole Mr. Fritz around to protect ya now!

I think ya need to go fer a little ride with us.

Joe Beeser laughed as he said, "Tee hee hee.

Yeth, I think we gots a little score to even up with ya.

Dwag her into the twuck, Butane.

We'll scare the pants off of this wittle twouble maker."

The meanness in their faces caused fear to grip her very soul.

All she could see was resentment and hostility in their eyes.

Slatter struggled with Mr. Craney as she tried to get away, but her foot steps faltered on the road making her easy prey. Due to the strong gusty wind, Mr. Craney could not get the truck door opened wide enough to pull her in. Mr. Beeser managed to turn the truck around and started driving slowly down the snow packed road. Mr. Craney held tightly onto Slatter's arms. The old truck's tires began smoking and the truck was zigzagging all over the icy road because Mr. Beeser was bearing down too hard on the accelerator.

Mr. Beeser bellowed out a hearty laugh, "Whewee! Ain't dis fwun Butane?

Ever dog has it's day.

Just hang onto that little brat for ath long ath ya can.

We'll teach her a lethon she ain't apt to ferget fer a while."

Slatter was scared to death. She started crying and pleading with the two men to let her go.

"Oh, please let me go!

Please I beg of ya!

I won't tell my grandpa ya are tryin' to hurt me.

If ya will just let me go I'll keep quiet.

I promise I will."

Slatter's pleading was useless.

The two men were laughing at her as she pleaded with them.

They thought it was funny they were dragging her through the snow drifts down the road. They figured she had it coming for making them get caught when they were stealing from her grandpa and because she threw firecrackers in their truck and blew it up. Because the muffler on the old truck was so noisy, Joe Beeser kept on yelling loudly, "We've got her thith time. Yeah boy. We got her now!"

After they had drug her on the road for about a mile, her face became completely numb from being bashed into the snow drifts. Her legs ached from being drug on the hard, icy road and her arms were in excruciating pain from Mr. Craney's tight grip. All at once the truck ran over a big chunk of ice causing Slatter's head to be slammed against the side of the outside mirror on the truck. She screamed with pain and passed out. Mr. Craney felt Slatter's body go limp and he said, "Uh Oh. Hey, Joe. Stop the truck. I think the kid's hurt."

Joe immediately stopped the truck and jokingly replied, "Ah. She ain't hurt. We was jest a havin' a wittle bit of fwun wif her. We weally didn't mean to hurt her bwad."

Mr. Craney replied with fear in his voice.

"I'm not joshin' ya.

Funin' or not.

I think she's really hurt.

She could even be dead."

Mr. Craney let go of Slatter's limp arms and she slid lifelessly down the side of the truck and into a deep snow drift beside the road. Her body was so cold and numb that she could not move. Joe Beeser's voice sounded panicky when he said, "Juth let her go Butane. She's a gettin' jest what she detherved."

Mr. Craney was nervous and his reply was shaky, "We ... we can't jest...... leave the kid.... here. She'll freeze to death Joe.

We gotta do somethin' quick."

Joe, hesitated as he bit his bottom lip like he was trying to think of a plan. He seriously replied,

"Well, thith here thnow storm is a gettin' worse and we beth be a gettin' on home before thumbody thees us.

The woad's a gettin' covered up and my old twuck ain't made to be out in dis here kind of weather."

He noticed Butane's worried look on his face.

"Ah c'mon Butane.

Ya have to stop a worryin' too much over dith."

He suddenly snapped his fingers and grinned great big as he said, "Hey!

I think I jeth thought of a good idea.

We'll dwive on up to J.E.'s store and make up a thory about how we theen her a comin' up the woad & theen her fall down in a gweat big thnow dwift.

Ya know old J.E. will go a wookin' fer her.

He'll fwind her."

Mr. Craney frowned as he kept staring into the ditch where he saw Slatter fall. He was very upset because he knew he was the one who had caused her harm. In just the few minutes she had been laying in the snow drift, the snow had completely covered her body. Mr. Craney wiped his chin with his hand. His voice quivered, "Er....Uh.. I don't know 'bout this Joe.

I'd feel real bad if'n she died.

I mean she's just a little kid."

He stuck his head out the window and looked around. Then he added,

"Ya know.

I've been a thinkin'.

The way I see it is if'n she was to get out of that ditch I reckon she could go into that grove of thick trees over there til somebody could come and get her.

Anyways, Joe.

We gots to be careful and hurry up and get on out a here before someone comes along.

Chances are somebody may have already seen us."

Mr. Craney once again leaned forward to look out the front window. He pointed as he asked, "Ain't that big thicket of woods over there what they call Humphrey's Lane?"

Mr. Beeser leaned out of the truck and in an uncaring tone, he half heartedly replied, "Yeah. I can't thee very good. I think maybe it ith. It's hard to tell with all of this thnow a coverin' up everthin'.

After he wiped his eyes a few times he said, "Oh, I can thee now. Yep.

That's Humphwey's Wane alwight.

There's the two bwig cwooked twees.

I'd know them anywhereths."

Mr. Craney was cold and scared. He wanted to be done with the whole situation. He reluctantly agreed to Mr.

Beeser's plan and they turned the truck around and headed for Slopey's store. The weather was so bad Mr. Beeser could not see to drive. Due to the freezing temperature, the windshield wipers on the old truck had frozen and the heavy wet snow was piling up on the window blocking his visibility. He couldn't tell whether he was still on the road or not. Suddenly the truck came to an abrupt halt. Mr. Beeser stomped on the throttle and tried to gain some speed. The truck began sliding on the ice and spun around in several circles before the hood of the truck plowed into a deep snow drift sending up a fantail of white as it came to an abrupt halt. Mr. Craney and Mr. Beeser's eyes met. With apprehension in his voice, Mr. Craney asked, "Well Joe. Ya done it now! Ya gave it way too much gas.

I bet we ain't even on the road anymore.

Ya pert near turned the truck over on us.

Ya idiot!

Ain't ya ever drove on ice before?

I'll bet we're stuck fer shore thanks to ya."

Mr. Beeser, with a worried look on his face replied, "Well. I think we're stuck and da engine is fwozen."

Mr. Craney angrily cried out, "What! Ya are plain stupid!

Do ya know that?

We could die out here.

This ain't no jokin' matter!

I'm freezing my buns off cause ya ain't got a heater in this jalopy and now ya go and get us stuck!

I should've known not to take up with the likes of ya!"

Mr. Beeser's had fear in his voice. He swallowed as he spoke,

"I wouldn't kid ya 'bout dis, Butane.

There's tho much thnow a blowin' in the air ........Even if'n we was still on the road, I think all thith thnow has cwogged up the twuck motor!"

They got out of the truck and were shocked to find they had driven off the road and were sitting in a huge snow drift in a corn field. They tried to push the truck out of the field, but it would not budge. They quickly grew weary from wrestling the strong bitter cold wind. Giving up, they buttoned up their coats and started walking toward Slopey's General store.

It was starting to get dark and the snow had not let up. Luckily, they were headed in the right direction and were just minutes away from their destination. Slatter's grandpa had just finished mopping up the melted snow in the entry way of the store when Mr. Craney came barging through the door. Mr. Beeser knew neither one of them would be welcomed there so he waited outside. He didn't want to be any where around when J.E. Slopey found out his granddaughter was missing.

As Mr. Craney pulled off his snow covered cap, he walked over to Slatter's grandpa and started apologizing. He was afraid to tell him the truth, so he made up a big lie. He could not look him in the eye as he told him his bogus story. He gave himself away when he started stuttering, "Er .. uh... J.E. I know ya ain't got much use for me or ...old Joe Beeser, but we just thought ya outa know that earlier today, we think we saw that granddaughter of yourn a walkin down the road."

He nervously twirled his hat in his hand and as he grasped for the right words, he continued to stutter, "And...er... uh, I.... uh...I mean..uh we.....Well, what I'm a tryin' to say is......... we think we saw her fall into a big ditch somewheres along side the road. Uh...Me and Joe.....er ...uh......well, we looked everywhere fer her, but we couldn't find her. We wanted to do the right thing and come here and tell ya 'bout it."

Slatter's grandpa's face became enraged with anger. He dropped the mop and grabbed Mr. Craney by the shirt collar. His eyes were big and wide and Mr. Craney knew he was in big trouble. Slatter's grandpa gritted his teeth together and hysterically shouted,

"Why ya ornery outfit!

Ya wouldn't know a right thing if it jumped up and hit ya smack dab in your face!

"What do ya mean ya think ya saw her?

Where did ya see her last!

Why didn't ya come to me earlier!"

His tone of voice sounded pleading.

"How in the world could ya just leave a little helpless child out there in this snow storm all alone!"

His voice changed to express deep anger.

"What kind of a man are ya!

Never mind!

I already know!

You and the likes of ya always hang around together and you're all jest plain old no count fer nothin'.

My daddy always said birds of a feather flock together.

I'll tell ya this much.

If somethin' happens to my little Slatter, I will hold ya personally responsible!

Lucky fer ya both, the good Lord commands me to turn the other cheek to youns, but I don't think that means fer me to keep turnin' it over and over.

I've tried to.

Lord knows I've tried."

Slatter's grandpa realized he was losing his temper. He let go of Mr. Craney's shirt and pointed his finger in his face. He tearfully said, "Time's a wastin'.

That blizzard out there is a gettin' worse.

I don't have time to mess with ya two right now, but I'll tell ya this. I'll not forget this and I promise ya I'll deal with ya later.

Right now, most important thing is to take care of business at hand. The business of findin' my little Slatter."

Then, he quickly put on his over shoes and grabbed his hat and coat. Gaining control of himself, he slid into his coat turning the collar up over his neck. In a calm but gruff voice he asked, "Where do ya say ya saw her last?"

Mr. Craney, with his hat still in his hand, looked down at the floor. He humbly whispered, "I think she was near that old road that goes down Humphrey's Lane."

Slatter's grandpa hurriedly turned out the lights and locked up the store. There wasn't any time to count down his cash drawer or do any of his other regular chores he did when he closed up his business. This was not a regular night. It was an intense relying on faith night. He had something much more important to accomplish tonight. He had to find his precious lost granddaughter. He fought back tears as he held onto his faith.

With each step, he whispered a prayer out loud.

"Oh my heavenly father in heaven.

Please watch over Slatter and keep her safe.

Please, please God I beg of ya.

Ya entrusted her care to me and I let ya down.

Please forgive me.

She's just a little child.

Help me find her before she freezes to death.

Please keep her warm and don't let anythin' bad happen to her. Please speak to her heart and direct her path.

All I know to do right now is pray.

I don't know where she is, but I know ya do.

I am trustin' in ya Jesus."

Walking toward the old blue goose, he wiped his tears off his face with his gloves.

# 15

# LOVE YOUR ENEMIES

As he started to get into the old blue goose, he saw the shadow of a man hiding behind the gas pumps. He recognized the man to be Joe Beeser. With the cold wind whipping his face, Slatter's grandpa slid into the car and drove over to where Mr. Beeser was standing. In a disgusted tone of voice he remarked, "I figured as much......I jest had a feelin' ya were out here somewhere. Trouble usually travels in two and you two are nothin' but trouble as far as I'm concerned.

If I find out you two had anythin' to do with my Slatter a gettin' caught out in this snow storm, jest rest assured.

I will press charges.

Now youns get on down the road and get home."

The two men stood there and looked at one another.

Mr. Slopey looked around for their truck.

He didn't see one.

He sarcastically asked,

"Where's your truck, anyway?"

Mr. Craney, acting embarrassed, earnestly replied.

"Well, I'm sorry to say, we kind of got it stuck out in a corn field a little ways down the road here.

That's what took us so long to get to your store J. E.

I don't think we can get it out until this snow storm passes.

It's stuck real good!

I'm afraid it's gonna take a snow plow to pull it out."

Grandpa compassionately looked at the two bewildered, shaggy men standing before him in the freezing temperatures with snow all over them. He shook his head and scoffed, "Well. This must be your lucky night fellows.

The good Lord jest spoke to my heart and He won't let me leave you two a standin' out here in this blizzard.

I'm goin' to show love to my enemies.

I don't hate you men, but I hate what ya two stand fer.

Ya know ya might learn a couple of lessons in this situation yet.

Get in the car."

The men were at his mercy. They quickly obeyed. They opened up the back doors of the car and jumped in. They were grateful for any kind of shelter from the storm. As the old blue goose weaved down the road, it plunged through the snow like an armored tank. It was all Slatter's grandpa could do to hold the car onto the slick impassable road.

Through the car's rear view mirror, he watched the two men as they snickered and made jokes about his old car. His heart filled with anger toward them. He had just about all he could take. He angrily shouted out, "By the way ya two no account yahoos!

I hear ya back there a makin' fun of my car.

Youns had best be a puttin' a stop to your mouths right now cause I've had all I'm goin' to take from both of ya.

I have a mind to jest stop the car and dump your old hind ends out right here in the snow.

I can't believe how ungrateful youns are.

As long as you're ridin' in my car and I'm a doin' the drivin', both of youns are goin' to listen to what I have to say. Ya ain't heard a sermon until youns have heard mine."

He was driving less than ten miles an hour. He couldn't use the brakes for fear of skidding. To keep the car idling slow, he kept changing gears from neutral to drive as he held his foot steady on the throttle. He kept leaning forward over the steering wheel to peer into the blinding snowfall, trying his best to see the road. The headlights only illuminated the big white snowflakes as they fell silently on the ground. The poor old blue goose, with it's roaring rock-hard, durable engine kept trudging along at a sluggard's pace, as it weaved down the slick road. It was all grandpa could do to keep the car on track while he preached a sermon to his ungrateful passengers in the back seat. With both hands gripped onto the steering wheel of the car, he kept glancing up into his rear view mirror as he talked. His back seat passengers had no choice, but to listen to his lecture. He used a disgusted, irritated tone as he spoke.

"First thing ya need to learn is one of these days ya will be a answerin' to a higher power than the likes of me. God tells us in his word that if ya harm one of his children, ya may as well have a millstone tied around your neck and dropped into the sea.

Huh.

Put that in her pipe and smoke it.

Ain't that somethin' fer ya to look forward to?

And youns can take that little statement to the bank.

Second thing is ya need to learn to be grateful.

Grateful that I am a Christian man and that obligates me to love my enemies.

Otherwise, ya both would be in a worse fix than ya are now.

I could've left your no account hides out in this blizzard with no way to get around.

Ya know.

I'll be honest with ya.

Right now, it's very hard for me to believe that God loves you two as much as he loves my little lost, granddaughter.

But I know He does."

Trying to keep one eye on the road and one in the rearview mirror was proving to be a difficult task. However he looked behind his right shoulder, pointed his finger at the men and warned, "I just got a sneaky feelin' youns know more about her bein' lost than what you're a lettin' on.

But right now as far as I'm concerned, I'm a thinkin' that ya both are my enemies.

I want youns to know that I feel like I've done my part in helpin' ya get back home tonight.

I've given youns a ride as fer as I can.

So, this is the end of the line."

Just as the men thought he was finished with his sermon, he added. "Oh jest one more thing. Ya both had better get your life in order, and get right with the good Lord.

Cause, like it or not, there's comin' a day when everyone, and I mean every person alive, will bow on their knees and confess God as King of Kings and Lord of Lords.

I'm afraid that's the only way ya two are ever goin' to turn your life around fer the better.

Only the good Lord can change someone from the inside out.

And, if ya haven't asked God into your life before that day, Well, then ya are for sure headed straight for a devil's hell."

He slammed on the brakes causing the car to skate unassisted down the road. Spinning a circle, the car's right front wheel slid off of the road. The old Blue goose had come to a screeching halt right in front of Humphrey's Lane.

"Well, I ain't got nothin' else to say to ya, except the next time I see youns, it might be in the county jail. From here on out, ya two are on your own.

Go on now. Get ta goin'.

Get out of my car before I really lose my temper!"

Thinking he may have been a little too hard on the men, as they got out of the car, he tried to speak in a calmer tone of voice.

"If ya get too cold a walkin, little Jimmy Dee's place is just down the road a piece from here. He might put ya up for the night."

The two men never said a word after Slatter's grandpa finished giving them a piece of his mind.

Grandpa had put the fear of God in them and they were afraid to utter a word. They finally expressed a small amount of appreciation by humbly saying, "Much obliged, J.E."

They pulled their coat collars up over their ears and started jogging down the road.

The snow had temporarily stopped. Slatter's Grandpa didn't waste any time getting out of the car. He opened the trunk of the car and pulled out a big flashlight. He immediately started walking and yelling out her name at the top of his lungs.

"Slatter...Slatter

Where are Ya?"

Every now and then he would stop and listen. The only sound he heard was the blowing of the cold chilling, gusty wind.

He left the car running to keep the motor warm. He wanted the car to stay warm so when he found Slatter, she could get warm quickly.

He walked with hope as he struggled against the horrid weather............He had hope he would find her alive and well.

He was afraid it might start snowing again at any time, so he desperately searched for Slatter while his visibility was good.

He kept walking up and down the road as he frantically continued to call her name.

"Slatter! ......... Slatter!
Where are ya?"

There was no response. All he heard was the sounds of the malicious, howling wind, and all he could see was white from the blowing snow. All at once, he was overwhelmed with the thought that he was one man out in a blizzard trying to find one small child in such an intense, vast area. His heart sank. He could feel doubt and fear ripping at his heart. He was overwhelmed with uneasiness as he tried to observe any sign of her in the tranquil scene of the freshly fallen snow. However, as far as he could see, there was not a trace of her to be found. It seemed as if she had somehow suddenly vanished. Emptiness and helplessness tugged at his heart.

After he had spent about half an hour fighting the cold wind and frigid temperatures, grandpa knew he had to go home and get on warmer dryer clothes. He would not be able to search for Slatter if he came down ill. As he drove home, he couldn't help but think if he was having a difficult time enduring the horrible weather, how could a frail little girl ever survive it. He would not let himself believe Slatter was dead. Instead, he kept praying, asking God to direct her path to a safe place and to please help him find her. He refused to entertain any negative impulses that came to mind. He realized that his chances of finding her in such inclement weather by himself were slim to none. He was anxious to find out how Slatter managed to get outside away from Granny B. At the same time, he dreaded telling Granny B he couldn't find their precious granddaughter and she was somewhere, all alone in the dark, out in the middle of a snow storm. When he arrived home, Granny B met him at the front door with a worried look on her face. She did not see Slatter with him. As she closed the door behind him, she curiously asked, "J.E. Where's Slatter?

Didn't she come up to the store this afternoon?

And why in this world are ya comin in the house all wet and covered with ................... snow?"

She suddenly paused. She could tell by the solemn, concerned appearance of her husband's face something was terribly wrong.

"I don't know."

He mildly replied.

"I've jest spent the last half hour searchin' for her."

"What do ya mean ya been searchin' for her!" exclaimed an enraged Granny B.

I thought she was at the store with you!"

He detected horror in Granny B's voice as her facial expressions reflected fear and anger.

"Why, I never dreamed she was out in this snow storm all by herself!"

She stood utterly still and buried her face into her hands. Grandpa walked over to her and put his arms around her. He tried to reassure his wife by being as composed and calm as he could. He held her in his arms because he knew at that moment, she needed to feel his inner strength.

"Look," he said in a wavering voice, trying not to cry.

"All I know is, those two worthless, disgusting men, Joe Beeser and Butane Craney came into the store a while ago and reported to me they thought they saw her a walkin down the road."

He couldn't hold back the tears any longer. He choked out the words, "At least the varmints had a shred of decency left in them to come and tell me they saw her."

As he wiped his eyes, he walked over to his chair and sat down. Granny B knelt down beside his chair and tried to be comforting as she listened ever so closely. He continued with his story, "They said the last time they saw her was in front of the road that turns off to go to Humphrey's Lane."

He made a fist with his hand and raising it to his mouth, bit at his knuckles.

"I tried to be nice to those two, but for the love of God, I wanted to smack 'em right in the face.

I know in my spirit that they are somehow responsible for Slatter being lost."

He rubbed his hands together as he sighed, "Can ya tell me what in the world she was doing out in this blizzard anyway, and why she'd be so far from home.

That's over a mile from here!"

My goodness Bernadine.

Didn't ya even see her go outside?"

Granny B didn't answer. She knew when her husband called her by her given name, he was thoroughly disgusted.

There was a moment of silence between them and then suddenly Slatter's grandpa angrily hit the side of the chair saying, "I jest can't sit her and do nothin'!

Dad burn it!

I've got to go look fer her."

He quickly raised up out of his chair and walked toward the bedroom. Granny B, trying to control her feelings, followed him. Her hands were shaking as she helped him out of his cold, wet clothes. Because she had a huge lump in the middle of her throat, her voice was broken. She managed to push her words out.

"All I know, is.... I....I ran out of flour while we were makin' some cookies.

So, I walked out onto the back porch to look in the pantry to see if I had an extra bag out there.

I only left her for a few seconds.

But, when I came back into the kitchen, I found her apron laying on the back of the kitchen stool she was standing on; She was just................ gone!

I looked all over the house for her.

Then I looked out of the window and saw her foot prints in the snow. They looked like they were a headin' down the road toward the store. I just figured she was tryin' to help me out and decided to walk up to the store to get me another bag of flour.

Oh J.E.

I feel so bad about all this!

I feel like this is all my fault.

I hope she ain't been kidnapped er somethin'."

As she talked, she frantically worked at getting clean, dry clothes for her husband to change into. She helped him put on two shirts, a sweater, two pair of pants, and an extra pair of socks to help keep his feet warm and dry. As Slatter's grandpa got dressed, Granny B grabbed a handkerchief from her top dresser drawer and sat down on the edge of their bed. Slatter's grandpa's heart went out to her. He sat down beside her and took her hands in his. He kissed away her tears from her face. Smiling, he looked into her eyes and confidently said, "Now. Now. I ain't a blamin' ya fer what's happened. Our fussin' ain't goin' to do anybody any good. We don't need to be at each other's throats about this thing. We must pull together. We've been through many bumps in the road together over the years and somehow, we'll get through this too. C'mon now.

Where's your faith.

God will get us through this.

I jest know He will.

Don't ask me how," his voice faded.

"I jest know he will."

Grandpa continued to encourage Granny B as he rambled on and on.

"We can't imagine why this is happenin' tonight," he assuredly remarked holding up his forefinger, "But I guarantee ya one thing.

God has a purpose in it and He will give us the strength to get through it."

He took Granny B by the hand and started giving her instructions.

"Now, while I'm gone," he sincerely said.

"Ya get down on your knees and pray.

And I mean pray hard," His voice sounded heavier. "Pray God will send someone to help her and keep her safe.

"People hear us talk about our faith everyday and we've both lived long enough to know there are times when ya have to apply your faith. We both know this situation is totally out of our control right now. This is one of those times we have to depend on what God has given us in his word. We are going to lean on that old scripture in Proverbs that says,

'Trust in the Lord with all your heart.
And lean not on your own understanding.
In all your ways, acknowledge Him, and He shall direct your paths.'

He'll direct Slatter's path too.
Always remember we're not like most folks.
Most folks think prayin' is a task and last resort.
We know it's a privilege and it's the first thing we do.
I believe we'll find Slatter, and until we do, we will trust God to take care of her.
We serve a great and wonderful God and He loves us just like we love our family.
In fact, He loves us even more.
Because he sent his only son to die for us so, we can have eternal life one day and be with Him in heaven."

He kept patting her hand as he talked. Granny B was speechless. She kept staring back into her husband's face like her soul was feeding off his words. She absorbed his strength into her breaking heart.

"Oh, I know ya know what I'm sayin' is true.
And I know you've heard it said a thousand times over the years.
But in difficult times our faith can be strengthened by hearin' God's truths.

I have already asked God to keep her safe and direct her path and I believe He is going to honor my prayer. We have to go on and do what we know to do.

We do know she's only been out there in this rough weather for a couple of hours.

We do know in our hearts that God has never let us down.

We must keep believin' she is alive and will somehow seek shelter in the cleft of the rock. We must go to God in prayer and keep on prayin' until she makes it back home. We can't lose hope.

Granny B, overwhelmed with emotions, nodded her head yes as she wrinkled up her handkerchief in her hands and blew her nose. Slatter's grandpa winked at Granny B as he grabbed his extra heavy wool coat, put his boots on, and walked out the door.

As he was opening the car door, he turned around and looked back at his house. Every room in it was lit up and he thought it had a welcoming, homey look to it. It wasn't a fancy looking house at all. It was a very comfortable home and what a home it was. He thought to himself. Many of his neighbors had more expensive homes than his, but no where in the town of Whitton could anyone find a more loving home than his.

"A house is not a home", he mumbled to himself.

It is a buildin'.

It's like a person's life.

A person's body is just a shell that he lives in.

It's what's in a person's heart that makes him a good or bad person. A home is like a church. It's only as good as the people who are a part of it. As he proceeded to back out of his driveway, his thoughts continued. Since Slatter had come to live with him and Granny B, she had added so much love to their home. He and Granny B had forgotten how much joy children can bring to a family. Children can make such a difference in a home, if their parents take time for them. He had thought he had been taking time to share God's ways, with Slatter. He realized, now he was older, one of his mistakes he had made with his own children was he was always too busy running a business. He didn't take enough time to explain God's ways to them and they had grown up resentful of him and Granny B. He realized too late in life when it comes to children the old saying 'As a twig is bent, so grows the tree' had proven itself to be true. He wanted to raise Slatter different. He didn't want her to grow up to be a crooked tree. He wanted to help her to grow up like a straight and narrow tree. Like a tree that's planted by the water. A tree that would always stand strong and couldn't be moved or uprooted by the strong winds of life. Maybe he should have spanked her more instead of trying to reason with her when she disobeyed. His thoughts were suddenly interrupted by an unexpected jolt. He jumped out of the car to see what he had hit.

The old blue goose had met it's match. There before him was a mound of snow about ten feet tall. It blocked the entrance way to his driveway. He couldn't back out to the main road. Even though the snow had stopped falling, the fierce north wind had quickly blown the newly fallen snow into huge drifts at the end of the driveway.

Suddenly, reality began to set in. He was not going anywhere to look for Slatter tonight. He drove the car forward and parked it as close to the house as he could get. He hurriedly got out of the car, hung his head and started walking toward the house.

Granny B was startled when the front door unexpectedly opened. When she saw it was her husband, she jumped up from her rocking chair, grabbed her chest and optimistically cried out,

"Did ya find her? Is she here yet?"

Grandpa slowly took his hat and coat off. As he handed them to Granny B, he shook his head back and forth. Granny B hung up his garments and walked over toward him. She continued to anxiously hound him with questions.

"What do ya mean by shakin' your head no?"

What happened to ya?

Why are ya here instead of out there searchin' fer Slatter?"

She glared into his eyes waiting for an answer.

He sank down in his chair and let out a big sigh,

"Well," he began, as his eyes dropped to the floor.

"Our driveway is blocked and I can't go anywhere.

The wind gusts have been blowin' so strong out there a huge snow drift has formed at the end of the driveway and I can't begin to try and walk against that strong, bitin' north wind.

Oh...............I'm just way too old."

Granny B dropped to her knees beside the chair. She had a frightened look on her face as she listened to her husband.

"I'm tellin' ya.

We are jest goin' to have to trust the Lord to keep her safe.

I have to wait until the wind quits blowin' before I can go back out there.

We have to keep believin' she was able to get to a shelter somewhere and she's alright.

She's a young girl and she not only listens to her heart, she's driven by it.

Now, what we have to do is pray..................pray really hard.

We both know there's no greater force on this earth than when two God fearing people pray in unison."

He tilted Granny B's chin with his hand and smiled as their eyes met. Her bottom lip trembled as she tried to smile back at him. In a whimpering weak voice she said, "Jest when I thought things was a goin' so good, somethin' like this had to happen. It seems life has a way of making us pay a penalty for every success it gives us."

Slatter's grandpa straightened his shoulders and confidently whispered, "Oh, now don't talk like that. Ya can't lose hope. Remember the words to the song we sing at church.

Christ the solid rock I stand, all other ground is sinkin' sand.

Our hope is built on nothing less than Jesus' blood and righteousness.

We must have faith God will speak to her heart and direct her path. He can and will deliver her from the wrath of this awful storm."

His eyes slowly gazed upward. He paused a few seconds then reverently declared,

"We need to remember God is well known for seekin' out the lost, findin' them and bringin' 'em home.

It has to be done His way and in His time.

His will must be done.

Slatter is lost.

But somehow God will help us to find her.

As soon as the weather breaks, I will walk up to the store and get Mr. Fritz. I'm sure he'll want to help us look for her. We'll walk down the road to Linda Jenson's place. Her place ain't far from here. We can surely make it to there as soon as the weather clears. Remember the other day when she was at the store a braggin' about gettin' one of those new fangeldy telephones put in her house.

We'll ask her to help us spread the word by calling people to come here and pray with us.

She can call everyone she knows that has a telephone. All we can do now, Granny B is pray.

I know it don't sound like much, but we'll pray all night if we have to. God knows our hearts and He will answer our prayers."

They both agreed that Slatter's grandpa had a good plan.

As they held onto their faith and each other, they knelt beside the couch and prayed for Slatter's safe return.

# 16

# LOST IN A WINTER WONDERLAND

After Slatter's grandparents prayed long and hard they got up off their knees and sat down in their chairs. Together they drank coffee and waited. Every now and then, Slatter's grandpa would quote his favorite bible scripture aloud.

"Be still and know that I am God."

They waited for the sun to come up so they could resume their search for Slatter.

They waited for some kind of sign their prayers were being answered.

They were unaware God had already heard their prayers and had everything under control. Slatter was providentially being kept safe, but under very unusual circumstances.

It was no accident the snow drift she had slid into was now all covered with snow, causing the hole she was laying in to become like an igloo. Her body temperature caused the snow drift to become warm enough to keep her from freezing. Because she had hit her head on the truck's mirror, she blacked out for a minute. When she awoke and realized what had happened, she used her hands to fervently dig out of the snow drift. As she clawed at the snow, she reminded herself of a big dog she once saw throwing dirt behind him as he frantically dug a deep hole to bury a bone. When she felt the rush of the cold north wind on her face, she knew she was free. She struggled to her feet. As she waded the deep snow, she stumbled and fell onto something hard. It was the cold hard pavement of the road. She forced herself to stand up and look around. The landscape she was once familiar with, looked very different now because it was covered up in a blanket of white snow. She didn't know where she was. The blustery wind had become her enemy because it was swirling the fresh snow in the air, making visibility impossible. She was unable to judge which direction was the right way home.

Confused and lost, she began stumbling around in the dark.

She hunched her shoulders and tightened the hood of her coat around her neck as she tried to walk against the freezing wind. She noticed she had a feeling of comfort like someone was walking along beside her, somehow leading the way. She even stopped a couple of times to look behind her to see if there were any other foot prints in the snow besides her own. She wondered why, for the first time in her life, she wasn't one bit afraid of the dark. She pressed on forcing herself to walk toward the closest shelter she could see...which was a thick wooded area right straight in front of her. At that moment, she had no idea she was headed down the wretched, desolated road that lead to Humphrey's Lane.

The farther she walked the deeper she went into the snowy wilderness. All she could see were trees and bushes with mounds of snow on top of them. Even though the trees offered some protection from the weather, she was still walking in snow almost waist high. She was so cold and miserable, it took all the strength she had to drag her frozen feet and legs through the deep snow. She was becoming weaker by the minute. Her left leg had a ache in it. It hurt so bad she couldn't tell which part of her leg was actually injured. She figured she had a nasty cut on her leg somewhere because every now and then she could see a trail of blood in the snow behind her. She didn't want to take the time to stop and examine herself, because she was afraid she would freeze into a solid piece of ice.

    Suddenly, just as she was about to collapse from exhaustion, she noticed a full moon had suddenly appeared from behind all of the snow clouds. As she clung to a small branch hanging from a big oak tree, she looked up into a clear, night sky. The dense forest she was in provided a windbreak from the strong cold blasts of air. The weather seemed so much calmer now that she was in the woods. Because of the moonlight, she could see in the short distance ahead of her, there was a big dug out area at the bottom of a steep hill. The trees surrounded the area like a big shield protecting it from the blowing snow. She managed to hang onto the tree limbs as she pushed on trying to get to what looked to be a safer place. She caught herself thinking she was so cold she wondered if she were going to die out in this wilderness and all because, she chose to disobey. She knew now her attempt to go to the store by herself in severe blizzard conditions was a very bad mistake. She couldn't believe how beautiful and serene the frigid weather looked from the warm side of a living room window. Now, she was finding out the hard way how harsh and ruthless winter weather can be.

    Just as she reached the edge of the hill, her foot slipped on a limb and she found herself tumbling head first down the steep slope. She abruptly landed beside a huge rock. Using the rock to steady herself, she managed to stand. Shivering, she tried to brush the snow off her coat. As she glanced out at the moonlit surroundings, she spotted a hollowed out place, like a cavern, behind the rock. It looked like a cubby hole just her size. Because snow kept falling off the hood of her coat into her eyes, she couldn't see if it was occupied or not. Out of desperation, she bravely used her hand to feel the inside of the cavern. She was very relieved to discover the place was empty. She took off her snow packed coat and gave it a shake. When she put her knee on the cold rock to lift herself up, she made grieving, grunting noises. She was able to use her coat as a blanket because the outside of it was water repellant and the inside of it was nice and dry. She huddled as close as she could get against the cold back wall of the small cavern. She lay there wadded up into a ball, shivering, longing to somehow get warm. She tried to make herself dwell on warm thoughts that were pure and good. She thought about her church choir singing a song about hiding in the cleft of the rock. She let her mind wonder about how she loved wading the ditches in front of her house after a warm summer rain and how pretty the meadows of wild flowers were behind the store when the shadow of clouds in midday sun passed over them. She attempted to think about everything she could, except how cold she was, the jabbing pain in her leg, and how much she wanted to go home. She tried not to cry, but every once in a while, she caught herself wiping icy tears from her face.

 Because the moon was so bright, she caught herself looking out at the beauty of the snowy woods. She was trying really hard to be brave. It was hard not be scared when she kept seeing silhouettes of moving tree limbs as they cast odd shaped shadows against the moonlit snow. The shadows looked like scary creatures closing in on her. As she gazed up into the starry sky, she noticed how unusually big the stars looked. She had never before seen such big, bright twinkling stars so closely suspended overhead. She was briefly entertained by some exotic patterns of light flashing across the cold dark December sky. As she lay there gazing up at the stars, she bravely closed her eyes and drifted off to sleep.

She had only dozed off a few minutes when she heard a dreadful noise close by. She thought it sounded like an animal's cry. Her body stiffened as she trembled with fear. All of a sudden, she saw four black furry legs that had paws with long claws. She instantly recognized the legs to be that of a big, black wild cat. It pounced up into the cavern with her. The cat's unexpected presence along with it's hissing noises and hypnotic stare, left Slatter transfixed for just a moment. She could hardly catch her breath. She could hear her heart pounding in her ears. She tried to calm down by telling herself it was only a cat. A cat sort of like, Shekoe, only one that lived out in the wild. Slatter was very quiet and didn't make any sudden moves toward the animal. After a few seconds, Slatter cautiously began talking to it. With trembling lips she managed to utter, "H....hello............ k...kitty, kitty.

Am ...I .....in... your... house?

I ...didn't mean to..... take over... y...your house.

Are ya....c...cold too?"

The cat's ears went flat and as it humped its back up in an effort to make itself look bigger, its thick black hair stuck straight out. Growling and hissing at Slatter, it's big yellow eyes glowed in the dark. Without warning, it sprang out of the cavern. It jumped out as quickly as it had jumped in. Slatter was wide awake now for sure.

# 17

# ILLUMINATED FOOT STEPS

As she collected her thoughts and tried to go back to sleep, something caught her eye. She saw a bright glowing green substance coming out of the ground. She rubbed her eyes and took another look. It looked like steam coming off of hot bath water....only a greenish color. At first, she was too scared to walk over and see what it was. She was afraid something else might jump out at her and scare her half to death. Then, she started thinking maybe it was a sign from God, showing her which way to go to get help. After she lay there a while staring at the green haze, her curiosity got the best of her.

She courageously jumped down from where she had been laying and put her coat back on. She made her way over to the green vapor she had seen from a distance.

She couldn't believe her eyes!
It was big, illuminating green footsteps.

The footsteps were glowing in the dark because of the way the moon was reflecting on them. Slatter's lips were getting numb. She thought she'd better try to move them. With trembling lips, she started talking out loud to herself,

"M...maybe... th...this ...is...a...s...sign... fr...from G... God.

I 'm....g... goin' ..t..to f...follow ..th...them.

S....somebody...h... had ..t...to...ha...have m...made ..'em."

She remembered a scripture from the book of Psalm, she had read in her Sunday School class once.

'And we shall make His footsteps our pathway.'

Slatter was absolutely desperate. She did not want to stay out all night in an old dirty, cold cubby hole if she didn't have to. So, she courageously started stepping into each of the footsteps. Because it had been so difficult to drag herself through the deep, wet snow, she was amazed at how much easier it was to walk in the hollowed out places in the snow.

# 18

# A FRIEND WITH IMMORTAL EYES

In hope of finding a path leading home, she followed the green illuminating footprints as far as they went. She had traveled quite a distance when she noticed she ran out of them. She looked all around as far as she could see. But there were no more green illuminating footsteps. Slatter was overwhelmed with disappointment. She didn't know which way to turn or what to do. Gazing up into the moonlit sky, she sensed an eerie quietness. The feeling of loneliness infiltrated her entire being. In the distance, she caught a glimpse of an old tree stump sticking out of the ground. She managed to drag herself through the deep snow and sat down on it. She had exhausted all of her resources for finding a way back home. She felt like she was at the end of a burning rope with no place to go. She started crying very loud. The sound of her pitiful whimpers echoed as they floated upward in the still crisp night air. Her tears became frozen drops of ice as she flung them off her numb, chapped face.

She was suddenly startled by a very unusual subtle sound.

It was the clear sound of a human voice that was not her own. The voice was clear and precise. It pleaded, "Please don't cry."

The unusual sounding voice startled Slatter so much she jumped up from where she was sitting and tried to run, but she couldn't. Her feet were so frozen she couldn't make them move. She hoped it was someone sent by her grandpa to look for her. She quickly dried her tears and looked around. She didn't see anyone around anywhere. For just a moment, her joy overcame her fear.

Then, out of nowhere, a big bulky shadow slowly emerged from behind a grove of trees. Slatter's was mesmerized as she stood and stared as the shadow approached her. She recognized the shape of the shadow to be a donkey. With The bright moonlight shining against his body, it had made his shadow appear larger than he really was. But as the donkey got closer, his shadow became smaller. She was so afraid she stood utterly still and waited for him to make the first move. She had no idea what his next move was going to be. She didn't know if he was going to be dangerous or friendly. The little bit of joy she had just experienced had vanished because fear once again engulfed her entire being to the point she wanted to scream. She didn't take her eyes off of the donkey as she watched his every move. Her eyes were so wide she could feel cold air seeping into the corners of them. Slatter instantly remembered Mingler the snake that spoke to her at the junk hole pond and how much she had feared him.

The donkey took a few steps toward her. She looked for a big stick or something to defend herself with in case he tried to hurt her. She watched his mouth as it began to jerk back and forth in a wiggling motion. Then his upper lip began to loosen exposing his big yellow teeth. She couldn't believe her eyes as she watched his lips move and sound came out of his mouth. It was the same sound she had just heard.

"I'm sorry if I've frightened ya.

Please, don't be afraid of me," spoke the donkey kindly.

Slatter couldn't control her knees as they knocked together. She found herself responding to his speech,

" W-h-o...who......a-r-e......y...y-o-u?"

The donkey bent his head down low, buckled one of his legs under him and bowed before her. He kept blinking his bright eyes as he replied, "Well, my name is ABOB. It's short for A Beast Of Burden, so my master just calls me ABOB."

Slatter, still scared half out of her wits forced her icy lips to move, "W...where...... is.... y..your.... m...master?"

ABOB, standing up straight again stepped a little closer to Slatter. "Oh, just across those fields a ways."

He looked as if he was almost smiling as he continued his conversation,

"I have been sent to find you and take you to my master's house." Slatter didn't know what to do. The donkey's intentions seemed honorable toward her. She felt she had no choice but to go along with what he was saying to her. If she didn't, she was for sure going to freeze death. She thought to herself, at the very least, maybe she could get inside a building and get warm. She was uncertain whether or not she was doing the right thing, but she knew she was ready to do almost anything in order to get in out of the cold harsh weather. Shivering all over, she slowly agreed.

"W...well......ok........ I........w...will.... g..go....w..with.. ya.

The donkey stiffly backed up beside her and proclaimed, "If you'll step up on that tree stump you were sitting on, you'll be able to climb onto my back. You will find I'm very warm and I can bear the burden of walking in the deep snow a lot better than you can. You can just rest for a while.

Slatter quickly grabbed a hold of the donkey's mane and pulled herself up on top of the tree stump. Then, she threw her leg over the donkey and positioned herself on his back. She immediately appreciated feeling the heat from his body. She didn't want to appear ungrateful for his help, so as soon as she started to warm up a bit, she did her best to thank him.

"Oh ya feel so warm to my legs.

I am beholdin' to ya fer helpin' me and I want to thank ya fer it now, jest in case I forget to thank ya later.

Say ............ABOB.

I'd like to know somethin'.

How come ya can talk like a real person?

I know donkeys aren't supposed to talk like people talk, yet here ya are talkin' to me.

I'm sorta confused."

ABOB kept on plowing through the snow drifts with ease as he continued to orally communicate with her.

"Well, I'm a little confused myself.

Before tonight, I have never talked like a human before.

I felt odd sounds gurgling down in my throat and then words started coming out of my mouth.

It was a strange, funny feeling.

I really don't know if I like this talking thing or not.

All I know is my master told me to go into the woods find a little girl that is lost in this snow storm, and take her to a safe haven." You know you will really like my master.

She is wonderful, gentle and caring.... She's like an angel to me."

Slatter was getting more scared by the minute. How in the world could anyone have known the exact location of where she was. She didn't even know herself. She wondered who this master person was and where was this ABOB talking donkey taking her. The farther they traveled the more curious she became about her destination. The warmer she got, the friendlier she became toward the donkey. Deep in thought, she once again began asking him questions.

"Say ABOB.

I'm wonderin' about somethin' else.

Ya mentioned the word angel a while ago.

I'm really a wonderin' about somethin'."

"Mmm mmm, go on," murmured ABOB in a positive tone.

Slatter took his response to mean for her to proceed with her question. Starting to feel very exhausted and drained, she looked up into the big dark sky and with a weak voice asked, "Have ya ever seen a real angel before? And how do I know, you're not an angel yourself."

ABOB, pushing his sides way out, breathed a sigh as he replied to her question.

"Mmm, "he murmured again.

"Yes......... and no."

Then he hesitated.

"Huh?" asked Slatter with a puzzled look on her face.

ABOB gruffly cleared his throat and said, "Hmmm.

Yes, I have seen many angels before.

And no, I am not an angel.

As you can clearly see, I am a very special, white donkey.

But I can tell you I see angels almost everyday; all the time.

Why, they fly right over the top of my head when I'm out in the pasture grazing.

They float around way up in the air.

They really are very beautiful to watch.

When they are gracefully flying like that, they remind me of small butterflies with very large transparent wings.

The higher they fly the smaller they look.

I think they're most beautiful in the early morning sun because that's when the sun catches their wings at a certain angle, and their wings become iridescent reflecting all of the many different colors from the earth.

Now let me tell you, that's a beautiful sight to behold.

I guess they're all out just taking care of God's business as he commands them.

They always look like they are on some sort of a mission."

ABOB giggled a little.

" You know ," he proudly stated, " I'm starting to enjoy this talking skill.

I never thought in a million years I would get to share with anyone what I just told you.

I really enjoyed sharing my words with you.

Do you enjoy sharing when you talk to others?"

Slatter nodded her head.

"Yeah," she humbly responded. She thought about the love she and her grandparents shared. She was getting wobbly and very sleepy as she listened to ABOB ramble on. Every now and then as if to demand her attention, he would stop walking. What he was really trying to do was keep her from going to sleep. He didn't want her to fall off his back and get hurt. He tried to explain to Slatter why he could see angels and she couldn't.

"You see young lady", gurgled ABOB as he pushed against the ferocious wind.

"God made animals able to see much more light than humans see, and that's why we can see with immortal eyes.

Do you not know that all things become visible when they are exposed to enough light?

Things which are seen are temporary, but the things which are not seen are eternal.

I can see many invisible things that humans cannot see.

That's how I have the ability to know when I am near danger.

I have a God given ability to sense danger."

Slatter's mouth dropped open as she couldn't believe what she had just heard.

She thought maybe that she was dreaming and when she woke up she would still be sleeping in that little cubby hole of a cavern back in the woods.

ABOB knew he had his work cut out for him keeping her awake. He did his best to walk as fast as he could as he kept on making conversation,

"I think all animals can see angels, they just don't realize what they see."

He chuckled to himself.

"I just wonder sometimes if God gave us immortal eyes since He didn't give us the ability to speak with our mouths.

I know I'm only speaking tonight because for some unknown reason, God caused me to. Maybe that's not so unusual after all. I mean, did you know that thousands of years ago, God caused another donkey to speak?"

"No."

Replied Slatter in a soft sleepy tone.

"I guess I don't remember hearin' about that story.

ABOB continued.

"Well, it's quite a story.

It's in the twenty second chapter of the book of Numbers. You need to read it some time.

If you think really hard about the story, I think you'll agree that God uses it to explain to people how they can avoid terrible obstacles in their life, if they seek Him first, because he can reveal ways to them that will prevent them from taking wrong turns in life which are contrary to His way.

Slatter curiously asked, "Oh my. Can ya read, too?"

ABOB snorted out a laugh.

"Noooooo way.

I can't read.

But I know my creator and somehow I know about that story.

I don't know how to explain it.

I just know it, that's all.

In that bible story, God opened up the mouth of the donkey and that donkey spoke, just like I spoke tonight.

God said it and that's enough for me."

Suddenly ABOB stopped and threw his head back. He vigorously shook his snowy mane slinging the snow in every direction. Flicks of the cold wet snow landed on Slatter's face startling her. She used the sleeve of her coat to brush it off. ABOB stumbled as he laughed at her, "Ha ha ha. Sorry about that, but you were almost asleep. I could tell by the limp way you were sitting on my back. If you would have become any more relaxed you would have fallen off. Hey! I had to do something to wake you. You got to admit, that's one sure way to be woke up. C'mon hang in there little lady.

We're almost there."

As an after thought he added, "Oh, by the way. Just so you'll know. I won't be able to talk like a human ever again, once I deliver you to my master. The moment you climb down off of my back, I will lose the ability to speak with an audible voice.

I don't know how I know this.

I just do.

It's been a real privilege to get to share this time with you.

I know in your world, an animal talking is totally unheard of. But, I want you to know something.

If I was ever given a choice, of whether to be able to speak in a human voice or see angels, I would choose to see angels.

From what I've seen, humans are way too busy to spend much time gazing up at the heavens.

That's the only sure way you're ever going to get to see an angel.

Slatter was so tired and confused by now, she was just wanted to get warm and go to sleep. Listening to the sounds of ABOB's soothing voice, the feel of his warm back, and feeling his hoofs as they rhythmically crunched the snow, caused her to dose off once again.

Just as she let her guard down, the unexpected happened.

Still trying to keep Slatter awake, ABOB started to trot. He didn't see the solid sheet of ice in front of him. When he stepped on it, he couldn't stop himself from sliding. All four of his legs flew out from under him and he slid into a deep, snow filled ditch. Slatter, quickly became alert and wrapped both arms around his neck so she wouldn't fall off ABOB's back. She felt him jerk and then helplessly, they sank down deep into the cold wet snow. ABOB landing on his side shouted,

"Hold on for dear life.

We're sinking to the bottom!"

Slatter, now wide awake, let go of ABOB's neck and clutched his mane with both hands. She screamed, "What's happening!"

ABOB, struggling to catch his breath tried to reply calmly so Slatter wouldn't think he was afraid, "We've .......we've sunk!

I ....... I.....lost my footing when I stepped on the ice!"

There they were stuck in the middle of a deep snow drift. The snow covered all of ABOB except for his head. They were up to ABOB's neck in trouble. Slatter had despair in her voice as she cried out, "Oh no ABOB!

We ain't got nobody to help us either.

We're really stuck big time ain't we?

Ooooooh!

What are we gonna do now!"

ABOB began to waiver back and forth as he tried to stand. He managed to pull himself up into a standing position.

"Oh my," he groaned.

"It feels soooo much better to be standing.

That snow was cold on my big belly.

Please.

Sit real still and try not to move.

Whew!

Give me just a minute to rest."

ABOB regained his composure and vigorously shook the snow off his neck. "I'm a very strong and sure footed animal and I know I can pull us out of this mess.

I need for you to have faith in me.

Just keep hanging on to me very tightly."

Slatter thought she had come to the end of the line. She started to cry as she quarreled with the donkey.

"What do ya mean hang on to ya?

I don't see how you and me are goin' anywhere.

You're standin' in snow all the way up to your neck!

How do you think you're gonna pull us out of this mess?"

ABOB grunted out a reply.

"Do you...do you think I'm just standing here doing nothing?

Don't be silly...............I've got a plan.

Just because you can't see me doing anything doesn't mean

I'm not.

I'm stomping down the snow with my hoofs.

In just a few seconds, I will have the snow packed down enough to get some traction."

The harder ABOB labored with his legs to compact the snow the more he groaned and moaned. Slatter could feel his legs moving up and down underneath the snow. She sat quietly upon his back. She was knocked about with every jolt he made. She was eager to help but didn't dare make any sudden moves until instructed. Finally, after a few minutes, ABOB yelled out to her.

"OK.

I believe we're out of here!

This snow drift is history!

Hang on!

Here we go!"

And sure enough with one big thrust, ABOB flung the heavy wet snow in every direction like a bulldozer. Using his muscular front legs to pull and his brawny back legs to push, he managed to heave himself right out of the snow drift.

# 19

# A HAUNTED LOOKING SANCTUARY

Stomping his feet on the ground, ABOB shook himself off and proceeded to move on. Both the donkey and the rider were very glad to be on the move again. Slatter mumbled under her breath, "Huh.

So much for your being sure footed and able to sense danger!"

They had only traveled a short distance when Slatter noticed they had come to a complete stop. Raising up her weary head, she found herself staring at a big old haunted looking house. The house looked empty except for a shimmer of light flickering in one of the windows. The distinctive quivering light, looked like it could be a burning candle. She hesitated to slide off of the donkey's nice warm back. After she sat there for a few minutes, she leaned over and whispered into the side of his big floppy right ear. Her voice quivered from the cold.

"I... r.-real..ly... don't know... w-what ..to do.

I.... am ..so...so...nervous... and ...so...so scared.

This...p-place.. is...s-so.... creepy... lookin'.

It...it's.... so... c-covered ...up ..in ..tr-trees.

It... even.. l-.looks.. like... it's...m-made ..out..of ..huge tr-ees!

Da...do... I... h.-have...t.-to....g.-go...inside...that..h-ouse?"

ABOB sensing how frightened she was, replied in a friendly reassuring voice.

"Oh, come on now.

You want to get warm don't you?

Haven't you figured out by now that God has taken care of you so far tonight.

Why do you think he would suddenly stop?

God takes care of his children all of the time, not just when they are in some kind of trouble. I'm sure that your loved ones are praying for your safety and believe me when I tell you this..........their prayers are being answered. Their prayers will see your through.

So please.

Have faith.

You've made it this far.

If everyone everywhere knows all the time exactly where they are going and the outcome of each and every day, there would be little need for faith.

Your faith in God must be applied in order for it to be of any use to you.

Be strong and make yourself proud.

Go along with God's plan and try not to be so scared.

I know it seems hard right now because you're lost and trying to find your way back home, but I encourage you to let go and let God take you back home His way.

I assure you by tomorrow evening, everything will turn out just fine.

I want you to remember these words from God from the book of Joshua:

Have I not commanded you? Be strong and courageous! Do not tremble or be dismayed, for the Lord your God is with you wherever you go."

Slatter's chafed lips managed to utter, "Thank you.

I'm sure that's what my grandpa would tell me if he were here. I will try and remember that verse."

ABOB stomped his back feet and swished his tail as he prepared to say goodbye to Slatter.

"I do not like having to leave you standing out here in the cold all alone, but time's getting away from us.

I've enjoyed our time together, but right now I need for you to be brave. Please slide down off of my back and walk straight up the path to that big wooden door.

We both need to get out of this frigid cold weather or we're going to end up sick.

My job is finished.

My mission is now complete."

He paused as he chuckled,

"And that's a good feeling.

I get to return to being a regular old donkey with immortal eyes. That probably doesn't mean much to you, but believe it or not, that makes me very happy.

I like who I am and what I do."

Slatter stared at ABOB. She noticed what a big thick tongue he had as it wrapped around the inside of his mouth when he talked.

She very much liked the way his long mane hung over his face and lay between his eyes. She found comfort in his eyes and she was encouraged by what he had said about God taking care of her and being with her. She remembered reading that scripture in Church, but just hearing it again lifted her spirits and made her heart feel encouraged. She thought ABOB to be a very special donkey. She thought it was possible God had sent him out into the snowy wilderness to rescue her, because only God could have known her exact location. Slatter was very cold and tense. She was looking for **ABOB** to give her some good advise. In a discouraging voice, she asked him a direct question, "Well, if I go in that old house, is there gonna be a real live person livin' in there or is there some kind of spook in it?"

**ABOB** showed his big strong teeth as if he was laughing, then politely answered,

"No.

Heavens no.

There's no spooks living in there.

I can't believe you asked me that.

After I went all the way out in those woods, and in a blizzard mind you, to bring you to safety, and you asked me a silly question like that. Now why would I, want to scare you or bring you harm?

I'll have you know, a very nice person lives in that house.

Things are not always as they appear to be. Sometimes things just look scary, when actually they're very pleasant.

Now when you slide off my back, I want you to walk over to the end of the sidewalk and open the wooden gate.

You'll see a black mail box hanging on an old wooden post there.

You'll find her name on the mailbox."

**ABOB** started to shiver and shake all over.

"Brrrrrrrrr.

I need to get back in the barn for a while and dry off.

I really do have to go now.

So go on, and slide down off of my back."

Slatter hesitated a few seconds.

She wanted to stay on **ABOB**'s back. She stubbornly inquired, "Why can't ya take me back home instead of me a goin' in that old house?"

ABOB shook his head and replied,

"Because if I don't get dried off pretty quick, I'll catch pneumonia.

Now you wouldn't want me to get sick would you?"

Slatter whispered,

"No."

She hung her head. She knew she had no choice. She slid down off of ABOB's warm back. She walked up to his head and cupped it in her hands. She affectionately rubbed her nose against his. She was so scared she had goose bumps. She didn't want him to leave her. Her voice quivered, "G..ood....b..bye .....ABOB.

Thanks for being my friend and helpin' me.

I'll never forget ya.

Thanks... f...for... f...finding...m..me.. and ..b..bringing.. me h...here.

Since Slatter had already slid off of ABOB's back, he could no longer speak. He shook his head up and down a couple of times and then buckled his two front legs under him as if he was bowing to her. Slatter took his gesture to mean.

"Your welcome."

She watched him turn and walk away toward a nearby barn. He quickly disappeared into the darkness. Slatter's thoughts quickly turned to the throbbing pain in her leg. Her need to get warm was stronger than her feeling of fear. She slowly limped over to the mail box. It was an old rusty, black metal box barely hanging on a splintered post. The box was so old, she could only make out the first name and the first two letters of the last name. The other letters were completely worn off.

She said the names aloud as she read them, "AGA........... PE....

I can't even read the name with so many letters a missin'."

She took the sleeve of her coat and tried to rub some of the dirt off of the box in hope of seeing the imprints of the rest of the letters of the last name. The dirty letters were covered with a solid sheet of ice preventing her from being able to make out any more of the letters. She finally gave up trying to figure it out and slowly made her frozen body, hobble to the front door of the old house.

When she went to knock on the door, out of the corner of her eye, she saw the shadow of a big fluctuating image flutter against the side of the house. She jumped backwards and stood real still. She felt like her heart was in her throat because it pulsated with each intense throbbing heart beat so loud it pierced her ears. She tried to show God her faith by saying aloud, " God is with me..... God is with me.... I can't see him.... but I know he's with me.

Things just seem spooky, but they're not."

When she saw the same movement a second time, she looked past the image and saw it was only a low hanging limb blowing against the house. She let out a big sigh of relief as she fell against the big door. Using the door for support, she pushed herself away from it. Again she looked around at the big frame of the old house. She could see it was covered with all kinds of ugly shadows reflecting against the bright moonlight. She convinced herself that the shadows were nothing to be afraid of because she could plainly see they were just dark reflections of the many different shapes of limbs and leaves hovering over the house. She once heard one of the old loafers at the store remark that there would be no shadows in heaven because there would not be any darkness. Right now, that was a very comforting thought.

She knew she had to get inside soon, or freeze to death. She had breathed in so much cold air, she had difficulty sucking in air to fill her frozen lungs. With great effort, she drew a big breath and pecked on the big heavy wooden door. She kept looking at the huge door as she repeatedly knocked harder with each stroke of her fist. She concluded the massive door had to have been made out of great big tree trunks. She realized her knocking was not being heard because she knew she didn't have the strength to make enough noise for someone on the other side to hear. She saw a small rock lying on the ground next to where she was standing. She grabbed it up and used it to bang on the door. Her hands were so cold and stiff she could hardly hold the rock in place. She tried to yell, but her half frozen lips wouldn't move. Knowing this was her last chance to arouse someone, she used all the strength she had left in her to pound the rock against the door. With each thrust, she became more desperate. She believed **ABOB** when he told her someone lived there. Besides, she could see light seeping through the crack underneath the door as well as a yellow glare streaming from the candle lit window.

Just as she was about to give up on anyone answering, she saw the shadow of someone's footsteps approach the door. Slatter watched the big knob on the outside of the door turn. The anticipation was more than she could bear. She thought what or who would be on the other side and would they try to harm her. Her knees were knocking together and she was breathing hard out of fear. She didn't know what to expect next.

# 20

# THE DOOR TO ANOTHER DIMINSION

As the door opened it made a slow squeaky sound. With widened eyes, Slatter was pleasantly surprised. In the faded light of a burning candle, she saw standing before her an old white headed woman. She closed her eyes and sighed as a rush of relief engulfed her icy cold body. She could feel the warm air from inside the house float past her face. The old woman's kind smile and compassionate look was like medicine to her soul. With great difficulty, she managed to make her icy cold lips form a smile back at her.

Slatter sensed a strange demeanor about the old woman, but wasn't sure what it was. She liked the way she looked. She was wearing eye glasses and her white hair was in a tight, neatly woven bun. She had on a bright blue house dress that buttoned all the way down the front with a white lacey shawl draped around her shoulders. She was very tall and slender. Her skin was a ghostly, light color and Slatter was amazed at how smooth and wrinkle free her face was. Her eyes were a beautiful, piercing blue and her cheeks were rosy red. Slatter couldn't help but wonder what an old lady like this was doing living way out in the wilderness all by herself. For a few seconds they stood and stared at each other. The old woman lowered the burning candle she was carrying as she looked Slatter over from the crown of her head to her feet. The short silence between them, only added to

Slatter's discomfort. Slatter assumed this old mysterious woman, standing in the entryway was ABOB's master. She remember the donkey telling her his master was an angel of a person. She took that to mean his master was full of kindness. She was hoping he hadn't deceived her.

The old woman could tell by the relieved expression on Slatter's face that she was grateful to find someone to help her. Slatter, totally exhausted and about to collapse, didn't know quite what to say first. With head bowed, she bashfully stated her name as calmly as she could. The dry skin on her dehydrated lips began to pull apart as she spoke softly,

"Uh, h...hello.

My name is Slatter S...Slopey."

She felt the need to explain who she was and why she was out in the middle of the night in a snow storm. Miss Peabody, with a concerned look on her face, kept staring at the helpless, pitiful looking little girl standing at her door. Slatter was so nervous she started talking too fast. With chattering teeth, She began pleading her case,

" Uh perhaps... y..ya.. have heard of my gr..grandparents, Granny B, er...uh.. I m..mean....Ber..Bernadine and J.E. ....Sl.. Slopey.

Th..they... own Slo..Slopey's General Store ...just a ....ways from h..here," Slatter paused trying to make her cold brain think of what to say next.

"I ... uh, sorta got lost in the woods... in this snow storm and I g..guess it ..w..was your donkey, ABOB, that b..brought me..here. M..may.. I ...c..come in?

I'm ...awfully c..cold and I have a cut on my leg."

She tried to point to the back of her leg. But, the old woman was looking at Slatter's blustery red face and patches of blotched skin where tears had trickled down and froze.

As she looked into Slatter's eyes, she noticed her pupils so dilated barely any color showed around the rim.

Slatter begged, "P..Please....won't ya.... let me...come in?

My.. legs are s..so.... Cold.

I ....can h..hardly... feel them."

The old woman had a shocked expression on her face as she waited for Slatter to quit talking. When Slatter finished introducing herself, the old woman, in a squeaky voice, kindly invited her inside, "Why of course you can come in," exclaimed the old woman.

You come on in here right now out of that awful weather.

Why I'm shocked to open up the door and find such a little child standing in my front door this time of night...and out there all alone in this raging blizzard!"

"And honey, you're as pale as salt!"

gasped the old woman as she put her hand to her chest.

I'll take those nasty wet outer garments of yours and lay them over by the fireplace so they can be a drying out."

Slatter felt an overwhelming sense of relief as she welcomed the opportunity to take off her slushy, wet boots. Still standing in the doorway, she removed her hat, gloves, and coat and handed them to the kind woman. Slatter thought the snow storm must have caused a power failure because she noticed there were no lights on in the house. She carefully followed this kind stranger, carrying a burning candle, into the living room of the big old spooky house.

She had no idea she had just stepped through the door to another dimension. She had plunged into the darkness of an unknown realm.

A dimension where only angels dare to trod.

Except for a loud ticking clock, there was absolute silence in the house. Slatter cleared her throat and bluntly said,

"Uh, excuse me. . ...............................

I've told ya my name, but ya didn't tell me yours."

The little old woman smiled as she replied, "Oh, I'm sorry. I didn't, did I.

I guess I haven't seen any folks in so long, I temporarily forgot my manners. My name is Aga Peabody."

Slatter, shivering all over, stood as close to the fireplace as she could without getting burned.

"Ya have no idea how very glad I am to meet you Mrs. Aga Peabody," shivered Slatter.

"I think I was about to freeze to death out there.

Now that I'm thawin' out, I'm a achin' all over."

Slatter was thankful to be by a warm fire.

"You will have to forgive me," continued Slatter.

"But I'm probably goin' to take a long to thaw out.

I'm so very thankful that you invited me into your nice warm house."

Miss Peabody and Slatter looked down at the same time at Slatter's cold purple, bare feet. Blood ,which had been seeping from the cut, was now frozen to her leg. Miss Peabody shook her head back and forth with a worried look.

"Oh my.

Mmm. Mmm, " moaned Miss Peabody with a worried look on her face.

"I suspect you just might have a touch of frost bite, little Miss Slatter Slopey."

Then she pulled a rocking chair up next to the fireplace and pointed to it as she demanded, "Now, young lady.

It would be in your best interest to do jest as I say.

Sit down right here in this rocker and rest."

Slatter, tickled to sit down anywhere, quickly plopped down in the chair. Miss Peabody then walked over and took a bright red wool blanket off the hook hanging beside the fireplace and wrapped it tightly around Slatter. She graciously advised, "I think what you need now, is a pan to soak your feet in.

Looks like your wounds need fixing right now so they don't take a turn for the worse."

She carefully picked up Slatter's wounded leg and examined it.

"If this nasty cut gets infection in it, it could get as serious as the frost bite."

Slatter raised her eyebrows as she questioned Miss Peabody, "I ain't never heard tell of frost bite. Is it somethin' very serious?"

Miss Peabody's eyebrows moved down toward her eyes, frowning she calmly replied, "Oh yes. I'm sorry to have to say in some cases it can be.

I've known people who have had their feet taken off because of it. But lucky for you, I have something very special to soak your little purple feet in.

I have to go in another room to get a pan.

I'll be back in just a minute.

You just sit there and close your eyes and relax.

God only knows what you have been through out there all by yourself in that nasty snow storm."

As she started to walk away from Slatter, she turned around and asked, "Say Slatter. Would you like me to bring you a cup of home made broth and bread? I know you have to be hungry."

Slatter thankfully replied.

"Oh yes thank you.

I would love some food, but please don't go to any trouble.

You've been way too kind to me already by lettin' me come into your home so late at night. It's gotta be way after midnight I'm sure."

Miss Peabody smiled and softly patted Slatter on the arm, then left the room.

Slatter looked around for a clock.

She noticed a big, beautiful grandfather clock in one corner of the living room. She had never seen anything like it. She was astonished at its rich looking beauty. It had explicit detailing. The wood all around it was embellished with detailed scrolls that resembled hand carved long stem roses. The legs on the clock had great big claws. It also had beautiful hanging golden weights behind the glassed in front cabinet. The clock began to chime.

It chimed twelve times.

"It's only twelve o'clock midnight," she said aloud.

"Whew.

It seems to me like I've been lost for days.

I wonder if that old thing's got the right time on it."

Too tired to really care about the time, Slatter rolled her eyes and slumped down in the rocker. The room was very quiet except for the ticking of the big clock.

She did her best to close her eyes and rest, but curiosity got the best of her. Sitting straight up in the chair, she inquisitively looked around the room. The first thing she noticed was the flicker of several burning candles. There were several different sizes sitting on top of the fireplace mantle and one sitting in each of the two big living room windows that had perfectly fitting red velvet swag curtains hanging on them. In the middle of each of the four walls hung a mysterious looking wall sconce with a big red candle in each one. The wallpaper was a golden color with huge, red velvet roses embellished on it. The ceiling was very high and was aligned with huge, dark cherry wood beams. Slatter thought the house belonged in another century. She remembered seeing pictures in a book at school of Abraham Lincoln's home and she thought Miss Peabody's living room looked similar to the way his looked. The house had a definite turn of the century look. She had never before, in her whole life, seen such furniture. The furniture in her own house was very modest and Slatter thought Miss Peabody's house looked like an old mansion. It sure looked a lot better on the inside than it did on the outside. She said to herself, Wow!

Only rich people could own this kind of stuff."

Because the house looked dilapidated on the outside and overgrown with trees, she expected the inside of the house to have a similar look; but it didn't. It was absolutely beautiful.

Slatter thought Miss Peabody to be very wealthy.

The couch, nestled in between two very small wooden end tables, was beautifully detailed with carved wood accents. Its' upholstery was a deep red velvet material. Slatter wanted to walk over and run her hand across its' neatly constructed nail head trim. A white hand crocheted afghan with colorful butterflies on it, was neatly spread across the back. Sitting on each of the end tables was a white, porcelain kerosene lamp with artistically painted luscious grapes on the vine. The lamp shades had six long teardrop crystal beads hanging off of them. In the middle of the room was a big, elegant, red and black wool rug with scalloped gold edging that added beauty and warmth. She noticed an old, wooden, trunk that sat between the two big windows. At one time it had been painted black, but now was discolored with scratches on it. It looked completely out of place sitting in a room full of luxurious looking antique furniture.

But, out of all of the beautiful furniture that she noticed, there was one item in particular that caught her attention. On the wall, right behind the red velvet couch was an antique looking, shiny, gold trimmed mirror that had scenery etched into it. The painting caused Slatter to instantly have a flash from the past. She felt as though she was looking into a mirror and once again, seeing the most unusual day of her life. Slatter stood in awe as she stared at the familiar scenery. What she saw in the picture was a barefooted, little blonde girl standing on one side of an old washed out wooden bridge, looking out over a body of water with a lot of junk floating around in it. On the edge of the bank, was a huge yellow snake with a big red tongue sticking out of his mouth. His big head was protruding high up in the air. The body of muddy water was surrounded by trees and the nearby bushes had red berries on them. There was a big angel sitting on a huge white fluffy cloud that seemed to swallow up a large portion of the sky. Slatter was intrigued with the painting. She felt compelled to get a closer look at it. Just as she was attempting to get up out of her rocker, Miss Peabody broke her concentration by walking back into the room carrying a cup of hot broth wrapped up in a neatly folded piece of white cloth.

# 21

# THE GOLDEN PITCHER

As Slatter sipped her hot broth, she focused her attention on another unusual looking item in the room. She noticed Miss Peabody had placed a large golden pitcher on top of the fireplace mantel. She closely watched as Miss Peabody reached over to pick it up and then set it down on the floor next to the rocking chair. Then, Miss Peabody kneeled down on the floor, picked up Slatter's little cold feet and place them into the porcelain dish pan. Slatter, eagerly leaned forward so she could see what was in the pitcher. She couldn't tell what it was. The liquid didn't look like anything she had ever seen before. Miss Peabody kept smiling as she slowly poured the liquid over Slatter's feet. Slatter was astounded at what she saw flowing out of the pitcher. A thick, warm, transparent golden substance slid over her feet like a spray of liquid silk. From the way her feet were feeling so soothed, Slatter knew it had to be some kind of a miraculous healing medicine. The golden liquid was so bright, she had to squint her eyes to look at it. She thought it very strange when the soothing scent of fresh flowers filled the room.

When her feet were completely covered with the golden substance, Miss Peabody sat the pitcher back down on the floor. She dipped her forefinger into the porcelain bowl and as she reached behind Slatter's leg, she rubbed the golden liquid off of her finger into the open wound. Slatter immediately felt a deep warmth come over her feet and legs.

She didn't know whether it was the golden liquid her feet were soaking in or the delicious hot broth that was making her feel so warm and relaxed. Slatter leaned back in her chair and sighed with relief. She moaned loudly, "Ooooooh. Man that stuff feels sooo good to my feet."

Miss Peabody just smiled a big your welcome smile and set the golden pitcher back on top of the fireplace mantel. Still smiling, she seated herself in one of the red velvet chairs next to her guest. Miss Peabody ordered, "You need to sit there for a little while and let your feet soak in that liquid. You'll be better before you know it."

Slatter had no intention of arguing with her. She thought Miss Peabody's suggestion was an extremely splendid idea. She laid her head back against the rocker and gave her an obedient nod.

Slatter was very warm and relaxed and full of questions. She wanted to ask Miss Peabody about the painting in the mirror behind her couch. After she had relaxed a few minutes, she opened her eyes and pointed at it as she boldly inquired, "I've been wonderin' 'bout somethin'," she asked. Where in the world did ya get that paintin' that's a hangin' over there behind your couch?"

Miss Peabody looked up at the painting and sighed as she answered Slatter's question.

"Well," began Miss Peabody.

"One day this last summer, there was a very pleasant young man that came by my house selling his paintings.

He asked me if I wanted to buy one of them, so, I looked through what he had and decided I liked that one the best.

We visited a while, and he shared some stories with me about some of his extensive travels.

He was an intriguing young man.

I enjoyed his company so much I fixed him a nice lunch and in return he gave me the painting.

I thought we made a pretty good trade.

Isn't it just beautiful?

I love the colors in it.

I really like the way the angel is sitting up there on that great big, fluffy, cloud.

He sure was talented when it came to painting the heavens.

To me, the expression on the angel's face says it all."

Miss Peabody stopped smiling and her face took on a serious look as she walked over and stood in front of the painting.

"I think his facial expressions reflect his total submission and obedience to God.

He seems to be saying something like here am I Lord............ send me.....wherever....whatever." She laugh quietly.

She then noticed Slatter had an odd look on her face. She could tell by the way her little visitor was looking at the painting, it was bothering her. Miss Peabody felt compelled to ask Slatter what was wrong.

"Is there something wrong with this painting or something?"

Miss Peabody softly asked.

"You've got a look on your face that's telling me you're seeing something that is upsetting you."

Slatter kept staring at the painting as if she were in some sort of daze. Once again Miss Peabody tried to get Slatter's attention by asking her another question.

"Uh mm," Miss Peabody cleared her throat.

"Slatter," she said her name louder.

Would you please care to share with me what you're seeing?"

You seem very fascinated with it."

After the second prompting, Slatter, with her eyes still affixed on the painting, swallowed as she finally, but reluctantly replied.

"W...well," she started stammering then regained her composure.

"I ...I was just wonderin' 'bout somethin'.

What's the young man's name that gave ya the paintin'?"

Slatter was hoping Miss Peabody would tell her the young man's name was Gappy. Miss Peabody, put her forefinger to her mouth like she was trying to remember his name. She paced back and forth in front of the mirrored painting. After what seemed like a long pause she answered using a young girl's giggle, "Oh, my.

You know, now that you mention it. I guess I must've forgotten to ask him his name. Why do you want to know his name?

Do you know someone who paints scenes on mirrors?"

She waited for Slatter's response.

Filled with disappointment, Slatter softly spoke in a low voice, "Oh...er.. uh... no I don't.

I guess his name ain't important after all."

Slatter felt like she had to explain her shocked reactions to the painting.

"Please don't think I'm silly, but I have the strangest feelin' I've been to the place in that paintin' before.

I mean, don't ya think that blonde headed girl standin' on the end of that old washed out bridge looks a whole lot like me? And do ya see that big yellow snake curled up on the bank? He looks jest like a big mean yellow snake I saw one time. Look at all that junky stuff a floatin' 'round in the old muddy water."

She kept pointing at the painting as she talked.

"I think that's the same old junk hole pond not too far from where I live."

Miss Peabody had turned her back to the painting to look at Slatter, so she turned around toward the painting and began studying it.

Acting puzzled and with a surprise look on her face she said, "Oh, honey. There's no junk floating around in the water and there's not a little girl standing on the end of the washed out bridge either. She ran her finger over the painting, as she continued talking.

"Now right there is a big, yellow snake and look up here on the cloud. Now that's a real looking angel sitting on that big, white cloud. Doesn't that cloud look beautiful and serene? It looks as soft as cotton and as big as a mountain. But that's all I see in the painting. I guess all that time you spent out in the cold must've caused you to start seeing things. I'm sure you'll see things differently in the morning.... things always look different in the daylight."

Miss Peabody dismissed Slatter's remarks and continued talking about the painting.

"I will tell you this much," she giggled putting her right hand over her mouth.

"One of the reasons I wanted the picture in the first place was because that big yellow snake is in it. I suppose that sounds silly to you, but it's true."

Miss Peabody noticed Slatter looked confused so she tried to get her mind off of the picture. She had excitement in her voice when she said, "Let me explain to you about the big yellow snake. Would ya like that?" Slatter nodded her head yes.

"Well, you see, I had a brother named Andy.

He lived in Africa for a very long time because he loved the jungle and all of the mystery it held.

He had a pet puff adder snake he named, Savo.

Puff adders are big yellow snakes that have crescent shaped markings on them and when they get excited, they have the ability to inflate their bodies. Sometimes, they get so large, they look deformed. I think they are somewhat related to the yellow side winder snakes. Andy was so very fond of big Savo. Over the years, he had developed a strange attachment to him. Andy told me one time that when he would talk to Savo, he would coil up into a big ball and stick his head straight up in the air. Then he said that Savo would flash his big red eyes at him like he was actually, somehow, understanding what Andy was saying. I'm sure that probably sounds ridiculous to you, but I was gullible enough to believe everything my brother told me.

One time Andy told me a story about old Savo.

It was about the time the snake became a security guard for him." Miss Peabody snickered a little.

"I know that sounds strange, but please bear with me because Andy swore up and down the story is true.

After you hear the story, you'll have to admit it makes sense.

During the time when Andy lived in Africa, he grew his own crop of tobacco. When it came time to harvest the tobacco crop, the natives would steal it for their own use. The natives loved to smoke tobacco in their special pipes they make themselves.

At that time, tobacco was a high price commodity within the villages.

Well," she put her hand to her mouth as she giggled, "Andy just had to find a way to stop the natives from stealing. He got the bright idea to find a baby puff adder snake, make it a pet and put it out in the middle of the tobacco field after dark to keep the natives out. He wanted a puff adder snake because it could make itself get great big and besides, all of the natives thought that particular snake to be possessed with bad spirits. He hunted and hunted until he found one. He made it a pet and named it big Savo. My brother even caught rats in specially designed cages just to feed Savo.

Everyone, but Andy was extremely afraid of big Savo. Each night about dark, Andy let old Savo roam around in his tobacco fields; then in the morning at the first break of daylight, he would go out and find him, put him in a big cloth bag and put him back in his glass cage.

So, it worked.

No one ever again stole any tobacco out of my brother's field once word got out that old Savo was living there. The natives called Andy bigoostra Midwan which meant Man with spirit of snake. When Andy came back home to live, he couldn't bare the thought of leaving his old friend behind, so he didn't. He loaded him up and brought him home to live here, with us. But, I guess old Savo didn't like it here. Because one day, he just up and disappeared. We never did know what happened to him. Oh, but that was a very long time ago."

Slatter kept staring at the painting as she listened to her story.

Her mind was drifting back to the junk hole pond when she had seen a very similar big yellow snake with red flashing eyes. She wondered if the snake in Miss Peabody's story was the same snake she had seen at the junk hole pond. Perhaps, Mingler had a second name and maybe his second name was.......................big Savo.

When Miss Peabody had finished her story, Slatter's eyes were wide with interest. She was still trying to figure out why the two of them saw different objects in the mirrored painting. She impatiently stated, "That's a very good snake story, Miss Peabody. But are ya tellin' me I am seein' a totally different picture in that painting than you are seeing?

How can that be?

That's way too weird!"

As Miss Peabody walked back over to where Slatter was sitting, Slatter noticed she did not have any reflection in the mirror. Fear gripped her stomach. She instantly remembered being down at the junk hole pond and how her friend, Gappy didn't have a reflection in the water either. She became very uncomfortable. But as she thought about how friendly and kind Miss Peabody had been to her, she became calm again. She couldn't help but wonder, Was Miss Peabody an angel dressed up as an old woman and could Gappy have been an angel too? How silly of me to think that. Maybe Miss Peabody is right. Maybe I was out in the cold way too long or maybe I'm havin' a bad dream and I'm goin' to wake up and find myself back at home in my own bed. Slatter shook her head like she was trying to wake herself up. If this was a dream, it sure felt awful real.

Miss Peabody wanted Slatter to feel wanted and welcome in her home, so she walked over to her and kindly touched her hand.

Shaking her head back and forth, she tried to console her with caring words, "You know, I think you are one very tired little girl.

And perhaps being out so long in the cold is causing you to imagine things."

Slatter could tell by the way Miss Peabody was acting that when they each looked into the mirrored painting, they were seeing two entirely different scenes. Slatter thought since the objects looked all too familiar, and she had gone so long without sleep, Miss Peabody was probably right about her imagining some very unusual things.

Miss Peabody's kind demeanor was very comforting to Slatter. She seemed so caring and easy to talk to. But there was something a little bit peculiar about her. Slatter began to get the same peaceful feeling she felt when she was around her old friend, Gappy. Slatter wanted to know more about her new found friend so she changed the subject.

"Have ya ever been married Miss Peabody?"

Still staring at the mirror painting, Miss Peabody responded.

"Oh, no child.

I never married.

As I mentioned to you earlier, I had a brother I lived with.

His full name was Andopholus Peabody.

I always just called him Andy.

He passed away several years ago and I miss him dearly.

I took care of him until he died.

You might say I took care of him all of his life because he never married either. He was a very well traveled, renowned man.

He did have a very good friend named Ossie Humphrey. Mr. Humphrey was the man that sold my brother all of this wooded land here where I live. My brother made him a cash offer on the land and Mr. Humphrey took the money and left the country.

I think all total, Andy bought about a hundred acres of woods from Mr. Humphrey. As odd as it seems, we never heard from him again."

Slatter's eyes lit up when Miss Peabody mentioned the name, Humphrey.

She felt her heart turn a flip flop out of fear, but not one time did she allow her fear to show to Miss Peabody.

She was trying very hard to act grown up and hold her fears inside. However, she suddenly realized that Miss Peabody had just confirmed her greatest fear;

Due to the harsh winter storm, she had become disoriented and walked into the woods that led to Humphrey's Lane.

Miss Peabody, with a far away look on her face, stared at the fireplace as she kept on talking. Slatter could tell how much Miss Peabody loved her brother because it seemed like he was all she talked about. Smiling to herself, she kept describing him to Slatter. "Poor old Andy.

He never seemed to be content and satisfied with anything.

He was always wanting more of everything.

More of this and more of that.

He wanted to buy all the land around him so he could be surrounded by trees, like it was when he lived in Africa.

He had this place built out of trees cut right here on his own property.

He was an outdoorsman and loved living way out here in the middle of no where. Because he led such a busy life dealing with all kinds of people in all walks of life, he got sick of dealing with them. He wanted to retire to a place where he could not be bothered by anyone. He became like a hermit... living out here in this wilderness."

Suddenly Miss Peabody paused and her face changed from happy to sad. Her eyes looked toward the floor when she said, "When my Andy became ill, he sent for me. I immediately came and took care of him until he died.

All of this furniture that you see here in this living room all came from his many travels.

He never did marry, so when he passed away, he left everything right here in this house to me.

Everything he owned in the world is right here."

As Miss Peabody nonchalantly took her eyeglasses off her face and cleaned them with her dress tail, she never stopped talking.

"I tried my best to tell him about God, but he just didn't want to listen.

I tried to tell him that he needed to store some treasures up in heaven instead of storing everything in this old house. Everything you see here, Slatter, will either rot, rust, or somehow ruin.

He just didn't believe in the hereafter.

He was a sad, selfish man.

He never really cared too much about anyone or anything outside of his own personal interests.

He was a mess, but I loved him very much."

Slatter, still sitting in the rocker soaking her feet, had a concerned look on her face as she respectfully listened to Miss Peabody.

"Oh dear.

I'm so sorry.

I have rattled on and on about my brother.

Am I boring you?"

Slatter nodded her sleepy head.

"Oh, No.

Of course not.

I have enjoyed hearing about your family.

What Slatter really wanted to do was ask Miss Peabody about the unusual looking trunk that was sitting between the two windows. Pointing at the trunk, she mustered up enough nerve to inquire, "Uh, if I might ask.

Why do ya have that old junky lookin' trunk sittin' in here with all of this beautiful furniture?

It looks so out of place."

Miss Peabody timidly smiled as she nodded her head.

"Well, now that you mention it, I guess it does look a little out of place.

That trunk is very old.

It belonged to my brother and I have not opened it since he died. I don't have a clue what's in it."

With renewed attention, Slatter scooted up to the edge of the chair. Miss Peabody noticed Slatter had taken a great interest in the trunk.

"Come to think of it," said Miss Peabody, "Andy spent the last days of his life right there on that couch."

She pointed to the beautiful red velvet couch Slatter had very much admired.

"Funny thing.

He always wanted that old trunk close by his side for some reason."

Slatter had an uneasy tone in her voice as she posed her question, "When did Andy, er...uh..I mean Mr. Peabody pass away?"

Miss Peabody hung her head.

"Well, it seems like only yesterday," She softly uttered.

"but it has been many years ago."

She got up out of her chair and dragged the trunk over beside Slatter and with a big grin on her face when she delightfully suggested,

"I know.

How about we just open it and see what's in it!

Now is a good of time as any!"

Miss Peabody observed Slatter's response. Slatter just stared at the trunk as a smile tugged at the corners of her mouth.

Miss Peabody asked again, "Well.

You didn't answer me.

You do think it would be fun ................to open the trunk."

Slatter shrugged her shoulders,

"I guess," she bashfully replied.

"I mean, I don't care.

It's your brother's stuff.

What do you think is in it?"

Miss Peabody grunted a little as she leaned over to tilt the trunk on its side.

"Oh I think there's probably just a lot of memories in that old thing, but we're going to find out right now."

She jerked a key off of the bottom of it.

"Here's the key, she said proudly.

Suddenly, she acted as if she remembered something. She dropped the key into the pocket on her dress and as she slowly rose to her feet she said,

"Oops!

Before we start this project," she held up her left forefinger, "we had better finish our first one."

Slatter carefully watched Miss Peabody as she walked out of the room and back in with a big fluffy towel to dry her feet.

Miss Peabody knelt back down on the floor and when she picked Slatter's feet up out of the golden liquid, they were no longer purple.

They were the same color as the rest of her skin.

Slatter excitedly yelled, "Well would ya look at that!

If I had frost bite, I certainly don't have it now!

Boy, do my feet feel great!"

Slatter, feeling all warm and cozy, was grateful to be in a house with a nice warm fire.

As soon as Miss Peabody left the room to clean up the dishpan, Slatter stood up and began wiggling her toes. It felt so good not to be numb. She noticed the pain from her leg was gone too. She reached to feel the cut, but it was completely gone. Her leg felt smooth and silky. She walked over to the fireplace mantel and peeked inside the golden pitcher to see what kind of miracle cure was in it. The pitcher was empty. Slatter's mouth dropped open. She was astonished. She wondered how the liquid could have vanished into thin air. When Miss Peabody came back into the living room, Slatter inquired about the substance in the golden pitcher, "Miss Peabody," she demanded, "What in the world was in that golden pitcher? Not only are my feet completely healed but so is the cut behind my leg.

There isn't even a scab or nothin'. I can't even tell where I had a cut. "

Miss Peabody, trying to avoid discussing the substance in the golden pitcher, gave Slatter a capricious smile as she answered, "Oh, it's just a secret concoction that I keep around.

I'm glad you are feeling all better now."

Slatter wasn't satisfied with Miss Peabody's answer, but to avoid sounding disrespectful, she didn't pursue her line of questioning any further. Miss Peabody went back into the kitchen and brought out a beautifully flowered tea pot and two tea cups. She poured them both a cup of hot tea and sat the tea pot down on a small wooden table in front of the couch. With great difficulty, she managed to sit down on the floor in front of the fireplace. She picked up her cup of hot tea and leaned up against the couch. Heaving a sigh of relief, she patted the floor beside her and contently requested, "Come here, my little friend and sit down beside me.

Let's drink some of my special hot herb tea together while we open up my brother's pitiful looking old trunk. Then, I am going to make you a nice warm bed on the couch so that you can get some rest.

Tomorrow is Christmas Eve and I want to make sure you get home before Christmas. I have an old sled, out back in the barn and come morning, I'll hitch up old **ABOB** and we will see to it you get home." Slatter became excited thinking about going home. She clapped her hands together and her face gleamed with joy. All at one, Miss Peabody noticed a worried look come over her face. Something disturbing had instantly crept into her mind and over powered her joy. Slatter was thinking about how worried her Granny B and her grandpa must be about her. Miss Peabody cocked her head to the side saying, "Did I say something wrong?" Slatter didn't answer. Instead, she plopped down on the floor next to Miss Peabody. Without saying a word, she picked up her tea cup and sipped a drink of tea.

"Yucky poo!" shrieked Slatter wrinkling up her nose with a disgusted look on her face.

"This tastes awful!

It ain't got no sugar in it!

Gee Whiz.

How do ya drink that stuff?

Whewee!

Granny B puts sugar in her tea.

I thank ya anyways, but I jest can't finish drinkin' that stuff."

Miss Peabody took the cup from Slatter and sat it down on the table.

"Oh, that's ok.

I drink my tea pretty strong and it probably tasted bitter to you."

Slatter missed her grandparents very much and she couldn't help but to express her feelings as she answered Miss Peabody's question.

"I didn't mean not to answer your question.

You didn't say anythin' wrong.

I just wish I could go home tonight and sleep in my own bed," whined Slatter. Her bottom lip started to quiver. She couldn't hide her home sick feelings any longer. She began to sob.

"I've been so scared and so cold for so long.

I think the only thing that was a keepin' me alive out in those cold dark woods was Granny B and my grandpa a prayin' for me. Sometimes I thought I could hear their voices callin' out to me."

I've lived with them since my mother died and they're the only mom and dad I've ever known.

I love them very much and I feel so bad cause I've brought heartache and grief to 'em because I disobeyed.

They must be worried sick about me.
They may even think I'm dead!"

Miss Peabody reached over and patted Slatter's hand, as she wiped away the tears from her face.

She whispered,

"There. There.

Now don't cry.

It's ok.

Save your tears for when you need them.

Everything is going to be alright."

She could see Slatter had backed out of her comfort zone. She decided to cheer up Slatter by saying nice things about her grandparents.

"You know, Slatter.

Over the years, I have heard some very nice compliments about your grandparents.

I have heard your grandpa is a man of God and your Granny B is a Godly woman.

Their faith in God is very strong.

Believe me.

They haven't given up hope of finding you."

Then in a matter of fact tone of voice she declared,

"I'm sure they are praying for you this very minute."

Startled, Slatter slowly scooted away from Miss Peabody. There was something about the way she patted her hand. It was at that moment, Slatter remembered sitting with her friend Gappy at the junk hole pond. She distinctly remembered how he patted her hand the very same way Miss Peabody had just patted her hand. Slatter didn't like the peculiar, uneasy feeling she had in the pit of her stomach. She remembered Gappy's bright blue eyes, his silky smooth skin, and his fluffy, shiny, white hair. She looked into Miss Peabody's bright blue eyes like she was trying to see through a window. She felt goose bumps pop up on her arms. For an instant, she thought she was looking right into the face of her long lost friend, Gappy. As she stared at Miss Peabody, she scarcely whispered, "Gappy............ is that you?"

Miss Peabody gave Slatter an odd look.

"Excuse me," she said with raised eyebrows.

What did you ask me?"

Slatter realized what she said must've sounded foolish.

Embarrassed, she just quickly glanced down at the old trunk sitting in front of them. Miss Peabody reached over and gave Slatter a reassuring hug.

"Oh, come on now.

Where's your faith?

Everything is going to be alright, you'll see.

Just remember Slatter, the one thing I've found out over the years, is **what is meant to be, will always find a way.**"

Slatter gave her a funny look and Miss Peabody giggled a little.

"Someday," she said as she shook her finger at Slatter.

"You'll understand a lot more things that you do right now. Nothing in this old world stays the same.

Just trust me on that.

Life is a book and everyday is a new chapter."

Then she handed Slatter the key to the trunk and said.

"Ok kiddo.

Let's move on to bigger and better things.

Dry your tears and let's have some fun.

You're the lucky one tonight.

You get to open the trunk."

## 22

# FINDING A VALUABLE TREASURE

Slatter excitedly stuck the key into the keyhole of the old trunk and the lid popped open. She immediately saw the trunk was full of old odd shaped newspapers dated May 23, 1854. Slatter began to think about where she had seen that date before. Then, she remembered that was the date on her secret map. A wonderful realization began to flood her mind. During the storm, could she have actually gotten lost in the wilderness down Humphrey's Lane? Could this house she is sitting in be the very house that was marked on her secret map? The more she thought about the secret map, the more she remembered about it. As Slatter's anticipation grew, she started whispering out loud to herself.

"Mmm.

Let's see now.

That name A. Peabody.

I'm sure that was the name on the secret map.

Let me think now. Oh my gosh! Andy Peabody. That's it! That's it! There were some letters too. Oh, now I remember the letters were D.I.T.

Maybe they meant that whatever kind of treasure it was, the IT stood for IN TRUNK.

Miss Peabody noticed Slatter talking to herself and she curiously asked, "What on earth are you jabbering about?"

Slatter was so excited she turned to Miss Peabody and in a pleading escalading tone asked, "Oh Could I please dig through the trunk?"

Laughing softly, Miss Peabody waved her hand downward, giving Slatter the go ahead to do as she pleased.

"Why sure," she answered.

"Go right ahead.

I said we were going to look inside the trunk didn't I?

What are you waiting for?

Be my guest.

I'm watching you stare at that old trunk like you think there is a buried treasure in it."

Slatter's face gleamed with excitement. Looking at Miss Peabody with hope in her eyes she seriously confessed, "Miss Peabody.

Please don't laugh at me, but I have a very good reason to think there is a hidden treasure somewhere inside this old trunk."

Slatter very carefully started taking each newspaper out of the trunk and carefully unfolded each one. When she pulled the last one out, she had a disappointed look on her face when she saw the trunk was empty. Suddenly, out of the corner of her eye, she saw something glimmer on the left side of the trunk. She ran her hand down the inside and felt another key. It was taped onto the side. She tore the tape off of the key and looked for a keyhole. Because the wood was so old, she couldn't see anything on the inside except black. Miss Peabody watched Slatter frown as she struggled to see inside the dark trunk. She reached over and picked up one of her porcelain kerosene lanterns that was burning and held it close to the trunk. Benefiting from the light, Slatter spotted a small keyhole on the bottom. With a surprised look, she smiled as she looked up at Miss Peabody. She happily yelled out, "Oh my gosh! Look what I found!"

There must be a secret compartment in the bottom.

Can I open it?

Miss Peabody, enjoying Slatter's excitement, nodded her head and very calmly replied, "Oh by all means, we should open it.

I mean we've come too far to turn back now."

Slatter was so excited her hands started to shake. She finally got the secret compartment unlocked. She reached inside and pulled out another old, folded up newspaper, only this time there was something in it. She slowly unfolded it. There lay a small, blackened rock about the size of a large marble. It glistened all over like it had glitter on it. Slatter kept turning the rock around and around in her hand as she frowned. She felt disappointed. Surely, the priceless treasure she so desperately sought, couldn't turn out to be just an ugly black rock. She didn't have a clue what the rock was or why it was so important that it needed to be hidden in a secret compartment in an old trunk. As she continued rolling it around in her hand, she curiously asked, "What in this world is it?"

Miss Peabody, acting surprised, raised her eyebrows as she reached over to touch the rock. As soon as she got a close look she knew exactly what it was. She exclaimed, "Well, well, my little friend. That is a real, unfinished, uncut, exquisite diamond."

Laughing under her breath Slatter spoke quietly to herself, "Oooooh............ now I remember what the letters on the map were.

D.I.T. The letters must stand for............. diamond in trunk.

Slatter couldn't take her eyes off the rock. She leaned over toward the light so she could see it better. She replied,

"Well, I ain't never seen nothin' like this thing."

Miss Peabody made a fist with her right hand and put it to her mouth like she was remembering something. Smiling at Slatter, she said,

"Well, come to think of it, I do remember the time Andy showed me that diamond.

Many years ago he brought it back from one of his diamond mines he owned in Africa.

He did his best to explain to me how unusual and valuable it was." Squinting her eyes, she marveled at the diamond as she made a clicking noise with her mouth.

"My oh my, I haven't seen that thing in years.

I thought perhaps he had sold it on the diamond market years ago. Mmmm.

I guess not."

It's kind of ugly isn't it?

I've seen many a diamond while they were in the rough.

They pretty much all look the same to me.

That's how my brother always had so much money. Boy did he love money. He centered his whole life around money."

She laughed and threw her hands up in the air.

"What can I say!

He owned a diamond mine in Africa.

At least he did for a while, anyway.

The mine is closed now.

All mined out.

All good things must come to an end I guess."

Slatter, still feeling disappointed, half heartedly agreed with Miss Peabody by saying, "Well, you're right about one thing Miss Peabody. It's kind of plain and ugly. It shore don't look like much to me. I can't see one pretty thing about this thing.

I thought diamonds were all shiny, and clear.

I didn't know a diamond could look ever look like this!"

It just looks like an old black rock to me."

Miss Peabody patted Slatter on the arm as she assuredly replied, "Oh, believe me, child.

It isn't just an old black rock.

It's got a name.

It's called a diamond in the rough."

# 23

# A DIAMOND IN THE ROUGH

Miss Peabody continued explaining to Slatter about diamonds.

"Well, little lady. Allow me to share with you some of the knowledge about diamonds that I've gained over the years.

You see Slatter. A lot of hard work goes into the making of a diamond."

Slatter drew her knees up to her chest as she attentively listened to Miss Peabody.

"Diamonds form down in the ground just like coal does," continued Miss Peabody.

"When a diamond is dug out of the earth, it is surrounded by a lot of waste material. Andy called this waste 'excess baggage.' The waste has to be separated from the diamond by a crushing procedure.

In fact, the waste has to be crushed several times in order to get to the diamond.

It is a very costly and lengthy procedure.

This diamond that we are looking at has only been partially crushed.

The diamond that is in the middle of that rock looking substance is about the size of a nickel; which is pretty extraordinary in itself.

How that diamond is cut out will determine it's worth."

Slatter was absorbing every word Miss Peabody was saying so she could learn all about the diamond. Still totally engrossed in their conversation, Slatter inquisitively asked, "What do ya reckon the diamond inside this rock is worth?"

Miss Peabody took the diamond out of Slatter's hands and examined it very closely.

"Oh, to me it looks like it could be cut very clear. Of course, I'm no diamond expert, but, I have seen several over the years.

It looks like it's going to be rather large, so....oh, I'd guess it should be worth somewhere in the neighborhood of ten to twenty thousand dollars give or take a few thousand. That is if you took it to a good master diamond cutter who knows how to cut it just right."

Miss Peabody handed the diamond back to Slatter.

With eyes bulging out of her head, she screamed,

"Ten to twenty thousand dollars! Holy Cow!

Wow!

I can't believe it!

I really did find a treasure!"

Miss Peabody tried to calm Slatter as she placed one hand on her arm. She repeated what she had just said, "Remember now what I said, Slatter. It is only worth that much money if it is cut properly.

If it is turned over to a master diamond cutter, he is the one who determines the value of the diamond."

Slatter pleaded with Miss Peabody to tell her more about diamonds. Miss Peabody, fully aware Slatter was thinking how rich she would become if she could sell the rock for a lot of money, cautioned her by saying, "Honey. You know there is an old saying that goes,

'Things that come too easily, have a tendency not to be of high value to the acquired.'

Everyone appreciates the value of money a lot more if they have to earn it. Always remember one must never use money to measure wealth. Acquiring wealth can become addicting. People who love money think only of adding to what they already have and spend their entire lives thinking of ways to protect it. Yet, when they die, they leave it all behind for others to squander as they see fit. Most of the time, they never take time to smell the roses or share in their loved ones' lives."

Slatter had an astonished look on her face when Miss Peabody finished speaking. Miss Peabody was glad Slatter was listening so closely to her advice.

Pouring herself another cup of tea, she continued to explain to Slatter about diamonds. As Miss Peabody spoke, Slatter watched her form her lips to sip her hot tea. Something about her mouth reminded Slatter of Mrs. Kohler, her school teacher.

"You see," remarked Miss Peabody, placing her cup in it's saucer, as she continued to explain further about a diamond's detailed clarification.

"Diamond cutting and shaping is an exquisite skill that takes years of experience to acquire.

In olden days, the meticulous skill was handed down from generation to generation.

Now a days, it's very difficult to find even one jeweler with remarkable diamond cutting expertise. In this generation, I understand one can even go to school to acquire the skill. There are many people who manage to cut a diamond, but there are very few master diamond cutters, with a steady hand, left in the world. One little sliver of a cut the wrong way and a precious diamond that could be worth thousands of dollars will be worth only a few hundred dollars.

Believe me.

One thing I learned for sure from my brother's adventures is a diamond cutter is the one that can make a diamond priceless or worthless.

He has a great power within his skill.

Because he is a creator, it is also within his realm to create a very expensive, dazzling stone that has superb clarity.

The more clarity a stone has, the more it sparkles, and the more it is worth. On the other hand, he can cut the diamond the wrong way and it will have a cloudy look. Cloudy diamonds don't usually sell very well because they always look dirty and they don't have a brilliant, twinkling sparkle. Sometimes a diamond can be so wrongly cut, it loses its' value totally. It becomes so worthless it has to be thrown away." Miss Peabody smiled.

"You know what?" asked Miss Peabody.

I just thought of something. Talking about this diamond and the important skill of a diamond cutter reminds me of a very special story. Have you ever heard the bible story about the Potter and the Clay?" Slatter thought for a few seconds before she replied, "No.

I don't think I have."

"Well," Miss Peabody said,

"It's a very good story. It would make a lovely bed time story. Slatter eagerly awaited her story, "Oh please do tell me the story. My grandpa always tries to tell me a story when he's tryin' to help me understand something real important.

I'll understand it better if ya tell me in your own words though."

Miss Peabody picked up her cup of tea and laughed a little as she took a sip. Then, she said, "Alright then, I will tell it to you in my own words. It goes something like this.

'God told Jeremiah to go to the potter's house.

When he got there, the potter was making something on the wheel.

The vessel of clay that the potter was making, was spoiled in the hand of the potter.

So he reshaped the clay and made it into another vessel.

When the second vessel turned out well, this pleased the potter.

Then God said to Jeremiah,

Can I not deal with you, O house of Israel, as this potter dealt with his clay?

Behold, like the clay in the potter's hand, so are you in my hand.'

When we give our heart to God, we become his vessel. God becomes the potter and we become the clay.

The clay is sort of like the diamond and the diamond cutter that we've been talking about is sort of like God.

God is your creator.

God determines your worth.

To be worth more to God, you must be willing to let Him guide and direct your path.

God could make everyone serve him if he wanted to.

But God wants people to use their own free will to come to him. I believe God directed your path here tonight.

He has a plan of salvation just for you.
He even gives you the faith to accept him.
Do you know what faith is Slatter?"
Miss Peabody had Slatter's full attention.
Slatter was fascinated with her story.
She enthusiastically replied.
"I think I do.
Slatter hesitated as she thought about the meaning of the story. Do ya think maybe that story also means that when somebody messes up in life, God gives em a second chance?
I mean if we're the clay and He's the potter, he can keep smashin' us down to a glob of clay and shape us into what he wants us to be."

"Well," said Miss Peabody as she gazed into Slatter's eyes.
For such a little girl, I think that is a very good analogy of that story.
God is a God of second chances.
Every time people mess up and ask him to forgive them of their wrong doings, he forgives.
People are going to continue to mess up in life, because they're not perfect. The key word here is **ASK**. People must acknowledge the fact God can and will forgive, but they have to ask.
You have not because you ask not."
Slatter, picking at her fingernails, acted a little embarrassed when she asked, "Miss Peabody, can I ask you a real serious question?" Miss Peabody kindly replied,
"Of course you can.
What is it?"
Slatter reluctantly asked,

What would ya say faith is."

Miss Peabody stood up and walked over to the fireplace mantel. She picked up an old, ragged bible and then sat down next to Slatter. As she opened up the bible, an old piece of paper with notes scribbled on it fell out. Slatter noticed the date on the top of the paper was dated December 24, 1854.

Miss Peabody picked up the piece of paper and began to read, "These are some notes I made from a sermon I heard one time a very long time ago.

I would like to read them to you."

With great compassion, Miss Peabody began to read her notes.

"Faith is the substance of things hoped for, the evidence of things not seen.

Faith is never easy.

Faith means clinging to the hope God will eventually be victorious over whatever difficult situation you may be going through.

Faith is the guide and love is the road as you travel down the highways of life.

You cannot please God without faith.

Faith is not a feeling.

Faith is an assurance.

Faith comes to you by hearing about it and hearing by the word of God.

For by grace, you have been saved through faith."

Miss Peabody could see Slatter was perplexed.
She put her notes back into her bible as she laid it on the floor beside her.
"You see Slatter.
You cannot get into heaven any other way except through accepting Jesus as your personal savior.
You must believe God sent to earth his only begotten son, Jesus, to die on a cross for your sins.
There's an old saying ' seeing is believing.'
Well.
When you believe in God and accept Jesus as your personal savior, He gives you a new set of eyes.
You learn to walk by faith, not sight.
God says believing is seeing.
You begin to look at circumstances in your life in a totally different way.
You realize that you only pass through this life but once, and then you are at the door to eternity.
When a person dies, all that matters at that moment is whether or not they have given their heart to God.
Anything else that a person has done during their lifetime, does not determine where they will spend eternity.
Slatter added to the conversation by saying.
"My grandpa and my Granny B are good people.
They do kind things for people all of the time.
They are Christian folks."
As Miss Peabody took another sip of her tea, she replied,
"I'm very glad to hear that they are Christians, doing Godly works. But some people think they can get to heaven just by doing good works.

No one can ever be good enough to go to heaven on their own accord.

Doing all the good you can for God while you're here on earth should be a Christian's goal, but good works cannot get you a ticket into heaven.

Jesus is the only ticket to heaven.

He paved the way, purchased your ticket for you, not with money, but with his own holy blood. He became the perfect sacrifice for your sins, and was crucified on a cross, rose again, and sits on the right hand of God.

This ticket is free to everyone who will accept Jesus.

You must have a total change of heart and turn your life over to Him. You are saved through grace by faith. When you pray to God, after you've accepted him into your heart, He forgives you of your sins. Because God cannot look upon sin, He somehow sees the blood of Jesus miraculously cover your sins. He not only forgives you, but also forgets them as he scatters them as far as the east is from the west. He remembers them no more."

Miss Peabody reached over and touched Slatter's arm cheerfully stating,

"Then my dear.

All of God's promises belong to you.

Isn't that wonderful?

Jesus has done it all for you.

Just remember, once you become a Christian, you become his child.................. a part of God's own family.

Just like an earthly family, when a child is disobedient and asks for forgiveness, his loving parents love and forgive him.

God is our heavenly loving parent that forgives us too when we ask.

Did you know when you become a member of the family of God, no one can snatch you out of the palm of his hand absolutely no one. What God does, he does forever. You belong to him forever and ever. He wants you to allow Him to take your life and mold it into whatever he wants you to be; just like the potter and the clay.

Oh, you will have struggles in your life 'cause it's your nature to try and do things your way, instead of God's way.

But when you mess up, all you have to do is be sincerely sorry for what you did wrong and ask God to forgive you.

He will.

Then, try your best not to do that wrong thing again.

You see Slatter.

Like the potter and the clay, God wants to make a beautiful vessel out of your clay body, but he won't come into your heart uninvited.

Have you invited the Lord to come into your heart yet?"

Slatter just stared at Miss Peabody and politely said, "No.

I guess I haven't."

She was surprised at Miss Peabody's boldness.

Slatter always talked to her grandpa about God, but not even her grandpa had asked her a question quite like the one Miss Peabody just asked her. Miss Peabody happily demanded, "Well, what in the world are you waiting on child? Time is a wasting.

Would you like to ask him into your heart right now?"

Slatter hesitated.

Even though she was feeling a tug on her heart from the Holy Spirit, she wanted to ask Miss Peabody a question.

She began to feel a little scared. She wished her grandpa was with her so she could ask him her heart felt questions.

She nervously asked, "What if I feel like I haven't done much sinnin' since I've been alive. I'm just a little girl and I know I haven't lived long enough yet to get into any real trouble. I guess what I'm askin' is, shouldn't I at least wait and ask God into my heart when I'm older and I'll know more about sin and stuff?

I thought becoming a Christian was for older folks, not little kids." Miss Peabody, reached over and placed her hand on top of Slatters as she modestly replied,

"Slatter.

Age has nothing to do with it. God sends his Holy Spirit to people of all ages. He seeks out the lost and gives them an understanding about faith. Sometimes people come to know the Lord at a very young age. Everyone's salvation is different and it occurs at different times.

Ya see honey. Everyone is born into this world a sinner, but they don't realize it until they become a part of God's family. God makes exceptions for little children and others that are not old enough or capable to understand about his salvation plan.

It's not anything they have or haven't done.

It has to do with Adam's sin.

Honey, if you know the difference between right and wrong, then you are old enough to choose where you will spend eternity.

You do not get to choose how or when you will leave this old world, but, one thing is for sure; because Jesus died for your sins, you can choose where you will spend eternity.

Believe it or not, some people reject Jesus, thus they choose not to go to heaven.

Let me ask you this.

Have you ever told a lie or deceived anyone?"

Slatter reverently nodded her head yes.

"Well, "continued Miss Peabody as she flung up her hands.

"There you have it.

You do know the difference between right and wrong.

To God, sin is sin; it's all the same.

One lie or five hundred lies.

Besides, everyone is born into sin. Because people in this life are born into this world, they are sinners from birth. They don't know they're sinners until they receive a beckoning from God's spirit. When people are born, they're little sinners and when they grow up, they're big sinners. Nobody's perfect.

You were born as a sinner into the world and you have to repent to God in order to become one of his forgiven children.

I know that's hard for a child to understand, but I don't know any other way to tell you about it. I am just laying it all out there for you and either you understand it or you don't. I am telling you the Gospel truth and the truth will set you free."

Slatter suddenly began to feel a strong tug on her heart.

She now had no doubt. She understood everything Miss Peabody was telling her. She had heard the preacher on many occasions, say everything Miss Peabody had said, but now, it was somehow making more sense to her. She knew her mother was a Christian and she wanted to become one too. She just wanted to make sure she was old enough to have a good understanding of it all.

She knew her heart felt heavy and she needed to repent and accept Jesus as her personal savior. She realized God's

Holy Spirit was knocking on the door to her heart. She felt a flutter in it, like the one she described in her poem she read at the princess pageant.

Slatter anxiously asked, "How...how do I do this? What do I say?"
Miss Peabody took Slatter's hands in hers and tenderly coached her by saying,
"My child.
It's the easiest thing you will ever do in your life.
Just close your eyes and I will lead you in what I call the sinner's prayer."
Slatter held up her hand and demanded, "Wait. Please wait jest a minute. I feel scared and nervous and I don't know why.
As her heart pounded in her ears, in an effort to calm herself, she put her hand on her throat. Miss Peabody put Slatter's hand in hers.
"Why are you so scared," asked Miss Peabody in a loving, calm voice."
Slatters wallowed as she replied, "I reckon I'm being a little bit like my daddy.
I'm scared of responsibility....ya know...... afraid I can't measure up to God's standards.
What if I can't be what He expects me to be?
I don't want to fail God."
Miss Peabody smiled, and immediately soothed her fears.
She said,
"Why Slatter.
You know some big words for such a little girl.

I can tell that your grandparents must talk to you a great deal.

Well let me put your mind at ease by assuring you about one thing.

God always makes it easy for you to turn to him about anything.

Everyone that has ever been born into this world, has fallen short of the glory of God.

No one is perfect.

It's human nature to do wrong things, but if you mess up, God will always make it easy for you to come to him and ask forgiveness.

You don't have to ever worry about being saved over and over again if you mess up.

What God does, he does forever.

He saves you forever.

Once you accept Jesus into your heart, nothing you can ever do whether it is bad or good can change his love for you.

He is a very loving and just God and you must always remember that."

Slatter, with tears in her eyes wanted to ask Miss Peabody another important question. It took her a few seconds but she finally spit it out. Picking at her fingers, she blurted out, "I reckon I have to be honest with ya and tell ya somethin' else; somethin' that I ain't never told anybody."

Miss Peabody curiously asked,

"Well, go right ahead. I'm listening. What is it?"

Slatter forced out words she didn't think she could ever say out loud. Sticking her lips out and folding her arms across her chest she ashamedly stated,

"I'm still mad at God for taking away my mommy.

He's the one who broke my heart.

Are ya sure He can heal my heart if'n He's the one who broke it?"

Miss Peabody smiled and hugged Slatter as she answered her question.

"Oh Slatter," replied Miss Peabody shaking her head.

"God is the only one who can heal your broken heart.

God will heal your broken heart if you give him all the pieces.

If you're holding onto anger toward Him then that's a very big piece of your heart and He needs it to put it all back together again. I know you are very young and cannot understand why God chose to take your mother, but I can tell you this much.

You can trust He knows what He's doing and He always has your best interest at heart regardless of how it looks to you.

One day you will see your mother again.

She is alive.

Her body got sick and died, but now she is happy and alive in a city named heaven.

She now has a new body and she will never be sick again or ever have to die again.

Heaven is a millions times more beautiful and wonderful than what you could ever imagine.

The bible says ear has not heard nor eye has not seen what God has in store for us in heaven.

You must believe me, when I tell you that God has saved the best for us for last.

Heaven... is... a ...real ....place," emphasized Miss Peabody.

You just can't see it while you are here on earth.

Death is like a special secret passageway you get to go through to get to heaven.

You don't remember being born and when you get to heaven you won't remember dying.

God takes care of all of that for you.

He has everything under control.

Please just let go and trust God.

Let God heal your heart so you won't be carrying a grudge against Him the rest of your life. That makes for a miserable life."

Feeling assured by her kind words, Slatter bowed her head and closed her eyes.

"Ok.

I will let go and forgive Him if He'll forgive me.

I will trust God to heal my heart.

My grandpa told me once that in order to be a Christian, a person has to have F...A...I...T...H.

He said that stands for Forsaking....All...... I .....Trust..... Him.

I'm ready to pray now."

The two of them held hands and Slatter sincerely repeated Miss Peabody's words as instructed.

"Dear Lord....I know that I have sinned against you ....and I am sorry for it.... I am asking you to forgive me of my sins. I am inviting you to come into my heart and live. I know in my heart you are the one and only true God. I believe you sent your only son Jesus to die for my sins. I believe He rose from the dead, and I believe you are coming back again to receive me unto yourself. I confess my sins to you and your word tells me you are just to forgive me of my sins and remember them no more. I thank you for accepting me into your family. I believe in you and I thank you for giving me the faith to be saved. In Jesus name..... Amen."

While they were praying, Miss Peabody looked upward and saw a sudden burst of white light appear in the heavens and slowly beamed down through the clouds. It extended down through the roof of the house and descended on Slatter. The room instantly filled with the bright radiant light as it completely engulfed her. She was being bathed in God's love. A divine, reverent, calmness hovered over the room. A feeling of holiness lingered in the air. Miss Peabody watched as a huge blanket of dense red fog, representing the blood of Jesus begin to form high above the ceiling. This delicate, luminously sheer, vapor-like veil floated downward and draped around Slatter's body like a well-fitted cloak. Then, it dissipated like millions of tiny sparkling diamonds as it sprinkled over her body. Miss Peabody smiled as she heard a merciful, thunderous voice from heaven announce,

"My child............I forgive."

Miss Peabody knew Slatter's prayer had approached the throne of God and she had just absorbed His holy spirit, through the blood of God's holy son, Jesus.

When Slatter opened her eyes, she was totally unaware that her body was radiating a white, angelic glow that could only be seen with immortal eyes. Miss Peabody knew the bright glow signified that through Jesus' blood God had forgiven Slatter of her sins. She was now a new creature in Christ. In God's sight, she was whiter and more pure than the freshly fallen snow that lies on the ground outside.

When Slatter had finished repeating the sinner's prayer, she began to whimper. Joy like she had not known before, filled her soul. She hugged Miss Peabody and thanked her for leading her to Jesus. Slatter felt like she was a new person inside. She knew without a doubt, her heart had been miraculously changed. She couldn't explain the wonderful, peaceful, soul satisfying way she now felt. She realized she now had a special personal relationship with Jesus. Before, she had the head knowledge of Jesus, now she had the heart knowledge of Him. For a couple of minutes, the two of them sat together in complete silence until Slatter regained her composure. She had not realized how much anger she had toward God for taking away her mother. She was now free of all of those hurtful feelings. She now had the assurance God will always be there for her. She was so ashamed of her sins, she didn't want Miss Peabody to know about them. Miss Peabody handed Slatter a handkerchief and broke the silence.

"Just one more thing child," said Miss Peabody as she comforted Slatter. I must tell you something else. You are very young and you will face many obstacles that will tempt you to abandon your faith, but don't ever be ashamed of the gospel of Jesus Christ.
Sometimes people will laugh at you and make fun of you.
But let God be the one to deal with them.
God will take very good care of you, if you'll let him."
Slatter stopped crying and stuttered, "I...I...will."
After Miss Peabody gave Slatter a little while to think about what she had just experienced, she hugged her and pointed at the diamond in Slatter's hand.

"Now Slatter, about this diamond," Miss Peabody kindly said.

"I want you to take it home in remembrance of what happened between you and God tonight."

The grandfather clock chimed two times signifying it was two o'clock in the morning. Miss Peabody retracted her words, "Or should I say what happened between you and God this morning." They both giggled. Miss Peabody put her arm around Slatter and exclaimed loudly, "You know what I think?

I think if I had a child, I would love to have a little girl just like you. You are an absolute delight.

"Know what else I think, Slatter?"

"What's that," asked Slatter wiping her red nose with the handkerchief.

"I think," continued Miss Peabody as she bragged on Slatter,

"you have something in common with this unfinished stone.

You are a diamond in the rough yourself."

God is going to be your master diamond cutter and He is going to mold you and make you into a wonderful, priceless jewel fit for his kingdom!

Isn't that wonderful news!

Oh, my little friend.

You have to know in your heart that God is real and He loves you very much. You are very young and impressible right now, but God has a wonderful plan for your life. He wants to mold you and make you into a shiny, clear, priceless vessel from the inside out all for his honor and glory. From this day forward you need to be looking for some wonderful gifts that he has in store for you, and I'll tell you a special little secret young lady.

Your eternity began at the moment you accepted Christ into your heart. In God's own time, He will give you a greater understanding about what eternity means."

Slatter, very tired and sleepy, was trying her best to stay awake because she didn't want to miss out on one word Miss Peabody had to say. She felt a warm glow all over because God had come into her heart and filled the empty, aching gap that had haunted her since her mother's death. She was so grateful she no longer felt anger toward God or anyone. She was at peace with God and herself.

After a few minutes of silence, Miss Peabody noticed Slatter's head start to bobble. She was about to fall asleep sitting up. She tiptoed quietly out of the room to get a pillow and blanket to make a bed for her on the couch. By the time she returned, Slatter had fallen fast asleep on the floor in front of the fireplace. She never made it to the beautiful red velvet couch. She had the unfinished treasure clutched tightly in her hand. Miss Peabody tucked a pillow under Slatter's head and covered her up with a warm blanket.

# 24

# DASHING THROUGH THE SNOW

Miss Peabody's antique grandfather clock chimed twelve times for the noon hour and woke Slatter from her sound sleep.

Wiping the sleep from her eyes, she slowly realized where she was and what had happened to her the night before. She felt refreshed and her heart felt light and peaceful. She could see through the slanted openings of the red velvet curtains that it was daylight and the sun was shining brightly. She quickly threw the blanket off of her and jumped to her feet. She ran across the room to look out one of the big windows. As if she was in a daze, she lifted a hand to her head. She brushed back one side of the soft velvet curtain and rubbed her hand across the frosted glass. She noticed a little blue bird sitting on the snowy ledge of the window. The bird did not offer to move. Instead, he cocked his head to one side and stared back at her. She pecked on the window at him, giggling at the bird's gestures. As she peered out the window, she was fascinated at the beauty of the unblemished snow covered scenery. The trees surrounding the old house looked wild and unrestrained. She wondered if God created snow in order to make the earth look pure and clean again; even it was just for a little while.

Slatter was glad to see the sun shining. The clarity of a cloudless sky was a very welcoming sight to behold. The snow was blinding as it glistened in the noon day sun. Huge, long icicles hung from the trees and the snow that lay on the trees was two or three inches thick. Every bush around the house was snow covered. She could barely see the top of Miss Peabody's old barn. Slatter noticed a couple of deer frolicking in the snow. She laughed out loud as she watched them ram their heads together and kick up snow with their back feet. She wished Granny B could see this winter wonderland. As she watched them struggle to run in the deep snow, she wondered how in the world she was going to get home. Home seemed so far away. She knew for sure she was somewhere down Humphrey's Lane, but other than that, she had no idea where on earth she really was.

She suddenly remembered Miss Peabody mentioning something about having a sled out in the back shed. Because the snow looked so deep, Slatter doubted even a sled would be able to get her home. She yelled for Miss Peabody.
"Miss Peabody.........Miss Peabody!
Where are ya?"
There was no response.
Slatter suddenly felt all alone in the big old house.
Then, she heard Miss Peabody come walking through the door.
She was carrying a load of firewood. Slatter was relieved to see her and she helped put more wood on the fire. Miss Peabody walked back over to the front door, took off her snow boots and put on a pair of men's house slippers. Slatter watched with a puzzled look on her face and curiously asked, "Miss Peabody.
Why do ya wear men's house slippers?"

Miss Peabody smiled as she looked down at them.

"Oh, I just like to wear them because they belonged to my brother.

He bought them overseas somewhere in Australia, I think."

She chuckled a little and said,

"I think of them as my Israelite shoes because they never seem to wear out.

They're made from Alpaca hides.

I've worn them for years and years.

Besides, they are the warmest shoes I own.

They keep my feet all warm and cozy."

Then, Slatter, all keyed up and ready to go said,

"I'm all rested up now.

Do ya think ya can take me home today?"

Miss Peabody grabbed her and gave her a big hug. She tickled Slatter under her chin causing her to giggle loudly. Miss Peabody, enjoying the sound of Slatter's laughter teasingly said, "Why, you can be sure me and old ABOB will get you home, but first let me fix you a cup of hot broth and another piece of my tasty bread.

You need nourishment and it's already after noon, you know.

You've slept the morning away.

You were so tired from last night that I didn't dare wake you this morning.

I don't think you made a move all night.

I trust you slept well."

Slatter, in such good spirits to be going home replied, "I sure did.

It felt so good to be warm!

Ya know.

After being out in the cold so long, I wonder if I'll want to play outside in the snow ever again.

As she clutched the diamond into her hand she eagerly said, "Oh, I just can't wait to get home and show my grandpa and my Granny B my new found treasure."

Miss Peabody walked out of the room to get Slatter some food. In couple of minutes she walked back into the living room with the broth and bread. She had Slatter sit down in the rocking chair and eat. Slatter reluctantly allowed Miss Peabody to take the diamond out of her hand and laid it on top of the fireplace mantel while she ate. Miss Peabody let out a big sigh, as she sat down in the chair next to Slatter.

" Well now," asked Miss Peabody, "which new found treasure are you referring to my dear?

Your diamond in the rough or Jesus?"

Slatter acted a little embarrassed because she didn't want Miss Peabody to think she didn't value her new relationship with Jesus.

So she smiled and timidly replied,

"Well, I reckon I have two new treasures, don't I."

Slatter felt a need to apologize to Miss Peabody.

"I didn't mean to sound like asking Jesus into my heart wasn't important," said Slatter with a serious look on her face.

"Jesus is very important to me.

In fact, He's the most important thing in the world to me now.

I am thankful for all God has done for me.

I know I would still be lost out in the woods, if wasn't for Jesus.

I am sure it was Jesus who sent your donkey ABOB to me.

I was so lost out in the woods last night, that if I hadn't found your house, I would've died out in the cold.

Jesus had ABOB bring me here so ya could take care of me.

I also know another meaning of being lost.

Before last night, I wasn't a Christian.

I was just a little kid, that went to church.

I didn't have Jesus in my heart at all.

Ya might say I was double lost.

I was lost from Jesus before I was lost in the woods."

She covered her mouth with both hands and giggled.

"Now," she said as she squirmed around in her chair, "Jesus found me out in the woods and I found him. We found each other.

Ya know what Miss Peabody.

I just remembered a song I sing sometimes at my church.

It's called Amazin' Grace.

Can I sing it for ya?

Miss Peabody whole heartedly replied, "I would dearly love to hear your song.

Please do sing it for me."

Slatter began to sing in a sweet, clear voice.

"Amazing Grace. How sweet the sound. that saved a wretch like me. I once was lost. But now I'm found. Was blind, but now I see."

When Slatter finished singing, Miss Peabody graciously applauded and complimented her, "My you sang that song so lovely.

Maybe you will be a singer when you grow up."

I know that beautiful old hymn too.

Slatter, was embarrassed a little by Miss Peabody's kind words.

No one had ever told her before that she sang lovely.

Because she didn't know how to receive a compliment, she giggled a little and tried to change the subject.

"Want to know a secret?" asked Slatter, acting bashful with her finger in her mouth.

Miss Peabody, watching Slatter's ever move, took a deep breath and replied, "Yes............ I like secrets."

Slatter confidently declared, "Well, I can't tell ya how.

But I know for a fact that God help me find this diamond in the rough that ya gave me."

Miss Peabody, gave Slatter a puzzled look as she pushed her glasses back on top of her sweaty nose. Patting Slatter on top of her head, she proudly said, "Well, now let me tell you a little secret.

I know for a fact that God gave you another precious stone to take home with you."

Slatter remarked.

"Oh, yeah.

What other stone is that? "

Miss Peabody putting on her hat and coat, cleverly responded to Slatter's question,

"God gave you the jewel of heaven, His only begotten son, Jesus.

Because God gave, you now have the priceless gift of eternal life.

Now that's a precious jewel to own.

Always remember my little one.

Jesus is more precious than jewels and nothing you can desire compares with Him."

Slatter was impressed. Her mouth dropped open as she said, "Wow. I never thought of it like that.

Gee Whiz. I didn't even know what I was really prayin' for when I prayed to God and asked him to help me find a valuable treasure. He answered my prayer. He gave me His jewel of heaven."

They both agreed what Miss Peabody had just said was true. Miss Peabody put her fur lined gloves on and in an insistent tone ordered, "Hurry up now and finish eating so we can get started.

I will go outside and hook up ABOB to the sled. It may take me a few minutes because I may have to go and get him out of the pasture. I tell you what. He wonders around so much, sometimes he's very hard to find. I know it may sound a little strange to you, but he's very fond of standing out in the pasture and gazing up into the sky."

Slatter grinned because that didn't sound strange to her at all. She knew exactly what he was doing when he was gazing up into the sky.

Miss Peabody pointed her finger at Slatter as she gave her additional instructions, "Now when I come back in the house, you be ready to go. Time is of the essence. In just a few short hours it will be dark again and we've got to make hay while the sun shines, if you know what I mean."

She leaned over to whisper to Slatter. In her own calm, reassuring way she said,

"There is something I must tell you.

You see.

We have quite a ways to go to get back to your house.

My donkey ABOB is old and while he is very sure-footed, he is not able to travel at a fast pace in such deep snow.

That's why we've got to get a move on."

Slatter was so excited to get to go home she jumped up and down and clapped her hands together.

Miss Peabody knew that Slatter needed to freshen up a little before they started their long journey, so she laid a comb beside her and winked. Slatter winked back at her and nodded her head as to let Miss Peabody know she would use it to comb her hair.

Slatter finished eating and combed her hair the best she could. With each forced stroke of the comb, she thought of her Granny B and the way she always fussed at her about looking presentable. She wished she had a mirror so she could see to comb her hair. Suddenly, she remembered the painted mirror in the living room and hurriedly ran to it. When she looked on the wall above the couch, the mirror was gone. A picture of a beautiful early century woman was hanging in its place. The woman reminded her of her Granny B. As she stood staring at the picture, Miss Peabody came back in from outside. Slatter could tell she was pleased with her newly groomed look by the way she lovingly smiled at her. Miss Peabody commented in a sweet voice, "Well. Well. You certainly look all refreshed and ready to go."

Then, she walked over and put her arm around Slatter commenting, "It didn't take me as long as I thought it would to find ABOB.

Are you ready to go for a ride in my sled?"

Slatter did not take her eyes off of the new picture as she smiled great big and nodded her head yes.

"Good," said Miss Peabody.

"I have ABOB all hooked up and ready to go."

Slatter pointed to the new picture hanging above the couch. She inquisitively asked,

"Miss Peabody.

What happened to the mirrored painting that was hangin' right there last night?"

Mrs. Peabody put her hands on her hips and gave her a look like do we have to talk about this now. Then after she thought for a few seconds, she half heartedly replied,

"Well, you were so upset by that painting last night, I took it down and went into the attic and got that one.

I was hoping you wouldn't notice.

C'mon now, we need to get going and make some tracks so we can get you home before dark."

Slatter seemed satisfied with her answer so they headed for the door.

As Miss Peabody helped Slatter put on her coat and boots, she started telling Slatter another story about her brother.

"You know when I was very young, my brother used to take me for a sleigh ride every Christmas Eve. He would fix us up a thermos of hot broth and then we would load up in this same big old sled we're going to ride in.

He would make sure I was all wrapped up tightly in a nice warm blanket, then, he would crack the whip at his two mules and off we would go.

Sometimes, he made the sled go too fast and I worried we might turn over but, we never did."

She paused and smiled as she thought of such pleasant memories then continued on,

"We always made it back home safe and sound.

I sure miss that, but those days are gone.

Now it's my turn to bring joy to someone else.

It's Christmas Eve and I get to take you for a sleigh ride."

Slatter was ecstatic.

She had never been on a sleigh ride before plus she was going home. She would get to see her grandpa and Granny B again! When she finished putting on her coat and boots, she noticed Miss Peabody had a basket of items sitting by the door. Each item was individually wrapped and Slatter couldn't tell what they were. She couldn't stand it. Her curiosity got the best of her and she had to ask,

"What's in the box?"

"Well, curiosity killed the cat you know," teased Miss Peabody.

Slatter didn't laugh. Miss Peabody noticed the pouty look on Slatter's face. She patted her on the back and said,

"Oh, I'm just joshing you.

That's supplies we might need on the journey.

We must go prepared.

As you found out, lady winter can show her wrath and without warning.

I have candles, matches, hot broth, some of my home made bread, and several blankets to spread over our legs."

Slatter, joyfully smiled at Miss Peabody and declared,

"Miss Peabody, I guess ya think of just about everythin'."

Suddenly, Slatter remembered Miss Peabody had laid her diamond on the fireplace mantel. She ran back into the living room and picked it up. She quickly slid the diamond into her coat pocket.

Miss Peabody watched Slatter as she ran back into the living room to get the diamond. When she ran returned to the entryway, Miss Peabody, shaking her head, was patiently waiting. She bent over to pick up the box and Slatter cheerfully said,

"Oh, please allow me Miss Peabody.
This is one thing I can do for ya."

Miss Peabody bowed and backed out of the way, allowing Slatter to carry the box outside to the sled.

When they walked outside, Slatter's eyes opened wide with excitement. There stood ABOB with a ring of bells hanging around his neck, hitched to a big wooden sled decorated with beautiful pine branches. The huge sled was made of sculptured wood infused with ribs of bark. The bottom had big, steal runners. Slatter lit up like a Christmas tree when she saw the lavishly way Miss Peabody had decorated the sled just for her. Miss Peabody was pleased that Slatter was delighted.

"I tried to fix it up for you", said Miss Peabody.
I think it's every kid's dream to go on a sleigh ride in the snow on Christmas Eve."

As Slatter looked toward the sky, her face turned from happiness to sadness.

She noticed the sun was no longer shining and the sky was dreary with dark snow clouds drooping down.

Miss Peabody carefully observed Slatter's worried face as she gazed at the darkening sky.

"Oh, c'mon now," said Miss Peabody in a fearless tone.
"Don't let that dreary sky worry you.
We'll be alright.
This could be your first test of faith!
Just remember, the Lord is on our side."

Slatter could see the snow flakes falling down onto her coat. Miss Peabody began giving precise instructions to Slatter.

"Go ahead and climb up into the sled.
Now, scoot on over and make room for me."

As Slatter climbed up onto the sled she noticed even the seat was a nicely sanded piece of art.

Slatter was absolutely stunned at how massive the big, old sled was.

She wondered how in the world could poor old, ABOB pull that much weight through such deep snow.

Miss Peabody noticed Slatter was still amazed at the big sled.

She proudly boasted, "You'll never see another sled like this one again. It's an original. My brother made it all by himself.

Miss Peabody hurriedly handed Slatter the box of goodies and Slatter sat it down in the seat between the two of them. Slatter scooted over on the seat as far as she could, so Miss Peabody could have enough room to sit beside her. Miss Peabody slowly climbed up into the sled and sat down. She reached into the box and pulled out the three blankets. She and Slatter then spread them over their shoulders and legs. Then, with everything situated, Miss Peabody picked up the reins and assuredly said,

"Well, Miss Slatter Slopey, my little friend.

I'm a thinking you might be home right around supper time."

Then, she made a clicking sound with her mouth and yelled,

"Get along now, ABOB!

Takes us to Slatter's home."

With one jerk of the reins, the seemingly unyielding sled took off like a shot, causing the snow to spray all over Miss Peabody and Slatter.

As they laughed, Miss Peabody pointed to a group of red birds as they flew overhead. They made a zigzag pattern as they did a dazzling dance high up in the air.

Slatter was impressed with ABOB's physical ability. She watched his strong, powerful back legs dig through the heavy snow, causing the sled to glide very smoothly. She was really enjoying the sleigh ride especially when they hit a big bump causing the snow to fly high into the air. She and Miss Peabody passed the time by singing Jingle Bells and other Christmas carols. She was having so much fun, she hardly noticed time was passing by very quickly.

After they traveled for a while, they came upon a clearing.

Miss Peabody thought it was a good time to eat something.

She knew it would be getting dark soon and she didn't want to waste time stopping the sled to eat. So, she reached down into the box and pulled out a piece of cloth she had her bread wrapped in.

As the sled kept trudging through the snow, she handed Slatter a piece of bread to eat and a container of hot broth to drink.

Slatter looked up at Miss Peabody and thankfully declined her offer.

"Thank ya just the same", said Slatter, "But I'm way too excited about goin' home to be hungry."

Miss Peabody would not take no for an answer.

"Eat," she insisted.

"This bread will give you strength."

Slatter didn't offer to argue. She took the food and drink from Miss Peabody and forced it down.

# 25

# CRYSTAL MOMENTS

As they neared the clearing, Slatter noticed big snow capped pine trees lining each side. The trees were so tall the tops were concealed by the low hanging snow clouds. Slatter had no way of knowing she and Miss Peabody were approaching an unusual place where they would embark on a new horizon. However, Miss Peabody knew exactly where they were. She knew they were on the edge of an unknown celestial sphere; A terrestrial hemisphere where only angels can pass through.

One of the few places on the earth where only the very elect are allowed to experience the union of realism and flights of the imagination into the unknown.

A place where the immortal and mortal merge.

Suddenly, a blinding flash of light streaked across the sky.

Slatter was absolutely awestricken as they came upon a scene that took her breath away. A bright haze in the atmosphere was causing a shimmering mist to glisten from the sky, like falling glitter. The mist containing a beautiful rainbow of pastel colors, shimmered as it sprayed to the ground. As the sun collided with the darkened clouds, speckles of the beautiful colors were reflected into the long, crystal clear icicles that hung from the very tall, snow packed, mysterious trees. For a few moments, all that could be seen was the reflection of the rainbow of colors on the snow, in the sky, and in every piece of ice. Everything around her was every color imaginable. Slatter was amazed at these beautiful crystal moments. It was like she was passing through the inside of a gigantic rainbow. She looked down at her coat and gloves just in time to see the fine droplets of ice land on them. She watched in amazement as her gloves repeatedly changed colors right before her eyes. One second they would be red, then yellow, then blue. They even changed into colors Slatter hadn't seen before. She thought the snow was prettiest when it changed to a dark purple color, but when the trees turned a glowing red outlined in gold with silver icicles hanging on them, Slatter clapped her hands together and gasped for air. Such miraculous beauty took her breath away. Miss Peabody had seen this sight before, but she found joy in watching Slatter's astonishment at this mystery of nature. Slatter stood up in the sled so she could get a better look at the beautiful, splendor of nature she was seeing. She felt a sense of supernatural happiness she had never felt before. She wondered if she could be at the thresh hold of heaven. She wondered if she looked hard enough, she could actually see her mother again. Her face glistened with serenity as her eyes scanned over the vast beautiful scenery. If what she was seeing was a taste of the beauty of heaven, she knew her mother was happy there. Maybe heaven really is closer to earth than anyone ever dared to imagine.

As ABOB slowly pulled the sled through the clearing, the beautiful colors slowly diminished. Slatter, still full of excitement, sat back down. She noticed the branches on the trees arched forward toward the sled as it passed by; as if they were bowing down to them. Slatter could not believe what she was seeing. She turned to look at Miss Peabody to see what her reaction was to all of this beauty. Miss Peabody had her head in the air looking straight ahead in front of her with a pleasant look on her face like she knew a secret Slatter didn't. Slatter noticed how the squirrels, the deer, and other animals of the woods stopped in their tracks to watch the sled as it slowly glided past. They showed no fear. In fact, they acted as if they were very familiar with the loud scraping sound of the sled's big steel blades.

After they had passed through the clearing, ABOB came to an unexpected halt. He was unwilling to proceed any further. He shook his head and used his hoofs to paw the ground. He had sensed he was approaching some kind of danger and stopped dead in his tracks. There before them was a big creek overflowing with deep icy water. The roaring sound of the water flowing down stream echoed through the woods. As Slatter sat silently in the sled, she looked all around her at the beautifully curved, unblemished snow drifts on both sides of the creek. Slatter looked over at Miss Peabody. With fear in her voice, she firmly probed her for an answer, "Why have we stopped," inquired Slatter.

"Is something wrong with ABOB?"

Miss Peabody twisted in her seat as she pointed to the old stone bridge in front of them. In a calm voice she replied, "Look right over there. That's why we've stopped. That old stone bridge has been partially washed out. ABOB is a very smart donkey.

Donkeys have a sixth sense for approaching danger and I can count on my ABOB to sense danger a mile away."

Miss Peabody looked all around as if she was trying to figure a way around the impossible situation. She pushed the blanket away from her as she remarked to Slatter,

"I don't like the way this looks.

Something is very wrong.

I've never known that stone bridge to be washed out before.

I'd better check this out.

You stay right here.

I'll walk on up to the bridge and get a closer look."

In an instant, Slatter's excitement had changed to fear. She sat in the sled huddled under a nice warm blanket watching Miss Peabody's every move. She run her tongue across her top lip to lick off the snow that had sprayed on her face when the sled stopped. She watched Miss Peabody walk up to the bridge and look around. Suddenly she noticed a scary change in the weather. The snow was quickly changing over to heavy sleet. Slatter quickly pulled the blanket tightly over her head to protect her from the freezing rain. She was puzzled when she saw Miss Peabody walk up to ABOB and bend over close to his big ears. She heard her whisper, "I was looking for the old devil to try and cause trouble on this little girl's first day of being a Christian. That's his style. But the good Lord has assured me through much prayer that He will make sure the devil's little plot to destroy Slatter will not work. C'mon ABOB let's try plan number one first and see which way God directs our paths.

We'll do our best to try to handle things on our own, but if our way doesn't work, then I'm sure He'll take care of us His way. Maybe you're sure- footed enough to walk along that widened edge of the bridge and then jump over the gap. I got faith in you. The boards under the sled are well balanced and I think we just might be able to get on across."

She patted ABOB's neck and grabbed hold of the reins. Then, she walked him over to the edge of the railing, pulling the sled behind him. When he was perfectly in line with the edge of the bridge, she commanded him with a loud shout, "Ok. Up....up. That's it ABOB.  Put your front feet up.... up.... good boy, good boy.

Now, walk on the edge of the railing of the bridge.

Easy... boy...easy."

ABOB started easing his way forward then stopped; causing the sled to wobble back and forth. Slatter, scared half to death, didn't know whether to jump out or stay in the sled.

She yelled to Miss Peabody, "Please stop!  I'm so scared!

This thing feels like it's goin' to turn over!"

She kept pleading, "Please don't leave me in this thing by myself!" No matter how hard ABOB tried to walk across the rail of the bridge, he couldn't. Miss Peabody could see that the sled was much too wide to balance on the rail. She also knew Slatter was scared half out of her wits. Realizing the danger she was putting Slatter in, Miss Peabody yelled for ABOB to stop.

"ABOB!.......... Whoa," she yelled.

ABOB obeyed her command and stopped immediately. She clicked with her mouth as she backed him down off of the ledge. Covered in ice from her head to her toe, she slowly eased herself into the sled and sat down. Slatter held the blanket up so Miss Peabody could get under it with her. Sliding under the blanket, Miss Peabody sighed as she looked over at Slatter. Humbly she said, "Looks like we're in a bad way, but we aren't licked yet by a long shot.

If this weather gets any worse, we will be in a worse way.

We had better do some prayin............real quick.

Without further prompting, Slatter grabbed hold of Miss Peabody's hand, closed her eyes and started praying, "Dear God, I hope Ya remember me. I'm Slatter Slopey, and I'm a new member of your family. Me and Miss Peabody here need your help.

Could ya please help us?

She's tryin' to get me home and we can't go no further.

This bridge has washed out and we can't get across.

There ain't nothin' we can do about our problem, so we're dependin' on ya to get us out of this mess.

I believe ya will come and help us yourself.

But, if ya are too busy with other stuff right now, it's alright with us if ya send somebody in your stead. Ya know sort of like ya did with Pydie. Ya couldn't come and play with me yourself so ya sent me Miss Pydie. I'm askin' ya for help in the name of Jesus and I believe you're goin' to help us somehow. I don't know how, but I just know that You will help us. Thanks.

Amen.

# 26

# WINDS OF WARFARE

As soon as Slatter had finished praying, a very strong gust of wind started to blow. The way the snow was blowing around in the air, it looked like another blizzard was on the horizon. Slatter was so scared she felt like she needed to hang onto something.  She grabbed a hold of Miss Peabody's heavy winter coat and clutched it tightly. The wind began roaring through the trees so loudly the sound was deafening. Slatter had to duck down into the sled to keep from being hit by the big chunks of snow and tree limbs being hurled into the air. The trees were so bowed they looked like they could snap in half. The wind was causing the sled to tip from side to side. Miss Peabody felt Slatter grip her coat.  She grabbed Slatter's hand and in order to make sure her voice could be heard over the roaring wind she yelled, "These winds are the strong winds of an ugly, angry war.

I've seen this kind of wind before.

I don't want to frighten you, but they are the winds of a great, spiritual war.

You cannot see there are two winds fighting against one another, but you can see the evidence of it.

The force of these turbulent winds are like two big cyclones fighting.

"Remember last night when we talked about faith!"

Slatter, speechless and crying with fear, nodded her head yes.

"Well, this is your first test of faith and it looks like it's a big one.
God will prevail though, you'll see."

Miss Peabody knew there was a lot more going on than two very strong forces of winds and a shattered bridge.

She knew there was an evil force lurking out in the wooded wilderness trying to prevent Slatter from getting home.

Then, without any warning, the wind died down and the ambiance became very serene and still. Even the clouds were not moving. Slatter felt an eerie feeling in the air. All of a sudden, Miss Peabody started sniffing the air like she was smelling something. As Slatter pulled the blanket off her head, she could smell something too.

The air was filled with the fragrance of freshly cut roses. Slatter gave Miss Peabody a puzzled look. She knew there couldn't be any flowers around because it was winter and the ground was covered in snow. Miss Peabody looked at Slatter and smiled, "See I told you so. God is always in control. It's always darkest before the dawn. He's not only answering your prayer, He's answering many prayers. Prayers of the people that are praying right now, pleading God for your safe return."
Slatter, still clutching Miss Peabody's coat, was in shock of what was going on around her. Her tense body stiffened

even more as she stuttered out her words. Petrified she asked, "H...how ....can ya... t...tell?"

Miss Peabody reverently replied, "Well, because the wonderful, sweet savory scents we are smelling are the prayers of God's people praying for you. God says in his holy word when his saints pray, he can smell their prayers like a savory burning incense."

All of a sudden the old wooden sled began to shake. Then it slowly began to rise up in the air. It kept rising higher and higher until ABOB's hooves were higher than the bridge. Slatter, wide eyed, looked at ABOB. She noticed he was standing perfectly still showing no fear. The sled started moving forward as it slowly floated over the broken down bridge. Slatter grabbed hold of the sides of the sled and screamed, "We're floatin'!

Oh my gosh!

We're actually floatin' in the air right over the bridge!

What if we turn over!

We'll fall down into the deep icy water!"

Miss Peabody, beaming with excitement, tried to comfort Slatter by pulling her close to her bosom. Miss Peabody threw her head back and shouted, "To God be the glory great things he hath done!

"Faith does not bring you to the edge of the river and stop.

It lifts you up....... into fellowship........ with an unseen God!"

"ALWAYS BELIEVE IN....... DIVINE INTERVENTION!"

Miss Peabody was not the least bit afraid and kept patting Slatter's arm to comfort her. As ABOB and the sled steadily floated high up in the air, Slatter looked down into the raging, icy waters. She closed her eyes and sobbed, "Why doesn't God do somethin' to calm the mean waters?"

Miss Peabody, hearing Slatter's question, responded by crying out in a loud voice,

"Because God doesn't always calm the troubled waters in your life. He has his own way of helping you build a bridge so you can cross over safely. There's a spiritual bridge between heaven and earth and it is called Miracle Bridge. God will always meet you there, no matter what.

As the perfectly balanced sled slowly floated over the old washed out bridge, it didn't wobble or waver; not even for a moment. The whole ordeal only lasted for a few minutes. Then the big sled softly landed on the other side of the bridge. Slatter, glad to be on the ground again, started to turn around to look behind her. Miss Peabody grabbed her arm and kindly demanded, "No need to look behind you. You need to keep your eyes on the trail before us. Don't waste time on what's behind you and don't worry about tomorrow. Let's concentrate on tonow so we can get you home. The old devil wants you to look back so he can throw up in your face all your past troubles and everything you've done wrong, but remember a good life has no time for past regrets; their only purpose is to stop you from enjoying today.

Concentrate on enjoying your forgiveness.

What difference does it make how you reached this point in your life as long as you are here?

Don't ever let the devil steal your joy by throwing your past wrongs up to you. We'll pick up and go on from here."

Slatter didn't understand what all Miss Peabody was trying to tell her, but because she saw trust in Miss Peabody's eyes, she obeyed her to the letter. She sat up straight in her seat and looked directly ahead.

Slatter noticed the dark dreary clouds had passed away and the sky had become clear. Still a little frightened, she wiped tears from her eyes. She thought she had experienced enough adventure to last her for a very long time. Time seemed to be passing by very slowly and it seemed like it was taking forever to reach their destination. She looked at Miss Peabody with a pitiful look on her face and stuttered, "Is.... it... m- much.. f-further.... t-to.. m-my.. h-house?"

Miss Peabody looked down at Slatter and winked. She patted her on the back and encouragingly replied,

"No.

It's not much further at all honey.

In fact, your house is just over the next big hill."

After the excitement was over and they were out of harm's way, Slatter once again filled with anticipation, began to enjoy the sleigh ride home. Her eyes were tired and she kept blinking them to keep herself awake. She also kept her eyes on **ABOB**. She thought him to be a most beautiful, unusual looking animal as she watched him plod tirelessly through the snow..........just as if nothing had ever happened.

## 27

## A LITTLE PIECE OF HEAVEN

Slatter began thinking warm thoughts about seeing Granny B and her grandpa again. She also thought about how much she missed Mr. Fritz and Pydie. She had wanted to buy them a Christmas present from Peddler Pete, but since it was already Christmas Eve she knew that was out of the question. She decided to ask Miss Peabody what she could do about getting her loved ones a Christmas present on such short notice.

"Miss Peabody," asked Slatter sincerely.

"Today is Christmas Eve and I don't have time to buy any presents for the people I love.

Any ideas what I can give them for a present?"

Miss Peabody, holding sturdy to ABOB's reins, quickly responded to Slatter's question in a confident manner, "Why don't you give them a little piece of Heaven?"

Slatter crinkled up her nose and gave her an odd look as she replied, "A little piece of heaven.

What kind of present is that?"

Miss Peabody lovingly softly replied, "Well, God is love and Love is God." I mean give them a little piece of God.

She went on to explain herself,

"You see Slatter. All people at one time or another go through hard times in life. Sometimes they lose their way due to all the trouble they're going through. Sometimes just a little act of kindness can restore their faith in mankind.

A kind word or deed at the right time can be a light at the end of the tunnel. I mean, people who are dealing with sickness and some kind of sadness are people in great need of hope.

Hope that everything will get better for them.

Hope that God is going to see them through their crises.

When you help others, you give them hope. Hope deferred makes the heart sick. Remember when I explained to you what faith is. Faith is the assurance of things hoped for. Without hope a person's spirit within them will die."

Miss Peabody poked her elbow into Slatter's side and winked as she said, "Ah, you know what I'm talking about.

You can take the time to bake someone some cookies, or rub their tired aching back. You can even help them with some of their chores around the house. How about making them a nice card telling them all of the good things you see in them or all of the good things you like about them. Make them a good list though. Give them all ya got. Do your best to help them see the good they do.

All people need encouragement. Discouragement is the most horrible disease known to man. The greatest gift you can ever give to anyone is a word of encouragement- good words stay with them forever....words are powerful. They can heal or destroy. The gift of loving kindness is priceless. The way you give a gift and the attitude in which you give it tells others what kind of person you really are.

The gift of yourself is a little piece of Heaven, Slatter.

God made you. You my dear were created out of God's own desire. You have been created fresh out of heaven. God doesn't make mistakes. You have a specific gift and purpose that is to be used in your lifetime. Since you have become a child of God, you are like your creator, just like you are somewhat like your parents.

Jesus is your heavenly father now.

The bible says you are now born again.

Only this time, you have been born into a spiritual life.

You can read in His bible and become more like Him.

When you are called on to judge or criticize others, always do your best to use your tongue as if it were God's. You can show God your love for Him by being willing to be used by Him; sort of like reaching out to others by becoming His hands and His feet.

You gave your heart to Jesus this Christmas. Now, you can give Jesus, as a love gift, to someone else.

Always remember Christmas is all about Jesus.

He's God's gift of love to the world. The greatest of all gifts.

God so loved the world that He **GAVE** His only begotten son and whosoever believeth in Him shall have the gift of eternal life.

What a Christmas gift!

You now have a gift that no one can ever take from you.

So, it's your job now to share your gift of love with everyone you can. You are a light in a dark world and you cannot hide it under a bush. You need to let your light shine so the whole world will see it."

She pulled the blanket up to Slatter's chin to make sure she was staying warm, as she continued talking,

"I guess what I'm really trying to impress upon you is when you give the gift of yourself, you are giving the most wonderful gift of all; a gift that is yours to give, and a gift that is as unique as yourself.

It is the gift from your heart that everyone remembers.

It is good to give materially, but remember when you do for others in God's name, you are storing up for yourself treasures in heaven where neither moths nor rust destroys.

All the other material possessions wither and pass away, but when you give a little piece of heaven to someone, it lasts forever.

You need to know, you have something to give to others even when you think you have nothing left to give."

When Miss Peabody finished talking, the sled topped the hill to Slatter's home. Even though Slatter's face lit up with joy, she began to feel a sweet sorrow. She was glad to be home, but sorry to leave her friend. She had grown to love Miss Peabody in the short time she had been with her. She had been a wonderful friend that had opened up her home to her. She had kept her safe and warm and had led her to Jesus.

As the sled slowly slid down the hill, Slatter could see many cars parked in her snow plowed driveway and down both sides of the highway as far as she could see.

She immediately wondered if something terrible had happened to her grandpa or Granny B.

Miss Peabody was watching Slatter and noticed her face took on a worried look. She reached under the blanket and patted Slatter's hands. She smiled at her and spoke reassuring words to her. Lovingly she said, "It's alright.

Everything is going to be all....right.

Your grandparents are doing fine."

Slatter took a relieving deep breath and nodded her head.

She knew this was probably the last chance she would get to ask Miss Peabody a question she desperately wanted to know the answer to. With all the courage she could muster up and fearing the answer she blurted out her question, "Miss Peabody.

How come ya know so much about God?

Are you a real angel?"

Miss Peabody laughed a hearty laugh then replied, "Well, my answer to that question is simple.

God and I have become very good friends over the years and I've talked to Him a lot.

I share everything with Him.

If you've ever had a very good friend, then I'm sure you know what I'm talking about.

Good friends share everything."

Slatter raised her eyebrows and smiled. That was not the answer she had been hoping for, but it caused her to immediately think of her good friend Pydie. She knew exactly what Miss Peabody was talking about. She softly said, "I know what it's like to have a good friend. It's like finding a valuable treasure."

Miss Peabody pointed to all of the cars that were and down the road in front of Slatter's house. and said, "Well, well, now would you look

That's one mystery solved.

I think we both see where all of those prayers of God's saints were coming from.

No wonder the fragrance was so strong.

Christians from all around have gathered here at your grandpa's house, and they're in there praying for your safe return.

The shadows of the night were lengthening fast and darkness was now upon them. The stars were shining brightly and the moon was trying to hide behind a transparent cloud.

Miss Peabody jerked on ABOB's reins and brought the sled to a sudden halt in front of the snow packed road in front of Slatter's house. She smiled as she brushed the snow off the blanket covering Slatter's shoulders.

"Well, young lady," announced Miss Peabody.

"This is it.

You are home safe and sound.

I think you've had quite an adventure, but as the old saying goes, all good things must come to an end!"

Slatter reached out her arms to hug Miss Peabody goodbye.

She could still smell the same sweet fragrance on Miss Peabody coat she had smelled back in the woods. Slatter had tears in her eyes as she affectionately sobbed, "I'm gonna miss ya and ABOB. I can't thank ya enough for all that you've done for me.

I know now that kindness is priceless.

Some day I will tell my grandpa and Granny B all about ya."

She wiped her tears on the blanket and in a sad voice she said, "I guess I'd better get goin' now."

As Slatter started to get out of her seat, Miss Peabody put her hand up and said, "Hold it. I almost forgot something. I want to give you something very special in remembrance of me."

She had a captivating smile as she spoke.

"Hold out your hand and close your eyes," demanded Miss Peabody.

Slatter extended her left hand out and closed her eyes real tight.

Miss Peabody reached into her coat pocket and pulled out a small, gold bottle that glowed with radiance. She dropped the bottle into Slatter's hand.

"Ok," said Miss Peabody confidently.

"You can open your eyes now."

Slatter opened her eyes.

She stared at the small, glowing, gold bottle.

"Oh, it's so beautiful and it glows!" gloated Slatter.

Is it perfume?"

"No," said Miss Peabody as she chuckled a little at Slatter's response.

"It's not perfume.

It's a very special Christmas gift from me to you."

Slatter let out a long sigh as she replied,

"Ya have already been so kind to me, and ya have already given me the diamond in the rough."

Miss Peabody, tired of the long ride, stood up in the sled and stretched her arms up in the air.

"Yes, so I did, but understand that gift was something that belonged to my brother.

I want to give you something special from me that is mine to give. Then she sat back down in the sled and put both of her hands on Slatter's shoulders.

With a very serious look on her face she advised, "My child.

Listen to me very, very carefully."

What Miss Peabody said next was mind-boggling to Slatter. Pointing to the bottle she said, "The substance is in this little bottle is absolutely priceless. I have put three drops of the same healing liquid that was in my golden pitcher into this special little bottle." Slatter, wide eyed, asked, "Ya mean it's the same shiny healin' stuff ya used on my feet and hurt leg?"

"Yes it is," replied Miss Peabody.

"You must remember to use the three drops very wisely and very sparingly.

The drops have great healing, life sustaining power.

You must cherish this gift and use it only in the most extreme circumstances."

Slatter nodded as she stared at the bottle. Then Miss Peabody added, "Oh, one more thing. No one must know you have this extraordinary gift. In fact, it would be a very good idea to put this bottle in a very secret place. It is yours to use as you see fit.

I trust you with this gift and place it in your care."

Excitement rippled in Slatter's voice when she said, Gee whiz………thanks."

Slatter didn't know what to think about receiving such a miraculous gift. She had no way of knowing that the gift in her possession was a phenomenal treasure. It truly was a unique gift. She had indeed just received a very precious little piece of heaven.

She dropped the bottle into the same coat pocket she had put her diamond in. Then, slowly slipped out from under the warm blanket. She hugged Miss Peabody one last time and Miss Peabody kissed her on the left side of her cheek leaving a permanent dimple on her cheek that wasn't there before. She then jumped down off of the big wooden sled. Tearfully she blurted out, "Thank you for my very special gifts, Miss Peabody. I promise to cherish them forever."

She walked over and gave ABOB a big hug. She kissed his warm, soft fuzzy face and he flashed his big bright eyes at her. He buckled his knees under him as a way of respectfully bowing to her; which was his way of saying goodbye. Miss Peabody's had one final word of advise to Slatter. As she situated herself in the driver's seat of the sled in preparation of the long ride home, she looked down at Slatter and insisted,

"Remember now.

As you grow up, no matter what, always look on the sunny side of life because you now know the secret of being truly happy.

When you have Jesus, you have everything."

Then, Miss Peabody made a very unusual statement to Slatter.

She threw her head back and said,

"Every time you see the light of a burning candle, please think of me."

Miss Peabody jerked on ABOB's reins and turned the sled around. As she waved goodbye the sound of her voice faded in the distance as she shouted, "You are now clothed in God's everlasting love for all of eternity!"

It was now pitch black outside and Slatter, anxious to get home, started running toward the highway. She turned back around to wave goodbye one last time to her friends. She wanted to say see ya later alligator, but when she turned around, they were gone. Slatter stopped running and stared in amazement. There was not even a sign of any tracks where the big wooden sled had been. It was as if they had just vanished into thin air. They had totally disappeared into the darkness and there was not one shred of evidence they had even been there. All she could see was the vapor of her warm breath as she exhaled into the bitter cold night air. For just a moment, Slatter wondered if she had dreamed the whole thing. She quickly felt into her coat pocket to see if the diamond in the rough and the little gold bottle were still there. They were.

## 28

# HOME AT LAST

Confused and little frightened, she quickly started running toward the house. She couldn't believe how many cars were parked down the road and in her driveway. The closer she got to her house, the more she noticed how all of the windows were glowing with light. As she loped through the snow, she said aloud, "My heart feels all aglow like the lights in my house. Oh God, I am so thankful to be home again."

As she ran down the driveway, she saw Mr. Kaneke's old tow truck parked next to the front door. His truck was easy to recognize because it was bright yellow with big purple letters on the side of it that spelled out the words **STUCK N THE SNOW.... WE TOW**. As she ran past the blue goose, she smiled to herself as she ran her hand across the front bumper, slinging snow high into the air.

As she approached the squeaky front screen door that led to the porch, she stopped and took a good long look at it. She was so glad to see it again. Shaking her head, she spoke aloud,

"How silly I am. I can't believe I'm glad to see an old squeaky door."

She opened and closed it several times just so she could hear it squeak. She dawdled onto the porch and rubbed her hand over the old porch swing. She smiled as she remembered sitting in it next to her grandpa after she had won the Whitton county princess pageant.

As she approached the front door, she could hear people praying inside the house. She felt loved because she knew the prayer meeting had been called by her grandparents. Many friends and neighbors had come together to pray for her safe return. She gently turned the door knob to go inside, but the door was locked. She softly pecked on it. When Granny B opened the door, Slatter was surprised at how many people were in her house. There were people kneeling beside the couch while others were knelt down beside kitchen chairs. She couldn't help herself. She jumped into Granny B's arms and bouncing up and down she cried out, "My Granny B! I've missed ya so much!" I'm home! I'm so glad to be home!"

Grandpa heard Slatter's voice and came running out of the kitchen with his arms extended out toward her. Slatter, crying her heart out, ran and threw her arms around him. Everyone else in the house stopped praying and applauded. Tears were rolling down grandpa's face as he cried out, "Oh, dear God. Thank ya God.

Sis, I'm so glad you're home.

We've looked and looked everywhere for you.

I wouldn't even let the snow plow clean off the highway fer fear ya were somewhere in a ditch along side the road.

It's........... like food and drink to have ya home again."

Mr. Fritz was the next one to walk over and pick Slatter up in his big strong arms. He has speechless as he kept crying and hugging her. Everyone came over and gave Slatter a hug. Granny B took charge and sternly said, "Enough of this huggin' business.

I've got to get this child's winter duds off.

Everybody jest back up and let me take care of her."

The smiling guests knew Granny B was right, and they went back to their seats.

Granny B helped Slatter take off her hat and coat. Then she made her sit down so she could take off her snow covered shoes. She took her afghan off the back of the couch and heated it by the fire, then wrapped it around Slatter.

After the rejoicing was over Granny B popped several big bowls of popcorn and heated apple cider. Everyone sat around the fire sharing stories about how God had answered their prayers in one way or another and sang Christmas carols. Slatter sat quietly next to Granny B and sipped on hot cider listening to the harmonious voices of their guests. She observed everyone's body gestures and closely watched their facial expressions. She was amazed at how different the people were, yet they shared a common bond. That common bond being they were all born again Christians that loved God and believed in miracles. Slatter was glad no one asked her any questions about where she had been during the time she was lost. She looked around the room. She knew no one there had ever heard a story quite like hers and she felt assured, her story would probably be laughed at. She didn't dare share it with anyone.

It started to get late and everyone started shaking hands with Granny B and Grandpa as they left to go home. Mr. Kaneke and his wife were preparing to leave when Slatter heard him comment to her grandpa about the farm implement.

He said, "Uh, say J.E.

I been meanin' to come over and thank ya fer bringin' that old implement by my place.

I've already fixed it up and got a buyer fer it.

As soon as I get the money, I'm goin' to come up to the store and pay my grocery bill."

"Oh really," replied grandpa with a big smile on his face.

"I reckon that'll be jest fine.

I'm always glad to get money, but truthfully, I ain't the one that brought the thing over to your place.

I'm glad ya could get some use out of it though.

Turns out we both are gettin' some good use out of it."

As Mr. Kaneke left, grandpa had a puzzled look on his face.

Mr. Fritz was the last one to leave. Wiping the tears out of his eyes, he had a big smile on his face as he slowly knelt down to talk to Slatter. He used a tender tone of voice as he said, "My little ole Miss Slatter. Youz gave old Mr. Fritz here quite a scare.

Iz jest can't believe that youz is back home.

Iz want ya to know I never gave up hope, and I knowed in my heart the good Lord was goin' to bring ya back home safe and sound.

Ain't no utter way it could've happened in dis here bad weather.

No sir.

It was da good Lord dat done brought ya back.

He heard everybody a prayin'.

Dat's all dare is to it. Iz told everyone heres tonight that day can mark it downs in their little black book that the good Lord has shone his face on dis Slopey house tonight 'cause He is still on the throne." He gently rubbed his big black hand across Slatter's soft cheek and kissed her hand. As he stood up to leave, he said, "Iz will see ya all tomorrow. Iz best be gettin' on home now too.

Have a good evenin'."

Slatter smiled back at him and waved goodbye. Walking out the door, he stopped to shake hands with Slatter's grandpa. He leaned over his shoulder, winked at him and whispered, "J.E. Iz been meanin' to talk to ya 'bout that farm implement.

Iz overheered Mr. Kaneke a talkin' to ya.

I seez ya already took care of thangs, so Iz will jest let things be."

Grandpa's eyebrows shifted downward as he made a face like he was having difficulty trying to figure out who moved the farm implement from his field to Mr. Kaneke's place. As soon as Mr. Fritz closed the door behind him, Slatter folded her arms across her chest and whispered under her breath, "I bet I know how the implement got over to Mr. Kaneke's place. If everyone only knew the real story about things I see and hear, but ain't no need in tryin' to tell anybody, anything. Ain't nobody ever goin' to believe me......cause I'm jest a kid. "

Slatter had new eyes now as she looked around at all of Granny B's Christmas decorations. She felt like she had aged several years in just one day. The tree lights were plugged in just like they were when she left; so were the lights on the homemade wreath she and Granny B had carefully made for the old front door. She looked at the fireplace mantel she had so proudly decorated all by herself.

Slatter was doing a lot of looking around and not saying much of anything to anyone. She noticed a Christmas gift under the tree, wrapped in plain brown paper that had her name on it. She wondered what was in it, but she wouldn't allow herself to get excited about opening it. She was concentrating on how she going to explain to Grandpa and

Granny B what had happened to her when she was lost in the storm.

After everyone left, grandpa and Granny B sat down next to Slatter. They didn't say a word. Slatter quickly stood up and walked over to the fireplace. She rubbed her hands together over the fire. Turning around to face them, she openly started explaining her actions.

"I 'm so sorry Granny B," she began in an exonerated tone of voice. "I mean fer disobeyin' ya about goin' out into the weather.

I jest had no idea how cold or how bad the weather really was until I got half way up to the store.

Those two old mean men, Butane Craney and Joe Beeser, came along in a truck and drug me by my arms through the snow, down the road."

She could still feel anger at the two men because of how awful they had treated her. Then as her thought shifted, her voice softened.

"I.........I must've hit my head cause it's still sore.

The next thing I remember was I was layin' in a deep snow drift.

I was so cold I thought to myself, is this what it's like to die?

But I knew I wanted to live.

Somehow, I knew I had to fight.

I had to fight to live.

I started digging, like this, her voice intensified as she made digging gestures with her hands.

"I dug harder and faster until I managed to dig my way out of the hole. The snow was blowin' so hard I couldn't see where I was goin'. I didn't know it, but I was walkin' a straight path right into the woods that led down Humphrey's Lane.

I was so cold and numb.

I called out to ya, but I knew nobody could hear me fer the loud noise the wind was a makin'."

She paused a minute to cry.

Grandpa shook his head in disbelief of the awful things she had endured and said, "Just take your time Slatter.

If ya would like, we can talk about this in the mornin'."

She composed herself and continued,

"No.

I want to tell youns about it now while it's still fresh in my mind."

She swallowed back her tears and continued with her story.

"I.....I finally got to a place in the woods where there wasn't as much snow and I tried to crawl in behind a rock to get out of the cold.

After what seemed a very long while, not too far from where I was layin' I saw some green stuff a floatin' up out of the ground. It looked like hot steam a comin' off hot water except it was green.

I couldn't imagine what it was, so I walked over to it.

The closer I got, the more I could tell it was great big footsteps and when the moon reflected on them, they somehow glowed a bright green color.

I thought maybe it was a sign from God or somethin', so I started steppin' into the footsteps.

I was hopin' they'd lead me to the way back home, but after a while, the footsteps just stopped.

I jest stood there in the snow a cryin'.

Suddenly, out of nowhere I heard a voice.

In the moonlight I saw a shadow of somethin' movin'.

I was scared stiff.

I was so cold and stiff I believe if I'd a fell down I would've broke in half.

Then you're never goin' to believe what I saw next."

Her eyes widened with excitement.

"I saw a small, white donkey step out from behind a grove of trees." Smiling, she exclaimed, "Come to find out, he was a talkin' donkey. He even told me his name was ABOB.

This donkey told me his master named him ABOB because he was a beast of burden."

Hesitating, her voice softened as she described the donkey. She looked down at the floor to avoid making eye contact with her grandparents because she didn't want to see disbelief on their faces. "ABOB, " she continued, "was very warm and comfortin' to me. I didn't know then, but I know now, he was a special messenger sent out to find me. He gave me a ride to a great big, old haunted looking house way out in the middle of the woods.

It was jest awful lookin' on the outside.

I was soooo scared."

She rubbed her hands over her arms as she shivered.

"The house looked liked it was made out of great big trees."

As Slatter relived what had happened to her, she rubbed her throat trying to relieve the painful lump in it.

"Once I got inside the house," she continued, "it looked like a beautiful old mansion.

A little old lady named Aga Peabody lived there.

She was real nice.

She fed me and took care of me and gave me words of hope.

And, I am proud to say, she talked to me about the Lord and then led me through the sinner's prayer."

She walked over to her coat and pulled out the diamond Miss Peabody had given her.

Slatter nervously rubbed her forehead as she kept telling her story, "See this," as she held up the diamond for them to see.

"Miss Peabody gave it to me.

It's a real unfinished diamond.

It's called a diamond in the rough.

I know it doesn't look like much, but she told me it's a real diamond and I believe her.

She should know 'cause her brother used to own a diamond mine a long time ago, but he died.

She told me if it is cut just right by a master diamond cutter, this diamond is worth at least ten to twenty thousand dollars."

She was so tired she started running her thoughts together and her story started sounding scattered.

"Then, " continued Slatter, "She told me the bible story about the potter and the clay.

Oh, and she is the one who gave me a ride home tonight in a great big beautiful wooden sled.

I know I'm just a kid, but ya have to believe me."

For a few brief moments, there was dead silence in the room.

Granny B and Slatter's grandpa stared at each other.

They didn't know what to think about such a wild, made-up story. Slatter was very perceptive. She could tell by the looks on their faces they didn't believe a word she had said.

Her grandpa tried to show Slatter some support, by asking, "May I take a closer look at your diamond in the rough?"

Slatter slowly dropped the stone in the palm of his hand. He held it up toward the ceiling light and examined it closely. Frowning, he cheerfully commented, "Well, your old grandpa jest don't know much about this sort of thing.

It looks jest looks like a shiny black rock to me, but I don't reckon I recall ever a seein' a real diamond before.

I've seen pictures of 'em in magazines.

They didn't look anythin' like this thing, but if ya say it's an unfinished diamond, then I reckon it is.

Maybe it just needs a lot of work in order to make it look sparkly and pretty."

Slatter acted desperate for her grandparents to believe her story. She knelt down and grabbed hold of the arm of her grandpa's chair. She looked up into his kind face. He felt she was telling the truth because she had a different demeanor about her. With tears streaming down her face, Slatter started telling about finding Jesus. She blubbered her words as she spoke, "I'm.....I'm.... tellin' ya grandpa. Miss Peabody told me about Jesus. She spoke about Him as if the two of them were very close friends. She knew all about the bible too. As I listened to her talk about God, I felt some kind of a flutter in my heart.

I just knew it had to be God a speakin' to me.

I knew He was drawin' me to him 'cause I could feel the warmth of his love fer me.

It was like a feelin I ain't ever had before.

Ya see, I'm different on the inside now.

I was lost, but now I'm found.

I was blind, but now I see."

Slatter's eyes lowered as she bowed her head. In a pouting tone, she whispered,

"I can tell by the way you are lookin' at me ya really don't believe a word I'm sayin'."

Then she jumped up and exclaimed, "I know what we can do.

When the snow melts, you and Mr. Fritz could take me down Humphrey's Lane and I can show ya where Miss Peabody's old house is. Then I can prove to ya that I am tellin' ya the truth. Then ya will have to believe me!

Grandpa and Granny B tried to comfort Slatter. They could tell she very much wanted them to believe her story. They thought she had hit her head when she fell in the snow bank and had dreamed about Miss Peabody and her donkey, ABOB. As grandpa looked into Slatter's eyes he could tell she was a changed person on the inside, but tonight he didn't care. He was thankful his precious little Slatter had safely returned home where she belonged.

Granny B was speechless as she listened to Slatter's story.

She got up out of her chair and started picking up the mess her guests had left behind. Grandpa rubbed his chin as he tried to collect his thoughts. He didn't want to say the wrong thing and hurt Slatter's feelings. He could tell she had lived her story even it was just in her mind. He chuckled a little and clapped his hands together as he carefully chose his words,

"Well, all I know is that God heard the prayers of his people and those prayers have been answered.

We have been a prayin' the whole time ya been gone." Grandpa raised up both of his hand in front of him and said,

"Our little girl is back home with us and that's all that matters; enough said."

Slatter nodded her head and lay back down on the couch. She pulled the warm afghan over her legs. When Granny B had finished picking up after her guests, she walked over and sat down on the couch beside Slatter. She thought maybe Slatter was being extra quiet because she was hungry. She tried to baby her by rubbing her feet and asking, "Is my little Slatter hungry fer somethin' special?

I'll be more than happy to go and fix ya anythin' ya want."

Slatter was so worn out from the sled trip home she had a weak tone in her voice when she replied, "No thanks Granny B.

I had some of Miss Peabody's home made bread just a little while ago.

I'm jest not hungry.

Right now, all I want to do is rest."

Granny B brushed Slatter's hair away from her face and lovingly stated, "Sounds to me like ya might've been taken care of by a real angel. It wouldn't surprise me none, cause it's just an out and out miracle God brought ya back home to us.

One things for sure, youngin.'

Your bein' here is livin' proof someone took care of ya.

Slatter, feeling like Granny B really did believe her story, grabbed her hand and smiled.

"Oh Granny B," said Slatter in a sleepy tone of voice.

I think you're right."

"I think I was taken care of by a real angel.

If ya only knew what all I've been through since I've been gone.

I can tell ya one thing.

I'm not worryin' 'bout my mommy anymore.

I know she's in heaven and I think while I was lost out in those woods, God showed me a little bit of heaven.

I think it's a very beautiful place and I know my mommy's happy there.

Someday, I'll tell ya about it, but believe me this is a Christmas I'll never ever forget for as long as I live."

Slatter looked up at the Christmas tree and noticed the Christmas angel was not on top of the tree yet. Feeling good because Granny B believed her story, she wanted to put the angel on top of the tree. She respectfully asked, "Hey ya two. Since it's Christmas Eve, could I please put the angel on top of the Christmas tree now?"

Granny B was most accommodating. She stood up and walked over to the fireplace mantel and picked up a small box with the words tree topper written on the top of it. As She walked back over to where Slatter was sitting she noticed the string that held the old box together, had been broken.

"J.E." she said as she glared at her husband with a puzzled look.

"Did you break the string on this box?"

He promptly replied, "Why no. I didn't even know where it was until I saw ya go over and pick it up jest now."

"Well I declare," said Granny B as she handed Slatter the box.

"That's very strange.

That box hasn't been opened since last Christmas. I had that heavy string tied as tight as I could get it. It would've taken a very strong hand to have broken that string.

Oh well.

I sure do hope the angel's not broken.

Be very careful Slatter when ya take it out of the box," persisted Granny B.

"'Cause remember my tellin' ya that this special angel has been in our family for several hundred years or more.

It belonged to my great grandmother and her great grandmother before her. Your grandpa can pick ya up so ya will be high enough to put it on top the tree. I want ya to know I wasn't goin' to put that angel up there until ya returned home to us, 'cause I'd already told ya that was your job."

Slatter smiled and slowly opened the box. She was so please at what was in it. There lay a porcelain angel about a foot long with beautiful white fluffy wings. Granny B was relieved to see it was perfectly in tact. The angel's white hair was in a neatly woven bun on top of her head and she had beautiful blue eyes. She wore a crown of beautiful multi-colored stones. In her left hand, she carried a white candle with a bulb on top of it. In her right hand, she carried a small banner with an inscription on it. The inscription read, 'Jesus is more precious than jewels and nothing you can desire compares with Him.'

The angel reminded Slatter of Miss Peabody. Smiling, Slatter stood up and very carefully took the angel out of the box. She looked on the back side of the ornament. She noticed some words written in very small letters. She squinted her eyes as she read the words out loud, "Always believe ......................in divine intervention."

She grinned to herself as she remembered Miss Peabody saying those very words. She walked over to the tree. Her grandpa picked her up by the waist and gave her a big boost up in the air. She carefully placed the angel on the very top of the tree and plugged it into one of the light bulbs on the tree. The candle in the angel's hand lit up. Slatter remembered Miss Peabody saying, when you see the light of a burning candle think of me. Grandpa then stood her back down on the floor. The three of them just stood there for a few moments, holding hands, as they gazed at the beautiful Christmas tree. With a far away look in her eyes, Slatter softly whispered, "Listen. Do ya hear that? Do ya hear what I hear?"

Her grandpa replied, "Hear what.

I don't hear anythin', do you Granny B?"

Granny B whispered, "No."

I don't hear anythin' either.

Grandpa asked, "What is it Slatter?

What do you hear?"

Slatter still had the same far away look in her eyes as she answered. "I hear a choir of angel's singin'.

They're singin' a Christmas song.

They're singin'................ 'O come All Ye Faithful.'

Oh my gosh!

I've never heard such beautiful singin' in all my born days!

She began to sing out loud,

"Glory to God...In the highest.... O come let us adore him.

O come let us adore him.......O come let us adore him.

Christ..................the Lord.

Slatter's grandpa gave Granny B an astonishing look.

The only angel that he heard singing in that room was his precious granddaughter.

With tears in his eyes, he proclaimed, "Yes.

I think I did hear an angel singin'.

I heard an angel singin' right here in this very room.

He smiled and winked at Granny B.

# 29

# A CHRISTMAS GIFT FOR SLATTER

When Slatter had finished singing, Granny B gave her a big hug. Then she reached under the Christmas tree to pick up the package wrapped in brown butcher paper with a red bow on top that had two big candy canes sticking out of the middle. Granny B giggled, "Your grandpa just can't wait until ya open up your Christmas present. He wrapped it himself."

Thinking Slatter would be very anxious to unwrap it, she handed it to her.

"Go on," she tenderly ordered.

"unwrap it."

Slatter replied in a whiny voice, "Oh Granny B. Do I have to?

I jest can't open it yet.

It jest wouldn't be fair.

I don't have a gift for either one of youns yet.

I had planned on gettin' youns a present from Peddler Pete.

That's why I left the house the day I got caught out in the snow storm. I was tryin' to catch the peddler at the store.

Now it's Christmas Eve and I don't even have a gift for youns from me under the tree."

Grandpa could tell Slatter was grumpy from being so tired and sleepy. He wanted her to go to bed and get some rest. He winked at Granny B and in a concerned voice he suggested, "Maybe Slatter is too tired for any more hoopla tonight, Granny B.

It's ok if she wants to wait until mornin' to open her gift.

After all, tomorrow is Christmas day.

Slatter, with weepy eyes, looked at Granny B and pleaded softly, "Please, can I wait til in the mornin'?

All I wanna to do right now is get in my very own bed.

Maybe I can come up with some kind of a present for youns n the mornin'.

I know now I can give a present to someone even when I don't have anything to give.

Slatter's grandpa said sternly, "Now honey.

Don't ya worry none about giving us any gifts.

You've already given me and Granny B the best present ya could've ever given us.

The gift of ya being returned home, safe and" ...............

Slatter frowned as she abruptly interrupted him.

"Say Grandpa.

Has old peddler Pete even been back to your store in the last couple of days?"

Grandpa shook his head back and forth as he answered, "No.

But there was another peddler that came by one evenin' last week jest as I was lockin' up.

He gave me one of his cards.

I laid it on the table there by my chair."

He walked over and picked up the business card off of the table beside his chair and handed it to Slatter.

"Here's his card.

This new peddler talked like he might come around a little more regular than old Peddler Pete.

His station wagon looked a might cleaner too."
Grandpa grinned as he confessed,
"I bought your Christmas present from him.
I think you'll like it.
It's somethin' practical, but ya can use and be proud of.
Ya know your old grandpa.
I'm not much on spendin' money on fancy things we don't need." He winked as he spoke proudly of his gift for her.
"I feel in my heart this present represents a new beginnin' for ya." "Thanks a million grandpa," Slatter kindly replied.
I'm sure I'll like my present no matter what it is."
Then, she took the card from her grandpa and kissed him on the cheek. She reached up and wrapped her arms around Granny B's neck and kissed her too.
"Goodnight.
I love you both so very much," she sweetly whispered.

When she turned to go to her room, she paused for a few seconds. She turned around and took a good, long look at both of them standing there in the living room in front of the Christmas tree.

They fondled with the ornaments on the tree unaware they were being watched. Slatter peeked behind the doorway, observing the loving kindness in their wrinkled faces. She glanced at their worn out looking hands. She knew she couldn't begin to imagine all of the hard work they had done during the course of their lifetime. She wondered how many times over the years their hands had extended out to people in need causing them to neglect their own comfort. How many times have their hearts been gashed by hurtful words and how many tears had their eyes cried over good times as well as bad. Her mind pondered further as she thought about how much of life's crushing, harsh elements they had endured over the years. Their lives had been crushed, sanded and refined, like a diamond in the rough; yet they still had the vitality and strength from within to live each day to the fullest; emerging from all of their life's experiences like new shiny diamonds. They were young at heart and always seemed encouraged to love like they'll never get hurt. Such virtues cannot be taught by humans, rather they are blessings extended to them, instilled in their hearts from their heavenly father. She thought about how grateful she was that God had put a desire in their hearts to take her into their home and raise her as if she was their very own child. She was so thankful they loved her and she had grown to love them. She emerged from behind the doorway and quietly stepped out into the open. She used a humbled, soft voice as she spoke,

"I.....I got somethin' else to say to both of youns before I go to bed."

Hearing her voice, they both turned around and faced her. Grandpa acknowledged her presence by saying, "Oh Slatter, we didn't know ya was still a standin' there. We thought ya was already in bed.

What is it ya need to say honey?"

"Well," said Slatter in a humbled tone as she picked at her fingers.

"I don't know how to say this, except to jest say it.

The whole time I was out there....stumblin' around in the dark, tryin' to find my way; I felt like someone was walkin' right beside me each step of the way.

I can't explain it, but I could feel your love fer me.

It was like I was surrounded by a cloud of love.

Somehow it kept me warm.

Somehow it kept me from freezing to death.

I jest want both of ya to know that ....... I knew in my heart youns were prayin' fer me and that God would see to it I'd get back home.

Don't ask me how I knew this......... I.. I just knew."

Slatter cocked her head to the side when she suddenly noticed Granny B had knitted some extra stockings for ornaments and had hung them on the tree. She slowly walked over to the Christmas tree and took off one of the extra stockings. Then she walked over to the fireplace and hung it next to her own. She then turned around and with tears in her eyes said, "There. I think it's a good idea to hang up a stocking for Baby Jesus. Every kid I know wants somethin' special in their stockin' and I'll bet nobody thought to hang up an extra one for baby Jesus and Christmas is His birthday. I think Jesus wants somethin' special in his stocking too and I got a pretty good idea what it is. It's somethin' that cannot be bought or sold. It's somethin' that we should give him because we want to, not because we have to. He wants us to put our hearts in his stocking. The secret to having peace deep down in your soul is having a heart full of mercy, kindness, and love. He already owns everything else in the world, 'cause he made everything. His gift to us is making a way for us to go to heaven to be with him when we die, so it only makes sense our gift to him should be our hearts; so he can prepare them for heaven."

She picked up a pencil and paper and wrote a note to God. The note read,

Dear God,

Merry Christmas. I give you my heart forever. Please make my heart like your son, baby Jesus.

With love from your earth.
Your new child, Slatter Slopey.

She folded the paper into a little square and stuck it inside the extra stocking. As she walked out of the living room, she waved her hand up in the air and said,

"Merry Christmas to both of ya!"

Leaving Granny B and grandpa absolutely speechless, she walked over and reached down into the pocket of her coat. She felt around for the small golden bottle Miss Peabody had given her. She quickly clenched the bottle in the palm of her hand making a fist to keep it hidden from her grandparents. Glancing over her shoulder to see if they were watching her, she grimly straightened her shoulders and ran to her room.

As she looked around her room, she felt a new sense of belonging and comfort. Her room wasn't fancy, but it was her room. It felt good to be back in it. She walked over to her dresser and picked up her old wooden hairbrush. As she twirled it around in her hand, she was amazed at herself because she didn't feel any hate for it anymore. She smiled and laid it back down on the dresser. She gently placed her diamond, and the business card her grandpa had given her, beside it. She spoke out loud to herself. "There.

Two good things beside one old bad thing.

Well, two out of three ain't so bad.

I don't hate my hairbrush anymore, but it's still the ugliest thing I've ever seen."

She reached under her mattress and pulled out her secret map.

She realized it didn't belong in a secret place any longer because it was no longer a secret. She ripped it into tiny pieces and threw it in the trash.

Then, she looked around her room. Her mind began to wander.

She had a new secret now. Where would she hide the little gold bottle? It had to be put in a very special place where no one would think to look. Her eyes skimmed over the room. Suddenly, she noticed one of the knobs were loose on her bed posts at the foot of her bed. She walked over and pulled on the unfastened knob. Sure enough, it came off easily and fell into her hand. She looked down into the bed post and saw a hollowed out place about three inches deep. She giggled a little as she wondered why she hadn't noticed the wobbly knob before now. It looked to be the perfect place to stash her new secret. She took the little bottle and dropped it down into the empty space.

"Ah ha," she said out loud to herself.

"A perfect fit."

Then she neatly placed the knob back onto the bed post. She was quite satisfied with her new hiding place.

She quickly got undressed and put on her old familiar pajamas. She collapsed on her bed. It felt good to her to be able to stretch out across her bed. For just a minute, she became curious about the name on the business card her grandpa had given her. She sat up on the edge of the bed, and picked up the card off of her dresser. As she stared at the card, she thought the letters in the name of the company looked very familiar.

The card read:

## A. GAPE CO.
## OUR GIFTS ARE OUT OF THIS WORLD.
## IT'S OUR BUSINESS TO SERVE YOU

She tried to remember where she had seen those same letters before. But this was one night that she was just too tired to do anymore thinking about anything.

She was tired of thinking.

She was tired of walking.

She was tired of being cold and afraid.

She had enough excitement over the last few days to last her for a very long time.

She was so thankful to be back home.
She shrugged her shoulders and laid the card back down on the dresser. She slipped in between the warm covers on her bed. The best Christmas present she could have right now was a good night's sleep in her very own room in her very own bed. She snuggled up to her very own favorite pillow. Because she was excited that tomorrow was Christmas morning, she found it difficult to say her goodnight prayer. Physical exhaustion took over her excitement as she closed her eyes and sincerely prayed.

"Dear God.
  Remember me?
  I'm your new child, Slatter Slo.............................."
She only managed to say a few words of her prayer, before she drifted off to a much needed restful sleep.

# 30

# AGAPE'S WATCHFUL EYE

As Slatter lay in a sound sleep, she had no idea her guardian angel Agape was present; invisibly sitting high above her head. He floated down to her bedside and tenderly touched her soft, rosy cheek with his big smooth hand. He pulled the blanket up next to her chin as he tucked her in for the night. He softly whispered aloud to her as she slept, "Sweet, sweet little Slatter.

You are all wrapped up in a nice warm blanket tonight, but I know that you are also wrapped up in God's everlasting love."

Agape looks forward to his third encounter with Slatter as he is pleased at how well everything is going with God's plan for her life. As he reflects back on her magnificent journey with him, he realizes she is maturing and becoming very much aware she has been entertaining angels unawares.

He was the one who sent, Pydie to become friends with Slatter.

When Slatter was lighting too many firecrackers and throwing them into Mr. Beeser's old truck, Agape was the one who tripped her so she would fall and roll underneath another parked car; preventing her from being injured.

He was the angel she saw standing behind her grandpa as he helped her grandpa pull the big farm implement off of her neck. He was also the one who supernaturally moved the farm implement down the road to Mr. Kaneke's tractor repair shop.

At the County fair, he was the one made the horse walk up and mess all over the mean bullies, Newton and Lodden as they made fun of Slatter.

Agape was the one who caused the same two boys to become stuck at the top of the rocko plane ride at the county fair.

Agape wanted to teach the two boys a lesson in obedience.

Agape flew high into the heavens and caused a meteorite to fall to earth. He wanted Slatter to keep the mind set that God is always at work in the heavens. Agape wants to keep her inquisitive so she will learn more about God.

When Slatter was playing in the leaves at school, he was the one who caused the big whirlwinds of leaves to swirl into Newton and Lodden, so they would leave Slatter alone.

He was the one who kept her from freezing in the snow drift after she hit her head on a rock and was knocked out. He sat in the ditch with her and held her next to his bosom with his big feathery wings wrapped around her; keeping her safe and warm, until she could wake up and regain enough strength to get out of the ditch.

He was the one who walked beside her through the snowy woods and directed her path. He also caused the snow clouds to blow over so the moon could shine down on her as she searched for a safe place to get out of the inclement weather.

He was the one who created a small cavern in behind a great big rock so she would be hidden from wild animals in the woods, while she took a short nap to regain her strength.

When Slatter was lying in the small cavern, gazing up into the sky, it wasn't big stars hovering close to the earth she saw. Agape had called ten thousand angels to watch over her while she slept. What Slatter was seeing, was the eyes of all of those thousands of angels watching her every move. The exotic patterns of light she saw were the multitude of angels flitting to and fro, finding their place in the heavens, as they obeyed Agape's command.

Agape was the one who made the big illuminating green footsteps she followed out of the woods to a clearing so ABOB the donkey could easily find her.

While she was lost, Agape presented himself to Slatter as Miss Peabody so he could take care of her and keep her safe. He was the one who actually told her about Jesus and with his immortal eyes, witnessed her salvation.

When Miss Peabody served Slatter homemade bread and hot broth, Slatter didn't have a clue she was actually eating real angel's food, prepared by one of God's own heavenly angels.

The golden substance that Miss Peabody poured from the golden pitcher was a healing liquid that will never be found in this world. It was created and sent directly from the throne of God.

Agape was also the one who loosened the knob on Slatter's bedpost at the foot of her bed, so she would have a new hiding place for her newly acquired heavenly gift.

And last, but not least, she didn't know Agape was the one who guided the big wooden sled through a spiritually darkened path. Satan, himself, the one God calls, the angel of light and the Prince of Darkness, tried to destroy her life and keep her from getting back home to her grandparents. He is a great lion who wants to destroy her soul. Agape knew that Satan's plan was to create a strong enough wind to make the sled topple off the washed out bridge and fall into the icy waters. God gave Agape powers to intercept Satan's plan. Satan's winds of warfare were unsuccessful because Agape with his God given power, blasted away the evil one. Then calmed the winds with a powerful wave of his big hand. God also gave Agape supernatural powers to make ABOB and the sled float over the bridge of troubled waters so they could safely land on the other side.

Agape turns a couple of circles and floats back up to the ceiling.

His rapid turns leave behind him reflecting streaks of white light.

He is very pleased with the creative ways in which he has been fulfilling God's instructions. He is being very clever with the way he is using his name and he always makes sure he tells Slatter ...........God is real and He loves her very much.

Agape knows his watchful eye has never left Slatter since his great commission was given to him by God. He looks toward Heaven and with his immortal eyes, he sees God sitting on his throne with his precious son Jesus sitting on His right hand side.

He lovingly smiles as he confidently bows down before God's throne.

Why is Agape smiling?

Because Slatter doesn't realize yet what a great plan of salvation she has inherited by being one of God's children. However, Agape knows all about it. God's faithful messenger is exceedingly joyful because he knows there is joy in the presence of God's multitude of angel's over one sinner who repents, and the name of the sinner who repented today is a child named Slatter Slopey. Her name has been written down in God's family book of life for all eternity by God himself.

As God's glory serenely shines down upon Slatter, all of heaven is silent as Jesus smiles and pronounces,

"Behold, I shall never forget thee, Slatter Slopey.

I have given you the gift of eternal life.

I have graven thy image upon the palm of my hand, and no one is able to snatch you out of my hand.

Neither death, nor life, nor angels, nor principalities, nor things present, nor things to come, nor powers, nor height, nor depth, nor any other created thing, shall be able to separate you from my love, which is in my son, Christ Jesus."

Agape respectfully closes his eyes and whispers,

"Amen."

ATTENTION READERS:

BE SURE AND READ THE CONCLUSION OF SLATTER SLOPEY IN THE THIRD AND FINAL BOOK OF THE SERIES ENTITLED

"SLATTER SLOPEY III
"THE VISION"
(THE ANGEL'S THIRD VISIT)

Coming Soon

Printed in the United States
77706LV00007B/106-117